NOTATION

Symbol	Concept
R_{fg}	Correlations between two sets of factor scores
R_{fs}	Correlations of the f theoretical factor scores and s obtained factor scores
R_j	Multiple correlation of variable j with the other $v - 1$ variables
R_{uf}	Correlations of the u unique factors with the f common factors
R_{uu}	Correlations among the u unique factors
R_{vv}	Correlations among the v variables
$R^*_{vv.A}$	Residual coefficients among v variables after the influence of factor A has been removed from R_{vv}.
S_{vf}	Factor structure matrix containing the correlations between the v variables and f factors
S_{ff}	Diagonal matrix of standard deviations for the f factors
S_{vv}	Diagonal matrix of the variances for the v variables
$T_{ff'}$	Transformation matrix to shift the factor pattern for f factors to the reference vector structure for the f' rotated factors
U_{nv}	Unique factor scores for n individuals on v variables
U_{vv}	Diagonal matrix with the squared unique factor loadings as elements
$V_{vf'}$	Reference vector structure matrix containing the correlations of the v variables with the reference vectors for the f' rotated factors
V_{vv}	Diagonal matrix of variances for the v variables
$W_{f'f}$	Weight matrix for calculating the f' rotated factor scores from the f initial factor scores
W_{vf}	Weights applied to the v variables to obtain the f factor scores
X_{nv}	Data matrix with raw or derivation scores for n individuals on v variables
Z_{nv}	Standard score data matrix for n individuals on v variables
λ_{fg}	Transformation matrix to shift the f factors' factor pattern to the g factors' reference vector structure

FACTOR ANALYSIS

Second Edition

FACTOR ANALYSIS

Second Edition

Richard L. Gorsuch
Graduate School of Psychology
Fuller Theological Seminary

LEA LAWRENCE ERLBAUM ASSOCIATES, PUBLISHERS
1983   Hillsdale, New Jersey   London

Lawrence Erlbaum Associates, Inc., Publishers
365 Broadway
Hillsdale, New Jersey 07642

Library of Congress Cataloging in Publication Data
Gorsuch, Richard L.
Factor analysis.

Bibliography: p.
Includes indexes.
1. Factor analysis.   I. Title.
QA278.5.G67 1983   519.5'354   83-1650
ISBN 0-89859-202-X

Printed in the United States of America
10   9

To Eric and Kay

Rotation:
    Oblique:
    Ortnogonal:
,.

Confirmatory F. A. - Ch. 7, Ch. 5
    (Rotation not used here? p.127

Exploratory F. A.

Be aware of F.A. misuse, poor use - p. 370

Variable Selection Process

why use FA - p. 2
    2 things I want:
        underlying structure of the variables &
        variable reduction - p. 4

Contents

*Advanced topic. May be considered optional reading.

*Advanced topic. May be considered optional reading.

---

*Advanced topic. May be considered optional reading.

PREFACE

The years since writing the first edition have seen a number of new developments of factor analysis. The purpose of the second edition is to include those new developments within the text without disturbing the successful features of the first edition. The style, general outline, and degree of mathematical sophistication required of the student have been kept the same as in the first edition.

To make room for the new materials, the first edition was carefully scanned for those techniques and procedures that have not been widely used and for which there does not seem to be as strong a case for their use as with other procedures. For example, the geometric representation of factor models has played almost no role in factor analysis in the past 10 years, and so the presentation of that material has been starred to indicate that it is not essential to the later materials. And because rotation has become almost exclusively processed by computer with only a very few computerized techniques being widely used, the two rotation chapters have been presented more simply in one chapter with an additional starred chapter for those interested in more detail or in visual rotation.

It is apparent that the common practice of factor analysis lags behind theoretical knowledge and the possible uses of it. To keep the lag to a minimum, this revision includes promising new developments, such as the new Chapter 7 on the use of confirmatory factor analysis. The discussions of continuing problems for which major new references exist have been revised, including the determinancy-of-factor-scores discussion. A reasonably complete set of references is given with introductory treatments to encourage the user to think through the techniques needed in a particular application.

A further purpose of this edition is to allow the book to be more readily used in multivariate courses as a supplementary text to a multivariate text. Such application allows a professor to spend approximately half a semester on other multivariate techniques and half a semester on factor analysis itself. I have had considerable success blending the chapters into such a course with a multivariate text so that students could take their pick of, for example, two presentations of matrix algebra and so that the role of factor analysis as compared to other multivariate techniques could be discussed from an examination of the last several chapters of this edition. Generally, I have used Chapter 1 as part of the general course introduction, Chapters 2, 3, 6, 8, 9, and 11 for an introduction to exploratory factor analysis, Chapter 7 with canonical correlations to test hypotheses, and Chapters 12 and 16 to discuss the relevance of scoring techniques and replicability for all multivariate techniques. Chapters 17 and 18 are used in a final overview of when each of the multivariate techniques should be used.

I deeply appreciate the many individuals who have provided feedback on the first edition. Included among those are the students who have taken the course from me, and have been generous with their reactions, as well as colleagues who have used the text. To the degree that I have been able to maintain or improve the quality of the first edition, the thanks go to them.

Finally, I would like to express my deep appreciation to secretaries—particularly Marilyn Lundberg—for the extensive time that they have spent doing the numerous tasks essential for an effort such as this. Their expertise and willing attitude have helped to make the revision much more pleasant than it would otherwise have been.

Richard L. Gorsuch
Graduate School of Psychology
Fuller Theological Seminary
Pasadena, California

PREFACE to the First Edition

Factor Analysis began the way many books do. When asked to teach a course in factor analysis in the late 1960s, I felt there was no truly appropriate text. The high-quality texts that were available seemed to me not to stress points I deemed critical when factor analyzing data or appeared to be too difficult for graduate psychology students with only an average mathematical background. My response was to develop a set of dittoed notes for use in my classes. The notes were part of my effort to make my course effective in teaching graduate students when and how to use factor analysis in their substantive research. To be frank, I also felt that using my own notes would keep the course from unduly imposing upon my substantive research, because it is often easier to present one's own ideas than it is to integrate those ideas with someone else's work. Once the notes had begun, they took on a life of their own. Revising the notes each time the course was taught eventually led to this book.

The first purpose of the present book is to enable an investigator to properly utilize factor analysis as a research tool. Such utilization requires an understanding of when the differences in possible mathematical procedures may have a major impact upon the substantive conclusions and when the differences might not be relevant for a given research study. In addition, one should also know when factor analysis is not the best procedure to be used.

Stressing the aspects of factor analysis that are important for research does not mean, however, that the mathematical foundations of factor analysis are ignored, because a basic understanding of the mathematical models is necessary to understand the application of those models. Hence, derivations are given for the many aspects of factor analysis; however, no calculus is used. If one has a working knowledge of basic algebra and patience, he will be able to follow the mathematics.

Any person completing the usual first year of graduate-level statistics will probably have the background necessary to pursue this text. I have assumed that the reader is familiar with correlation coefficients, the rudiments of multiple correlation, and the basic concepts of significance testing. Some familiarity with social science research is also helpful so that the importance of the research-oriented discussions may be readily apparent.

Some sections are of greater interest to the more mathematically oriented or advanced reader. These sections, which can be skipped on the first reading, are identified by an asterisk preceding the section title.

In addition to increasing the student's sophistication in factor analysis, it is hoped that this book will increase the reader's general research sophistication as well. Studying factor-analytic procedures requires one to ask and to explore basic questions about how an area is to be conceptualized. These basic questions exist in every scientific endeavor, whether or not factor analysis is used as a formal tool. Studying factor analysis may therefore help the reader to better understand the basic questions and provide possible rationales for improving scientific models. An increase in research sophistication has been one of the prime benefits that I have personally derived from my contact with factor analysis.

There are several ways in which this book can be used. First, it can be used to help decide if factor analysis is relevant to one's research program. If this is your interest, I suggest that you read Chapter 1 carefully and then scan Chapters 17 and 18. These three chapters can be read more or less independently of Chapters 2 through 16 and should provide a basis for deciding if factor analysis would be useful in your research program. The rest of the text can then be read if factor analysis is likely to be used.

Second, the present book can serve as the text for a graduate-level course on factor analysis or for a section of a course in multivariate statistical techniques. In some situations, it may be appropriate to use the book in its entirety. In other courses, Chapters 14 and 15 may be skipped along with the starred sections. The latter option will allow more time for pursuing outside readings, practice problems, and so forth. Chapters 11, 13, 16, 17, and 18 are essential to a complete understanding of factor analysis and should not be treated lightly simply because they occur later. They are critical for understanding the role of factor analysis in research.

The third way in which this book can be used is as a reference. It is hoped that the detailed Table of Contents, the Subject Index, the starred sections, the references to and discussions of computer programs, the appendix on computer program libraries, and Chapters such as 14 and 15 will be particularly useful to investigators actively engaged in factor-analytic research. To increase the book's usefulness as a reference, citations are made to the factor-analytic literature so that further pursuit of any particular topic is possible.

In writing about factor analysis, I find that I have been extensively influenced by my former professors. I am especially indebted to Raymond B. Cattell. Not only did he involve me in factor-analytic research, but the types of questions that he raised concerning both the factor-analytic procedures themselves and the usefulness of factor analysis in theory building have had a lasting impact upon me. The ideas of my former professors are so interwoven with mine that I find it difficult to know if I have unduly appropriated their constructs while considering them to be my own. Indeed, I am sure that I have not referenced professors such as Wesley Becker, Lloyd Humphreys, S. B. Sells, and Ledyard Tucker sufficiently throughout the text.

Among those who have helped with the manuscript itself are Anthony Conger, John Horn, and Jum Nunnally. The thoughtful, detailed reviews that they provided of an earlier draft are deeply appreciated. Their comments have certainly resulted in a higher-quality product; if I have failed to achieve my goals in writing this book, it is probably because I have not properly interpreted their reactions.

I also deeply appreciate the contributions that my associates and friends have made to my thinking in the area of factor analysis. In particular, numerous students have contributed their reactions to earlier drafts of the materials included here. They are, as is usually the case, the unsung heroes in the development of this book.

In turning ideas into a manuscript, numerous errands need to be run, pages typed, and proofreading conducted. Without the able assistance of Mrs. Betty Howard, such tasks would have kept the book from being published. Her professional expertise as well as her cooperative, responsible attitudes are assets that most authors need in secretarial support, but only a few are privileged to have.

During the period that this book was being written, I held a Kennedy Professorship in the John F. Kennedy Center for Research on Education and Human Development at George Peabody College for Teachers. I deeply appreciate the gracious support provided by the Joseph P. Kennedy Jr. Foundation.

Several of the book's examples are based on reanalyses of previously published data. Therefore, I would like to thank the University of Chicago Press for their permission to use data from the Holzinger and Swineford (1939) monograph, as well as the *British Journal of Psychiatry* for their permission to use data from an article by Rees (1950).

RICHARD L. GORSUCH

FACTOR ANALYSIS

Second Edition

1 Introduction

A basic review of the role of factor analysis in scientific endeavors is necessary background for the presentation of factor-analytic procedures. The overview is begun in Section 1.1, Science and Factor Analysis, where factor analysis is placed within a general perspective of science. In Section 1.2 it is noted that factor analysis—like any statistical procedure—is simply a logical extension of methods people have always used to understand their world. Some common-sense procedures often used to achieve the goals of factor analysis are noted. This section is concluded by pointing to the limitations of these elementary procedures and by indicating that some of the limitations are overcome through the more powerful factor-analytic techniques. The chapter concludes with background on examples that are used throughout the book (Section 1.3).

1.1 SCIENCE AND FACTOR ANALYSIS

A major objective of scientific activities is to summarize, by theoretical formulations, the empirical relationships among a given set of events. The events that can be investigated are almost infinite, so any general statement about scientific activities is difficult to make. However, it could be stated that scientists analyze the relationships among a set of **variables** where these relationships are evaluated across a set of **individuals** under specified **conditions.** The **variables** are the characteristics being measured and could be anything that can be objectively identified or scored. For example, a psychologist may use tests as variables, whereas a political scientist or sociologist may use the percentage of ballots cast for different candidates as variables. The **individuals** are the subjects, cases,

1

voting precincts or other individual units that provide the data by which the relationships among the variables are evaluated. The **conditions** specify that which pertains to all the data collected and sets this study apart from other similar studies. Conditions can include locations in time and space, variations in the methods of scoring variables, treatments after which the variables are measured, or, even, the degrees of latitude at which the observation is made. An **observation** is a particular variable score of a specified individual under the designated conditions. For example, the score of Jimmy on a mathematical ability test taken during his fifth-grade year in Paul Revere School may be one observation, whereas Mike's score on the same test at the same school might be another. (Note that observation will not be used to refer to an individual; such usage is often confusing.)

Although all science falls within the major objective of building theories to explain the interrelationships of variables, the differences in substantive problems lead to variations in how the investigation proceeds. One variation is the extent to which events are controlled. In traditional experimental psychology and physics the investigator has randomly assigned subjects to the various manipulated conditions, whereas astronomers have, until recently, been concerned with passive observations of naturally occurring events. Within any broad area, some scientific attempts are purely descriptive of phenomena, whereas others seek to generate and test hypotheses. Research also varies in the extent to which it utilizes only a few variables or utilizes many variables; this appears to be partly a function of the complexity of the area and the number of variables to which a discipline has access.

Regardless of how the investigator determines the relationships among variables under specified conditions, all scientists are united in the common goal: they seek to summarize data so that the empirical relationships can be grasped by the human mind. In doing so, constructs are built that are conceptually clearer than the a priori ideas, and then these constructs are integrated through the development of theories. These theories generally exclude minor variations in the data so that the major variations can be summarized and dealt with by finite beings.

The purpose in using factor analysis is scientific in the sense previously discussed. Usually the aim is to summarize the interrelationships among the variables in a concise but accurate manner as an aid in conceptualization. This is often achieved by including the maximum amount of information from the original variables in as few derived variables, or factors, as possible to keep the solution understandable.

In parsimoniously describing data, factor analysts explicitly recognize that any relationship is limited to a particular area of applicability. Areas qualitatively different, that is, areas where relatively little generalization can be made from one area to another, are referred to as *separate factors*. Each factor represents an area of generalization that is qualitatively distinct from that represented by any other factor. Within an area where data can be summarized (i.e., within an area where generalization can occur) factor analysts first represent that area by a factor and then seek to make the degree of generalization between each variable and the factor explicit. A measure of the degree of generalizability found between each variable and each factor is calculated and referred to as a **factor loading.** Factor loadings reflect quantitative relationships. The farther the factor loading is from zero, the more one can generalize from that factor to the variable. Comparing loadings of the same variable on several factors provides information concerning how easy it is to generalize to that variable from each factor.

Example

Numerous variables could be used for comparing countries. Size could be used by, for example, counting the number of people or the number of square kilometers within the borders of that country. Technological development could be measured by the size of the transportation systems or the size of the communications systems. Indeed, the number of variables is almost infinite by which countries could be compared. To what extent can this large number of variables be considered as manifestations of more basic constructs or factors? To the degree that the variables are interrelated and represent a few factors, then, it will be possible to develop a theory for each factor but still explain a large number of variables.

Table 1.1.1 presents the results of a typical factor analysis. Cattell and Gorsuch (1965) correlated demographic variables across countries, and factored them by the iterated principal axis procedure described in Chapter 6. The factors were then rotated to visual simple structure, a procedure described in Chapter 9. The factor loadings relating each variable to each factor are given in Table 1.1.1.

TABLE 1.1.1
Factor Pattern Loadings of Demographic Variables
on Two Factors

| | *Factors* | |
Variables	*Size*	*Development*
Population	.84	−.09
No. of Government Ministries	.63	.00
Area	.86	.57
UNICEF Contributions per capita	.58	.91
Miles of Railroad per capita	.41	.94
Income per capita	−.17	.94
Telephones per capita	.00	.89
Physicians per capita	−.01	.02

Note: The Table is based on data collected in the 1950s from 52 individual countries. The elements in the table are the weights given to the factor standard scores to reproduce or estimate the variable standard scores. (Adapted from Cattell & Gorsuch, 1965.)

From the set of variables having large loadings, it can be easily seen that the factor labeled *development* is distinct from the factor representing the size of the country. If it is known that the country has a high score on an operational representative of the development factor, then it can be concluded that the national income per capita, telephones, and the other variables with high loadings on this factor will also be prominent. A different set of generalizations can be made if the size of the country is known, because that is an empirically different content area.

Some variables overlap both of the distinct factors, for example, the miles of railroad per capita. Others may be unrelated to either factor, as is the physician rate; no generalizations can be made to it from the factors identified in this analysis.

Some Uses of Factor Analysis. A statistical procedure that gives both qualitative and quantitative distinctions can be quite useful. Some of the purposes for which factor analysis can be used are as follows:

1. Through factor-analytic techniques, the number of variables for further research can be minimized while also maximizing the amount of information in the analysis. The original set of variables is reduced to a much smaller set that accounts for most of the reliable variance of the initial variable pool. The smaller set of variables can be used as operational representatives of the constructs underlying the complete set of variables.
2. Factor analysis can be used to search data for possible qualitative and quantitative distinctions, and is particularly useful when the sheer amount of available data exceeds comprehensibility. Out of this exploratory work can arise new constructs and hypotheses for future theory and research. The contribution of exploratory research to science is, of course, completely dependent upon adequately pursuing the results in future research studies so as to confirm or reject the hypotheses developed.
3. If a domain of data can be hypothesized to have certain qualitative and quantitative distinctions, then this hypothesis can be tested by factor analysis. If the hypotheses are tenable, the various factors will represent the theoretically derived qualitative distinctions. If one variable is hypothesized to be more related to one factor than another, this quantitative distinction can also be checked.

The purposes outlined above obviously overlap with purposes served by other statistical procedures. In many cases the other statistical procedures can be used to answer the question more efficiently than one could answer them with a factor analysis. For example, if the hypothesis concerns whether or not one measure of extroversion is more related to a particular job performance than another, the investigator can correlate the two variables under consideration with an operational representative of the job performance. A simple significance test of the difference between the correlation coefficients would be sufficient. This is actually a small factor analysis in that the same statistics would result by defining the operational representative of job performance as the first diagonal factor (see

Chapter 5) and determining the loadings of the two extroversion variables on that factor. Although the result would be exactly the same, proceeding factor analytically would be to utilize an unnecessarily complex approach.

Many traditional statistics can be viewed as special cases of the factor-analytic model where, because of their limited nature, detailed statistical theories have been developed that greatly enhance the statistic's interpretability. In particular, probability testing is widely available in the traditional statistical areas, although it is more limited in factor analysis. Therefore whenever the decision is between other statistical procedures and factor analysis, the choice will usually go to the former if they both answer the same question. This should not, however, obscure the fact that the basic rationale and problems are often the same.

1.2 ELEMENTARY PROCEDURES FOR FACTORING

Although factor analysis is a term usually applied to the mathematical models discussed in Chapter 2, the logical process is often utilized on an intuitive basis. For example, common observation has identified four dimensions of position. These include the three dimensions of space and the dimension of time. The use of six or seven variables to mark the location of a plane in flight would be redundant because four variables can give all the unique information necessary to locate it. Quantitative comparisons can be made within one of these dimensions but seldom across the dimensions because the dimensions are qualitatively distinct. Fifty feet of altitude does not offset a change in latitude in describing the position of an airplane.

A formal factor analysis is not needed to discover the four dimensions of position because the distinctions are obvious. Many scientists can, fortunately, operate upon such easily observed distinctions. However, many others find the distinctions in their areas to be difficult to identify and turn to statistical aids.

After the variables are subjectively classified along obvious dimensions, the next improvement is classification by joint presence or absence. One notes the number of times A occurs in relation to the occurrence of B for the cases at hand that are under the specified conditions. If the percentage is high enough, the variables are considered related (i.e., they are manifestations of the same factor). If a number of such variables are found together, then they are classified under the same rubric and an implicit factor results. As Royce (1958) points out, such thinking in the area of psychology can easily be traced back at least to the Greek philosophers.

Example

In his studies of the Old Testament, Wellhausen (1885) noticed that passages from the Pentateuch had varying characteristics. Going from one passage to another led to a shift in style, names, and concerns. Furthermore, he noted that these characteristics covaried together; if one appeared, then another was also likely to be found in that passage. He identified several "factors" from his "variables."

The variables are given in Table 1.2.1 in the form of questions asked of a given passage of scripture. The answers are entered in the table under the factors that they are generally assumed to measure (Gottwald, 1959). The factors—E, J, P and D—are named for the principal characteristics by which they are identified. Because of the differences in writing style, the factors are attributed to different traditions or sources that were combined into the present Pentateuch. In writing an Old Testament text, it would be appropriate to devote separate sections to each of the factors, and a final section to how the traditions (factors) were integrated into the Pentateuch.

There is no universal agreement on the exact number of factors, or on their characteristics. The data can support different theories, as is true in any scientific enterprise. Old Testament scholars cannot, unfortunately, test their rival theories by gathering new data although they can reanalyze the existing data more thoroughly.

TABLE 1.2.1
Pentateuch Factors

Variables	Factors			
	E	J	P	D
Is God's name Elohim?	Yes	No	No	No
Is the passage anti-monarchic?	Yes	No	No	No
Is God's name Yahweh (German *Jahweh*)?	No	Yes	No	No
Is it anthropomorphic?	No	Yes	No	No
Is it concerned with priestly affairs?	No	No	Yes	No
Does it have a labored style?	No	No	Yes	No
Is it from Deuteronomy?	No	No	No	Yes
Is it explicitly monotheistic?	No	No	No	Yes

Note: The first factor, *E* (for Elohim), is hypothesized to consist of the stories and writings that came from the northern tribes of Israel. *J* (for Jahweh) appears to be a southern source giving somewhat different traditions. *P* represents the Priestly content, and *D* is the Deuteronomic material.

A slightly more sophisticated implicit-factoring procedure is to group variables together from an examination of appropriate statistics. These statistics could be correlation coefficients, covariances, measures of distance, or any other measure of the degree of association that would summarize the empirical relationships. When several variables are consistently found to be associated, then they are grouped and discussed together. This means that they are considered a factor and the concept underneath which these variables are jointly discussed would be the factor itself. Hierarchical clustering schemes (Ward, 1963; Johnson, 1967) also fall within this general category.

Example

It is apparent that many psychological tests measure almost the same thing as others do. Those that do measure the same underlying construct, or factor, need to be so identified so that we know that they are—despite differences in names—reasonably

TABLE 1.2.2
Correlations Among Six Psychological Variables

	1	2	3	4	5	6
1. Information	1.00					
2. Verbal Ability	.67	1.00				
3. Verbal Analogies	.43	.49	1.00			
4. Ego Strength	.11	.12	.03	1.00		
5. Guilt Proneness	−.07	−.05	−.14	−.41	1.00	
6. Tension	−.17	−.14	−.10	−.48	.40	1.00

Note: Individuals were 147 high school girls. (Adapted from Gorsuch, 1965.)

interchangeable. This can be determined by examining the correlations among psychological variables. Those variables that correlate highly together are basically interchangeable, and so measure the same factor. Do several intelligence tests measure the same factor? Do several anxiety tests measure the same factor?

Table 1.2.2 gives the correlations among six psychological variables. The correlations are low because the tests were not very reliable. From this table, an informal factor analysis can be readily completed: variables 1, 2, and 3 form a verbal comprehension factor whereas 4, 5, and 6 form a personality factor. The personality factor is traditionally called *anxiety* but may also be called by some similar name, such as *emotionality*. Table 1.2.3 summarizes the conclusions from Table 1.2.2 in a factor matrix. The factor matrix contains Xs where substantial relationships occur and a dash where the variable is basically unrelated to the factor.

TABLE 1.2.3
An Intuitive "Factor Matrix"
Showing the Relationship of
the Variables to the Factors

	Factors	
Variables	Verbal Comprehension	Anxiety
1. Information	X	—
2. Verbal Ability	X	—
3. Verbal Analogies	X	—
4. Ego Strength	—	X
5. Guilt Proneness	—	X
6. Tension	—	X

Limitations of Intuitive Factor Analyses.   Some areas have been thoroughly researched on the basis of such intuitive factoring. Where this is possible, it would be ridiculous to utilize highly sophisticated procedures. However, more sophisticated procedures are necessary when the limits of the intuitive approach are reached. The primary limitations of the intuitive approach that may be overcome by factor-analytic procedures are as follows:

1. In the case where there are numerous variables, it is difficult to examine any matrix of association indices for the intuitive factors. The task simply becomes too great. The number of indices of association between each pair of variables in a set is equal to $v(v-1)/2$ where v is the number of variables. Whereas the six-variable example had only 15 correlation coefficients to examine, a 20-variable problem would have 190 coefficients and a 50-variable problem would have 1,225 coefficients. Most of us find some difficulty in integrating 1,225 interrelationships by an intuitive analysis.

2. With the intuitive approach, it is difficult to indicate varying degrees of association with the factors. For example, a variable could have correlations of .35 with the first three variables and .0 with the last three in Table 1.2.2. It would thus be related to the first factor but at a lesser level than the first variable. Varying degrees of relationship could be represented by using upper- and lower-case xs, but making still finer distinctions would soon result in a numerical system much like a correlation coefficient. A correlation between the variable and the factor is one of the basic indices of association produced by a factor analysis.

3. The problem presented in Table 1.2.2 was deliberately selected because it is a relatively clear example. Despite our hopes and desires, empirical data are usually far from clear. Generally, many variables have borderline relationships. In the case of Table 1.2.2, what would happen if variable 3 was replaced with variable 3', when 3' correlated moderately (e.g., .3) with all the other variables? In this case, variable 3' would probably load on both factors in either an intuitive analysis or an actual factor analysis, but this agreement only occurs because the rest of the matrix is relatively small and well-defined. If the analysis were of a 1,225 correlation coefficient matrix, a variable such as 3' could be impossible to place on an intuitive basis.

4. Intuitive factor analyses do not necessarily produce the most parsimonious results. The number of concepts developed will often be more than necessary to represent the vital distinctions in the domain. Inasmuch as more concepts are created than are necessary, it simply means extra work for those investigating the area. It is also a failure to apply Occam's Razor.[1]

---

[1]William of Occam a fourteenth-century English scholastic philosopher, stated that the simpler theory is to be preferred over the more complex theory when both are equally accurate summaries of the data.

Overcoming the Limits of Intuitive Factor Analyses.   Factor analysis is simply a statistical procedure that has been developed out of the intuitive approaches. Because of the power gained from the use of mathematics and computers, most of the immediate problems of the unsophisticated approaches have been overcome. Factor analysis allows one to analyze numerous variables at a time, to unravel relationships among variables correlated in highly complex ways, to report gradated relationships of variables to factors, and to stress parsimonious solutions. From the old maxim that "you don't get something for nothing," the reader might suspect that factor analysis has some problems of its own. It has. **However, the problems in factor analysis are implicit in the intuitive approaches to the same set of data,** so its advantages offset the disadvantages.[2]

1.3 EXAMPLES

The simple examples included in the previous sections of this chapter could all be reasonably solved on an intuitive basis. Not all of the examples used in the rest of the book will have obvious solutions, but the major examples used will be a compromise between easy interpretability from a common-sense basis and realistic factor-analytic problems.

In factor analysis, examples have traditionally played an even more important role than that of illustration. Due to the complexities of the procedure, it has occasionally been difficult to derive the methodological conclusions needed to proceed with the research at hand. In such cases, a number of examples have often been run to check the validity of the proposed method of analysis. The examples have occasionally shown that the suggested procedure breaks down in practice whereas on other occasions they have shown the potential usefulness of factor-analytic procedures. We shall rely on studies analyzing sets of examples to help us identify those elements of factor analysis that are critical to research.

---

[2]A halfway house between an intuitive approach to factoring and use of the full factor-analytic stable of techniques is that of primitive cluster analysis. While clustering procedures vary from simple ones, like the example of Table 1.2.3, to the complex (Bromley, 1966; Tryon & Bailey, 1970) they are similar in that the goal is to identify those variables that are related enough to be placed under the same label. The variables that are placed together are considered a cluster. In some of the more sophisticated procedures, a measure of the central thrust of the variables is used to define the cluster; each individual variable is then correlated with that index of the cluster. In that case, the results of the cluster analyses are essentially the same as the results from what is called factor analysis. Technically, the process is that of multiple-group factors, diagonal factors or some other variant depending upon how the central thrust of the cluster of variables has been determined. More sophisticated procedures for clustering diverge from the factor-analytic model. In many cases, the results are quite similar to those of a factor analysis, but this is not always so.

Some examples have been artificial ones constructed to fit the theory of factor analysis. These have been termed **plasmodes** (Cattell, 1966c, p. 223f) and are analyzed as a check on the validity and robustness of the procedures. The classic plasmode is Thurstone's box problem (Thurstone, 1947). He measured different characteristics of boxes, for example, the interdiagonal of the box. He then factored the data and was able to show that the three dimensions of space were found by his procedures. This occurred in spite of the fact that practically all of his variables violated a basic assumption of factor analysis noted in the next chapter: they were not linear combinations of the underlying factors but were multiplicative functions! A *new* box problem is presented in Section 1.3.1 as a plasmode to be analyzed several times in later chapters which follow the assumptions more closely.

In substantive research, factor analysis has generally been used for exploratory purposes. This has been true in the area of human abilities where factor analysis originally developed. In Section 1.3.2 we present an ability problem that is a widely used factor-analytic example.

Other types of data may also be factored. Section 1.3.3 contains a physique example where the interest has been in the structuring of the data (i.e., determining the quantitative and qualitative generalities that can be made).

Analyses of the examples are principally oriented toward illustrating factor-analytic procedures. No one theoretical perspective is consistently used with a set of data because that would limit the example's usefulness for this book. If the data were being analyzed for a substantive purpose, that purpose would restrict the analyses. The theory producing the purpose would also lead to more interpretations of the results than are made here. The discussions of the examples are at a common-sense level and ignore many sophisticated theories on which they might reflect but with which the reader may not be familiar.

The same examples are analyzed at several places in the text to illustrate factor-analytic procedures. At this point background information for each example is presented. That background information will allow referral to the problems as appropriate later in the text.

1.3.1 Ten-Variable Box Plasmode

The spatial dimensionality of boxes is obviously three. Many measurements calculated on a box can be reproduced from knowing solely the height, width, and depth of that box. Therefore, these three dimensions are considered the factors for this example; giving appropriate weights to each of these dimensions will reproduce other box measurements provided that the measurements are weighted combinations of length, height, and width. Many of the possible measurements that could be taken from boxes are not weighted combinations and, as we shall see later, these measures would be only approximated by the three underlying dimensions. It would be hoped that factor-analytic procedures would be able to adequately recover the three original dimensions from appropriate box data. Naturally, the box plasmode has an intuitive answer, and it is included to show how commonsense results are given detail through a factor analysis.

The box example was developed by simply measuring 100 boxes found in and around the homes of graduate students. As in the case of Thurstone's example, few variables were purely linear composites. Also, each value was taken in inches, rounded, and converted to rounded centimeters to introduce a touch of error. The shape of some variable distributions was altered by squaring them. These imperfections were introduced to add realism by keeping the data from following the factor model perfectly. The correlations among the box variables are given in Table 1.3.1. As can be seen, the plasmode has been developed so that the three dimensions of space would not be intuitively abstracted from the correlations.

If the dimensionality of space were not known, then a factor analysis of the box data would provide an empirical estimation of the dimensions and how they affect the measurements taken. Given the nature of the variables, it is apparent that the data can only be used to evaluate spatial dimensionality. Non-spatial characteristics of boxes, such as color, materials used in construction, aesthetic appeal, and the like have not been included. Nothing can come from a factor analysis that was not measured among the variables.

The means and standard deviations of the box variables are given in Appendix A.

TABLE 1.3.1
Correlations Among Box Measurements

Variables	1	2	3	4	5	6	7	8	9	10
1. Length squared	10000									
2. Height squared	6283	10000								
3. Width squared	5631	7353	10000							
4. Length plus width	8689	7055	8444	10000						
5. Length plus height	9030	8626	6890	8874	10000					
6. Width plus height	6908	9028	9155	8841	8816	10000				
7. Longest inner diagonal	8633	7495	7378	9164	9109	8572	10000			
8. Shortest inner diagonal	7694	7902	7872	8857	8835	8884	7872	10000		
9. Space inner diagonal	8945	7929	7656	9494	9546	8942	9434	9000	10000	
10. Thickness of edge	5615	6850	8153	7004	6583	7720	6201	6141	6378	10000

Note: Decimal points are not given. Four digits are given instead of the usual two so that additional calculations can be based on this matrix.

1.3.2 Twenty-Four Ability Variables

Holzinger and Swineford (1939) gave 24 psychological tests to junior high school students at two schools. The data are typical of the ability tests that have been used throughout the history of factor analysis. The factor-analytic problem itself is concerned with the number and kind of dimensions that can be best used to describe the ability area.

From the ability data come factors such as intelligence. Such a factor has no more "reality" than the simple sum of a set of items that is given the same label, or measurements established in any other way. An intelligence factor represents a construct that has been found by some to be useful in summarizing data and would therefore, it is hoped, be useful in theory-building. The fact that a construct may be factor-analytically based may or may not add to its scientific viability, which depends upon the rationale for and methods of factoring as well as the long-term usefulness of the construct.

However, the Holzinger and Swineford data are of interest not only because they represent the substantive area out of which factor analysis developed but also because they have been widely used as an example in factor analysis. Whenever any new procedure is recommended, it is often accompanied by an analysis of these data.

The 24 variables with their means, standard deviations, and reliability coefficients for the two schools are given in Appendix A. The raw data are given in Holzinger and Swineford (1939), and the correlations among variables in Chapter 6.[3]

It should be noted that the raw data do not always produce the same statistics as Holzinger and Swineford gave. We have assumed the raw data were correct. Our results therefore differ slightly from the results of those who have assumed the correlations were correct.

1.3.3 Twelve Physique Variables

An early and continuing problem to which factor analysis has been applied is that of physique. What is the best way to describe and distinguish the basic characteristics of physique? The answer is not only worthwhile in its own right but has implications for personality–physique studies and for medicine as well as other areas.

---

[3]Unless otherwise noted, the examples use only the data from the Grant-White School. The common practice of including variables 25 and 26 but not variables 3 and 4 is followed here. (Variables 25 and 26 were attempts to develop better tests for variables 3 and 4). However, when both schools are involved in an analysis, the original variables 3 and 4 are used so that all subjects will have scores from identical tests (tests 25 and 26 were given only at one school).

Because physique characteristics are measured in three-dimensional space, an example from this area provides some parallels to the box plasmode. However, Eysenck and others (Burt, 1944, 1947; Eysenck, 1969, Chapter 9; Rees, 1960) have argued that two dimensions are more appropriate for describing physique than the three of length, height, and width (later chapters give some of this evidence). Thus the problem is not as close to the box problem as one might initially think and adds an interesting degree of complexity to the analyses and interpretation.

The manner in which data are factored reflects the theoretical interests of the investigators. The physique data could be factored from other perspectives than that of typing physiques. For example, in Chapter 5 the data are factored from the viewpoint of a women's garment business. Different perspectives can, and often should, produce different factor analyses of the same data.

The data used are taken from a study by Rees (1950). He collected his data from English armed service personnel being treated for emotional disturbances. The means and standard deviations for the 200 women are given in Appendix A. Our analyses will generally begin from the correlations published by Rees (which are given in Chapter 5).

2 Basic Factor Models

In Chapter 1, basic goals of a factor analysis and common-sense approaches to achieving the same goals were presented. In the present chapter factor analysis is presented within the framework of the multivariate linear model for data analysis. The general nature of multivariate linear models is presented in Section 2.1.

The multivariate linear factor model has several variants. One class of variants is the **full component model,** which is based on perfect calculation of the variables from the components. The other class of variants, the **common factor model,** includes sources of variance not attributable to the common factors.[1] Both classes of multivariate linear factor models, discussed in Sections 2.2 and 2.3 respectively, can be subdivided according to whether the factors are assumed to be correlated or uncorrelated (Section 2.4), giving a total of four basic variants: correlated components, correlated common factors, uncorrelated components, and uncorrelated common factors. Each variant of the multivariate linear factor model has its own peculiarities although they do blend into each other.

In the concluding section, 2.5, the role of the models in factor analysis is discussed.

2.1 MULTIVARIATE LINEAR MODELS AND FACTOR ANALYSIS

A considerable amount of contemporary research can be subsumed under the multivariate linear model (Section 2.1.1), although that model has its limitations (Section 2.1.2). Techniques such as analysis of variance and multiple regression

---

[1]Factor analysis as a term is occasionally used with only the common factor model, but then there is no term to use with the broader model of which both components and common factors are a part.

solve for certain unknowns within the model whereas factor analysis solves for other unknowns (Section 2.1.3). Therefore, factor analysis can be approached as one method of analyzing data within the broader multivariate linear model.

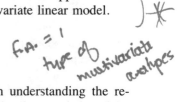

2.1.1 Multivariate Linear Models as a Basis for Behavioral Science Research

Research in the behavioral sciences is concerned with understanding the responses of individuals. The responses are explained by the characteristics of the particular situation and the characteristics of the individuals. The result is seen as arising from some combination of these two sets of influences. Some psychologists, for example, summarize this relationship by the following:

$$X_{ij} = f(S_j, O_i) \tag{2.1.1}$$

where X_{ij} is individual i's response in situation j, S_j summarizes the characteristics of situation j, and O_i summarizes the characteristics of organism i. The relationship between S and O is unspecified because the equation only states that the response is a function of both S and O. From a broader perspective, the organism involved need not be an individual person, but could be a society, a street-corner gang, an economic unit, or any other entity. In each case, the group or unit has certain characteristics it brings to the situation and the situation also contributes to the result.

Within any one situation, some characteristics of the organism will be more closely related to the responses than will others. These characteristics can be weighted so as to indicate which ones have the strong relationships. A simple weighting system consists of zeros and ones, but more complex weights can be easily developed. When the characteristics are weighted, Eq. (2.1.1) becomes:

$$X_{i1} = w_{1A}A_i + w_{1B}B_i + \cdots + w_{1f}F_i + c \tag{2.1.2}$$

where X_{i1} is individual i's response in situation 1, w_{1A} is the weight given in situation 1 to characteristic A, A_i is individual i's score on characteristic A, and $w_{1f}F_i$ is the last weight and score whose relationship is determined. A constant, c, is also added to adjust the mean. Because Eq. (2.1.2) is linear or additive in form, we have introduced a linear model of behavior. Using a linear model for behavior allows use of the mathematical and statistical linear models to guide data analyses. Using weights in the model necessitates assuming that they can be applied across the range of the scores on the characteristics.

Equation (2.1.2) is only for one specific situation. Factor analysis has usually operated within the individual differences model in which all individuals are assumed to be in a similar situation. If different individuals are in different situations, then a single set of weights could not be used. The factors influencing the hitting of a stationary target on a shotgun range would not be of the same relative importance in determining the accuracy of using a shotgun on geese, and so the usual factor analysis should use data from either one situation or another.

The statistical linear model is widely used. It includes all of regression analysis and, as Cohen (1968b) and others have shown, all of analysis of variance.[2]

The linear model becomes the multivariate linear model when it is used to predict more than one dependent variable, that is, when several different kinds of responses (X's) are predicted. Each separate response has its own set of weights. For example, one might want to determine not just a single response but the responses to a wide range of variables, X_1 to X_v. The multivariate linear model would consist of a series of equations:

$$X_{i1} = w_{1A}F_{iA} + w_{1B}F_{iB} + w_{1C}F_{iC} + \cdots + w_{1F}F_{if}$$

$$X_{i2} = w_{2A}F_{iA} + w_{2B}F_{iB} + w_{2C}F_{iC} + \cdots + w_{2F}F_{if}$$

$$X_{i3} = w_{3A}F_{iA} + w_{3B}F_{iB} + w_{3C}F_{iC} + \cdots + w_{3F}F_{if} \qquad (2.1.3)$$

$$\cdot \quad \cdot \quad \cdot \quad \cdot \quad \cdot \quad \cdot$$

$$\cdot \quad \cdot \quad \cdot \quad \cdot \quad \cdot \quad \cdot$$

$$\cdot \quad \cdot \quad \cdot \quad \cdot \quad \cdot \quad \cdot$$

$$X_{iv} = w_{vA}F_{iA} + w_{vB}F_{iB} + w_{vC}F_{iC} + \cdots + w_{vF}F_{if}$$

where X_{iv} is the response of individual i to dependent variable v, w_{vA} is variable v's weight for characteristic A, F_{iA} is individual i's score for the first characteristic and F_{if} is individual i's score for the f'th characteristic. The characteristics are usually referred to as factors.[3] Characteristics that are irrelevant to a particular response are included in the general equation but given a zero weight. All scores are assumed to be deviations from the mean so that the constant, c, of Eq. (2.1.2) can be dropped.

Within the multivariate linear model, **any scores that are given weights and added together are defined as factors of the resulting variables.** (The weights are often referred to as "factor coefficients" or "loadings," although both of these terms are occasionally used to refer to the correlations between the variables and factors as well.) The weights may be as simple as 0 and 1, and the factor scores need not have any specified mean, standard deviation, or distribution. Although various procedures for finding the factors make additional assumptions, **the basic factor model assumes only that the variables are additive composites of the weighted factors.**

The multivariate linear model can also be used to analyze situations. To do so, we simply reverse the words "individual" and "situation" in the preceding

---

[2]Gollob (1968a) and Boruch and Wolins (1970) explore the relationships between factor analysis and analysis of variance.

[3]Some writers reserve the phrase "scores on factors" for only those scores that are generated in a formal factor analysis. However, because some scores on factors come from simply adding appropriate test items (cf. Chapters 5 and 12), they therefore blend into other types of scores. The important distinctions among scoring systems are, of course, the degree to which the scores used in a study are directly observed, are replicable, and are integrated into a substantive theory so that they may be meaningful. Scores from a factor analysis can meet all of these requirements.

discussion. If both situations and individuals are to be examined in the same analysis, then three-mode factor analysis is available (Chapter 15). The multivariate linear model, therefore, can be applied to a considerable amount of contemporary research.

It is important to distinguish between theories concerning ''laws of nature'' and mathematical models. In beginning this section, a theory of behavior was introduced that involved a linear mathematical model to show that model's relevance. However, the linear mathematical model, which includes factor analysis, is usually developed separately from any substantive theory of behavior. Investigators in any given area evaluate the applicability of such mathematical models to their domain of interest.

2.1.2 Limitations of Linear Models

In a linear model, some variables—which are often called dependent variables or criteria—are assumed to be a weighted combination of a set of factors, which are also referred to as independent variables or predictors. There are three cases in which the linear model may not give the best representation of the relationships between factors and variables.

First, it may be that the relationship is nonlinear. The dependent variable may be low, for example, whenever the factor is either high or low. Or, the variables may be a function of the log of the factor score, of two factors multiplied times each other, and so forth. Many of the variables investigated by science have turned out to be nonlinear functions of their factors.

If nonlinear relationships are involved, no statistical analysis within the linear model is truly adequate. Only those relationships that can be approximated by a linear model will appear and other models may be necessary. (Nonlinear factor analysis is discussed later.) However, if a nonlinear relationship is expected, then a variable might be transformed so that the relationship between the derived variable and the factors is linear (cf. Section 14.2.5; Bottenberg & Ward, 1963; Kelly, Beggs & McNeil, 1969).

Second, the relationship between the variable and the factor may not be the same for all levels of the factor. Table 2.1.1 presents one such situation. Low

TABLE 2.1.1
Job Performance as a Function
of Ability

Ability Levels	Range of Observed Job Performance
High	Poor to Good
Medium	Poor to Good
Low	Poor to Fair
Very Low	Poor

ability predicts poor performance in most jobs, but high ability is less related to performance. Low ability means the person simply does not have what it takes to handle the intricacies of the job. However, after a minimum level of ability has been reached, everyone can perform the tasks. Whether or not a person performs well is then a function of motivation.

In Table 2.1.1, a weight would be needed for the ability factor only if the person were below the critical level on the factor. For all others the weight given ability to estimate job performance should be zero. Because the linear model uses a single weight for all levels of the factor, analyses would produce a single weight to be applied in all cases.

Third, the relationships of several factors to a single variable may be interchangeable. For example, one can satisfy some job requirements by being either fast or accurate. Some people would score high on the performance variable by being accurate but slow while others would be fast but careless. The linear model assumes that each factor is related to the variable in the same manner for all individuals. In the present example, an analysis under the linear model would give some weight to both the speed and accuracy factors, and this would lead to the false interpretation that some of both factors were needed to perform well.

The aforementioned three cases are situations in which the linear model should be used only after appropriate changes are made so that the variables can be linear functions of the factors. Although the three problems exist because the linear model is used, they are not unique to factor analysis. All methods of analyzing the linear model have the same problems when the linear model is not the best for the data.

Note that the three problem cases arise out of the factor-to-variable relationship. The only assumption made in using the linear model is that the variables are linear functions of the factors. **The variables are not assumed to be linearly related. Variables may be related in any manner whatsoever so long as that interrelationship is a function of each variable being linearly related to the factors.**

2.1.3 Analysis of the Multivariate Linear Model

Analyzing the multivariate linear model takes on various forms depending on what is known and what is unknown. Obviously, if the variable scores, weights, and factor scores are known, there is no problem and no calculation. When the scores on the variables are unknown but the weights and scores on factors are known, then the process is that of simple calculation.

Example

Hollingshead and Redlich (1958) gave the following equation for their two-factor approach to the measurement of social class:

$$C_i = 7O_i + 4E_i$$

where C_i is individual i's social class index, O_i is his occupational level rated on a seven-point scale, E_i is the educational level rated on another seven-point scale, 7 is the weight for occupation and 4 is the weight for education. The resulting class score can range from 11 to 77 and is subdivided into social classes. To determine a person's social class from the occupation and education ratings, one simply puts them into the formula and computes C_i. O and E are factors of C; O_i and E_i are an individual's scores on the factors.

If the scores are available for both variables and factors, then weights can be found by a series of multiple regression analyses. Each such analysis finds the weights for one variable. This procedure is commonly used when, for example, the same set of variables is used to predict high school grades, admission to college, and the probability of dropping out of high school. Each of the predictors is given a nonzero weight if it makes a significant contribution; otherwise it is given a zero weight. Zero weights are implicitly given whenever a variable is dropped from a particular equation.

It may be that no set of weights can be computed that will exactly reproduce the scores on the variables. In that case, the weights that produce the best least-square estimates of the variables are used.[4]

In calculating variables from factors and weights or calculating weights from variables and factors, we assume that scores are available for the factors. If this is not so, then the data must be analyzed for the factor scores. Computing factor scores would not be difficult if the weights were known, for then a process analogous to the typical multiple regression could be used. However, neither the weights nor factor scores may be known and the solution is solely from the variables themselves. This is the domain of factor analysis. (Note that the phrase "factor analysis," the gerund "factoring," and the infinitive "to factor" refer to solving for the factors when and only when the factor scores and the weights are both unknown.)

To solve uniquely for the weights and factors at the same time is impossible without further assumptions, for an infinite number of weight/factor sets exist by which the variables can be calculated. Factor analysis is possible only if some restrictions are placed on the solution. A prime source of differences in procedures for factoring lies in the restrictions they place on the weights. (Chapters 5 through 10 present some restrictions that are commonly used.) Such restrictions include assumptions concerning what is important, the model, and the relationships among the factors. Varying these restrictions will vary the nature of the weights and factor scores.

In a mathematical sense, the particular restrictions imposed to find a unique set of weights and factors are arbitrary, although each has its own characteristics. However, it is not an arbitrary decision when factor analysis is used in research.

---

[4]Least-square estimates occur when the sum of the squared differences between the observed scores and those estimated under the model is minimized. This procedure is discussed in greater detail in statistical texts.

The particular restrictions placed on the solution are legitimatized by the theoretical stance the investigator adopts. Different theories make different sets of restrictions appropriate.

Several mathematical models will usually reproduce one particular set of data equally well. In such cases, different resolutions of the factor-analytic problem will be equally accurate and the most appropriate factor-analytic restrictions will not be known until critical experiments are developed for deciding among the substantive theories that follow from each mathematical model. In addition, factor-analytic research may contribute directly to the evaluation of competitive theories. The investigator can place mathematical restrictions as required by the competitive substantive theories and examine their relative efficacy. Some sets of restrictions derived from one theory will increase the explanatory power more than those derived from other theories.

Inaccuracies in reproducing the variables may occur in two basic forms. On the one hand, the model may be exactly correct in the population. However, a model is almost never developed from or applied to a population, but is used with only a sample from the population. Chance fluctuations in sampling will virtually guarantee that the model will be partially inaccurate. Model error occurs regardless of whether the factor model contains a term for unique sources of variance.

On the other hand, theoretical considerations may suggest that only part of the variables could be fit by the factor model. For some variables, past research may be the basis of an expectation that factors other than those in the model may be important. The other factors may be ones of substantive interest but which are not being examined in that research study, or the other factors may be considered contaminants in the measurement of the construct. In addition, some variables may not be expected to be reproduced under the model because the measurement operations do not exclude sources of random error. These sources of inaccuracy can be taken into account in the factor model (see Section 2.3).

2.2   THE FULL COMPONENT MODEL

In the multivariate linear model of Eq. (2.1.3), it was assumed that the model would lead to perfect reproduction of the variables because no error term appeared in the equation. The variables can be directly calculated from the factors by applying the weights. The same factor scores produce all variables simply by altering the weights. This mathematical model is referred to as the **full component** model. When one factors for all components, the existence of a set of factor scores that produce the original variables **exactly** is assumed. Any observed error is a reflection of the inaccuracy of the model in that particular sample. It is obvious that empirical research is seldom a case of full component analysis because observed data are usually known to be fallible. Nevertheless, the full component model may, in the light of sampling error, give such an excellent approximation as to be useful. Additionally, it may be used to produce a set of uncorrelated variables from a set of variables containing moderate correlations.

Truncated components occur whenever some, but not all, of the components are used to estimate the original variables. In truncated components the smaller components are dismissed as due to inaccuracy in the model's fit for a particular sample. Truncated components are the usual form of a component analysis.

2.2.1 Defining Equation

The full component model is defined by the following equation for deviation scores:

$$X_{iv} = w_{v1}F_{1i} + w_{v2}F_{2i} + w_{v3}F_{3i} + \cdots + w_{vf}F_{fi} \tag{2.2.1}$$

where X_{iv} is individual i's score on variable v, w_{vf} is the weight for variable v on factor f, and F_{1i} to F_{fi} are subject i's scores on the f factors. The number of factors is, for reasons explained in Chapter 8, usually the same as the number of variables in a full component analysis although less in truncated components. The weights may be presented alone for a variable and are then called the **factor pattern** of that variable. The factor pattern summarizes the relative contribution of each factor to that variable for all the subjects.

Example

Table 2.2.1 represents the factor scores used to illustrate the component model. Each of ten individuals has a score on both factor A and factor B. The factor scores are in

TABLE 2.2.1
Component Scores
for 10 Individuals

	Component Scores	
Individuals	A	B
1	1	−1
2	1	1
3	1	−1
4	1	1
5	1	1
6	−1	−1
7	−1	1
8	−1	−1
9	−1	1
10	−1	−1
Mean	0	0
Standard Deviation	1.0	1.0

Note: The correlation between the two sets of scores is .20

TABLE 2.2.2
Component Factor Patterns for
Four Variables

	Factors	
Variables	A	B
1	.96	.15
2	1.02	−.15
3	.29	.90
4	−.65	.90

Note: The entries in the table are the weights by which the factor scores
are to be multiplied to produce the variable scores.

standard score form, with means of zero and variances of one, but are simplified by being
only + 1s and − 1s. They have a slight correlation of .20.

Table 2.2.2 contains the weights for calculating scores for four variables from the
factor scores; the weights are scaled so that the resulting variables have variances of one.
Both Tables 2.2.1 and 2.2.2 were selected arbitrarily for illustrative purposes.

The factor scores in Table 2.2.1 are neither continuous nor normally distributed but
dichotomous and bimodal. In addition, one of the weights is greater than unity. These are
legitimate because the multivariate linear model requires only the application of a linear
equation such as (2.2.1), but some statistical procedures discussed later could not be
applied here because of their more restrictive assumptions.

Equation (2.2.1) requires that the factor scores be multiplied by their weights and
summed to obtain any one individual's score on any one variable. Individual 1's score on
variable 1 is calculated as follows:

$$X_{11} = (.96)\,(1) + (.15)\,(-1) = .96 - .15 = .81.$$

Note that the score is calculated perfectly from the components. The full set of variable
scores is given in Table 2.2.3.

TABLE 2.2.3
Component Variable Scores

		Variables		
Individuals	1	2	3	4
1	.81	1.17	− .61	−1.55
2	1.11	.87	1.19	.25
3	.81	1.17	− .61	−1.55
4	1.11	.87	1.19	.25
5	1.11	.87	1.19	.25
6	−1.11	− .87	−1.19	− .25
7	− .81	−1.17	.61	1.55
8	−1.11	− .87	−1.19	− .25
9	− .81	−1.17	.61	1.55
10	−1.11	− .87	−1.19	− .25

2.2.2 Characteristics of the Variables as a Function of the Full Components

In the multivariate linear model, the variables are defined as linear functions of the factors. The dependence of the variables on the weights and factors means that all of a variable's statistics are a function of the weights and factors. In Sections 2.2.2 and 2.3.2 as well as in the two following chapters are presented the relationships between characteristics of the variables and the weights and factors under the multivariate linear model. It is assumed that scores are known for both variables and factors and that the weights are also known. Knowing the theoretical relationships will enable us to select appropriate starting points for a factor analysis (i.e., to find weights and factors when only scores on the variables are known).

Table 2.2.4 contains the equations showing the characteristics of a given variable, X, as a function of its components. The equations are derived in the next chapter. The assumptions made in those derivations are for the population of individuals. The assumptions are as follows:

1. The variables are calculated from the factors by multiplying each factor by the appropriate weight and summing across all factors. (The term *calculated* is used rather than estimated; all of the variance of a variable is from the factors. This identifies it as a component model).

TABLE 2.2.4

Characteristics of the Variables as a Function of
Their Components

Mean of X:

$$\bar{X} = \sum_{k=1}^{f} w_k \bar{F}_k = 0 \qquad (2.2.2)$$

Variance of X:

$$V_x = \sigma_x^2 = \sum_{k=1}^{f} w_k^2 + \sum_{j=1}^{f} \sum_{k=1}^{f} (w_j w_k r_{jk}) \qquad (2.2.3)$$

(where j is not allowed to equal k)

Correlation between variables X and Y:

$$r_{XY} = \frac{\sum_{k=1}^{f} w_{X_k} w_{Y_k} + \sum_{j=1}^{f} \sum_{k=1}^{f} w_{X_j} w_{Y_k} r_{jk}}{\sigma_x \sigma_Y} \quad \text{(where } j \neq k\text{)} \qquad (2.2.4)$$

Correlation of X with component k:

$$r_{XF_k} = \frac{w_{X_k} + \sum_{j=1}^{f} w_{X_j} r_{jk}}{\sigma_X} \quad \text{(where } j \neq k\text{)} \qquad (2.2.5)$$

2. The factors have means of zero and standard deviations of one. This assumption simplifies the equations and results in little loss of generality because data from the behavioral sciences are, at best, only interval scales where the means and standard deviations are arbitrary.[5]

Note that nothing is said about the distribution of either the factor scores or the variable scores. They can be of any form so long as the two preceding assumptions are not violated and the equations—including those involving Pearson product-moment correlation coefficients—will still hold true.

The formula for the mean, Eq. (2.2.2), of X indicates that X is always a deviation score in this model, and so the variables to be factored are to have means of zero. If the mean of an observed X is not zero, the model cannot take that information into account. Although the model is expanded in Chapter 14 toward allowing both the factors and the variables to have means other than zero, the model normally used is that presented here. Thus, observed scores are implicitly or explicitly converted to deviation scores before being factor analyzed.

From Eq. (2.2.3) it is apparent that shifts in the variance of X can be from changes in the weights or correlations between factors. If the variance of X is to remain constant, any shifts in some weights must be offset by shifts in other weights or in the correlations among factors, r_{jk}.

From Eq. (2.2.4) it can be noted that the correlation between two variables is a function of the patterns of weights of the two variables. The more similar their weights—that is, the more often both variables have high weights for the same factors and low weights for other factors—the higher their correlation. The extent to which this holds true is seen in Eq. (2.2.4) to be a function of the correlations between factors. The higher the correlations, the less important the differences in weights become because the weights are multiplied by each other and by the correlation between the two factors. Also note that the correlations will, if nonzero, become relatively more important as the number of factors increases because the number of elements of which they are a part increases faster than those of which they have no part.

The correlation between two variables can be calculated with no knowledge of factor scores or any other data on individuals. Only the weights and the correlations among the factors are necessary. This holds true regardless of the variances of the variables, but the correlation must be "corrected" by dividing by the two standard deviations if the variances are not 1.0.

Equation (2.2.4) can be examined from another point of view. If the correlations between variables are available and suitable restrictions are placed on the weights and correlations among factors, the correlations can be analyzed to find the weights. **Analyzing correlations is the basis for most factor-analytic calculation procedures presently in use. One begins with the product-moment**

---

[5]Cattell (1972) has suggested methods for removing this assumption.

correlations among variables, makes appropriate restrictions, and solves for the weights (factor pattern). Factor scores can then be computed (cf. Chapter 12).

The correlations between a variable and its factors are calculated by Eq. (2.2.5). Again the impact of the correlations among the factors should be noted. A variable's correlations with a set of factors is called its **factor structure.** Note that the factor structure becomes identical to the factor pattern (i.e., the weights given the factors to compute the variable, when the variance of the variable is 1.0 and the correlations among factors are zero). Otherwise, they are different even though terms such as "factor coefficients" and "factor loadings" may be used for both the pattern and structure.

Equations (2.2.4) and (2.2.5) make no assumptions regarding distributions. These assumptions are made only when questions concerning how well the coefficient represents the "true" relationships or significance levels are involved.

Examples

The following examples use the data in Tables 2.2.1, 2.2.2, and 2.2.3, to compute the statistic by the usual formula and by the appropriate one in Table 2.2.4.

Variance of a variable. The usual formula for the variance when all scores are deviates from the mean gives the following results:

$$V_1 = \frac{\Sigma\, x^2}{N} = \frac{10.0017}{10} = 1.00$$

Applying (2.2.3) should give the same result:

$$V_1 = (.9216 + .0225) + .96\,(.15)\,(.20) + .15\,(.96)\,(.20)$$
$$= .9451 + .0288 + .0288$$
$$= 1.0017 = 1.00$$

Correlation between two variables. Because both variables 1 and 2 from Table 2.2.3 are in standard score form, the calculation of their correlation from the variable scores is simplified to the following:

$$r_{12} = \frac{\Sigma\, x\, y}{N} = \frac{9.585}{10} = .96$$

Equation (2.2.4) would be the appropriate one to calculate the correlation without knowledge of the individual's actual variable scores:

$$r_{12} = (.96\,(1.02) + .15\,(-.15)) + (.96\,(-.15)(.20) + 1.02\,(.15)\,(.20))$$
$$= (.9792 - .0225) + (-.0288 + .0306)$$
$$= .9585 = .96$$

Correlation of a variable and a factor. The correlation between variable 1 and factor A can be calculated from the scores on the variable and the factor:

$$r_{XA} = \frac{\Sigma_{XA}}{N\sigma_X\sigma_A} = \frac{9.9000}{10\,(1)\,(1)} = .99$$

From Eq. (2.2.5), it is:

$$r_{XA} = .96 + .15 \ (.20) = .96 + .0300 = .99$$

2.3 THE COMMON FACTOR MODEL

In the common factor model, the factors are divided into two groups. The first group, the **common factors** themselves, consists of those factors which contribute to two or more of the variables (i.e., several variables have these factors in common). However, the variables will seldom be calculable from the common factors alone, for each variable will be influenced by sources independent of the other variables. These sources may be legitimate causal influences that are not affecting the other variables, systematic distortions in the scores (usually called *bias*), or random error from inaccuracies of measurement. For most factor-analytic purposes, all of these sources simply detract from the accuracy of computing the variable scores from the common factors. The noncommon factor variance for each variable is summarized in a **unique factor** that contains the scores necessary to complete the prediction of that variable.

In Section 2.3.1 appropriate elements are added to the basic equation of the linear model to represent unique factors and several definitions are presented which arise specifically out of this model. The next section, 2.3.2, presents some statistics that are appropriate to the common factor model. Section 2.3.3 considers the characteristics of the variables, including their intercorrelations, as a function of both the common factors and the unique factors.

2.3.1 Defining Equation

The traditional common factor model is defined by the following equation:

$$X_{iv} = w_{v1} \ F_{1i} + \cdots + w_{vf} \ F_{fi} + w_{vu} \ U_{iv} \tag{2.3.1}$$

where the first elements are the same as in the component model, w_{vu} is the weight given variable v's unique factor, and U_{iv} is individual i's unique factor score for variable v. The unique factor includes the random errors of measurement, influences that affect only this variable and all other sources of error and bias that prevent the common factors from completely defining that particular variable. The subscript for U will change for each variable; this means that each variable's unique factor affects only that variable.

Note that the term *unique,* as used in the present discussion of common factor analysis, does *not* include error of the model, which might, for example, arise from attempting to generalize from a sample of individuals to the population. Sampling theory has not been extensively developed for factor analysis; to use the equations in this and most other chapters, all samples of individuals must be sufficiently large so that sampling error can be ignored (Chapter 16 contains a more detailed discussion of sampling problems).

Each U_v can be conceptualized as another factor that has a mean of zero, a standard deviation of 1.0, and is assumed to be uncorrelated with each of the common factors as well as each of the other unique factors. With f common factors and v unique factors, the solution technically has $f - v$ factors in it. Usually, only the common factors are evaluated. Having $f + v$ factors can cause an occasional problem. For example, scores on common factors can be only estimated (cf. Chapter 12).

Example

The common factor example begins with the same factor scores as used in the components example (Table 2.2.1). To these factors are added unique factors in keeping with the common factor model. Each unique factor can be considered the sum of all errors and specific influences contributing to only that variable. The unique factor scores for four variables are given in Table 2.3.1 for the same ten individuals as before. They are uncorrelated with each other and with the factors.

The weights to calculate the scores for the variables are the same as used in the component model but with the addition of weights for each unique factor. Table 2.3.2 contains the weights.

The scores for each individual on each variable are found by applying the weights to the common and noncommon factor scores.

Entity 1's score on variable 1 is:

$$X_{11} = .96(1) + .15(-1) + .40(-1.58)$$
$$= .96 - .15 - .632 = .178$$

Table 2.3.3 lists all of the scores on the four variables.

TABLE 2.3.1
Unique Factor Scores

Individuals	U_1	U_2	U_3	U_4
1	−1.58	.00	1.58	.00
2	1.58	.00	.00	−1.58
3	.00	1.58	−1.58	.00
4	.00	−1.58	.00	1.58
5	.00	.00	.00	.00
6	.00	.00	.00	.00
7	.00	1.58	.00	1.58
8	.00	−1.58	−1.58	.00
9	−1.58	.00	.00	−1.58
10	1.58	.00	1.58	.00
Mean	.00	.00	.00	.00
Standard Deviation	1.00	1.00	1.00	1.00

TABLE 2.3.2
Common and Unique Factor Weights

Variables	Common		Unique			
	A	B	U_1	U_2	U_3	U_4
1	.96	.15	.40	.00	.00	.00
2	1.02	−.15	.00	.60	.00	.00
3	.29	.90	.00	.00	.80	.00
4	−.65	.90	.00	.00	.00	1.00

From some perspectives, the common factor model can be considered a special case of the component model. In Eq. (2.3.1), the variable scores are calculated directly by the same weighted summation method used in components; the only difference is that one factor is called unique in the common factor model. Or, the component model could be considered a special case of the common factor model where all unique factors are given weights of zero. For this reason, both models are varieties of factor analysis.

However, the distinction between common factors and unique factors is often important when the variable scores are given and the factor pattern and scores are to be computed. In common factor analysis, the factors sought are broken into common factor and unique factor sets, and different assumptions are made about each. In the component model, perfect prediction is implied and the same assumptions are made for all the factors.

Although the present discussion has included all noncommon factor sources of variance in one unique factor, this need not be done. The unique contribution

TABLE 2.3.3
Variable Scores for Common Factor Example

Individuals	Variables			
	1	2	3	4
1	.178	1.170	.654	−1.550
2	1.742	.870	1.190	−1.330
3	.810	2.118	−1.874	−1.550
4	1.110	− .078	1.190	1.830
5	1.110	.870	1.190	.250
6	−1.110	− .870	−1.190	− .250
7	− .810	− .222	.610	3.130
8	−1.110	−1.818	−2.454	− .250
9	−1.442	−1.170	.610	− .030
10	− .478	− .870	.074	− .250

to the variable can be subdivided into one part arising from unreliability of measurement and another part arising from systematic sources in addition to the common factors. The latter component is a composite of all of that variable's reliable variance that does not overlap with a factor in that analysis, and is called a **specific factor** because it is specific to one variable. Both of these sources are assumed to be uncorrelated with the common factors and with each other.

Variants of the common factor model are possible depending upon how the unique factors are defined. In image analysis, for example, uniqueness is that part of a variable that is not predictable from the set of other variables. We shall not distinguish the variants of the common factor model in this and the next two chapters so that the basic concepts do not become overly complex. The variants will be introduced where their calculation procedures diverge from those used with the traditional common factor model.

2.3.2 Statistics for the Common Factor Model

By definition, the **communality** of a variable is that proportion of its variance that can be accounted for by the common factors. For example, if the communality is .75, the variance of the variable as reproduced from only the common factors would be three-fourths of its observed variance. It can then be shown that the communality for variable X, h^2, is:

$$h^2 = \frac{\Sigma w_k^2 + \Sigma \Sigma w_j w_k r_{jk}}{V_x} \qquad \text{(where } j \neq k\text{)} \qquad (2.3.2)$$

Given Eq. (2.3.2), the variable's **uniqueness,** u^2, is defined as that proportion of the variance excluding the variance attributed to the common factors or the extracted components in a truncated component analysis:

$$u^2 = 1 - h^2 \qquad (2.3.3)$$

To subdivide u^2 further, it is necessary to have a measure of the variable's variance that is nonrandom. This is given by a reliability coefficient, r_{XX}, which is an estimate of the true score variance, r_{Xt}^2 (Nunnally, 1978).

Because r_{Xt}^2 is the proportion of nonerror variance and the communality gives the proportion of the variance from the common factors, the specific factor's proportionate contribution to the variance, s^2, is given by:

$$s^2 = r_{Xt}^2 - h^2 \qquad (2.3.4)$$

In the model, the communality can never be greater than the true score variance except by capitalizing on chance or because of the fallibility in methods of estimating each statistic because negative specificity has no meaning. The error contribution, excluding the specific factor, is e^2 and is calculated by:

$$e^2 = 1 - r_{Xt}^2 \qquad (2.3.5)$$

The following equations also hold true:

$$u^2 = s^2 + e^2 \qquad\qquad (2.3.6)$$

$$1.0 = h^2 + s^2 + e^2 \qquad\qquad (2.3.7)$$

Example

The communality for variable 1 by Eq. (2.3.2) is (where V is taken from the next example):

$$h_1^2 = \frac{.96^2 + .15^2 + (.96)\,(.15)\,(.20) + (.15)\,(.96)\,(.20)}{1.1617}$$

$$= \frac{.9216 + .0225 + .0288 + .0288}{1.1617}$$

$$= \frac{1.0017}{1.1617} = .8623 = .86$$

From Eq. (2.3.3):

$$u_1^2 = 1.0 - .8623 = .14$$

Assume that variable 1's reliability is .97. Then Eq. (2.3.4) is:

$$s_1^2 = .97 - .8623 = .11$$

The error contribution to the variance of the variable can also be computed by Eq. (2.3.5):

$$e_1^2 = 1.00 - .97 = .03$$

As a check, Eq. (2.3.6) can be used:

$$u_1^2 = .1077 + .0300 = .14$$

In Eq. (2.3.7) the total variance is partitioned into components of interest:

$$1.00 = .86 + .11 + .03$$

Obviously, most of the variance of 1 is from the common factors. The specific factor accounts for some variance but the random error is quite small.

The interest is often in the total set of variables. The proportion of the total variance contributed by the common factors is important in determining if the factors can reasonably reproduce the variables. This is obtained as follows:

$$\text{Proportion of total variance extracted} = \frac{\Sigma\, h_j^2}{v} \qquad\qquad (2.3.8)$$

where v is the number of variables. The closer Eq. (2.3.8) comes to 1.0, the more accurately the variables can be reproduced from the common factors.

2.3.3 Characteristics of the Variables as a Function of the Common Factors

The basic equations for the common factor model are given in Table 2.3.4. The derivations, presented in the next chapter, assume the following is true for the population of individuals:

1. The variables are estimated from the common factors by multiplying each factor by the appropriate weight and summing across factors. The variables are only calculable if both common and unique factors are included.
2. The common factors correlate zero with the unique factors.
3. The unique factors correlate zero with each other.
4. All factors have means of zero and standard deviations of 1.0.

In Eqs. (2.3.9) and (2.3.10), it can be seen that unique factors do not affect the means but do affect the variances. The unique factors increase the variance of the variables. By increasing the variances, the unique factors add to the divisor in both formulas for correlations and thus lower each as compared to a component model containing only the common factors.

TABLE 2.3.4
Characteristics of the Variables as a Function of the
Common Factors

Mean of X:

$$\bar{X} = \Sigma\, w_k\, \bar{F}_k = 0 \qquad (2.3.9)$$

Variance of X:

$$V_X = \sigma_x^2 = \Sigma\, w_k^2 + \Sigma\Sigma\, w_j\, w_k\, r_{jk} + u_x^2 \text{ (where } j \neq k) \qquad (2.3.10)$$

Correlation between X and Y:

$$r_{XY} = \frac{\Sigma\, w_{X_k}\, w_{Y_k} + \Sigma\Sigma\, w_{X_j}\, w_{Y_k}\, r_{jk}}{\sigma_X \sigma_Y} \text{ (where } j \neq k) \qquad (2.3.11)$$

Correlation of X with factor k:

$$r_{XF_k} = \frac{w_{X_k} + \Sigma\, w_{X_j}\, r_{jk}}{\sigma_x} \text{ (where } j \neq k) \qquad (2.3.12)$$

Note that both the $j = 1$ to f and $k = 1$ to f have been dropped. This simplification is used when the summation sign appears obvious.

If the variables are in standard score form, then the variance must be 1 and:

$$1 = \Sigma\, w_k^2 + \Sigma\Sigma\, w_j w_k r_{F_j F_k} + u_k^2 \text{ (where } j \neq k) \qquad (2.3.13)$$

Because the correlations among the factors remain constant independent of scaling, the weights will shift as a function of arbitrarily changing the variable's variance. The weights can be changed to produce a variable with a variance of 1 by dividing by the original variance:

$$\frac{V}{V} = \Sigma \frac{w_k^2}{V} + \Sigma \Sigma \frac{w_j}{\sigma} \frac{w_k}{\sigma} \, r_{F_jF_k} + \frac{u^2}{V} \qquad (2.3.14)$$

From Eq. (2.3.14), it can be noted that the weights are converted from those giving raw scores to those giving standard scores by dividing each weight by the variable's standard deviation. In multiple regression analysis, the former are commonly referred to as the b weights and the latter as the beta weights. The weights in the factor pattern are beta weights whenever correlations are factored since correlations implicitly convert all scores to standard scores. From this point on, the terms *weights* and *factor pattern* will only refer to beta weights unless otherwise noted.

Examples

Variance of a Variable. Applying Eq. (2.3.10) to variable 1:

$$V_1 = .96^2 + .15^2 + .96 \, (.15) \, (.20) \, .15 \, (.96)(.20) + .40^2$$
$$= .9216 + .0225 + .0288 + .0288 + .1600$$
$$= 1.1617 = 1.16$$

The variance of variable 1 was increased over variable 1 in the component example by the square of the unique b weight. If a particular sample had error that was correlated at chance level with one of the factors, then the equation would not simplify so readily and the variance could increase even more.

Effect of Unique Factors on Factor Weights. The beta weights, or factor pattern elements, for the last variable of the example are:

$$W_{4F_A} = \frac{-.65}{1.9985} = -.33$$

$$W_{4F_B} = \frac{.90}{1.9985} = .45$$

$$W_{4U_4} = \frac{1.00}{1.9985} = .50$$

When the factor-analytic solution is for variables in standard score form, error lowers the common factor pattern weights in comparison to component weights.

Correlation Between Two Variables. The correlation of variables 1 and 2 in the previous example requires the variances for both variables. The variance for variable 1 was calculated previously; the variance for variable 2 is 1.3617. Using these variances with Eq. (2.3.11):

$$r_{12} = \frac{(.96(1.02) + .15(-.15)) + (.96(-.15)(.20) + 1.02(.15)(.20))}{\sqrt{1.1617} \, \sqrt{1.3617}}$$

$$= \frac{.9792 - .0225 - .0288 + .03608}{1.0778 \times 1.1669} = \frac{.9585}{1.2577} = .7621 = .76$$

Correlation of a variable with a Factor. The correlation of variable 1 with factor A by (2.3.12) is:

$$r_{1A} = \frac{.96 + .15\ (.20)}{1.0778} = \frac{.96 + .300}{1.0778} = \frac{.9900}{1.0778} = .9185 = .92$$

This is somewhat smaller than the component correlation of .98 due to the introduction of a little error. Note that it is also distinct from the weight for variable 1 on factor A.

2.4 CORRELATED AND UNCORRELATED FACTOR MODELS

Component and common factor models each have two forms. In the first and more general case, the common factors or components can be correlated with each other. For example, if measures of abilities are being analyzed, verbal and numerical ability factors could occur that would be related to each other. The prior sections contained the models for correlated factors.

The correlation between two factors can theoretically range up to an absolute value of 1.0. However, factors with high intercorrelations (e.g., .7 or .8) are seldom allowed in a factor analysis because highly overlapping factors are not of great theoretical interest. The problem when a correlation between two factors is "too high" can only be resolved by considering the impact of high correlations on the future use of the factors in practical situations or in theory development. (Further discussion of the proper level of correlations among factors is given in Chapter 9. The implications of correlated factors are discussed in Chapter 11.)

In the uncorrelated models, the equations are simplified because the investigator assumes the factors are independent of each other. Then the elements in the equations that reflect these correlations become zero and drop out. Comparing Table 2.4.1, which contains the basic equations relating characteristics of the variables to uncorrelated factors, with Tables 2.2.4 and 2.3.4 illustrates that fact. Equations assuming uncorrelated factors are easier to compute than the others. Terms such as *factor coefficient* and *factor loading* are clear when the factors are uncorrelated because, as can be seen in Eq. (2.4.5), the factor structure is equal to the factor pattern for standard scores.

The equations in Table 2.4.1 apply to either the component or common factor model except where noted. However, the factor weights are seldom identical when the same data is analyzed under both models due to the presence of u_X^2 in Eq. (2.4.3) and σ_X in Eqs. (2.4.4) and (2.4.5). Therefore, a real difference between a component analysis and a common factor model will exist in the case of the uncorrelated factor models as well as in the case of the correlated component and common factor models.

TABLE 2.4.1
Characteristics of the Variable as a Function of
Uncorrelated Factors

Mean of X:

$$\bar{X} = \Sigma \, w_k \, F_k = 0 \tag{2.4.1}$$

Variance of X:
Component model

$$V_X = \Sigma \, w_k{}^2 \tag{2.4.2}$$

Common factor model

$$V_X = \Sigma \, w_k{}^2 + u_X{}^2 \tag{2.4.3}$$

Correlation between X and Y:

$$r_{XY} = \frac{\Sigma \, w_{X_k} \, w_{Y_k}}{\sigma_X \, \sigma_Y} \tag{2.4.4}$$

Correlation of X with component/factor k:

$$r_{XF_k} = \frac{w_{X_k}}{\sigma_X} \tag{2.4.5}$$

2.5   WHICH FACTOR-ANALYTIC MODEL?

The correlated and uncorrelated, full component and common factor models provide a basis for understanding the relationships between the variables and the factors. Given one of these models and appropriate data, it is then possible to solve for the unknown elements of the model. For example, when the scores on the variables and factors are both known, then multiple regression procedures are used to solve for the weights for all four models. If one asks for a reasonable set of weights and factor scores for a given set of variable scores, then a factor analysis results.

With both weights and factor scores unknown, an infinite number of solutions is possible. To obtain a unique solution, restrictions must be placed upon the solution. The different models provide some of the restrictions. The exploration of these and other suggested restrictions forms the bulk of this book and provides factor analysis with its more interesting problems.

From the equations showing the relationship of the correlation between two variables to the factorial compositions of the variables, it is apparent that the correlations are a function of the factor weights regardless of the model. As a result, the weights can be calculated from a sufficiently large set of correlations as is done, for example, in Chapter 5. Once these weights have been computed, procedures are available to compute the factor scores (cf. Chapter 12). The interrelationship of correlations and weights is the starting point for all major factor-analytic procedures where the correlation (or covariance) matrix is examined to determine weights for each variable. If scores on factors are desired, then these are computed in a later step. The same general approach is used with all the models because the same relationship between correlations and weights is found in all four models.

The selection of a model is based on the answers to two questions:

1. Would using different models produce noticeable differences in the results? If so, which mathematical model is most appropriate given the substantive theory of the area?
2. Are there major differences in the computational difficulty or other costs associated with using the models?

These questions would be answered sequentially with the first being of major importance and the second used to resolve ties. With modern computers, there are only a few procedures that are so prohibitively expensive that the cost question would be a major one.

The supporters of an uncorrelated, truncated component model usually argue that there are no important differences between the models and therefore one should use the simplest model. Others are inclined to argue that there are major differences between the models. The latter, for example, might ask how one can assume that the factors in a given area are uncorrelated without even testing that assumption, or they might suggest that using a model for social science research where the data are initially assumed to be perfectly reproduced is inappropriate.

Because the models do involve different assumptions, they can produce different results. The proper question is not to ask if the different results mean that only one model should ever be used, but to ask *when* different models lead to interpretations sufficiently different to alter theories. With this knowledge, it is then possible to evaluate the appropriateness of each mathematical model for a given situation.

The conditions under which the models do produce different results will be explored at several points in later chapters. By the time readers finish this book, they should be able to select the appropriate model for their substantive research. As a byproduct of this understanding, the reader should also be able to design a study where two models whould give noticeably different results, and design another study where the same two models would give virtually identical results.

The simplification from using the uncorrelated models is often great, and, indeed, may make the difference between being able to present a reasonable derivation of complex phenomena and not presenting any derivation at all. It also leads to easier calculations; even with the advent of today's mighty computers, some calculations with correlated factors are both difficult and time-consuming. Similarly, the interpretation of the results may be easier if the factors are uncorrelated. However, whether or not these gains in ease of use are sufficient to offset the possible distortion in the theoretical conception of the area is not a question a factor analyst can answer. The proper conclusion depends on a substantively based theoretical analysis, an analysis that can be performed only by a person intimately acquainted with the past research in the area.

Because the uncorrelated models are special cases of the correlated models, derivations in this book are for correlated models. The equations can easily be simplified for the special case of uncorrelated factors, but it is not always apparent how to generalize from an uncorrelated to a correlated model. At those points in our discussion where nothing but problems are gained by working within the correlated model, an uncorrelated model is used.

Note that the models are only variants of the general linear model. The basic characteristics of factor analysis arise from the general model and the objectives of factoring, not from differences in the variants of the general linear model.

3

Matrix Algebra and Factor Analysis

The equations presented in Chapter 2 were often complex owing to the numerous elements and subscripts involved. Matrix algebra is a simpler procedure for handling such equations. It is *the* approach to factor analysis. Section 3.1 (Matrix Definitions and Notation) contains the basic notation system of matrix algebra. Matrix operations that parallel the usual algebraic addition, subtraction, multiplication, and division are given in Section 3.2 (Matrix Operations).[1]

An understanding of the basics of matrix algebra permits a simpler presentation of the material in Chapter 2. In Section 3.3, the component model is described in matrix algebra; the common factor model and uncorrelated models are developed in matrix algebra form in Sections 3.4 and 3.5.

3.1 MATRIX DEFINITIONS AND NOTATION

A **matrix** is a rectangular array of numbers or functions. A capital letter is used to signify the entire array, or table, and brackets are usually placed around the numbers to indicate that they are to be considered as a unit. When it is necessary to refer to individual elements within the matrix, lower-case letters are used.

---

[1]Bisher and Drewes (1970), Owen (1970), and Horst (1963) discuss matrix algebra in more detail. In the first two, matrix algebra is placed in the broader context of general mathematical principles applicable to the behavioral sciences, whereas the last is particularly concerned with matrix algebra applications to factor-analytic problems.

Example

The following is a simple matrix of three rows and two columns.

$$A = \begin{bmatrix} 1 & 2 \\ 3 & 4 \\ 5 & 6 \end{bmatrix}$$

Its elements are designated as follows:

$$\begin{bmatrix} a_{11} & a_{12} \\ a_{21} & a_{22} \\ a_{31} & a_{32} \end{bmatrix}$$

A number of matrices appear in developing factor-analytic concepts. The capital letters that are used to signify frequently used matrices are as follows: (1) X, a data matrix in deviation score form or Z if it is in standard score form; (2) F, the factor score matrix in standard score form; (3) C, the variance–covariance matrix where variances form the diagonal elements and covariances appear in the off-diagonals; (4) R, a correlation matrix among a set of variables or factors: (5) P, a factor pattern matrix giving the weights by which the factor scores are to be multiplied to give the standardized variable scores; and (6) S, the factor structure matrix that contains correlations of each variable with each factor. Other matrices will be defined as needed.

Examples

Chapters 1 and 2 contain several matrices. The set of numbers in 1.1.1 are a P or factor pattern matrix, the factor scores of 2.2.1 form an F matrix, the elements of 2.2.2 another P matrix, and 2.3.3 a data or X matrix.

3.1.1 Order of the Matrix

The **order** of the matrix refers to its size, that is, the number of rows and columns of the matrix. In the present notation, subscripts are used to indicate the rows and columns of a matrix. The first subscript gives the number of rows found in that matrix while the second indicates the number of columns it has. An individual element is indicated by changing the upper-case letter for the matrix into a lower-case letter; its subscripts identify that row and column which locate it in the array.

Example

Consider the following matrix:

$$A_{42} = \begin{bmatrix} 3 & 2 \\ 1 & 4 \\ -2 & -3 \\ 4 & -1 \end{bmatrix}$$

The subscript 4 indicates that A has four rows; the subscript 2 indicates that A has two columns. Element a_{42} is the number where the fourth row and second column intersect; it is -1. Other elements are:

$$a_{11} = 3$$
$$a_{12} = 2$$
$$a_{32} = -3$$

The following lower-case subscripts are used to symbolize the size of frequently used matrices: (1) n, the number of individuals across which indices of association are calculated; (2) v, the number of variables which are being factored; and (3) f, the number of factors. For example, the usual data matrix is noted as X_{nv}, whereas the factor structure matrix, containing the correlations of the variables with the factors, is represented by S_{vf}. In X_{nv}, individuals are represented as rows and variables are represented as columns. The number of rows is equal to the number of individuals, and the number of columns is equal to the number of variables. In S_{vf}, the correlation matrix has the variables as rows and the factors as columns. Other subscripts will be defined as needed.

Vertical matrices have more rows than columns; this is the conventional form of matrices used in factor analysis. Because the number of individuals is (we hope!) larger than the number of variables, the data matrix is presented as the vertical matrix X_{nv}, instead of X_{vn}. The factor structure matrix almost always has more variables than factors and is therefore the vertical matrix S_{vf}.

Square matrices have the same number of rows and columns. The most widely used square matrix is the matrix of correlations. The correlation matrix is symbolized, R_{vv} (i.e., it is a matrix where the number of rows and number of columns both equal the number of variables). The elements whose two subscripts are equal (e.g., $a_{11}, a_{22}, a_{33}, \ldots, a_{vv}$) form the **main diagonal** of a matrix.

Occasionally, a matrix may be used which has only one row or one column; this is referred to as a **vector.** It will be symbolized in the present notation by using a 1 as one of the subscripts. If a particular vector is a **row vector** (i.e., a vector with only one row) then it could be symbolized, for example, as V_{1f}. If it is a **column vector** (i.e., has only one column) then it could be symbolized as V_{v1}.

Examples

A row vector:

$$X_{14} = [1 \; 6 \; 5 \; 3]$$

A column vector:

$$X_{41} = \begin{bmatrix} 1 \\ 6 \\ 5 \\ 3 \end{bmatrix}$$

If both the number of rows and the number of columns are one, the matrix is a single number. Such a matrix is called a **scalar.** It is symbolized by a lower-case letter, usually without subscripts. For example, the number of individuals often appears in factor-analytic equations and is represented by n, and would be a single number, for example, 4.

When the rows and columns of a vertical matrix are interchanged so that it is then a horizontal matrix, the matrix is said to be **transposed.** It is symbolized by adding a prime to the capital letter designating the matrix and *also* interchanging the subscripts. The transpose for the data matrix, X_{nv}, is X'_{vn}.

Example

When:

$$A_{42} = \begin{bmatrix} 3 & 2 \\ 1 & 4 \\ -2 & -3 \\ 4 & -1 \end{bmatrix}$$

Then the transpose is:

$$A'_{24} = \begin{bmatrix} 3 & 1 & -2 & 4 \\ 2 & 4 & -3 & -1 \end{bmatrix}$$

3.1.2 Special Matrices

In addition to matrices defined with reference to their order, several matrices have special characteristics and are therefore given unique titles. The following matrices are frequently used in factor analysis:

A **symmetric** matrix is one where $a_{ij} = a_{ji}$. This can occur only when the matrix is square and when the elements above the diagonal are equal to their counterparts below the diagonal. A correlation matrix is a symmetric matrix. Note that a symmetric matrix is its own transpose. Because the elements above the diagonal in a symmetric matrix are the same as those below the diagonal, it is common practice to give only half the matrix. Thus Table 1.2.2 actually represents a 6-by-6 square, symmetric matrix.

In a **diagonal** matrix, all off-diagonal elements are zeros and at least one of the diagonal elements is nonzero. It is a special case of the symmetric matrix.

An **identity** matrix is a diagonal matrix (i.e., all off-diagonals are zero) where all the diagonal elements are equal to 1.0. One example would be a matrix of the correlations among the factors in an uncorrelated model. In that case, the diagonal elements are 1.0 because factors correlate perfectly with themselves, but all off-diagonal elements are zero because the factors are uncorrelated.

Examples

A 6-by-6 diagonal matrix:

$$D_{66} = \begin{bmatrix} 9.8 & 0 & 0 & 0 & 0 & 0 \\ 0 & 7.6 & 0 & 0 & 0 & 0 \\ 0 & 0 & 8.8 & 0 & 0 & 0 \\ 0 & 0 & 0 & 5.3 & 0 & 0 \\ 0 & 0 & 0 & 0 & 6.4 & 0 \\ 0 & 0 & 0 & 0 & 0 & 0.0 \end{bmatrix}$$

A 4-by-4 identity matrix:

$$I_{44} = \begin{bmatrix} 1.0 & 0 & 0 & 0 \\ 0 & 1.0 & 0 & 0 \\ 0 & 0 & 1.0 & 0 \\ 0 & 0 & 0 & 1.0 \end{bmatrix}$$

3.1.3 Equal Matrices

Two matrices are defined as equal if and only if each and every corresponding element is identical. If $A = B$, then $a_{11} = b_{11}$, $a_{12} = b_{12}$, and, in general, $a_{ij} = b_{ij}$. To be equal, the two matrices must have the same number of rows and columns. A matrix is not equal to its transpose unless that matrix is symmetrical. If $A = B$, but subsequently two rows, or two columns, of A are interchanged, then A will no longer be equal to B unless the interchanged rows, or columns, happen to be equal.

Examples

Equal and unequal matrices:

$$A_{31} = \begin{bmatrix} 1 \\ 2 \\ 3 \end{bmatrix}, \qquad B_{31} = \begin{bmatrix} 1 \\ 2 \\ 3 \end{bmatrix}; \qquad A_{31} = B_{31}$$

$$A_{32} = \begin{bmatrix} 1 & 4 \\ 2 & 5 \\ 3 & 6 \end{bmatrix}, \qquad B_{32} = \begin{bmatrix} 1 & 4 \\ 2 & 5 \\ 3 & 6 \end{bmatrix}; \qquad A_{32} = B_{32}$$

$$A_{31} = \begin{bmatrix} 1 \\ 2 \\ 3 \end{bmatrix}, \qquad B_{13} = \begin{bmatrix} 1 & 2 & 3 \end{bmatrix}; \qquad A_{31} \neq B_{13}$$

$$A_{32} = \begin{bmatrix} 1 & 4 \\ 2 & 5 \\ 3 & 6 \end{bmatrix}, \qquad B_{32} = \begin{bmatrix} 2 & 5 \\ 1 & 4 \\ 3 & 6 \end{bmatrix}; \qquad A_{32} \neq B_{32}$$

3.2 MATRIX OPERATIONS

The more important matrix operations are those corresponding to the simple algebraic operations of addition, subtraction, multiplication, and division.

3.2.1 Matrix Addition and Subtraction

To add two matrices, add each element of one matrix to the corresponding element of the other matrix. Thus, $c_{12} = a_{12} + b_{12}$, $c_{13} = a_{13} + b_{13}$, etc. In subtraction, the corresponding element of one matrix is subtracted from that of the other. For addition or subtraction to take place, the two matrices must have the same number of rows and the same number of columns.

Matrix addition and subtraction follow the associative and commutative laws, that is:

$$A_{ij} + (B_{ij} + C_{ij}) = (A_{ij} + B_{ij}) + C_{ij} \tag{3.2.1}$$

according to the associative law, and

$$A_{ij} + B_{ij} = B_{ij} + A_{ij} \tag{3.2.2}$$

according to the commutative law.

The addition of two matrices does not give the same result if one of the matrices is transposed, unless the transposed matrix happens to be square and symmetrical. Thus:

$$A_{jj} + B_{jj} \neq A'_{jj} + B_{jj} \text{ unless } A_{jj} = A'_{jj}. \tag{3.2.3}$$

However, the transpose of a sum is equal to the sum of the transposes:

$$(A_{ij} + B_{ij})' = A'_{ji} + B'_{ji} \tag{3.2.4}$$

Examples

Given:

$$A_{32} = \begin{bmatrix} 1 & 4 \\ 2 & 5 \\ 3 & 6 \end{bmatrix} \qquad B_{32} = \begin{bmatrix} 6 & 5 \\ 4 & 3 \\ 2 & 1 \end{bmatrix}$$

Then:

$$A_{32} + B_{32} = C_{32} \text{ where } C_{32} = \begin{bmatrix} 7 & 9 \\ 6 & 8 \\ 5 & 7 \end{bmatrix}$$

Also given:

$$D_{32} = \begin{bmatrix} -1 & 1 \\ 1 & 1 \\ -1 & 1 \end{bmatrix}$$

Then:

$$A_{32} + B_{32} + D_{32} = E_{32} \text{ where } E_{32} = \begin{bmatrix} 6 & 10 \\ 7 & 9 \\ 4 & 8 \end{bmatrix}$$

So:

$$C_{32} + D_{32} = E_{32}$$

And:

$$A_{32} + (B_{32} + D_{32}) = E_{32}$$

3.2.2 Matrix Multiplication

Matrix multiplication could be defined in a number of different ways. The manner in which it is defined is such as to maximize its usefulness for solving simultaneous equations and for developing formulas such as those used in factor analysis.

Matrix multiplication proceeds by computing the sum of cross-products of the elements in the first **row** of the **first** matrix with the elements of the first **column** of the **second** matrix, then with the second column of the second matrix and so on for every column. The same operation is then performed using the second row of the first matrix and the columns of the second matrix. The procedure is continued until all rows of the first matrix have been multiplied by all the columns of the second matrix. The elements of the product matrix are as follows:

$$
\begin{aligned}
c_{11} &= \Sigma a_{1k} b_{k1}, \\
c_{12} &= \Sigma\, a_{1k} b_{k2}, \\
c_{21} &= \Sigma a_{2k} b_{k1}, \\
\end{aligned}
\tag{3.2.5}
$$
etc.

Matrix C will have the same number of rows as A, the first matrix, and the same number of columns as B, the second matrix.

In order for matrix multiplication to occur, the number of columns in the first matrix must equal the number of rows in the second matrix. If they do not, then one or more of the last elements in the sum of cross-products would have no number defined by which it would be multiplied.

Examples
Given:

$$A_{32} = \begin{bmatrix} 1 & 4 \\ 2 & 5 \\ 3 & 6 \end{bmatrix} \qquad B'_{23} = \begin{bmatrix} 1 & 2 & 3 \\ 2 & 1 & 2 \end{bmatrix}$$

And:

$$A_{32}\, B'_{23} = C_{33}$$

Then:

$$\begin{bmatrix} 1 & 4 \\ 2 & 5 \\ 3 & 6 \end{bmatrix} \cdot \begin{bmatrix} 1 & 2 & 3 \\ 2 & 1 & 2 \end{bmatrix} = C_{33}$$

C_{33} is formed by summing cross-products. The elements of C are calculated as follows:

$$c_{11} = a_{11} b_{11} + a_{12} b_{21}$$
$$= 1(1) + 4(2) = 9$$

$$c_{12} = a_{11} b_{12} + a_{12} b_{22}$$
$$= 1(2) + 4(1) = 6$$

$$c_{13} = a_{11} b_{13} + a_{12} b_{23}$$
$$= 1(3) + 4(2) = 11$$

$$c_{21} = a_{21} b_{11} + a_{22} b_{12}$$
$$= 2(1) + 5(2) = 12$$

$$c_{22} = a_{21} b_{12} + a_{22} b_{22}$$
$$= 2(2) + 5(1) = 9$$

$$\cdot \quad \cdot \quad \cdot$$
$$\cdot \quad \cdot \quad \cdot$$
$$\cdot \quad \cdot \quad \cdot$$

$$c_{33} = a_{31} b_{13} + a_{32} b_{23}$$
$$= 3(3) + 6(2) = 21$$

In algebra, $a \cdot b = b \cdot a$, a fact known as the commutative law of multiplication. Also $a(bc) = (ab)c$, which is known as the associative law of multiplication. Matrix multiplication is associative, that is:

$$A_{ij}(B_{jk}C_{kk}) = (A_{ij}B_{jk})C_{kk}. \tag{3.2.6}$$

However, matrix multiplication is not commutative since, in general,

$$A_{ij}B_{ii} \neq B_{ii}A_{ii}. \tag{3.2.7}$$

Because matrix multiplication is not commutative, **the order in which the matrices are multiplied is extremely important.** One can multiply two matrices in either order, but the result will seldom be the same. Both multiplications can be performed with the same two matrices only if their orders are appropriate.

Matrix multiplication follows the distributive law:

$$A_{ij}(B_{jk} + C_{jk}) = A_{ij}B_{jk} + A_{ij}C_{jk} \tag{3.2.8}$$

$$(B_{ij} + C_{ij})A_{jk} = B_{ij}A_{jk} + C_{ij}A_{jk}. \tag{3.2.9}$$

Examples

It was just shown that:

$$A_{32}B'_{23} = C_{33}$$

If A is premultiplied by B, the result is:

$$B'_{23} A_{32} = D_{22} \text{ where } D_{22} = \begin{bmatrix} 14 & 32 \\ 10 & 25 \end{bmatrix}$$

Obviously, $C_{33} \neq D_{22}$

Given:

$$E_{32} = \begin{bmatrix} -1 & 1 \\ 1 & 1 \\ 1 & -1 \end{bmatrix}$$

Then:

$$E_{32}\, B'_{23}\, A_{32} = F_{32} \text{ where } F_{32} = \begin{bmatrix} -4 & -7 \\ 24 & 57 \\ 4 & 7 \end{bmatrix}$$

This can be calculated by either first postmultiplying E by B' and then postmultiplying the result by A or by postmultiplying E by D where $D = B'A$.

Whenever two or more matrices are multiplied together, the orders must be appropriate. In the following,

$$A_{ij}B_{kl}C_{mn} = D_{op}$$

j must equal k, and l must equal m for multiplication to be possible. Note that **the number of rows of the final matrix is always given by the first subscript and the number of columns by the last subscript in the multiplicative series.** that is, o equals i and p equals n.

If several matrices are multiplied together and the product is transposed, this is the same as transposing each of the original matrices before multiplication and then multiplying them in reverse order:

$$(A_{ij}B_{jk}C_{kl})' = C'_{lk}B'_{kj}A'_{ji}. \tag{3.2.10}$$

Because a scalar is a one-element matrix, a special rule of multiplication has been established for it. **A matrix can be multiplied by a scalar by simply multiplying that scalar times each element in the matrix.** This kind of multiplication is associative, commutative, and follows the distributive law.

Example

The result of premultiplying the component score matrix of Table 2.2.1 by its transpose is:

$$F'_{2,10}F_{10,2} = A_{22}$$

$$\begin{bmatrix} 1 & 1 & 1 & 1 & 1 & -1 & -1 & -1 & -1 & -1 \\ -1 & 1 & -1 & 1 & 1 & -1 & 1 & -1 & 1 & -1 \end{bmatrix} \cdot \begin{bmatrix} 1 & -1 \\ 1 & 1 \\ 1 & -1 \\ 1 & 1 \\ 1 & 1 \\ -1 & -1 \\ -1 & 1 \\ -1 & -1 \\ -1 & 1 \\ -1 & -1 \end{bmatrix} = \begin{bmatrix} 10 & 2 \\ 2 & 10 \end{bmatrix}$$

Then if $C_{22} = A_{22}n$ where $n = .1$,

$$C_{22} = \begin{bmatrix} 1.0 & .2 \\ .2 & 1.0 \end{bmatrix}$$

(As will be seen in Section 3.3.4, we have just computed the correlations between the factors.)

3.2.3 The Inverse of a Matrix: Matrix Algebra "Division"

In regular algebra, the reciprocal of a number plays an important role. It allows the function of division to be carried out by multiplicative procedures. The reciprocal of a is defined such that:

$$aa^{-1} = 1 = a^{-1}a \tag{3.2.11}$$

where the -1 superscript identifies the reciprocal of a.

The **inverse** of a matrix is defined by the same type of equation:

$$A_{jj}A_{jj}^{-1} = I = A_{jj}^{-1}A_{jj}. \tag{3.2.12}$$

That is, a matrix's inverse is that matrix which, when pre- or postmultiplied by the original matrix, gives an identity matrix as its product. Only square matrices have inverses. However, not all square matrices have inverses.

It is possible to compute the inverse of a small matrix of even five or six rows by hand, but it is laborious. Procedures for doing so are given in Bisher and Drewes (1970) and Owen (1970). A computer is recommended for a matrix of more than five or six rows, and it comes in handy for even the small ones.

Examples

Given:

$$A_{33} = \begin{bmatrix} 1 & 1 & -3 \\ 2 & 5 & 1 \\ 1 & 3 & 2 \end{bmatrix}$$

Then its inverse is:

$$A_{33}^{-1} = \begin{bmatrix} 7 & -11 & 16 \\ -3 & 5 & -7 \\ 1 & -2 & 3 \end{bmatrix}$$

And $A_{33}A_{33}^{-1} = I_{33}$

$$\begin{bmatrix} 1 & 1 & -3 \\ 2 & 5 & 1 \\ 1 & 3 & 2 \end{bmatrix} \begin{bmatrix} 7 & -11 & 16 \\ -3 & 5 & -7 \\ 1 & -2 & 3 \end{bmatrix} = \begin{bmatrix} 1 & 0 & 0 \\ 0 & 1 & 0 \\ 0 & 0 & 1 \end{bmatrix}$$

Here is a scalar matrix:

$a = 10$

Its inverse, a^{-1}, is that number that makes it equal to 1.0.

In this case, $a^{-1} = \dfrac{1}{10} = .1$.

The inverse of a matrix is particularly useful in solving for other elements within an equation. For example, if:

$$A_{ij}B_{jk} = C_{jk} \qquad (3.2.13)$$

then one can multiply through by the inverse of A to solve for B where only A and C are known:

$$A_{jj}^{-1}A_{ij}B_{jk} = A_{jj}^{-1}C_{jk} \qquad (3.2.14)$$

Because the inverse of a matrix multiplied by that matrix is an identity matrix and multiplying a matrix by an identity matrix leaves the matrix unchanged, then:

$$B_{jk} = A_{jj}^{-1}C_{jk}. \qquad (3.2.15)$$

Therefore, B can be calculated from A and C when the relationship is defined as in Eq. (3.2.13).

The following characteristics of inverses, derived in texts on matrix algebra (cf. Footnote 1), are often useful:

1. The transpose of an inverse equals the inverse of the transpose:

$$(A_{jj}^{-1})' = (A_{ij}')^{-1}. \qquad (3.2.16)$$

2. The inverse of a sum, for example $(A + B)^{-1}$, cannot be easily simplified.
3. The inverse of a product equals the product of the inverses when taken in reverse order:

$$(A_{ij}B_{jj}C_{jj})^{-1} = C_{jj}^{-1}B_{jj}^{-1}A_{jj}^{-1}. \qquad (3.2.17)$$

Example

Given:

$$A_{33} = \begin{bmatrix} 1 & 1 & -3 \\ 2 & 5 & 1 \\ 1 & 3 & 2 \end{bmatrix}, \qquad B_{33} = \begin{bmatrix} -1 & 1 & -1 \\ 1 & 1 & -1 \\ -1 & 1 & 1 \end{bmatrix}$$

$$C_{33} = \begin{bmatrix} 1 & 1 & 1 \\ -1 & 1 & 1 \\ 1 & -1 & 1 \end{bmatrix}.$$

Then $A_{33}\,B_{33}\,C_{33} = D_{33}$ where:

$$D_{33} = \begin{bmatrix} -1 & 7 & -3 \\ -12 & 16 & 4 \\ -8 & 8 & 4 \end{bmatrix}$$

The inverses of A, B, C and D, as calculated by a computer, are:

$$A_{33}^{-1} = \begin{bmatrix} 7 & -11 & 16 \\ -3 & 5 & -7 \\ 1 & -2 & 3 \end{bmatrix} \qquad B_{33}^{-1} = \begin{bmatrix} -.5 & .5 & 0 \\ 0 & .5 & .5 \\ -.5 & 0 & .5 \end{bmatrix}$$

$$C_{33}^{-1} = \begin{bmatrix} .5 & -.5 & 0 \\ .5 & 0 & -.5 \\ 0 & .5 & .5 \end{bmatrix} \qquad D_{33}^{-1} = \begin{bmatrix} -2.00 & 3.25 & -4.75 \\ -1.00 & 1.75 & -2.50 \\ -2.00 & 3.00 & -4.25 \end{bmatrix}$$

The product of $C_{33}^{-1} B_{33}^{-1} A_{33}^{-1}$ is:

$$(C_{33}^{-1} B_{33}^{-1})A_{33}^{-1}) = \begin{bmatrix} -.25 & .00 & -.25 \\ .00 & .25 & -.25 \\ -.25 & .25 & .50 \end{bmatrix} \cdot \begin{bmatrix} 7 & -11 & 16 \\ -3 & 5 & -7 \\ 1 & -2 & 3 \end{bmatrix}$$

$$= \begin{bmatrix} -2.00 & 3.25 & -4.75 \\ -1.00 & 1.75 & -2.50 \\ -2.00 & 3.00 & -4.25 \end{bmatrix}$$

which is the same as D_{33}^{-1}

Most computer programs for inverting matrices will usually give an inverse even when a unique inverse does not actually exist. One check for an inversion program is to invert the inverse; from the equations previously given, it follows that the inverse of the inverse is the original matrix itself if the inverse exists. If the inverse of the inverse agrees only with the original matrix for the first digit of each number, the program probably will need to be made more accurate. Many inverse programs currently in operation are not as accurate as they should be.

3.3   DEFINITIONAL EQUATIONS IN MATRIX ALGEBRA FORM

The following definitions are of statistics already used in Chapter 2. They are given in both standard and matrix algebra forms to enable the student to relate the two notational systems. The definitions are for population parameters, as are the derivations in later sections of this chapter.

3.3.1 Mean

The mean of a single variable is:

$$\bar{X}_1 = \frac{\Sigma \, x_i}{n} = X'_{1n} \, I_{n1} \, n^{-1} \tag{3.3.1}$$

where n^{-1} is the reciprocal of n in scalar form and I_{n1} is a column of 1's.

Example

The scores for five individuals are 2, 4, 3, 5, and 4. Calculating the mean by matrix algebra gives:

$$\bar{X} = [2 \quad 4 \quad 3 \quad 5 \quad 4] \begin{bmatrix} 1 \\ 1 \\ 1 \\ 1 \\ 1 \end{bmatrix} \cdot \frac{1}{5}$$

$$= 18\left(\frac{1}{5}\right) = 3.6$$

3.3.2 Variance

The variance of a single variable when the raw scores are deviations from the mean is:

$$\sigma_1^2 = \frac{\Sigma \, x_i^2}{n} = X'_{1n} \, X_{n1} \, n^{-1}. \tag{3.3.2}$$

3.3.3 Covariance

The covariance between variables X and Y when the raw scores are deviations from the mean is:

$$c_{XY} = \frac{\Sigma \, x_i y_i}{n} = X'_{1n} \, Y_{n1} \, n^{-1}. \tag{3.3.3}$$

3.3.4 Correlation

The correlation between variables X and Y when the raw scores are deviations from the mean is:

$$r_{XY} = \frac{\Sigma \, x_i y_i}{n\sigma_X \sigma_Y} = X'_{1n} \, Y_{n1} \, n^{-1} \, \sigma_X^{-1} \, \sigma_Y^{-1}. \tag{3.3.4}$$

The correlation when the two variables are in standard score form is:

$$r_{XY} = \frac{\Sigma \, z_{X_i} z_{Y_i}}{n} = Z'_{X_{1n}} \, Z_{Y_{n1}} \, n^{-1}. \tag{3.3.5}$$

Example

Here is the correlation between the deviation scores for five individuals on two variables:

$$
X_{n1} = \begin{bmatrix} -1 \\ 1 \\ 1 \\ 0 \\ -1 \end{bmatrix} \qquad Y_{n1} = \begin{bmatrix} 1 \\ 1 \\ -1 \\ -1 \\ 0 \end{bmatrix} \qquad \sigma_X = \sigma_Y = .8944
$$

$$
r_{XY} = \begin{bmatrix} -1 & 1 & 1 & 0 & -1 \end{bmatrix} \cdot \begin{bmatrix} 1 \\ 1 \\ -1 \\ -1 \\ 0 \end{bmatrix} \cdot 5^{-1} \cdot .8944^{-1} \cdot .8944^{-1}
$$

$$
= -1 \,(.2)\,(1.118)\,(1.118) = -.25.
$$

3.3.5 Covariance and Correlation Matrices

The real power of matrix algebra occurs when a number of variables are involved. In that case, the deviation score definition for all the variances and covariances is simply:

$$
C_{vv} = X'_{vn} X_{nv} n^{-1} \tag{3.3.6}
$$

where the variances are in the main diagonal and the covariances are in the off-diagonal elements (this is a symmetric matrix).

Example

An example of a covariance matrix is as follows:

$$
C_{vv} = \begin{bmatrix} 1 & -1 & 2 & -1 & -1 \\ -2 & 1 & 1 & 1 & -1 \\ 3 & -1 & 2 & -2 & -2 \end{bmatrix} \cdot \begin{bmatrix} 1 & -2 & 3 \\ -1 & 1 & -1 \\ 2 & 1 & 2 \\ -1 & 1 & -2 \\ -1 & -1 & -2 \end{bmatrix} \cdot 5^{-1}
$$

$$
= \begin{bmatrix} 8 & -1 & 12 \\ -1 & 8 & -5 \\ 12 & -5 & 22 \end{bmatrix} \cdot .2 = \begin{bmatrix} 1.6 & -.2 & 2.4 \\ -.2 & 1.6 & -1.0 \\ 2.4 & -1.0 & 4.4 \end{bmatrix}
$$

The deviation score definition for a correlation matrix is:

$$
R_{vv} = S_{vv}^{-1} C_{vv} S_{vv}^{-1} \tag{3.3.7}
$$

where S_{vv} is a diagonal matrix of the standard deviations for the variables. If the variables are in standard score form, then:

$$R_{vv} = C_{vv} = Z'_{vn} Z_{nv} \, n^{-1}. \tag{3.3.8}$$

3.4 THE FULL COMPONENT MODEL EXPRESSED IN MATRIX ALGEBRA

In matrix algebra, the component model can be defined by the following equation:

$$Z_{nv} = F_{nf}P'_{fv} \tag{3.4.1}$$

where Z_{nv} is the standard score data matrix of n individuals and v variables, F_{nf} is the standardized factor score matrix for the same n individuals but with f factors and P'_{fv} is the factor by variable weight matrix (i.e., the transposed factor pattern). Deviation scores could have been used, but standard scores simplify the equations and are usually the basis for a factor analysis.

3.4.1 The Correlation Matrix as a Function of the Factorial Compositions of the Variables

By definition [(3.3.8)]:

$$R_{vv} = Z'_{vn}Z_{nv}n^{-1}. \tag{3.4.2}$$

Substituting the factorial definition of Z Eq. (3.4.1) into Eq (3.4.2) gives:

$$R_{vv} = (F_{nf}P'_{fv})' \, (F_{nf}P'_{fv})n^{-1} \tag{3.4.3}$$

Using the principle of Eq. (3.2.10), removing parenthesis, and moving the scalar:

$$R_{vv} = P_{vf}F'_{fn}F_{nf}n^{-1}P'_{fv}. \tag{3.4.4}$$

Substituting by the definition of a correlation matrix in Eq. (3.3.8):

$$R_{vv} = P_{vf}R_{ff}P'_{fv} \tag{3.4.5}$$

where R_{ff} is the correlation between the factors. This, of course, is the same equation as (2.2.4) but in matrix algebra notation for standard scores.

Note that **any procedure that decomposes the correlation matrix into a pair of matrices in the form of Eq. (3.4.5) provides a possible P_{vf} and R_{ff} for R.**

Example

The correlations among the variables in the component example can be computed by Eq. (3.4.5). The factor pattern is from Table 2.2.2 and the correlation between the factors from Table 2.2.1:

$$
R_{vv} = \begin{bmatrix} .96 & .15 \\ 1.02 & -.15 \\ .29 & .90 \\ -.65 & .90 \end{bmatrix} \begin{bmatrix} 1.00 & .20 \\ .20 & 1.00 \end{bmatrix} \begin{bmatrix} .96 & 1.02 & .29 & -.65 \\ .15 & -.15 & .90 & .90 \end{bmatrix}
$$

$$
= \begin{bmatrix} .990 & .342 \\ .990 & .054 \\ .470 & .958 \\ -.470 & .770 \end{bmatrix} \begin{bmatrix} .96 & 1.02 & .29 & -.65 \\ .15 & -.15 & .90 & .90 \end{bmatrix}
$$

$$
= \begin{bmatrix} 1.00 & .96 & .59 & -.34 \\ .96 & 1.00 & .34 & -.59 \\ .59 & .34 & 1.00 & .56 \\ -.34 & -.59 & .56 & 1.00 \end{bmatrix}
$$

3.4.2 Correlation of the Variables with the Factors as a Function of Their Factorial Compositions

The correlation matrix of the variables with the factors, that is, the factor structure, contains only the correlations between the set of variables and the set of factors. It is not a symmetrical correlation matrix because the correlations among the variables and the correlations among the factors are not included. It is defined by the factor score and data matrices substituted into the definitional formula for a correlation matrix [Eq. (3.3.8)]:

$$
S_{vf} = Z'_{vn}F_{nf}n^{-1} \tag{3.4.6}
$$

when the factors and variables are assumed to be in standard score form. Substituting Eq. (3.4.1):

$$
S_{vf} = P_{vf}F'_{fn}F_{nf}n^{-1}. \tag{3.4.7}
$$

By definition of a correlation matrix:

$$
S_{vf} = P_{vf}R_{ff}. \tag{3.4.8}
$$

A comparison of the equations in this section with those in Chapter 2 illustrates the usefulness of matrix algebra in factor analysis.

3.5 THE COMMON FACTOR MODEL IN MATRIX ALGEBRA

For the common factor model, the factor score matrix can be divided into two sections: common factor scores and unique factor scores. The weight matrix is also divisible into a section containing the common factor weights and the unique weights. The composite score and weight matrices can be represented as follows:

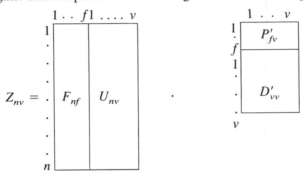

where U_{nv} is a matrix of unique factor scores with one unique factor for each variable, and D_{vv} is a diagonal matrix giving each unique factor weight for reproducing the variable with which the weight is associated. Whereas U and D are the unique factor scores and weights, F and P are the common factor scores and weights. Standard scores are again assumed.

From an examination of the preceding diagram it is apparent that the definitional equation for common factor analysis is:

$$Z_{nv} = F_{nf}P'_{fv} + U_{nv}D'_{vv}. \tag{3.5.1}$$

These equations also hold for a deviation score matrix if X is substituted for Z. The Ps will then be b weights rather than beta weights.

Example

Using Eq. (3.5.1) with the common factor example of Chapter 2 gives:

$$X_{10.4} = \begin{bmatrix} .81 & 1.17 & -.61 & -1.55 \\ 1.11 & .87 & 1.19 & .25 \\ .81 & 1.17 & -.61 & -1.55 \\ 1.11 & .87 & 1.19 & .25 \\ 1.11 & .87 & 1.19 & .25 \\ -1.11 & -.87 & -1.19 & -.25 \\ -.81 & -1.17 & .61 & 1.55 \\ -1.11 & -.87 & -1.19 & -.25 \\ -.81 & -1.17 & .61 & 1.55 \\ -1.11 & -.87 & -1.19 & -.25 \end{bmatrix} + \begin{bmatrix} -.632 & 0 & 1.264 & 0 \\ .632 & 0 & 0 & -1.58 \\ 0 & .948 & -1.264 & 0 \\ 0 & -.948 & 0 & 1.58 \\ 0 & 0 & 0 & 0 \\ 0 & 0 & 0 & 0 \\ 0 & .948 & 0 & 1.58 \\ 0 & -.948 & -1.264 & 0 \\ -.632 & 0 & 0 & 1.58 \\ .632 & 0 & 1.264 & 0 \end{bmatrix}$$

$$X_{10.4} = \begin{bmatrix} .178 & 1.170 & .654 & -1.550 \\ 1.742 & .870 & 1.190 & -1.330 \\ .810 & 2.118 & -1.874 & -1.550 \\ 1.110 & -.128 & 1.190 & 1.830 \\ 1.110 & .870 & 1.190 & .250 \\ -1.110 & -.870 & -1.190 & -.250 \\ -.810 & -.222 & .610 & 3.130 \\ -1.110 & -1.818 & -2.454 & -.250 \\ -1.442 & -1.170 & .610 & -.030 \\ -.478 & -.870 & .074 & -.250 \end{bmatrix}$$

3.5.1 Correlations among the Variables as a Function of the Factorial Compositions of the Variables

Substituting Eq. (3.5.1) into Eq. (3.4.2):

$$R_{vv} = (F_{nf}P'_{fv} + U_{nv}D'_{vv})' (F_{nf}P'_{fv} + U_{nv}D'_{vv})n^{-1}. \tag{3.5.2}$$

Then:

$$R_{vv} = [(F_{nf}P'_{fv})' + (U_{nv}D'_{vv})'] (F_{nf}P'_{fv} + U_{nv}D'_{vv})n^{-1}. \tag{3.5.3}$$

And:

$$R_{vv} = (P_{vf}F'_{fn} + D_{vv}U'_{vn}) (F_{nf}P'_{fv} + U_{nv}D'_{vv})n^{-1}. \tag{3.5.4}$$

Expanding terms:

$$R_{vv} = P_{vf}F'_{fn}F_{nf}n^{-1}P'_{fv} + D_{vv}U'_{vn}F_{nf}n^{-1}P'_{fv}$$
$$+ P_{vf}F'_{fn}U_{nv}n^{-1}D'_{vv} + D_{vv}U'_{vn}U_{nv}n^{-1}D'_{vv}. \tag{3.5.5}$$

By definition of a correlation matrix:

$$R_{vv} = P_{vf}R_{ff}P'_{fv} + D_{vv}R_{uf}P'_{fv} + P_{vf}R'_{fu}D'_{vv} + D_{vv}R_{uu}D'_{vv} \tag{3.5.6}$$

where R_{uf} is the matrix of correlations between the unique factors and the common factors, and R_{uu} is the matrix of correlations among the uniquenesses (note that u equals v; a separate subscript is used as an aid in distinguishing the several correlation matrices).

In this model, it is assumed that the unique factor scores correlate zero with the common factor scores and among themselves. Therefore R_{uf} is a matrix of zeros and the middle section of Eq. (3.5.6) disappears. The matrix of uniqueness correlations, R_{uu}, becomes an identity matrix. Equation (3.5.6) then becomes:

$$R_{vv} = P_{vf}R_{ff}P'_{fv} + U_{vv} \tag{3.5.7}$$

where U_{vv} is a diagonal matrix of the squared unique factor loadings (i.e., it contains u_j^2 as diagonal elements). $P_{vf}R_{ff}P'_{fv}$ is the **common factor correlation** matrix.

In solving for common factors, the common factor correlation matrix (i.e., that reproduced by PRP') is factored instead of the one with unities in the diagonals. However, this matrix can only be estimated by subtracting an estimate of U_{vv} from the observed correlation matrix. The reduced correlation matrix can then be factored into P and R_{ff}.

Because the diagonals are equal to the communalities, the need to estimate U_{vv} gives rise to the **communality problem** of estimating the proper diagonals. This problem is discussed in Chapter 6.

Equation (3.5.7) is a description of the situation in the population and not in any given sample. In a particular sample, the assumptions made at Eq. (3.5.7) are invalid. Chance correlations occur between the unique and common factors and among the unique factors. The chance correlations mean that the off-diagonal elements of the correlation matrix are inaccurate. Fortunately, with large samples, these effects should be small. The common factor example being used is a pure one that represents only the population situation.

3.5.2 Correlations of the Variables with the Factors

Substituting Eq. (3.5.1) into the defining equation [Eq. (3.4.6)] gives the correlations between variables and factors:

$$S_{vf} = P_{vf}F'_{fn}F_{nf}n^{-1} + D_{vv}U'_{vn}F_{nf}n^{-1}. \tag{3.5.8}$$

By definition of correlation matrices:

$$S_{vf} = P_{vf}R_{ff} + D_{vv}R_{uf} \tag{3.5.9}$$

when R_{uf} is the correlations between the unique and common factors. In the population, this is assumed to be a matrix of zeros and so the equation becomes:

$$S_{vf} = P_{vf}R_{ff}. \tag{3.5.10}$$

Again note that the assumption upon which Eq. (3.5.10) is based is never completely true in any given sample.

3.6 UNCORRELATED FACTOR MODELS AND MATRIX ALGEBRA

In matrix algebra terms, the restrictions placed upon the solution to obtain uncorrelated factors is that of orthogonality. **Orthogonality** means that the factor matrix premultiplied by its transpose gives a diagonal matrix (i.e., $F'F = D$). *Because the factor scores are assumed to be standardized and uncorrelated, dividing the resulting diagonal matrix by the reciprocal of* the number of individuals gives an identity matrix. The equations developed under the component and common factor models are simplified for the uncorrelated models by dropping all R_{ff} terms, because they are now identity matrices. Otherwise, the derivations and conclusions remain the same.

One equation of historical importance is:

$$R_{vv} = P_{vf}P'_{fv} = S_{vf}S'_{fv} \qquad (3.6.1)$$

which indicates that the correlation matrix can be reproduced simply from the factor pattern/factor structure when the factors are uncorrelated. (As can be seen from Eq. (3.5.10), $S = P$ in the orthogonal case.) This equation is of importance because it means that most procedures that decompose a symmetric matrix into another matrix that fulfills this condition can be used for factor-analytic purposes. It also means that one can solve for the factor pattern independently of the factor scores. In the literature, Eq. (3.6.1) is often written as:

$$R = F\,F' \qquad (3.6.2)$$

because many writers have used F to symbolize the factor pattern matrix. Practically all factor-analytic solutions begin by solving this equation, and it has been referred to as the fundamental equation of factor analysis. Using Eq. (3.6.2) as the definitional one means that our Eq. (3.4.1) can then be derived. However, the relevance of Eq. (3.6.2) to research is less apparent than the definitional equations given in the present chapter and is more restrictive because it does not include the case of correlated factors.

4 Geometric Representation of Factor Models

In the history of factor analysis, geometry was used in developing many of the principles of the factor models. The impact of geometry is still found in phrases such as "rotation of factors." Although factor-analytic principles and procedures are now generally developed by matrix algebra, a brief overview of the factor models from the geometric viewpoint can add greatly to one's intuitive understanding. It is particularly helpful when considering such problems as the number and placement of factors. More detailed presentations of the geometric approach to factor analysis are given in Harman (1967, Chapter 4) and in Thurstone (1947, pages 32–50, Chapter 3). These references provide the derivations for this chapter.

To understand the factor models geometrically, a brief introduction to the representation of variables and factors as vectors in space is given in Section 4.1, Representing Variables and Factors Geometrically. Section 4.1 is a presentation of the multivariate linear model where it is assumed that scores for factors and variables are known in addition to the factor pattern.

The simplest factor model to see geometrically is that of uncorrelated, or orthogonal, components, which is presented in Section 4.2. In Section 4.3, the Correlated (Oblique) Component Model, the geometric principles are expanded to apply to the case where factors can be correlated. In Section 4.4, the Common Factor Models, the effect of unique factors on the variable vectors is presented. Sections 4.2, 4.3, and 4.4 contain variants of the factor model, but also include a discussion of the nature and problems of solving for factors and weights from each of these perspectives. All variables and factors are assumed to be in standard score form.

*May be considered optional reading.

4.1   REPRESENTING VARIABLES AND FACTORS GEOMETRICALLY

To represent factors and variables geometrically, one identifies the factors as the axes and the variables as lines, or vectors, drawn in what is called a Cartesian coordinate space. When the plot shows the variable to be physically close to a factor, they are highly related. The direction and length for the line representing the variable are determined by the factor pattern of the variable; the factor pattern gives the coordinates of each line's end point. To keep matters simple, we will assume, in this section and the next, that the factors are uncorrelated with each other. Because uncorrelated factors form 90° angles with each other, they are **orthogonal** to each other.

Plotting the variables and factors in space can proceed in two ways. On the one hand, the variables can be plotted as a function of the factors. This procedure is given in Section 4.1.1 and can be used to represent the multivariate linear model in which variables, factors, and weights are all known. On the other hand, the variables can be plotted alone. Factors and weights are then determined as additional steps. This is the case of factor analysis; the procedures are presented in Section 4.1.2.

4.1.1 Plotting the Multivariate Linear Model

In developing the geometric representation of a particular data set, the factors are assumed to be the coordinate axes. The number of factors determines the number of axes, or geometric dimensions, required to plot the variables.

Plotting a Variable.   Once the orthogonal factors have been drawn arbitrarily, each variable is drawn as a line from the **point of origin** (i.e., from the point where the factors intersect). The location of the end point for a variable is determined by its factor weights or coordinates. The factor weights form a row of *P,* wherein each of the elements is one of the coordinates necessary to define the end point. The line itself is referred to as the **vector** for the variable.

Example

In Fig. 4.1, one variable is plotted as a function of two factors. Its weight on the first factor is .8; this means that its end point lies on the dotted line that crosses factor *A* at .8. The variable's weight on factor *B* is −.6, and so its end point also lies on the dotted line that crosses factor *B* at −.6. The two dotted lines intersect at only one point and that is where the vector ends.

The Roman numerals in Fig. 4.1 identify the quadrants formed by the abscissa and ordinate. In the first quadrant, all weights are positive. In the second, they

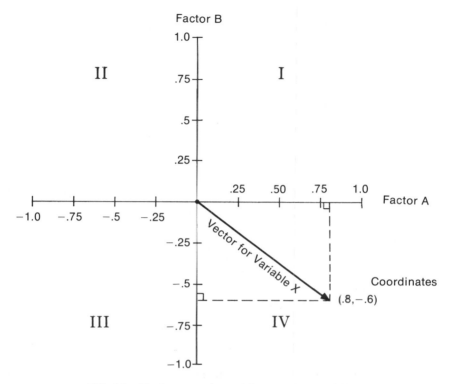

FIG. 4.1. Plotting two orthogonal factors and one variable.

are negative on the first factor, A, and positive on the seccnd, B. The third quadrant is the reverse of the first with all weights being negative. Vectors in the fourth quadrant have negative weights on B and positive ones on A.

Length of the Variable Vectors. The length of the vector can be computed from the Pythagorean theorem: the square of the length of the hypotenuse of a right triangle is equal to the sum of the squares of the other two sides. In Fig. 4.1, the right angle is formed by the intersection of the dotted line from the factor to the end point of the vector with the factor. The squared hypotenuse, h^2, is $.8^2 + (-.6)^2$, or 1.0, with the length being the square root of 1.0. The length of each vector is also its communality (symbolized by h). Because the two factors are the sole basis for this variable (i.e., a component model is used), the variable is drawn to unit length. If the length of the variable were less than unity but the variable scores had an observed standard deviation of 1.0, then these two factors would not perfectly reproduce the variable scores.

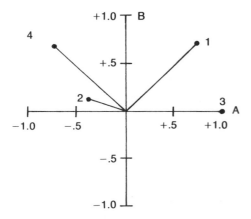

FIG. 4.2.   Sample representation of three variables and two factors.

Example

Figure 4.2 contains a diagram of two factors, *A* and *B*, and four variables. The factor matrix from which this figure was constructed is given in Table 4.1.1. Each variable was plotted by drawing a line from the point of origin (i.e., the point where all weights are zero) to the point identified by the coordinates.

In Table 4.1.1 variables 3 and 4 have communalities of 1.0, but variable 2 has a communality of only .13. Therefore, variable 2's vector is considerably shorter than the vectors for variables 3 and 4 in Fig. 4.2. (The plotted length is equal to the square root of h^2.)

The fact that the squared length of a vector represents that part of its variance that is estimated by the factors can be illustrated by dropping factor *B* from Fig. 4.2. In this case, the factor matrix would be one-dimensional and would be represented as a straight line. This is shown in Fig. 4.3. The length of a variable such as 4 has decreased because the variance accounted for by factor B is no longer included; however, the length of variable 3 is unchanged because *B* did not contribute to it.

Representing More Than Two Factors.   Figure 4.1 represents two factors in two dimensions. Three factors would require three-dimensional representation, which could be made by projecting the new factor off the paper or by building a three-dimensional physical model. Four dimensions are mathematically possible

TABLE 4.1.1
Factor Pattern for Figure 4.2

Variables	A	Factors B	h^2
1	.7	.7	.98
2	−.3	.2	.13
3	1.0	.0	1.0
4	−.6	.8	1.0

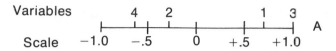

FIG. 4.3.   One factor representation of Table 4.1.1.

but they cannot be represented in three-dimensional space, unless the representation is subdivided into a series of two- or three-dimensional models.

Regardless of the limitations of space, geometric principles can be utilized for more than three dimensions; indeed, an infinite number of dimensions can be conceptualized. The number of factor-analytic dimensions often exceeds three-dimensional space, and the multidimensional space is referred to as **hyperspace.** All of the principles for two- or three-dimensional space hold for hyperspace. For example, a plane is a two-dimensional surface in three-dimensional space and a **hyperplane** is an $(f - 1)$-dimensional plane in f-dimensional space. The concept of a hyperplane will be used in Chapter 9.

Reversing a Factor or Variable.   Some simple changes can be made in the factor matrix without altering the plots in any dramatic way. One simple change is that of multiplying all the loadings on one factor by -1. This multiplication changes the sign of that factor's loadings and the resulting figure becomes a "flip-flop" of the initial figure.

Example

In Fig. 4.4 is a geometrical presentation of Table 4.1.1 but after factor A has been reversed; each of its loadings has been multiplied by -1. None of the relationships among the variables is altered in any major way, as can be determined by comparing this figure to Fig. 4.2.

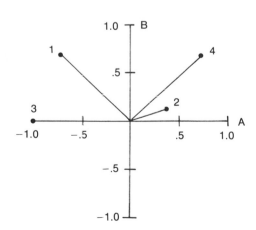

FIG. 4.4.   Figure 4.2 with factor A reversed.

The reversal of the signs for one variable does change the graph somewhat but the impact of the change is usually trivial. The reversal of the variable's direction can happen easily in data, such as that of sociology and psychology, where the scale is bipolar and the original positive end is chosen for mathematically irrelevant reasons. One could score a political activism scale with liberalism being positive or conservatism being positive; although one's personal preferences will probably be reflected in the choice of the positive pole, the scale still measures the same thing regardless of the direction in which it is scored.

Example

If variable 4 in Fig. 4.4 were scored in the opposite direction, then it would extend from the origin in the opposite direction (i.e., in the third quadrant instead of the first. This change would affect neither the factor nor its identification providing the label on the variable was also reversed.

The Correlation Between a Vector and Another Vector or Factor. When variables are represented in hyperspace as vectors, the correlation between that vector and one of the axes (i.e., factors), or with another vector (i.e., variable), can be readily determined as a function of the angle between them. The formula is:

$$r_{12} = h_1 h_2 \cos \alpha_{12} \tag{4.1.1}$$

that is, the correlation between any two vectors in space (including a factor as a vector) is equal to the length of the first times the length of the second times the cosine of the angle (α) between the two vectors.

Because each factor is represented as a coordinate and all its variance is included in the dimension that it defines, its length is always 1.0. Hence, when the correlation of a variable with a factor is being determined, the resulting formula is:

$$r_{1k} = h_1 \cos \alpha_{1k} \tag{4.1.2}$$

where r_{1k} is the correlation of variable 1 with factor k. Further simplification is possible by substituting the definition of the cosine of an angle:

$$r_{1k} = h_1 \frac{\text{length of the adjacent side}}{\text{length of the hypotenuse}}. \tag{4.1.3}$$

However, the hypotenuse is the same as h_1 in this case, so:

$$r_{1k} = h_1 \frac{\text{length of the adjacent side}}{h_1}. \tag{4.1.4}$$

Then:

$$r_{1k} = \text{length of the adjacent side.} \tag{4.1.5}$$

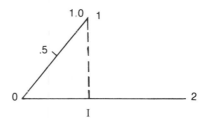

FIG. 4.5.   Forming a right-angle triangle between two vectors.

The length of the adjacent side is none other than the factor weight. Therefore, the correlation of the variable with its factor is its factor pattern element. This applies only to rectangular Cartesian coordinates (i.e., uncorrelated factors).

The length of the variable, h, may be any positive value. The variable's length squared, h^2, is also called the variable's communality.

The cosine of the angle between two vectors is determined by, first, drawing a line from the end point of one vector to the other vector in such a manner that the line is perpendicular to the second vector. The result is a right triangle. Figure 4.5 gives two variables with the line dropped from variable 1's end point to variable 2; it intersects variable 2 at point I.

The cosine is then the length of the adjacent side of the right triangle divided by the length of the hypotenuse. In Fig. 4.5 this is the length of variable 2 when measured only from the origin to the intersection, I, divided by the length of the other vector (which happens to be 1.0 in this example). The same cosine would occur if the line had been dropped from the end of vector 2 and intersected vector 1.

If the angle between the two variables were greater than 90^c, one vector would be extended through the point of origin. The usual right triangle would then be drawn with the extended vector. The cosine would be negative.

Equation (4.1.1) can also be used to determine the correlation between any two variables being represented as vectors. In the simplest case where each

TABLE 4.1.2
Angles for Cosines

Cosine	Angle	Cosine	Angle
1.00	0°	.41	66°
.966	15°	.31	72°
.90	26°	.26	75°
.87	30°	.21	78°
.80	37°	.10	84°
.707	45°	.00	90°
.60	53°	−.50	120°
.50	60°	−1.00	180°

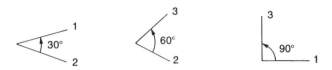

FIG. 4.6.   Correlations and the angles between vectors.

variable is completely represented in the hyperspace, the length of each vector is then 1.0 and the formula becomes simply:

$$r_{12} = \cos \alpha_{12}. \tag{4.1.6}$$

The correlation coefficient therefore equals the cosine of the angle between the two variables. The angles of some sample cosines (correlations) are given in Table 4.1.2.

Example

Variables 1 and 2 correlate .87, 2 and 3 correlate .5, and 1 and 3 correlate 0.0. All vectors have communalities of 1.0. They are plotted in Fig. 4.6. These may all be drawn together as in Fig. 4.7.

A positive correlation is represented as an angle ranging from zero to 90° and a negative correlation by angles from 90° to 180°. Because no other information is given, the first vector can be drawn in any direction. The second vector must be drawn to be consistent with the first.

Example

In Fig. 4.8, positive correlations are found between, for example, 1 and 2, 3 and 4, 5 and 6, and 1 and 7. Negative correlations are found between 1 and 4, 2 and 5, and 7 and 4.

4.1.2 Developing a Geometric Representation from Only the Variables

The fact that a plot of variable vectors can be developed independently of the factors and weights leads to factor analysis itself. The analysis begins by considering the correlations as cosines and plotting the resulting vectors. After the plot

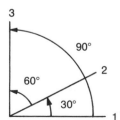

FIG. 4.7.   Plotting three-variable vectors.

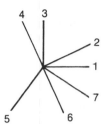

FIG. 4.8.   Plotting positive and negative correlations.

is made, coordinates (factors) are added according to a rationale determined by the investigator. The factor weights can then be read off the plot.

Example

In Fig. 4.9, three variables are represented geometrically. Variable 1 was drawn first and then the positions of variables 2 and 3 determined by their correlations with 1 and with each other. Factor *A* was drawn at random. It could have been drawn in at any position and the variable configuration would not have been altered. The position is not given mathematically until the principle for placing the factor is selected on theoretical grounds. One principle by which factor *A* could be placed is to have it correlate as high as possible with *one* variable (cf. Chapter 5) or with *all* variables (cf. Chapter 6). The second factor would then be placed orthogonal to the first. Here factor *A* correlates with all variables.

The result of this plotting is shown in Fig. 4.9. By measuring the end point of a vector in relationship to the uncorrelated factors, the weights can also be determined for each variable. For example, these are .99 and −.15 for variable 2. Because the factors are unit length, the projections also equal the cosine of the angles between the factors and the variable (i.e., the correlations).

What if the correlations are such that all of the angles cannot be plotted in two-dimensional space? Then one of two courses of action can be followed: On the one hand, more dimensions may be added until all the coefficients are

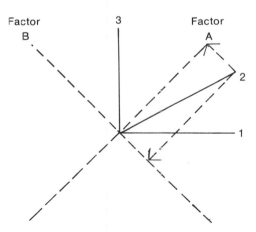

FIG. 4.9.   Adding coordinate axes
(factors) to the variable vector plot.

represented accurately. Adding more dimensions means that the number of factors are increased by moving to a space with three or more coordinates but that the variables would be completely represented. Complete representation is the full component model.

On the other hand, not all of the vector need be represented. Instead, only that part compatible with representing the other variables as vectors may be included. Because the variable's original communality was assumed to be 1.0, it will now be less than 1.0; therefore, the length of the variable will be less than unity in the hyperspace. The cosine would be calculated from the correlations by Eq. (4.1.1), which takes the reduced lengths into account. The common factor model generally represents only that portion of the variable which is associated with the common factors.

Example

In Fig. 4.6, variables 1 and 3 could correlate .5 instead of 0.0. They would then form an angle of 60° instead of 90°. In this case, variable 2 in Fig. 4.7 would need to extend out from the page somewhat so that all the angles could be properly represented. This can be illustrated more graphically by cutting out sheets of paper in triangular shape with the angle being appropriate to the correlations represented. By laying the sheets of paper on each other, it quickly becomes apparent whether they can be represented in two dimensions or whether a third dimension is needed.

In the figures used in this section, each variable is represented by a line drawn from the point of origin to the end of that vector. If large numbers of vectors are represented on the graph, a "blacking out" of some variables would occur due to a large number of lines being drawn through or near their position. Another way of representing the same information is to simply enter a dot on the graph for the end point of the vector. Figure 4.10 contains 14 variables in two-dimensional space, a case where it is necessary to plot only the end points.

FIG. 4.10.   Representing vectors by only their end points.

4.2   THE UNCORRELATED (ORTHOGONAL) COMPONENT MODEL

This model follows directly from the preceding discussion. In the model the entire variable is represented in space (i.e., the variable's communality is 1.0 and is represented in hyperspace by a unit-length vector). Therefore, the correlations in the correlation matrix should give the cosines between the vectors directly. Inasmuch as they do not, the model fails to account for the data. In most component analyses, unit-length vectors are not preserved. However, the attempt is made to represent the variables in a sufficient number of dimensions so that the reduction in vector length is minor. Determining the exact number of dimensions that will produce this "next to best" situation is the problem of determining the number of factors (cf. Chapter 8).

When the variables have been plotted, the factors can be added as deemed best so long as they are all orthogonal. Usually, a factor is placed near the center of a cluster of variables so that it can be identified by the conceptual central thrust of the variables.

Once several factors have been added, however, they need not remain in the same position. Instead, they can be shifted or **rotated** to any position for which the investigator can present an appropriate rationale (cf. Chapter 9). Further research and thought are often necessary to determine which position is the most scientifically useful.

Example

In the case of a small number of variables where it is obvious that there are only two factors, the relationship between the variables can be drawn on paper as, for example, in Fig. 4.11 and 4.12. Because each of the vectors is unit length, the component model is obviously appropriate for these data. All the information from the correlation matrix is represented in each of these figures.

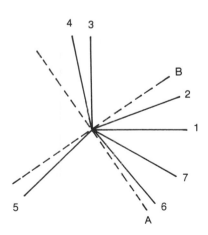

FIG. 4.11.   One investigator's coordinates for seven variables.

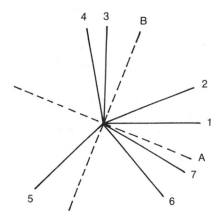

FIG. 4.12. Another investigator's coordinates for seven variables.

TABLE 4.2.1
Factor Matrix for Figure 4.11

	A	B
1	.55	.80
2	.25	.95
3	−.80	.55
4	−.95	.35
5	.45	−.90
6	.99	.10
7	.90	.50

Note: the entries are only approximate since they were developed from the plots.

TABLE 4.2.2
Factor Matrix for Figure 4.12

	A	B
1	.90	.40
2	.75	.70
3	−.40	.90
4	−.55	.85
5	−.40	−.90
6	.75	−.65
7	.95	−.30

Note: the entries are only approximate since they were developed from the plots.

Figure 4.11 gives the coordinates for an initial solution for Fig. 4.8. Another investigator examined the plot of the variables, however, and felt the factors needed to be shifted approximately 30°, and he rotated (or shifted) them accordingly. Figure 4.12 gives his solution. In each of these two cases, a different factor matrix would be determined. Tables 4.2.1 and 4.2.2 give the factor matrices for the two figures. Both are legitimate uncorrelated component solutions because all the vectors are unit length and the factors are uncorrelated. The factor matrices contain the weights/correlations relating each variable to each factor.

4.3   THE CORRELATED (OBLIQUE) COMPONENT MODEL

In representing correlated components, the general Cartesian coordinate system is used instead of the rectangular Cartesian coordinate system. The former allows the axes (or factors) to form an oblique angle and thus are correlated. The latter allows only orthogonal factors that are therefore uncorrelated. In the general Cartesian system, the correlation between two factors plotted in hyperspace is still defined by Eq. (4.1.1). Because both factors are defined as unit length, this equation becomes (4.1.6) (i.e., the cosine of the angle is equal to the correlation between the two factors). Because the angle between the factors is oblique, they are referred to as **oblique** factors.

It should be noted that the plotting of the vectors that represent the variables is identical to that in the uncorrelated component model. Each correlation coefficient is converted to a cosine and, if two dimensions are adequate, the variable vectors are plotted in a plane. The use of correlated coordinates does not alter the configuration of the variables.

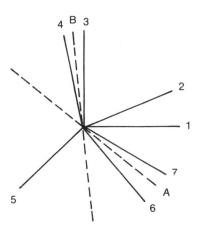

FIG. 4.13.   Correlated components.

TABLE 4.3.1
Factor Pattern for Figure 4.13

	A	B
1	1.20	.60
2	1.10	.90
3	.15	1.05
4	−.20	.90
5	−.85	−1.20
6	.60	−.50
7	.95	.30

Note: $r_{AB} = -.6$.

Example

In Fig. 4.13 the data from Fig. 4.12 have been entered into the same space but A and B correlate −.6.

Table 4.3.1 gives the approximate factor weights read from Fig. 4.13. Note that whenever the factors are correlated, it is possible to have weights greater than 1.0.

When plotting a two-factor matrix, one factor is arbitrarily drawn. The other factor is then drawn in accordance with its correlation with the factor already represented. The variable vectors can then be plotted by their relationships to the factors. In the general Cartesian coordinate system, the end point of each vector is again determined by its factor pattern. However, in this system, the weights are applied by extending a line from the factor at the point of the value given by the weight parallel to the other factor. A second line is extended from the point on the second factor equal in value to the weight and parallel to the first factor. The end point for the variable vector is the intersection of both lines from the factors.

Example

Figure 4.14 gives a case where factor A and B correlate .707 (i.e., they have an angle of 45°). Variable 1 is composed of $1.25A$ and $-.90B$ and is plotted accordingly.

Because the vectors are full length insofar as the component model is accurate, the correlation between each variable vector and each factor is generally equal to the cosine of the angle between the variable and the factor. Because the cosine is defined as the adjacent side over the hypotenuse in a right triangle, a line is dropped from the end point of the vector for the variable to the factor so that it forms a right angle upon intersecting the factor. The hypotenuse is the variable vector, which is 1.0, and the adjacent side is the distance from the origin that the perpendicular dropped from the point creates on the factor. Therefore, the correlation can be read off the factor scale simply by noting where the perpendicular line cuts the factor.

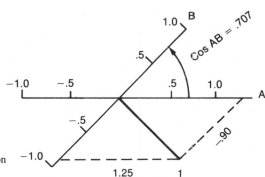

FIG. 4.14. Plotting variables on correlated coordinate axes.

Example

Determining the correlation of a variable with correlated factors is illustrated in Fig. 4.15. The correlation of variable 1 in Fig. 4.15 with A is .8 and with B is $-.2$. **In a correlated factor model, correlations are distinct from the weights and can even be of opposite sign.** (The weights were $1.25A$ and $-.90B$).

The possibility of correlated factors in the correlated component model allows the factors to take many more possible positions. In the two-factor systems being used here for illustrative purposes, the position of the second factor is fixed in the uncorrelated models. Once the position of the first factor is decided on, the second factor can only be placed 90° from the first factor. In the correlated component model, the placement of one factor places no theoretical limitation upon the other factor. However, in actuality, a correlation of .7 between two factors would be extremely high and seldom allowed. Most correlations between factors in empirical studies are not allowed to go above .5 or so (i.e., an angle of 30°).

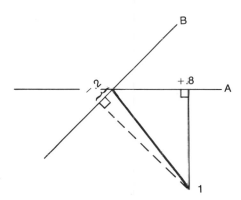

FIG. 4.15. Correlations between a variable and correlated factors.

4.4 COMMON FACTOR MODELS

The common factor model also comes in uncorrelated and correlated versions. Differences are exactly the same as between the orthogonal and the oblique component models and therefore will not be discussed. For simplicity's sake, only the uncorrelated common factor model is discussed but the principles apply equally to the correlated common factor model.

The common factor model consists of two sets of factors: common and unique. The length of the variable vector is assumed to be unity only if *all* of these dimensions are plotted. Because there is one unique factor for each variable in addition to the common factors, the number of dimensions necessary for the variables to be unity would be quite high. However, there is little interest in plotting the variable in the total hyperspace. Only the common factors section of the hyperspace is of general interest.

To plot a variable, only the common factor weights are used. Once the vector has been plotted, its length can be measured. The exclusion of specific factors and random factors does not affect the location of the vector with reference to the common factors, but does reduce the length of the vector.

The problem is more difficult, however, when the geometric representation is proceeding from the correlation matrix. Because the vectors are not assumed to be unit length, the correlations are not directly equal to the cosines of the angles between the vectors. Instead, each correlation is multiplied by each of the associated vector lengths. The communalities are not known but can only be estimated. They are usually estimated so as to leave the correlations as unaltered as possible for that number of factors. Communality estimation procedures are discussed in later chapters, particularly Chapter 6.

After the correlation is multiplied by the vector lengths, it is then the cosine of the angle between the two vectors. From the lengths and the cosines, the vectors can be goemetrically represented in as many dimensions as needed to prevent undue distortion of the angles. Factors are then added to the plot.

5 Diagonal and Multiple-Group Analysis

The equation $Z_{nv} = F_{nf} P'_{fv}$ has an infinite number of solutions when both F and P are being solved for simultaneously. There is no unique solution unless restrictions are placed on the solution. Several kinds of restrictions can be made; the type of restriction used is based on the nature of the desired factors. The restrictions can refer to the way in which the set of factors explains the total correlation matrix or can apply to one or only a few of the variables in the total matrix. This chapter contains simple solutions where the factors are defined as a function of only a limited subset of the variables.

Because only the variable scores are known, they are used as a starting point and the factor scores are defined in terms of the variables. This means that the factors are defined as a linear function of the variables, just as a test score is defined as the sum of the items.

Once a factor has been defined as a composite of the variables, the relationship of all the variables to the composite factor can then be found. For example, scores on the factor could be computed from the data matrix, and then each of the variables correlated with the factor scores. Although the factor scores could actually be calculated, this is usually not necessary. Instead, formulas are derived to compute factor pattern coefficients, factor structure elements, and the correlations among the factors.

In this chapter, simple definitions of factors are used. In Section 5.1, Diagonal Analysis, the solution is restricted by allowing only one variable to define a factor, which is about as "simple" as a factor can be. In Section 5.2, diagonal factor analysis is generalized into multiple-group factor analysis by allowing two or more variables to be the factor. The situations where diagonal and multiple-group factor analyses appear useful are in hypothesis testing, in a covariance analysis analog, in reducing the number of variables for further analyses or for future studies, and in item analysis (Section 5.3). Special complications arising under the common factor model are given attention throughout.

Because the procedures are simple, derivations will be presented. This is the last chapter where it is possible to derive all the equations without advanced mathematics. The fact that the procedures can be derived with relatively simple mathematics and can be calculated by hand allows for the development of an intuitive "feel" for factor-analytic procedures, but the simplicity does not mean that multiple-group factor analysis is less powerful than the more complex procedures (Guttman, 1952).

5.1   DIAGONAL ANALYSIS

In the simplest of factor analyses, the first factor is assumed to be the equivalent of one variable. The extent to which this one factor can account for the entire correlation matrix is determined. The next factor is then set equal to a second variable and the variance that it can account for is then determined for the correlation matrix from which the variance for the first factor has been extracted. The process is continued until all the factors of interest are extracted.

The procedure is referred to as **diagonal** factor analysis because the calculations for each factor begin with the diagonal element of the variable defining that factor. It has also been referred to as square-root factor analysis because the component version takes the square root of the diagonal element; other names for it include triangular decomposition, sweep-out method, pivotal condensation, solid-staircase analysis, analytic factor analysis (DuBois & Sullivan, 1972), maximal decomposition (Hunter, 1972), and regression component analysis (Schönemann & Steiger, 1976).

5.1.1 Extraction of the First Factor

In extracting the first diagonal factor, one variable is designated as the first factor. The problem is to determine the correlation of the variable with itself as a factor and the correlation of the other variables with the factor. The correlations are the same as the weights in the factor pattern matrix.

Because the variable is considered to be error-free in the component model, the defining variable *is* the factor, and the weight/correlation for that variable must be:

$$p_{1A} = 1.0 \qquad\qquad (5.1.1)$$

where the variable 1 is the defining variable. The loadings of the other variables on the first factor are simply their correlations with the defining variable 1:

$$p_{jA} = r_{j1}. \qquad\qquad (5.1.2)$$

Because the correlations of the other variables with the factor are simply the correlation coefficients, these factor loadings can be tested for significance by the ordinary test of a correlation coefficient (Guilford, 1965a). Diagonal component analysis is implicitly performed whenever one variable is correlated with another.

Example

The correlations for the physique data are given in Table 5.1.1. From a casual consideration of the nature of the problem, one might decide to classify people by height. Then within each height category, people would be further subdivided into "stout," "average," and "slim." This is one approach used by suppliers of ready-made women's clothing, most of whom use euphemisms such as "half-size" (for stout) and "petite" (for slim) to represent the classification. The height/weight approach defines a two-diagonal factor solution.

All variance attributable to height is accounted for by using it as the first measurement. Differences that still exist between physiques of the same height are accounted for by the weight category. So the first diagonal factor extracted is that of height, and then a diagonal factor of weight is removed. It is then of interest to see how well all of the physique measurements are reproduced by this approach; inasmuch as they are not adequately represented, coats, hats, and other apparel would not fit everyone equally well. Because both of these variables are highly reliable, a component model can be assumed with little loss of accuracy in reproducing the measurements.

Following Eqs. (5.1.1) and (5.1.2), the first factor's structure coefficients and pattern weights are simply the correlations of height with the other variables. These form the first column of Table 5.1.2. This table will be discussed later in the chapter where the weights for factor B are defined.

The First Diagonal Common Factor. Because the diagonal element of the correlation matrix is the communality of the variable, the diagonal element is the proportion of the variable's variance that can be attributed to the factors. For the

TABLE 5.1.1
Physique Correlations

	1	2	3	4	5	6	7	8	9	10	11	12
1. Stature	10000											
2. Symphysis height	8957	10000										
3. Breadth of skull	1098	1889	10000									
4. Length of skull	2860	4168	0500	10000								
5. Biacromial diameter	4529	3616	2764	4259	10000							
6. Transverse chest diameter	2668	1494	2280	1593	4881	10000						
7. Sagittal chest diameter	3335	2764	0000	3051	3523	2764	10000					
8. Bicristal diameter	2668	1889	1889	2860	2085	2571	3802	10000				
9. Length of sternum	5480	3616	1593	1692	3335	1296	4969	3894	10000			
10. Chest circumference (at expiration)	3146	0998	1889	1692	5480	5563	6131	4706	2860	10000		
11. Hip circumference	3429	1889	2860	0200	3523	4529	6594	6816	3802	7103	10000	
12. Weight	4969	3429	1593	3051	3395	6594	6518	4349	3802	7466	7103	10000

Note: Decimals omitted. Normally only two places would be reported; four places are reported here so that the reader can reproduce analyses in later chapters or experiment with other solutions. Adapted from Rees (1950).

TABLE 5.1.2
Diagonal Physique Factors: Height and Weight

	A. Height	B. Weight	h^2
1. Stature	1.00	.00	1.00
2. Symphysis height	.90	−.12	.82
3. Breadth of skull	.11	.12	.03
4. Length of skull	.29	.19	.12
5. Biacromial diameter	.45	.36	.34
6. Transverse chest diameter	.27	.61	.44
7. Sagittal chest diameter	.33	.56	.42
8. Bicristal diameter	.27	.35	.19
9. Length of sternum	.55	.12	.32
10. Chest circumference (at expiration)	.31	.68	.56
11. Hip circumference	.34	.62	.50
12. Weight	.50	.87	1.00

first diagonal common factor, all of the variance of the variable that is not measurement error could be defined as the factor. The reliability coefficient is, by definition, the proportion of nonerror variance, and so an estimate of the variable's reliability can be used as its diagonal element in the correlation matrix.[1]

The solution follows directly from Eq. (2.4.4); it is assumed that all variables are in standard score form. Equation (2.4.4) states that each element of the correlation matrix is reproduced by multiplying factor loadings for standard scores together. The sum of the squares of a particular variable's loadings is then equal to its diagonal element in the correlation matrix when the variables are in standard score form.

When the first factor is defined as identical with the defining variable, all of that variable's communality will be accounted for by that factor. Because the communality is given in the diagonal of the matrix being factored, the square of the defining variable's single loading on the first factor must reproduce the diagonal element. Therefore, the loading of the defining variable on the first factor, p_{1A}, is:

$$p_{1A} = \sqrt{r_{jj}}. \tag{5.1.3}$$

The next step is to find the loadings of the other variables on this first factor. From Eq. (2.4.4) the correlation between the defining variable and any other variable is equal to the product of their two loadings, that is,

$$p_{jA} \, p_{1A} = r_{j1}. \tag{5.1.4}$$

---

[1]Although a model could be used that would correct for specific factor contribution as well as unreliability of measurement by using other communality estimates (cf. Section 6.3), this is seldom if ever done.

To find p_{jA}, one would simply divide through by p_{1A} to obtain:

$$p_{jA} = r_{j1}/p_{1A}. \qquad (5.1.5)$$

The loading for each variable is therefore calculated by dividing the correlation by the loading of the defining variable.

5.1.2 Extraction of Successive Factors

If another diagonal factor is desired, a second variable is selected to define that factor. At this point, two choices are possible: correlated factors could be extracted or the solution could be so restricted that all the factors are uncorrelated with each other. The correlated factor case leads to a trivial solution for the component model. If, for example, one defined each succeeding factor by another variable and allowed the factors to be correlated, there would be as many factors as variables and each factor would be equal to a particular variable. The correlations among factors would be the correlations among variables. Therefore:

$$R_{vv} = R_{ff}. \qquad (5.1.6)$$

The correlation, or factor structure coefficient, of each variable with each factor would be the raw correlation of each variable with the defining variable. No new information would be gained from a diagonal factor analysis under a correlated component model.

In the correlated common factor model, the only alteration in the correlations would be that they would be corrected for the estimated unreliability in the defining variable. This too appears to be so simple as not to warrant further discussion. Only the uncorrelated models generally give nontrivial diagonal factors.

In diagonal analysis with uncorrelated factors, the factor being extracted after the first factor—or any number of diagonal factors—accounts for variance in the correlation matrix that is not accounted for by the first factor. Working from Eq. (2.4.4), it follows that the reproduced correlation matrix is:

$$\hat{R}_{vv} = P_{V1}P'_{1V} \qquad (5.1.7)$$

where P_{V1} is the first column from P_{vf}'. The matrix of coefficients representing variance not accounted for by the first factor is then equal to:

$$R_{vv.A} = R_{vv} - P_{V1}P'_{1V} \qquad (5.1.8)$$

where $R_{vv.A}$ is the correlation matrix with one factor removed. In $R_{vv.A}$, commonly referred to as the **residual** matrix, the influence of the first factor has been removed and the correlations of the first defining variable with all other variables are zero in the uncorrelated component approach. The other residuals are partial covariances where all the variance overlapping with the first variable has been removed.

Example

The residuals after height has been removed from Table 5.1.1 are calculated by Eq. (5.1.8). Some of the individual elements are:

$$r_{1,2 \cdot A} = r_{1,2} - r_{1A} (r_{2A})$$
$$= .8957 - 1.0000 (.8957)$$
$$= .0000 = .00$$

$$r_{4,5 \cdot A} = r_{4,5} - r_{4A} (r_{5A})$$
$$= .4259 - (.2860) (.4529)$$
$$= .4259 - .1218$$
$$= .3041 = .30$$

$$r_{12,8 \cdot A} = r_{12,8} - r_{12,A} (r_{8A})$$
$$= .4349 - .4969 (.2668)$$
$$= .4349 - .1326$$
$$= .3023 = .30$$

$$r_{12,12 \cdot A} = r_{12,12} - r_{12,A} (r_{12,A})$$
$$= 1.0000 - .4969 (.4969)$$
$$= 1.0000 - .2469$$
$$= .7531 = .75$$

Another diagonal factor can now be extracted from the residual matrix. Because none of the diagonal elements will necessarily be unity even in the component model, the equations used are (5.1.3) and (5.1.5). These may be rewritten for the second factor as follows:

$$p_{2B} = \sqrt{r_{22 \cdot A}} \qquad (5.1.9)$$

where the p_{2B} is the second defining variable's loading on its own factor. Then:

$$p_{jB} = \frac{r_{j2 \cdot A}}{p_{2B}} . \qquad (5.1.10)$$

The variable defining the second diagonal factor will have loadings on the first diagonal factor as well as the second. This means that the factor from the second defining variable is not equivalent to the original version of that variable even in the component model. Rather, all of the variance of the second defining variable that can be attributable to the first defining variable has been partialed out.

Example

For the physique data, the second factor is to be defined by weight. Using Eq. (5.1.9) the defining variable's loading is:

$$p_{12,B} = \sqrt{r_{12,12 \cdot A}}$$
$$= \sqrt{.7531}$$
$$= .8678 = .87$$

This is the correlation of weight as a raw score with weight after the variation due to height has been extracted. In adult women, weight is not a strong function of height. If the data were from children of varying ages, the overlap of height and weight would be greater.

The loadings of the other variables on the weight factor can now be calculated by Eq. (5.1.10), that is:

$$P_{8,B} = \frac{r_{12,8 \cdot A}}{P_{12 \cdot B}}$$

$$= \frac{.3023}{.8678}$$

$$= .3484 = .35.$$

The second column of Table 5.1.2 gives the complete set of loadings.

The next residual matrix is defined by either of the following two equations:

$$R_{vv \cdot A \cdot B} = R_{vv \cdot A} - P_{v1} P'_{1v} \tag{5.1.11}$$

where the elements of the column vector P are from the second column of the P_{vf}. Or:

$$R_{vv \cdot A \cdot B} = R_{vv} - P_{vB} P'_{Bv} \tag{5.1.12}$$

where P_{vB} is the factor pattern for the first two factors.

The third factor would be extracted from the second residual matrix in the same manner as the second factor was extracted from the first residual matrix. This process of factoring would continue for as long as diagonal factors were to be extracted. In this manner, all of the columns of P can be built up.

The first diagonal factor is the essence of simplicity to interpret because it is one of the variables itself. However, succeeding factors become more difficult to interpret because each succeeding factor has had the variation overlapping the previous factors removed. The elements of P_{vf} are a series of correlations, in this uncorrelated model, where each successive column has all the variance from the previous factors removed (i.e., the semipartial (or part) correlations of the original variable scores with the defining variables after that part of the defining variable correlated with the previous defining variables has been removed, see Nunnally (1978) for a discussion of semipartial correlations. **Unless the variables used to define the earlier factors are conceptually clear, the later factors and extraction procedures will be based upon essentially unknown components of the defining variables.**

Example

In the two-diagonal factor solution for the physique data, the question of how well the two factors predict individual measurements can now be evaluated. Examining Table 5.1.2, one finds that height can be used as an excellent estimate of symphysis height, because it correlates .9, and as a moderate estimate of several other measures of physique. For example, length of sternum has a factor loading of (i.e., correlates) .55 and weight correlates .5 with the height factor.

Weight also adds additional accuracy to several variables. In particular, and rather oddly, the three measures of chest diameter and the hip circumference can be more accurately estimated from weight than from height. It is interesting to note that hip circumference might be an even better second factor for reproducing this set of variables (the student may want to work out the solution needed to test this hypothesis). The closest measure to waist, bicristal diameter, is much less predictable from these two factors. Hence, weight definitely adds to height in predicting two out of three vital statistics.

The last column of Table 5.1.2 gives the communalities (i.e., the proportion of the variance of each variable that is accounted for by the two factors). Using height and weight to determine size of clothing could be expected to lead to reasonable fits, as shown by the high communalities, in some areas (e.g., coats) but not others. In particular, never guess a hat size by a person's height and weight.

In general, these two factors do not account for an impressive amount of the variance in physical measurements.

5.2   MULTIPLE-GROUP FACTOR ANALYSIS

The diagonal approach to factoring is a simple way of defining factors because each factor is defined as a single variable. **Multiple-group** factors are defined as linear, weighted composites of two or more of the variables, and thus are a generalization of the diagonal procedure. Indeed, diagonal factors can be defined as multiple-group factors where one variable is used as the "linear composite."

In most multiple group factor analyses, the *factor* is defined as the sum of the scores from a group of variables accepted as defining the factor with each variable given equal weight. For example, the standard scores from all the defining variables may be simply added together and this total score is considered the factor. Correlated multiple-group components (Section 5.2.1) follow the summed standard score definition exactly. In uncorrelated multiple-group components (Section 5.2.2), one defines the first factor in exactly this manner; the other factors follow the same definition but are kept uncorrelated with all previously extracted factors. A common factor version of multiple-group analysis is considered in Section 5.2.3.

Multiple-group factors could be defined by summing differentially weighted variables. Weights may be given the defining variables on the basis of an explicit conception of the factors, or the weighting could be accidental. For example, a common procedure is to add item scores together to obtain a variable. In this case, the items with the larger variances will influence the variation of total scale scores more than their colleagues. Each variable is therefore weighted and the total score, or factor, is the sum of the weighted item scores. Summing across items is a legitimate, correlated multiple-group component analysis. Everyone who uses a multiple-item scale, and correlates the items or other variables with the scale, has performed a simple factor analysis.

All of the equations developed in this section apply regardless of the weights used. The only difference is that the weight matrix to define the factors would consist of a wide range of weights instead of only the zeros and ones portrayed in the following sections. Because the principles are the same, the generalization simple, and the zero–one approach the most widely used, only the latter will be formally discussed.

Centroid factor analysis is a variation upon multiple-group factor analysis. In the full centroid method, all the variables are assumed to belong to the first group and to define the first factor. The factor is then extracted and a residual matrix calculated. Variables within the matrix are then "reflected," (i.e., reversed in sign) so that another centroid factor can be extracted (Thurstone. 1947). Factors are extracted one after another until a sufficient amount of the variance in the correlation matrix is accounted for. This is not hypothesis testing; rather, it is exploratory and is generally used with rotation procedures. Since the advent of high-speed computers with relatively large storage, this procedure has been replaced by the more sophisticated one of principal factors for many exploratory analyses. Multiple-group factor analysis is, however, still useful in several situations (cf. Section 5.3).

While the total score found by summing raw items is a legitimate way to define a multiple-group factor, it is not a multiple-group centroid factor because each item is indirectly weighted as a function of its variance. A centroid factor explicitly gives each defining variable equal weight regardless of its original standard deviation. If the scale is to be a multiple-group centroid factor, the individual items would need to be weighted equally in defining the total score. Equal weighting occurs when the item standard scores are added together.

5.2.1 Correlated Multiple-Group Components

If correlated multiple-group components are sought, then each factor is simply the sum of the standardized scores for the variables defining it. The factor structure, S_{vf}, is found by correlating the original variable scores with these multiple-group factor scores. Because the factor pattern, P_{vf}, is not the same as S_{vf} in the correlated factors case, each is calculated separately. The factor pattern is defined as a set of weights by which each variable can be predicted from the set of factors. With the scores available for the factors and variables, this becomes a series of multiple regression analyses where the original variable is the dependent measure and the factors are the independent measures. By running as many multiple regressions as there are variables, the entire factor pattern matrix, P_{vf}, can be built up.

As one would suspect, there are easier ways to compute S_{vf} and P_{vf} than to calculate actual factor scores for each of the multiple-group factors. These procedures do not produce scores for the factors but will give all the relationships of the variables with the factor scores, as well as the relationships among the factors themselves. The formulas are derived from the fact that one is correlating each original variable with a linear composite of a subset of other variables.

When the variables are in standard score form, the formula for the correlation of all variables with the multiple-group factors can be specified in terms of the factor structure. Thus:

$$S_{vf} = Z'_{vn}A_{nf}n^{-1}S_{ff}^{-1} \qquad (5.2.1)$$

where S_{vf} is the factor structure containing the correlations between the variables and the factors, Z contains the variable scores, and A_{nf} contains the observed factor scores that are not in standard score form. S_{ff}, the factor standard deviation matrix, is also needed.

Let W_{vf} be a weight matrix indicating which variables form which group factor. Those variables defining the group factor are given weights of 1 and the other variables are given weights of 0. The observed factor score matrix is given by:

$$A_{nf} = Z_{nv}\,W_{vf}. \qquad (5.2.2)$$

Example

In a four-variable problem, the first two variables can be used to define the first factor and the last two variables can be used to define the second factor. The weight matrix is then:

		Factors	
		A	B
	1	1	0
	2	1	0
Variables	3	0	1
	4	0	1

The standard score data matrix is postmultiplied by W. The following matrix is, we shall assume, three individual's scores for the four variables:

		Variables			
		1	2	3	4
	1	1.0	.5	0	0
Individuals	2	0	0	$-.3$	-1.2
	3	.5	.5	$-.5$	.3

The factor scores for the three individuals are computed by Eq. (5.2.2). The result is:

		Factors	
		A	B
	1	1.5	0
Individuals	2	0	-1.5
	3	1.0	$-.2$

As can be seen, the scores on the first factor are the sum of the individual's scores on the first two variables. The scores on the second factor are the sum of the scores on the last two variables. Although using a weight matrix may seem cumbersome at this point, it simplifies derivations and later calculations.

Substituting Eq. (5.2.2) into Eq. (5.2.1) gives:

$$S_{vf} = Z'_{vn} Z_{nv} \, n^{-1} \, W_{vf} \, S_{ff}^{-1}. \tag{5.2.3}$$

By definition of a correlation matrix, $Z' \, Zn^{-1}$ is R_{vv} and Eq. (5.2.3) is:

$$S_{vf} = R_{vv} \, W_{vf} \, S_{ff}^{-1}. \tag{5.2.4}$$

The standard deviations of the factors, S_{ff}, will be a function of the variances of each of the defining variables as well as their weights. By following a derivation analogous to that given above for the correlations between factors and variables, one finds that the variance–covariances of multiple-group factors in the component case are:

$$C_{ff} = W'_{fv} \, R_{vv} \, W_{vf} \tag{5.2.5}$$

which can be calculated directly from the correlations among variables and the weight matrix. S_{ff} is formed by taking the square roots of the diagonal elements of C for its diagonal elements and setting all off-diagonal elements to zero. S_{ff}^{-1} for Eq. (5.2.4) is easily calculated by dividing each of the elements of S_{ff} into unity.

The correlations among the factors can be calculated independently of the scores on the factors. The derivation of this formula begins from the definition of the correlation among the factors as a function of the covariance matrix:

$$R_{ff} = S_{ff}^{-1} C_{ff} S_{ff}^{-1}. \tag{5.2.6}$$

Substituting from Eq. (5.2.5) and Eq. (5.2.4):

$$R_{ff} = S_{ff}^{-1} W'_{fv} S_{vf}. \tag{5.2.7}$$

Example

In Table 1.2.2, three verbal comprehension variables and three anxiety variables formed a correlation matrix. The question can be asked: what would happen if each set of three variables were used to form a multiple-group factor? This is the same as asking what would happen if verbal comprehension were defined by summing the standard scores of the first three variables, and anxiety by summing standard scores for the last three. The hypothesis being tested could be one of asking whether variable X is a better measure of verbal comprehension than anxiety, of asking for the correlation between verbal comprehension and anxiety, or of asking if a particular variable (or item) is a better measure of one concept than another.

Extracting two multiple-group factors from the six variables is a worthwhile exercise for the student. To allow checking, a step-by-step solution for the correlations among the factors and the factor structure is given here; the factor pattern is computed later.

To find the factor structure, the factor variances are needed. These are calculated by Eq. (5.2.5):

$$C_{2,2} = W'_{2,6}R_{6,6}W_{6,2}$$

$$= \begin{bmatrix} 1 & 1 & 1 & 0 & 0 & 0 \\ 0 & 0 & 0 & -1 & 1 & 1 \end{bmatrix} \begin{bmatrix} 1.000 & .666 & .432 & .107 & -.074 & -.172 \\ .666 & 1.000 & .493 & .125 & -.047 & -.145 \\ .432 & .493 & 1.000 & .034 & -.142 & -.103 \\ .107 & .125 & .034 & 1.000 & -.409 & -.484 \\ -.074 & -.047 & -.142 & -.409 & 1.000 & .402 \\ -.172 & -.145 & -.103 & -.484 & .402 & 1.000 \end{bmatrix} \begin{bmatrix} 1 & 0 \\ 1 & 0 \\ 1 & 0 \\ 0 & -1 \\ 0 & 1 \\ 0 & 1 \end{bmatrix}$$

$$= \begin{bmatrix} 2.098 & 2.159 & 1.925 & .266 & -.263 & -.420 \\ -.353 & -.317 & -.279 & -1.893 & 1.811 & 1.886 \end{bmatrix} \begin{bmatrix} 1 & 0 \\ 1 & 0 \\ 1 & 0 \\ 0 & -1 \\ 0 & 1 \\ 0 & 1 \end{bmatrix}$$

$$= \begin{bmatrix} 6.182 & -.949 \\ -.949 & 5.590 \end{bmatrix}$$

The correlations between factors will be needed later. Using a standard formula gives:

$$R_{2,2} = S_{2,2}^{-1} C_{2,2} S_{2,2}^{-1}$$

$$= \begin{bmatrix} 1/2.4864 & 0 \\ 0 & 1/2.3643 \end{bmatrix} \begin{bmatrix} 6.182 & -.949 \\ -.949 & 5.590 \end{bmatrix} \begin{bmatrix} 1/2.4864 & 0 \\ 0 & 1/2.3643 \end{bmatrix}$$

$$= \begin{bmatrix} 2.4863 & -.3818 \\ -.4014 & 2.3643 \end{bmatrix} \begin{bmatrix} 1/2.4864 & 0 \\ 0 & 1/2.3643 \end{bmatrix} = \begin{bmatrix} 1.0000 & -.1615 \\ -.1614 & 1.0000 \end{bmatrix}$$

Anxiety and verbal comprehension are found to have a slight negative correlation. Then the factor structure is given by Eq. (5.2.4):

$$S_{vf} = R_{6,6} W_{6,2} S_{2,2}^{-1}$$

$$= R_{6,6} \begin{bmatrix} 1 & 0 \\ 1 & 0 \\ 1 & 0 \\ 0 & -1 \\ 0 & 1 \\ 0 & 1 \end{bmatrix} \begin{bmatrix} 1/2.4864 & 0 \\ 0 & 1/2.3643 \end{bmatrix}$$

$$= \begin{bmatrix} 1.000 & .666 & .432 & .107 & -.074 & -.172 \\ .666 & 1.000 & .493 & .125 & -.047 & -.145 \\ .432 & .493 & 1.000 & .034 & -.142 & -.103 \\ .107 & .125 & .034 & 1.000 & -.409 & -.484 \\ -.074 & -.047 & -.142 & -.409 & 1.000 & .402 \\ -.172 & -.145 & -.103 & -.484 & .402 & 1.000 \end{bmatrix} \begin{bmatrix} .4022 & 0 \\ .4022 & 0 \\ .4022 & 0 \\ 0 & -.4230 \\ 0 & .4230 \\ 0 & .4230 \end{bmatrix}$$

$$= \begin{bmatrix} .8438 & -.1493 \\ .8683 & -.1341 \\ .7742 & -.1180 \\ .1070 & -.8007 \\ -.1058 & .7661 \\ -.1689 & .7978 \end{bmatrix} = \begin{bmatrix} .84 & -.15 \\ .87 & -.13 \\ .77 & -.12 \\ .11 & -.80 \\ -.11 & .77 \\ -.17 & .80 \end{bmatrix}$$

Each variable is highly related to its factor and trivially related to the other factors.

Given the factor structure and the correlations among the factors, the factor pattern is given by beginning with Eq. (3.4.8):

$$S_{vf} = P_{vf} R_{ff}. \tag{5.2.8}$$

Then multiplying by the inverse of R—the matrix algebra method of dividing through by one element of the equation—gives the pattern:

$$P_{vf} = S_{vf} R_{ff}^{-1}. \tag{5.2.9}$$

Example

Calculating P for the personality problem:

$$P_{6,2} = S_{6,2} R_{2,2}^{-1}$$

$$= \begin{bmatrix} .8438 & -.1493 \\ .8683 & -.1341 \\ .7742 & -.1180 \\ .1070 & -.8007 \\ -.1058 & .7661 \\ -.1689 & .7978 \end{bmatrix} \begin{bmatrix} 1.0268 & .1658 \\ .1657 & 1.0268 \end{bmatrix}$$

$$= \begin{bmatrix} .8413 & -.0134 \\ .8694 & .0063 \\ .7754 & .0072 \\ -.0229 & -.8044 \\ .0183 & .7691 \\ -.0412 & .7912 \end{bmatrix} = \begin{bmatrix} .84 & -.01 \\ .87 & .01 \\ .78 & .01 \\ -.02 & -.80 \\ .02 & .77 \\ -.04 & .79 \end{bmatrix}$$

The differences between the elements of P and S are minor because the correlation between factors is not large. The elements would shift more with a higher correlation. If several factors are correlated, the interactions among the factors make the shifts between S and P difficult to predict.

From the S, R_{ff}, and P, appropriate conclusions can be drawn. For example, with an N of 147, the correlation between the factors is significantly greater than zero ($p < .05$). The anxiety variables are all equally good measures of that factor and the differences in correlations of the verbal comprehension tests with their factor could have arisen by chance (i.e., the correlations are not significantly different). All the variables are equally representative of their factors. The factors appear to be highly appropriate for the data.

5.2.2 Uncorrelated Multiple-Group Components

Uncorrelated multiple-group components are found by a successive extraction procedure like that used to extract uncorrelated diagonal factors. The first factor is identified by a set of defining variables. The factor loadings of all variables with that factor are then found. From the resulting factor pattern, the reproduced correlation matrix is calculated. This matrix is then subtracted from the original correlation matrix to form the first residual matrix. The factor extraction process is then repeated on the residual matrix and the second factor will be uncorrelated with the first.

The equation used to calculate the first factor's set of correlations/weights is Eq. (5.2.4). Note, however, that the weight matrix consists of only one column because only the first factor is being extracted. The residual matrix is then formed by Eq. (5.1.8).

The next factor is defined by another set of variables. The column of the factor pattern/factor structure for the second factor is calculated from the residual matrix by the same formula used to calculate the original loadings for the first multiple-group factor, but the formula is now applied to the residual matrix. More uncorrelated factors can be computed in the same manner from a succession of residual matrices.

Example

Uncorrelated multiple-group components can also be extracted from the personality variables. Two solutions are possible. The verbal comprehension factor could be extracted before the anxiety factor, or vice versa. These two results are as given in Table 5.2.1.

The difference between the two solutions lies in how the overlapping variance is distributed. In the first case, the overlapping variance is given to verbal comprehension, whereas the overlap is given to anxiety in the second case. With a higher correlation between factors, the differences would be more dramatic.

5.2.3 Multiple-Group Common Factors

When the common factor model is used in multiple-group analysis, estimates of the "proper" diagonal elements for the correlation matrix need to be made. What is appropriate for a diagonal element depends, of course, on how the multiple-group factors are to be defined. If all of the variances of the defining variables should be included except for random errors of measurement, then

TABLE 5.2.1
Uncorrelated Multiple-Group Factors

Variables	A. Verbal Factor Extracted First		B. Anxiety Factor Extracted First	
	Verbal Comprehension	Anxiety	Anxiety	Verbal Comprehension
1. Information	.84	−.01	−.15	.83
2. Verbal Ability	.87	.01	−.13	.86
3. Verbal Analogies	.77	.01	−.12	.77
4. Ego Strength	.11	−.79	−.80	−.02
5. Guilt Proneness	−.11	.76	.77	.02
6. Tension	−.17	.78	.80	−.04

reliabilities will probably be the choice. However, if only that part of the variance that a variable has in common with the rest of the set of defining variables is to be used to define the factor, then a more traditional communality estimate would need to be used. The communality estimation procedures for multiple-group common factors would be similar to those given in Chapter 6, where the communality problem is discussed more fully. In the present case, however, **only the defining variables for a given factor would be used in calculating the communality for a variable within that subset.** For example, if squared multiple correlations were going to be used as communality estimates, these would be calculated from the other variables within the subset defining the factor and not from the total variable pool. This means that only those variables used to define factors would have communality estimates (the communalities of the other variables would result from the analysis).

The calculation of factor pattern, structure, and correlation matrices is the same as given in the previous section except that the original correlation matrix is not used. Instead, it is replaced by the correlation matrix with communalities in the diagonals.

Example

The personality variables are mostly short forms or "quickie tests." Most of the scores are from only about a dozen items. They cannot be expected to have exceptional reliability and so the common factor model is appropriate. One theoretical perspective therefore suggests that reliability estimates could be used as communality estimates.

The uncorrelated solution with verbal comprehension as the first factor was recalculated for a common factor solution. The internal consistency reliability coefficients were used as the communalities. These were .92, .76, .55, .50, .53, and .42. Using the same formulas as were used for the uncorrelated component model but applying them to the correlation matrix with reliabilities in the diagonals gives Table 5.2.2.

The differences between the present solution and the first half of Table 5.2.1 arise from the component model assumption that each variable is perfectly reliable. Given the low reliabilities of some of the variables, these generally lower loadings are probably more appropriate estimates of the underlying relationships.

TABLE 5.2.2
Uncorrelated Multiple-Group Common Factors

Variables	Verbal Comprehension	Anxiety
1. Information	.87	.00
2. Verbal Ability	.82	.01
3. Verbal Analogies	.63	−.01
4. Ego Strength	.11	−.68
5. Guilt Proneness	−.11	.66
6. Tension	−.18	.63

5.3.   APPLICATIONS OF DIAGONAL AND MULTIPLE-GROUP FACTOR ANALYSIS

Diagonal and multiple-group analyses are both dependent upon the selection of variables for the definitions of the factors. Neither can be used intelligently without strong theoretical guidance. In Sections 5.3.1 through 5.3.4 four situations are presented in which the purpose of the factor analysis may give sufficient theoretical guidance for one of these procedures to be used.[2]

5.3.1 Hypothesis Testing

A situation in which multiple-group analysis is particularly appropriate is where a theory states that certain variables will load on the same factor and others on another factor (i.e., hypothesis testing). A multiple-group factor structure is computed that includes the hypothesized factors. The correlation of each of the variables that are supposed to load the factor with the factor would indicate how much they actually contributed to that factor's definition. The correlation of the other variables with that factor would reflect upon hypotheses concerning those variables, and could be tested for significance by the usual formulas for the significance of a correlation coefficient. The correlation between two factors can also be observed and tested for significance. If this correlation is significantly larger than the theory states it should be, the factors would not be considered sufficiently independent. Many investigators implicitly use this approach but actually calculate factor scores (they call them "test" or "variable" scores); their task would be eased by the formulas of this chapter. Others use path analysis, which is based on the same rationale.

The order in which the extraction takes place is crucial whenever uncorrelated factors are extracted. The basic question is that of which factor gets the overlapping variance. If factor A is extracted first, the overlapping variance will be given to A; if factor B is extracted first, then B will get the overlap. If uncorrelated factors are to be extracted, the theory must specify the order of extraction so that the hypotheses are given a fair test. If successive diagonal or multiple-group factors are extracted, the order of extraction will not affect the residuals after all of them have been extracted.

All factors need not be hypothesized. One or two multiple-group factors could be extracted in keeping with past studies or theory. The residuals would then be factored by procedures such as those of Chapters 6 and 7.

As long as the defining variables are identified before the data are collected, **tests of significance are available for the component model.** Multiple-group

---

[2]Diagonal or multiple-group factors could also be rotated by any of the procedures described later. To do so, however, would destroy their most useful properties.

factor analysis is therefore a useful procedure for testing hypotheses about factors. If oblique components are calculated, the correlation of each nondefining variable with each factor can be tested by the usual significance test of a correlation coefficient. If successive uncorrelated factors are extracted, the correlations of the variables with the first factor can be tested as ordinary correlation coefficients, but later factor structure elements will need to be tested as partial correlations (Nunnally, 1978). The correlations among the factors are also tested for significance by the usual formulas.

Example

Quereshi (1967) hypothesized that human abilities become more differentiated with age. His theoretical analysis led to the following proposition to be tested: a general ability factor (i.e., one which correlates with all measures of human ability) should account for less variance as age increases, whereas other ability factors should account for more of the variance as age increases. In addition, the factors should intercorrelate less with increasing age if the hypothesis is true.

The investigator reported defining his factors by identifying each with a particular variable and extracting correlated diagonal factors (actually, they were multiple-group factors because each of his defining variables was a sum of scores from several other variables in the analysis; for example, the general factor was defined by one variable formed by adding all nine tests of special abilities to the Stanford–Binet mental age). One analysis was conducted for each of seven age groups; the youngest group was $2\frac{1}{2}$ to 3 years of age and the oldest was $8\frac{1}{2}$ to 9 years of age.

His hypothesis was confirmed by statistical tests of significance. The general factor accounted for 41% of the variance for the youngest group but only 23% for the oldest group. The other factors generally contributed more with increased age, and their average intercorrelations decreased from .68 for the youngest group to .38 for the oldest. He therefore concluded that abilities do become more differentiated with age.

Quereshi's study illustrates hypothesis testing by the procedures advocated in this chapter. The illustration also shows that the factor pattern may not be the most relevant output from a factor analysis, but that relative size of the factors (i.e., the sum of the squared loadings on the factor) and the correlations among the factors may be of crucial theoretical importance.

5.3.2 A Factor-Analytic Parallel to Analysis of Covariance

Another situation where diagonal factor analysis appears useful is when it is used as a factor-analytic parallel to analysis of covariance and as an alternative to partial correlations (Brewer, Campbell, & Crano, 1970). The first factor extracted is passed through the variable measuring that which is to be held constant. The residuals can be examined and can be converted to partial correlations if this is deemed advantageous, or the residual matrix can be factored by any of the regular procedures discussed in this or succeeding chapters. Factors extracted from this residual matrix will all be uncorrelated with the variable held constant. This procedure has the advantage of controlling for one variable across many variables and factors simultaneously.

The procedure also has all the problems of any statistical control or matching procedure. One such problem is whether to use a component or a common factor model for the diagonal factor. If the defining variable's communality is assumed to be 1.0, then extracting that factor will not control for a sufficient amount of variance if the assumption is erroneous. Because the variable can seldom be expected to perfectly measure the construct, the actual underlying hypothetical variable may still produce some correlation between other variables in the matrix, a correlation that could be easily misinterpreted. If the common factor model is used, then the random error of measurement is taken into account and more variance is extracted from the matrix. The value of this procedure depends upon the accuracy with which the reliability is estimated. If the reliability coefficient is inaccurate or inappropriate, the results could be misleading. Those attempting to use diagonal factoring as an analysis of covariance analog should be well acquainted with critiques of analysis of covariance (Elashoff, 1969; Lord, 1960).

Multiple-group analysis could also be used to partial out a construct measured by several variables. The multivariate definition of the construct would be the basis of the weight matrix used to define the factor. The residuals after the covariate factor had been extracted would be treated in the same manner as if a diagonal covariate factor had been extracted.

5.3.3 Selection of a Reduced-Variable Set

Reducing the number of variables to a more reasonable subset is often a prime goal of a factor analysis. A reduced-variable set is sought that will contain as much of the information in the initial set of variables as possible. For example, if an area is being factored to identify basic constructs, a prime product is a small set of variables that can be used as operational representatives of the factorial constructs in future studies. Or if a set of criteria (dependent variables) is being factored to simplify the analyses, it may be best to identify each factor with one or two variables that would be useful in future studies and easily understood by the average reader of the report. Or perhaps a set of potential predictors (independent variables) is being factored so that another study can relate the reduced-variable set to the criterion (dependent variable). **The identification of only a few variables that can be used to represent the factors in other analyses or in future studies is one of the more important aspects of factor analysis, and is readily achieved through the use of diagonal and multiple-group factor analysis.**

Hunter (1972) has described a procedure that identifies the subset of variables that best reproduces the standardized data and correlation matrices. The procedure is as follows:

1. Add the sum of squared correlations for each column of the correlation matrix. The sum of squared correlations with the other variables indicates how much of the other variables can be predicted from a diagonal factor defined by the variable associated with the column.
2. Select the variable with the highest sum of squared correlations with the other variables. The selected variable defines the first diagonal factor and is the variable that best reproduces the other variables.
3. Compute the residual matrix after the diagonal factor of step 2 has been extracted. Sum the squared residual elements for each column and select the variable that has the highest relationship to the other variables (i.e., has the highest sum of squared covariances) after the first diagonal factor has been extracted.
4. Use the variable selected in step 3 to define the second diagonal factor.
5. Repeat steps 3 and 4 for as many factors as are deemed necessary (cf. Chapter 8).

The resulting factors will be those that best reproduce the original data matrix from a given number of variables.

In many cases the differences between the sum of squares for two columns will be trivial or probably insignificant. In that case, choosing the variable with the highest sum of squares will be about the same as choosing randomly from among the tied variables. In selecting a set of representative variables, random selection is appropriate for deciding among ties, and so the slight capitalization on chance that might occur will be irrelevant for most problems.

In special cases, the investigator may wish to choose among variables with essentially the same sums of squares on the basis of external information. The variable with the best-known validity might, for example, be chosen. Such a variable would have a more extensive background of proven usefulness in research. It would also be better known to the readers and would better communicate the nature of the dimension being measured.

Instead of choosing among variables with essentially the same sums of squares, two or more of the variables could be used to define a composite variable. A composite variable would be particularly desirable if the variables forming the composite all correlated well with each other. The variables would be essentially parallel forms. Adding parallel forms together increases the reliability with which a dimension is measured and therefore leads to increased correlations with the other variables in the analysis over the correlations which any one variable has.

Another principle could be used to decide ties if the validities were essentially the same, namely, cost. To be useful as a representative of the entire variable set, the selected variables should be usable. Usefulness generally decreases as the costs of collection and scoring the variable increase. A variable that is easily gathered, objectively scored, and does not inconvenience the individuals from whom the data are collected would be preferable to one not meeting these criteria.

The same variables would be selected under either a component or common factor model if the communality estimates did not differentially affect the sums of squares. The communality estimates will lower all sums by a constant if they are the same but not 1.0, but this effect will not alter the variable selection. If the communality estimates differ greatly, the variable that has a higher estimate would tend to be chosen over those with lower estimates. Because the number of communalities relative to the total number of elements in the matrix decreases as the number of variables increases, differences in communality estimates will be most influential on the selection of variables when the total number of variables is small.

A correlated model is generally used because the concern is with using the original variables in another study where, when collected, they could be correlated. However, selecting variables on the basis of the sums of squares of the residuals leads to defining the factors by variables with low intercorrelations.

5.3.4 Item Analyses

Multiple-group factor analysis is an appropriate procedure for item analysis when there are several subscales in a total scale (or several tests in a battery). Items defining a particular subscale (or particular test of the battery) are given weights of one and items defining other subscales (or tests) given weights of zero to define the factor for that subscale (or test). The same is done for each of the other subscales (or tests). The correlated multiple-group solution is computed from this weight matrix.

The multiple-group factor structure contains the correlation of each variable with all subscales as represented by the factors. Items that correlate higher with another subscale than that for which they are a defining variable can be identified as well as items that fail to correlate with the factor they are supposed to measure. Further, the correlations among factors—and thus among the subscales—are computed as well. Thus one has comprehensive information on the items as a function of the multivariate context, a result not given directly through ordinary item analysis. (Although the structure coefficients are uncorrected for the part—whole effect, that correction can be built into a program following Henrysson, 1962.)

A major difference between multiple-group and ordinary item analysis—in addition to the multivariate nature of the former—is that zero/one standard score weights define the multiple group solution. *This system weights each defining item's standard score item equally, whereas item analysis weights each raw score equally.* Multiple-group factoring gives the raw-score based item analysis exactly when the reciprocal of the standard deviation for each item is substituted for the weight of one and weights of zero are kept as weights of zero. Each item–factor correlation is then the correlation of each item with the total subscale score calculated by adding together the raw scores for those items.

6 Principal Factor Solutions

In Sections 3.4.1 and 3.5.1 it was shown that a correlation matrix could be decomposed to find factor matrices.[1] The most widely used mathematical method for such decomposition is principal factor analysis. Several characteristics make the principal factor solution desirable as an initial set of factors (Section 6.1, Characteristics of Principal Factor Methods). Although this solution could be rotated to from another solution (Thurstone, 1947), the principal factor procedure is generally used to extract factors from a correlation matrix. The principal factors are usually rotated (cf. Chapters 9 and 10).

The basic principal factor procedure can be applied in different situations to slightly different correlation matrices. If it is applied to the correlation matrix with unities in the diagonal, then principal components (Section 6.2) result. If it is applied to the correlation matrix where the diagonals have been adjusted to communality estimates, common factors result (cf. Section 6.3, Communality Estimation and Principal Axes).

Several variants of the common factor model utilize the principal factor procedures in their calculations. These procedures include image analysis (Section *6.4) as well as other related techniques (Section *6.5). In each case the principal factor procedure is applied but to an altered correlation matrix; they therefore depart from the traditional form of common factor analysis. For this reason, their originators have tended to distinguish between image and other analyses and factor analysis as traditionally conceived. In their terminology, *factor analysis* is reserved for the traditional variant that we have been calling the common factor

---

[1]It is assumed that the correlation coefficient is an appropriate index of association; other possible indices are discussed in Chapter 14.

model. However, common usage subsumes the component and all common factor models under the general phrase *factor analysis*. This would seem appropriate because the purposes and resulting solutions are much the same although some differences do exist. Names such as *image analysis* and *alpha analysis* will be used to distinguish variants of the common factor approach. *Principal axes* will refer to principal factors in the usual common factor tradition. Departing more radically from principal factor solutions are nonlinear and nonmetric factor analysis considered in Section *6.6. Applications of principal factors are noted in Section 6.7 and exploratory solutions are compared in Section 6.8.

The principal factor procedure has become widely used in the past decade. Earlier usage was infrequent because it required a month of desk calculator computations to extract principal factors from a moderately large matrix. Because of the difficulties of doing such factor analyses by hand, it is apparent that all of them will be done by high-speed computer in the future. Therefore, in this chapter we will discuss neither hand nor desk calculator procedures for extracting principal factors. Instead, it will be assumed that appropriate computer programs are available.

All the procedures presented in this chapter are *exploratory* factor solutions. It is assumed that there is no theoretical knowledge that is relevant to guiding the factor extraction or to serve as hypotheses to be tested. Without such information the procedures for extraction are solely based upon mathematical criteria. (Chapters 5 and 7 include alternative approaches that allow for hypotheses to be tested.)

6.1 CHARACTERISTICS OF PRINCIPAL FACTOR METHODS

The principal factor method extracts the maximum amount of variance that can be possibly extracted by a given number of factors (Section 6.1.1). It is a characteristic roots-and-vectors analysis of the correlations (Section 6.1.2), and involves extensive calculations. The principal factor method is a general one that can be used with either the component or common factor model.

6.1.1 The Maximization of Variance Extracted

The prime characteristic of the principal factor extraction procedure is that **each factor accounts for the maximum possible amount of the variance of the variables being factored.** The first factor from the correlation matrix consists of that weighted combination of all the variables that will produce the highest squared correlations between the variables and the factor because the squared correlation is a measure of the variance accounted for. One result is that the sum of the squares of the first column of the factor structure will be maximized.

The second factor is extracted so that it is uncorrelated with the first factor. This factor maximizes the amount of variance extracted from the residual matrix after the first factor has been removed. Each succeeding factor is extracted in like manner, and so a given number of factors accounts for as much of the variance as that number possibly could.

When principal factors are extracted, the solution has an additional property of interest. The resulting reproduced correlation matrix is the best least-squares estimate of the entire correlation matrix including diagonal elements (i.e., the sum of the squared differences between the original and the reproduced correlations is minimized). The diagonal elements may, of course, be communality estimates rather than unities.

There is no correlated version of the principal factor procedure, because if each of the correlated factors was to account for the maximum amount of variance, they would all be the same factor and correlate 1.0 with each other. However, limiting principal factors to uncorrelated factor models is not problematic because those interested in correlated factors invariably rotate the principal factors to what are considered more desirable positions (cf. Chapter 9).

Example

Two diagonal factors were extracted from the physique factors in the last chapter and were presented in Table 5.1.2. Principal factors were also extracted. In fact, the analysis of physique characteristics was one of the earliest problems for which Pearson recommended a principal factor solution (MacDonell, 1902). The principal factors are in Table 6.1.1. They are seldom interpreted but, instead, are the basis of further analysis.

The percentage of variance extracted by the first two factors extracted by each procedure is given in Table 6.1.2. These percentages were calculated by finding the sums of

TABLE 6.1.1
Principal Factors for Twelve Physique Variables

| | Factors | | | |
Variables	A	B	C	D
1. Stature	.63	.60	−.10	.12
2. Symphysis height	.55	.75	−.01	.11
3. Breadth of skull	.30	−.03	.51	.70
4. Length of skull	.43	.42	.19	−.47
5. Biacromial diameter	.66	.17	.46	−.16
6. Transverse chest diameter	.62	−.28	.48	−.14
7. Sagittal chest diameter	.73	−.15	−.37	−.23
8. Bicristal diameter	.62	−.21	−.27	.20
9. Length of sternum	.60	.24	−.40	.26
10. Chest circumference (at expiration)	.78	−.42	.08	−.14
11. Hip circumference	.79	−.42	−.18	.21
12. Weight	.85	−.20	−.01	−.15

TABLE 6.1.2
Variance Extracted by Different
Component Procedures

| | *Physique Data* | |
	Diagonal Factors[†]	*Principal Factors*
A	26%	42%
B	21%	14%
Total	47%	56%

[†]From solution given in Table 5.1.2.

squared loadings on a given factor and dividing by the sum of the diagonal elements in the matrix. In this case, that sum was the number of variables, or 12, because the correlation matrix had 1.0 for each diagonal element.

Table 6.1.2 shows that the first principal factor is definitely larger than the first diagonal factor. This is the same with the total extracted variance after the second factor. If the maximum amount of information is to be extracted by two factors, the principal factors are to be preferred.

Some of the reasons for the popularity of the principal factor extraction procedure are now apparent. With it, the most variance can be accounted for with the fewest factors. The correlation matrix can be reproduced with the greatest accuracy for a given number of factors. Because factor analysis is generally undertaken in order to reduce the number of variables while still maximizing the amount of information retained, the principal factor approach is a good solution.

However, *all* variables are needed to compute any principal component score, whereas only two variables, for example, are needed to obtain the scores for two diagonal factors. If the purpose is to identify preexisting variables to use as representatives of the variable pool in another study, a diagonal factor solution might be more appropriate, particularly an analysis like that described in Section 5.3.3. It will account for the maximum amount of variance possible with preexisting variables.

6.1.2 Principal Factors as Characteristic Roots and Vectors

The principal factor solution is one application of what is known in general mathematics as the solution of **characteristic roots and vectors** (other names are **latent roots** and **vectors,** or **eigenvalues** and **eigenvectors**). The general problem considered by mathematics is that of finding a vector, A, and a scalar, s, such that the following condition is fulfilled:

$$R_{vv}A_{v1} = A_{v1}s. \tag{6.1.1}$$

A and s are, respectively, a characteristic vector and characteristic root of R. When the problem is concerned with finding the complete set of vectors and roots for the correlation matrix in the component model, the equation becomes:

$$R_{vv}A_{vv} = A_{vv}S_{vv} \tag{6.1.2}$$

where S is now a diagonal matrix with the characteristic roots in the diagonal and A contains the vectors. R generally has as many roots and vectors as there are variables (cf. Sections 8.3.1 and 8.3.2).

The characteristic vectors have the following helpful property:

$$AA' = I. \tag{6.1.3}$$

Therefore, Eq. (6.1.2) can be multiplied on the right by A'_{vv} *to give:*

$$R_{vv} = A_{vv}S_{vv}A'_{vv}. \tag{6.1.4}$$

If the square root of each characteristic root is taken and these are used to form two diagonal matrices, we can define the following:

$$S_{vv} = S_{vv}^{.5}S_{vv}^{.5}. \tag{6.1.5}$$

Substituting from (6.1.5) into (6.1.4) gives:

$$R_{vv} = A_{vv}S_{vv}^{.5}S_{vv}^{.5}A'_{vv}. \tag{6.1.6}$$

By letting $P = AS^{.5}$, then

$$R_{vv} = P_{vv}P'_{vv} = (A_{vv}S_{vv}^{.5})(S_{vv}^{.5}A'_{vv}) \tag{6.1.7}$$

where P has as many factors as variables. This means that **principal factors are rescaled characteristic vectors.** Harris (1964) has shown that principal components, principal axes (and therefore minimum residual analysis), and image analysis produce the same vectors but different roots. Therefore, these solutions will show the same pattern of high and low loadings of variables.

The characteristic roots have several interesting characteristics of their own. First, the characteristic root is equal to the sum of the squared loadings on the principal factor. It is, therefore, a direct index of how much variance is accounted for by each factor. Second, the **trace** is equal to the sum of the characteristic roots, which is equal to the sum of the communality estimates used in the diagonal of the correlation matrix:

$$\text{Trace} = \Sigma h_j^2 = \Sigma s_j \tag{6.1.8}$$

If the correlation matrix has unities in the diagonal, it is equal to the number of variables.

Third, the characteristic roots are all positive and nonzero only if there are as many factors as variables and the determinant of the correlation matrix is nonzero. In component analysis, this is almost always the case. Where the diagonal elements are less than unity, there will be fewer factors than variables, but Eq.

(6.1.8) still holds true so that the sum of the characteristic roots equals the trace of the matrix. The characteristic roots are of importance in determining the number of factors to extract from the correlation matrix in Chapter 8.

The results from the same principal factor analysis performed with different programs at different computer centers may vary, particularly in the latter factors. In a 50 to 60 variable problem, it is not unusual to have no relationship between the pattern of the tenth factor from one program and that of the tenth factor from another program. The difference may arise from calculation and computer error, from extracting almost equal-sized factors in different sequences, or from the iteration sequence giving only an estimate to the actual solution. However, it will usually be found that the programs give factors that account for the identical amount of variance and that the rotated results are quite similar.

6.2   PRINCIPAL COMPONENTS

Principal component analysis is the extraction of principal factors under the component model. The principal factor method is applied to the correlation matrix with unities as diagonal elements. The factors then give the best least-squares fit to the entire correlation matrix, and each succeeding factor accounts for the maximum amount of the total correlation matrix obtainable. Because the main diagonal is unaltered, the procedure attempts to account for all the variance of each variable and it is thus assumed that all the variance is relevant, and component factors result.

Using the full component model means that as many factors as variables are generally needed. However, the full component model is seldom used because so many of the smaller factors are trivial and do not replicate. The smaller factors are generally dropped, and a **truncated component** solution results. The inaccuracies in reproducing the correlations and variable scores are attributed to errors in the model in that sample.

A correction has been suggested (Kazelskis, 1978) for the unreliability of variables in a component analysis. The result is to reduce loadings for variables with poorer reliabilities when those loadings are on smaller factors (e.g., those with a sum of squared loadings less than 3.00).

Example

Principal components can be extracted from the 24 ability variables. The correlation matrix for these variables is given in Table 6.2.1. The characteristic roots of that matrix are: 8.16, 2.06, 1.70, 1.48, 1.01, .92, .89, .83, .78, .73, .64, .54, .54, .51, .47, .42, .39, .36, .33, .32, .31, .25, .20, and .17. The first four principal components are given in Table 6.2.2. The roots and components were calculated by a computer program by applying the principal factor method to a correlation matrix with unities as the diagonal elements.

TABLE 6.2.1 (Part 1)
Correlations Among 24 Ability Variables

	1	2	5	6	7	8	9	10	11	12	13	14
1	10000											
2	3258	10000										
5	3277	2751	10000									
6	3416	2280	6217	10000								
7	3091	1595	6539	7186	10000							
8	3261	1560	5739	5205	6327	10000						
9	3171	1947	7203	7145	6853	5367	10000					
10	1042	0664	3142	2089	2539	2966	1787	10000				
11	3060	1509	3425	3596	2480	2936	2871	4676	10000			
12	3082	1675	2100	1042	1981	2905	1220	5864	4225	10000		
13	4868	2479	3434	3144	3556	4051	2718	4183	5271	5284	10000	
14	1297	0819	2614	2863	2332	2427	2499	1570	3239	1310	1935	10000
15	2228	1349	2191	2490	1573	1698	2133	1500	2384	1648	1381	3870
16	4194	2892	1768	2882	2007	2987	2360	1370	3144	1284	2771	3817
17	1690	0110	2127	2758	2506	2707	2851	3013	3571	2790	1906	3721
18	3641	2639	2593	1672	1756	2576	2126	3198	3463	3478	3254	1987
19	2672	1104	1957	2510	2414	2613	2755	1989	2897	1089	2523	2187
20	3601	2944	4000	4332	4585	4303	4515	1619	2035	2526	2476	3090
21	3706	2937	3192	2632	3144	3608	2720	4018	3964	3572	4309	1823
22	4137	2344	4446	3893	4005	3632	4917	1549	3170	2026	2901	2494
23	4687	3411	4340	4324	4080	4941	4958	2553	2510	3538	3836	2508
24	2734	2059	4156	4329	4400	3886	4177	5294	4112	4146	3570	2945
25	3990	3128	2489	2684	2272	3727	1766	-0750	0853	1436	3162	1771
26	4651	2272	2336	3304	3408	3850	3166	0908	1101	1687	3378	0621

Note: Decimals omitted. Normally only two decimal places would be reported; four places are given here to enable the reader to reproduce other analyses based upon this matrix. Variables 3 and 4 were not included since they were parallel forms of variables 25 and 26.

TABLE 6.2.1 (Part 2)
Correlations Among 24 Ability Variables

	15	16	17	18	19	20	21	22	23	24	25	26
15	10000											
16	3133	10000										
17	3464	3395	10000									
18	3181	3549	4524	10000								
19	1833	2538	3274	3578	10000							
20	2631	3939	2785	3048	1702	10000						
21	2322	3541	1889	3570	3313	4066	10000					
22	2455	2912	2958	3178	3468	4770	3740	10000				
23	2524	3548	3000	2671	2982	5152	4473	5079	10000			
24	1609	2702	3429	4050	3737	3691	4481	3778	4311	10000		
25	0669	2619	1761	2106	3118	3073	1645	2555	3865	2026	10000	
26	1261	3389	1934	2528	1346	3458	3519	3790	3365	2533	2989	10000

Note: Decimals omitted.

TABLE 6.2.2
Truncated Principal Components of the
24 Ability Variables

Variables	Factors			
	A	B	C	D
1. Visual Perception	.61	−.02	.43	−.21
2. Cubes	.40	−.06	.41	−.22
5. General Information	.69	−.33	−.33	−.06
6. Paragraph Comprehension	.69	−.41	−.26	.08
7. Sentence Completion	.69	−.41	−.35	−.06
8. Word Classification	.69	−.24	−.16	−.12
9. Word Meaning	.69	−.45	−.30	.07
10. Add	.47	.54	−.45	−.19
11. Code	.57	.42	−.21	.02
12. Counting Groups of Dots	.49	.54	−.12	−.35
13. Straight and Curved Capitals	.62	.28	.03	−.38
14. Word Recognition	.44	.10	−.03	.57
15. Number Recognition	.40	.16	.10	.52
16. Figure Recognition	.54	.10	.40	.29
17. Object-Number	.50	.27	−.06	.48
18. Number-Figure	.55	.38	.19	.14
19. Figure-Word	.48	.13	.10	.21
20. Deduction	.65	−.19	.14	.08
21. Numerical Puzzles	.62	.24	.10	−.19
22. Problem Reasoning	.65	−.15	.11	.07
23. Series Completion	.71	−.11	.15	−.09
24. Woody-McCall Mixed Fundamentals, Form I	.67	.20	−.23	−.05
25. Paper Form Board	.44	−.20	.47	−.10
26. Flags	.51	−.18	.33	−.21

If this solution were of direct interest, the first factor would then represent general ability. Each and every variable loads positively on it, and all the loadings can probably be considered significant. Some of the variables correlate higher with the first component than they would be expected to correlate with another parallel form. For example, variable 6's reliability coefficient is .65 (Holzinger & Swineford, 1939), and its first loading is .69.

The later factors consist of subsets of the variables. Factor 2 might be interpreted as distinguishing between clerical and verbal ability, 3 as involving perceptual ability, and 4 as most related to word and number recognition. Later factors are more difficult to interpret than the first because the interpreter must mentally remove the variance attributable to the first factor from each variable's meaning.

Tables 6.1.1 and 6.2.2 are based on correlation matrices with few negative signs and moderate to high correlations. In other correlation matrices, all variables need not load the first factor. If, however, a position exists where all variables load highly on the first factor, the first principal component will be there.

6.3   COMMUNALITY ESTIMATION AND PRINCIPAL AXES

The common factor model differs from the component model in that the principal factors of Eq. (6.1.7) reproduce the correlation matrix, R, only when U of Eq. (3.5.7) is added to PP'. Subtracting U from R gives a matrix to which the principal factor method can be directly applied to obtain principal common factors. Because U is a diagonal matrix, subtracting it from R only alters the diagonal elements. These altered diagonal elements are the communalities.

A popular procedure for extracting the common factors from a correlation matrix over the past decade has been that of extracting the principal factors from a matrix with communality estimates in the diagonal, a procedure that identifies it as a common factor approach. Once the diagonal elements are replaced with communality estimates, the extraction procedure is identical to that of principal components and the same program can almost always be used. The results are then called **principal axes.** The problem, of course, is to estimate the unknown communalities. This section is primarily concerned with communality estimation. **The information on communality estimation is not, however, limited to principal axis analyses, but applies to all factoring procedures with estimated communalities.**

In Section *6.3.1, some bounds or limits within which the communality should logically fall are given. Section 6.3.2 contains several of the more useful methods for estimating communalities when solving for only the common factors. Included in the final section, *6.3.3, is a discussion of the amount of variance attributable to specific factors as estimated after the common factors have been extracted.

*6.3.1 Upper and Lower Bounds for Communalities

The extreme limits that the communalities could take are, on the one hand, 0.0 if the variable has no correlation with any other variable in the matrix and, on the other hand, 1.0 if the variance is perfectly accounted for by the set of factors underlying the matrix. Negative communalities have no meaning and do not occur except as rounding errors from a communality of zero. Some procedures for estimating communalities do, however, result in diagonal elements greater than 1.0. Such results are referred to as **Haywood cases.** The usual procedure is to arbitrarily set any estimated communalities greater than 1 equal to .99 or 1.0 but it would be better to limit any communality estimate to the reliability coefficient.

A more accurate lower bound than 0.0 for the communality of a particular variable is its squared multiple correlation with all the other variables in the population (Roff, 1935). The squared multiple correlation gives the percentage of variance that the variable has in common with all the other variables in the matrix. That the squared multiple correlation is the lower bound follows from the fact that all of the correlations in the matrix are reduced to zero when all factors are extracted, so all the variance of the variable that overlaps with any other variable is included in one of the factors. The variable's total overlap with the other variables is, of course, the squared multiple correlation. However, the squared multiple correlation should not be considered *the* communality. The population R^2 gives only the overlap with the other variables, and not the overlap the variable might have with the factors in addition to that indicated from the overlap with the other variables.

Mulaik (1966) has argued that the reliability of a variable is both the upper and lower bound for the communality of that variable when the universe of variables is considered. For our purposes, it is sufficient to note that the reliability of the variable is a more accurate upper bound than unities for the communality of that variable. The unreliable portion of the variance is, by definition, random error and therefore could not be related to any factor whether common or specific. The reliability used as an estimate of the upper bound for the communality should be an appropriate one (cf. Section *6.3.3.; Nunnally, 1978).

6.3.2 Estimation of Common Factor Variance

The communality of a variable is defined as that part of its variance that overlaps with the factors being extracted. By placing the proper communality estimate in the diagonal of a correlation matrix, the diagonal elements give meaningful information about the extent to which the variables can be attributed to the common factors. No mathematical solution exists to solve for communalities, and so all estimates are just that: estimates. The initial estimates differ from the communalities computed from the factors since the former are seldom completely consistent with the correlations.

The communality for a variable interacts with the number of factors extracted. The effect depends upon whether or not an individual variable is related to the new factor extracted. If it is, the communality for the variable increases; otherwise it remains the same. Hence, communality estimates will change depending upon the number of factors that are being extracted from the matrix as common factors. Most estimation procedures are dependent upon the knowledge of the number of factors to be extracted. We shall generally assume that the number of factors is already set. (Chapter 8 is devoted to procedures for determining the number of factors.) Some communality estimation procedures are independent of the number of factors extracted; it is assumed that one is extracting as much of the common variance among the variables as possible.

When estimates of communalities are used in the diagonal of the correlation matrix, the correlation matrix may not maintain those mathematical characteristics that it is assumed to have when the principal factor extraction procedure is used. This does not prevent the principal factor extraction procedure from operating upon the matrix and usually has little impact on the interpretations. If it is desired to restore the properties of the matrix, Irwin (1966) gives a procedure for doing so.

It should be noted that the observed communalities resulting from a factor analysis will differ slightly from the communality estimates used in the diagonal. If the highest correlation in the column, the squared multiple correlation, or unity is used as an initial communality estimate, the actual communality is that resulting from the factor analysis and is thus one iteration away from the initial estimate.

The number of methods for estimating the communalities is legion. Only four methods will be given here. They are among the more popular ones and vary from simple approaches to procedures that, although being more time consuming to compute, are probably more accurate.

Unities as Initial Estimates: Truncated Components.   Unities can be used for initial communality estimates with several principal factors extracted. The result has been previously discussed as a truncated component solution, because unities are appropriate estimates only if the component model is used. However, the actual communalities resulting from a truncated component solution are unities only in rare cases. Instead, the resulting communalities often diverge considerably from unity. Truncated components can therefore be considered a "backdoor" common factor analysis where the initial communality estimate is 1.0 but the actual communality is the result of the extraction procedure. The computed communalities may then be used with reliability coefficients to determine specific factor contributions just as any other common factor communality. **However, the procedure is often inaccurate and may produce communalities considerably higher than the reliability estimates.** If the use of a common factor model is deemed critical, this procedure should not be used.

Largest Correlation.   A simple procedure for estimating the communalities is to select the largest correlation without regard to sign that each variable has with any other variable in the matrix. The absolute value of the largest coefficient is entered as the variable's diagonal element or communality estimate. This procedure's rationale seems to be as follows: The square of the largest correlation in the column is a lower bound for the amount of variance attributable to a factor defined by those two variables. Taking the correlation coefficient itself gives a result that is well above that minimum and yet is also seldom close to 1.0. Thus, it is probably close to the actual communality.

Experience indicates that the highest correlation is generally high when the communality is actually high and generally low when the communality is actually low. However, this procedure underestimates a communality when the highest correlation of one variable with other variables is high and overestimates it when the highest correlation is a low one.

Example

The 24 ability variables factored by the truncated principal component procedure were also factored by the principal axes approach. The highest correlation of each variable with any other variable was used as the communality estimate. The resulting factors are given in Table 6.3.1.

When the principal axis factor loadings are compared with those in Table 6.2.2, the first factor appears relatively unchanged. Some of the loadings are even identical. But in the third and fourth factors the differences are large enough to possibly affect interpretations. Table 6.3.2 gives the initial communality estimates and the resulting communalities for both the truncated principal component and principal factor solutions. It can be seen that the principal component communalities that actually result from the analysis are much less than one, suggesting that the component model may not be adequate for this data. The differences between the initial principal axis communality estimates and the actual or resulting communalities are often small; they would be closer if more factors had been extracted. This suggests that the common factor model is appropriate for these data.

TABLE 6.3.1
Principal Axes of 24 Ability Variables
(Highest Correlations Used as Communality
Estimates)

	Factors			
	A	B	C	D
1. Visual Perception	.59	.04	.36	−.20
2. Cubes	.38	−.01	.29	−.17
5. General Information	.69	−.33	−.27	−.05
6. Paragraph Comprehension	.69	−.41	−.19	.07
7. Sentence Completion	.69	−.41	−.27	−.07
8. Word Classification	.68	−.21	−.10	−.12
9. Word Meaning	.69	−.45	−.21	.07
10. Add	.46	.46	−.45	−.11
11. Code	.56	.35	−.20	.06
12. Counting Groups of Dots	.48	.49	−.17	−.27
13. Straight and Curved Capitals	.60	.27	−.01	−.31
14. Word Recognition	.42	.07	.00	.43
15. Number Recognition	.38	.12	.09	.39
16. Figure Recognition	.51	.11	.33	.21
17. Object-Number	.48	.21	−.03	.41
18. Number-Figure	.52	.33	.14	.14
19. Figure-Word	.45	.11	.09	.17
20. Deduction	.63	−.14	.17	.05
21. Numerical Puzzles	.59	.22	.06	−.13
22. Problem Reasoning	.63	−.10	.14	.06
23. Series Completion	.69	−.06	.15	−.08
24. Woody-McCall Mixed Fundamentals, Form I	.65	.17	−.20	.00
25. Paper Form Board	.42	−.11	.38	−.11
26. Flags	.49	−.10	.30	−.20

TABLE 6.3.2
Communality Estimates after Four Factors

	Truncated Principal Components		Principal Axes	
	Estimate	Resulting	Highest Correlation	Resulting
1	1.00	.60	.49	.51
2	1.00	.38	.34	.26
5	1.00	.70	.72	.66
6	1.00	.72	.72	.68
7	1.00	.77	.72	.72
8	1.00	.58	.63	.54
9	1.00	.78	.72	.73
10	1.00	.76	.59	.64
11	1.00	.55	.53	.48
12	1.00	.67	.59	.58
13	1.00	.61	.53	.53
14	1.00	.53	.39	.37
15	1.00	.47	.39	.32
16	1.00	.54	.42	.43
17	1.00	.56	.45	.44
18	1.00	.50	.45	.42
19	1.00	.30	.37	.25
20	1.00	.48	.52	.44
21	1.00	.49	.45	.42
22	1.00	.46	.51	.43
23	1.00	.54	.52	.50
24	1.00	.55	.53	.49
25	1.00	.46	.40	.35
26	1.00	.45	.46	.38

Squared Multiple Correlations.   Because squared multiple correlations are a lower bound for the communality in the population, they are often used for conservative communality estimates. With modern computers, the squared multiple correlation of any given variable with the other variables can be computed rather simply. When the inverse of the correlation matrix (with unities in the diagonal) has been calculated, the squared multiple correlation is:

$$R_v^2 = 1 - \frac{1}{r^{vv}} \tag{6.3.1}$$

where r^{vv} is the diagonal element from the inverse of the correlation matrix, and R_v^2 is the squared multiple correlation for variable v. As previously noted, the multiple correlation is the population lower bound for the communality. However, the relationship of R^2 to the communality in any given sample will vary as a function of the number of variables and the sample size. As the number of variables increases, the probability of the variable having overlap with a common factor over and above its overlap with other variables in that matrix is decreased and R^2 comes closer to the communality itself. The R^2 given in Eq. (6.3.1) is, however, a biased estimate of a population multiple correlation. It is spuriously high due to capitalization upon chance, and this effect increases as the number of variables increases and the sample size decreases. Because R^2 is used in its biased form as an estimate of the communality, it is higher than the best estimate of the lower bound and therefore closer to the population communality itself.

Iteration.   When the number of common factors can be assumed, another procedure is that of iterating for communalities. Simple communality estimates are first entered into the diagonal of the correlation matrix and the appropriate number of principal factors extracted. The observed communality is then calculated from the resulting factor solution by summing the squared loadings for each variable. The observed communality will be somewhat different from the original estimates, and are generally closer to the "true" communalities. The observed communalities calculated from the principal factor solution are then inserted into the diagonal of the correlation matrix and a second set of principal factors extracted. A new set of observed communalities is then calculated from the second factor analysis and these communalities become new estimates to be entered into the diagonal of the correlation matrix.

The iteration process of placing estimates into the diagonal and then finding new estimates on the basis of a complete factor analysis is continued until the maximum change between communalities from one estimate to the next is below some arbitrary level. The degree of accuracy of the iterated communalities is approximately related to this criterion.

Although the communalities do appear to converge towards appropriate values, **no proof has yet been presented to show that they either must converge or that the value to which they converge is either the theoretical communality or less than the variable's reliability.** Wrigley, Hemmerly, and McDonald (McDonald, 1970) report that they have always found convergence. I have seen an occasional instance where the iterations wobbled back and forth from one estimate to another with no improvement. On one wiggle of the wobble, one variable would be higher than another, whereas on the next wiggle the other variable would be higher. These appeared to be alternative solutions where the data were inadequate to specify which should be chosen. For this reason, and because the iteration sequence can consume a fair amount of time even on modern computers, it is common to limit the number of possible iterations.

From the limited amount of empirical work that has been done (Browne, 1968b; Hamburger, 1965; Jenkins, 1962; Wrigley, 1958), it appears that lower estimates converge more quickly than higher ones and that unities may converge to values considerably higher than those found from other estimates. The research also suggests that beginning with the highest correlation in the diagonal and iterating twice produces good estimates with relatively little cost. Squared multiple correlations with a few iterations also produce good estimates. If good reliability estimates are available, the communality estimates should be no greater than the reliabilities for the same variables. Extensive iteration does not seem necessary.[2]

Importance of the Communality Estimate.   The effect of error in the estimation of the communalities varies as a function of at least two other parameters. First, as the number of variables in the correlation matrix increases, the number of off-diagonal elements increases relative to the number of communality estimates in the diagonal elements. For example, the diagonal elements of a nine-variable correlation matrix form 10% of the entire matrix, whereas the diagonal elements of a twenty-variable matrix are 5% of the total number of elements. After 30 or 40 variables are reached, the effects of using reasonable but different communality estimates in the diagonal of the correlation matrix are minimal. This is probably why Howard and Cartwright (1962) concluded their empirical evaluation of several procedures for estimating communalities by noting that they all give quite similar results; they had 47 variables.

The other major influence on the effect of error in estimating communalities would be the magnitude of the actual communalities. For example, if the communalities range from .8 to 1.0, estimation procedures will give similar estimates and similar results. But if the communalities are low (e.g., .4), then the estimates may range more widely and so influence the results. **If communalities are reasonably high (e.g., .7 and up), even unities are probably adequate communality estimates in a problem with more than 35 variables.**

Communality estimation can be quite crucial in the case of a small problem. With less than 10 or 20 variables, the interpretations of the factors will often shift if the estimates are distinctively different. Cureton (1971) offers suggestions for communality estimation in small problems. But a very small matrix may not need to be factored because it can be so easily scanned.

Example

The differences in truncated principal component and principal axis (R^2 with two iterations) loadings will occasionally be quite dramatic because of their different assumptions about communalities. Table 6.3.3 gives both solutions for a set of four variables. If the sample size was not large, the principal axes would probably not be interpreted. But who could resist interpreting a factor with loadings of .6 and .7? The three highest correlations upon which that principal factor was based were −.17, .11 and −.07. The correlation matrix was insignificant by Bartlett's significance test (which is given in Chapter 8). With such a small matrix, the correlations should always be presented to prevent errors such as could occur here if only the components were presented.

---

[2]If it is extremely important to have good estimates of communalities, the iterative procedure suggested by Irwin (1966) should be considered.

TABLE 6.3.3
First Principal Component and
Principal Axis Loadings for a
Small Matrix

Variable	Principal Component	Principal Axis
1	−.56	−.29
2	.52	.24
3	.74	.41
4	−.33	−.13

Some writers (Nunnally, 1978) lean heavily toward a component model because they feel the communality estimation approach is inherently illogical because common variance is difficult to define. From this perspective, reliabilities would be the population communalities in the universe of variables (if "universe of variables" can be defined), and so might be used as communality estimates. However, such writers usually minimize the communality problem by extracting components from correlations among 30 or so variables.

*6.3.3 Estimation of Specific Factor Variance

The traditional common factor model divides the variance of a variable into three sections according to the theoretical nature of the source of that variance:

1. Common factor variance that is contributed by those factors loading two or more variables in the analysis.
2. Specific factors that contribute variance only to one particular variable. (Although the specific factor for a given variable could be theoretically divided into a number of different sources of influence, they are summarized as one factor.)
3. Error variance that is random and therefore can be assumed to belong to neither the common factor nor specific factor domains.

When the variance of each variable is to be divided among common factors, specifics, and error, communality estimates are used and common factors extracted. After the factors are extracted, the proportion of variance attributable to common factors is calculated and subtracted from the reliability coefficient of the variable. This is because the reliability coefficient is, by definition, an estimate of the proportion of the variable's nonerror variance (see Nunnally (1978) for a discussion of reliabilities). Subtracting the proportion of variance attributable to the common factors from the total nonerror variance gives the variance attributable to the specific factor, which can be converted to a specific factor loading by taking its square root. That is:

$$p_{vs}^2 = r_{vv} - h_v^2 \qquad (6.3.2)$$

where p_{vs} is variable v's loading on specific factor s, r_{vv} is that variable's reliability, and h_v^2 is the variable's communality.

In using reliabilities to estimate specific factor loadings, the results will vary depending upon which reliability estimate is used. Test–retest reliabilities seldom equal those calculated from parallel forms or from the internal consistency of individual responses. Each reliability coefficient commonly calculated could be appropriate depending upon the kind of variance that is assumed to be meaningful for the set of variables and the error variance in that analysis. The major kinds of reliability coefficients are as follows:

1. When the stability, or test–retest, coefficient is used, error is defined as nongeneralizability over the period of time between the initial measurement and a second measurement using the same procedure.
2. In the homogeneity, or internal consistency, approach to reliability, error is defined as nongeneralizability across various ways of measuring the concept within the same limited block of time.
3. In parallel form reliability, error may be defined in several different ways. If the parallel forms are both collected within a very limited time span, this reliability can be considered another approach to internal consistency reliability. If, however, the parallel forms are separated in time, then this reliability is defining error as both nongeneralizability over time and nongeneralizability from one way of measuring the variable to another similar way of measuring it.

The proper reliability to use is a function of the kinds of errors that affect the intercorrelations among the variables. In the usual factor-analytic study, the variables are collected on each individual over a very limited period of time. Therefore, they are not attenuated by shifts over time but the coefficients are attenuated in that each measurement can generally only sample its content area. In this case, the homogeneity or parallel form reliability would usually be the most appropriate. However, if variables are collected at different points in time but each variable's score is assumed to remain constant across the data collection time period, then a parallel form reliability involving both sources of error would probably be used. Note, however, that some factor-analytic studies purposefully gather data from different points in time because the theory states that the earlier variables should influence the later variables. Although the question of which reliability is appropriate for each variable needs to be thought through carefully, reliabilities stressing stability over time would not be appropriate for those variables where change is expected. Because specific factor loadings are seldom calculated, the major uses for reliabilities are: (1) to determine an upper bound for the communality; and (2) to indicate when the variable's lack of loading on factors may be attributable to poor measurement.

The specific factors may be of some interest when including additional variables in future research to move variance with theoretical potential from specific to common factor status. If the specific factor loading for a given variable is quite high, then it may load on other factors not in this particular analysis, or other variables may be needed in the analysis to increase the common factor variance that this particular variable represents.

Example

Reliabilities were computed for the 24 ability variables (Holzinger & Swineford, 1939). The psychological testing took place over several days and so the correlations among variables include error variance due to both lack of homogeneity and instability over short time periods. Unfortunately, all the reliabilities reported do not involve both of these sources of random error. Only variables 5, 11, and 14 through 20 had reliabilities calculated from parallel forms given in two sessions; the rest of the reliabilities were from materials all given on the same day. Because the calculation of specific factors was not of interest to the investigators, the lack of adequate reliabilities was no major problem. However, the current example will be restricted to those variables whose reliabilities cover both sources of random error.

In Table 6.3.4 the reliability, initial communality estimate (its highest correlation with another variable), the observed principal axes communality, and the specific factor loading are presented. The latter was calculated by Eq. (6.3.2). These specific loadings would be lower if another factor or two were extracted. Even so, they would not reduce to zero and indicate some systematic sources of variance outside of the common factors.

TABLE 6.3.4
Reliabilities, Communalities and Specific Factor
Loadings of Several Ability Variables

Variables	r_{XX}	Estimated h^2	Observed h^2	Specific Factor Loading
5	.81	.72	.66	.39
11	.71	.53	.48	.48
14	.65	.39	.37	.53
15	.51	.39	.32	.44
16	.60	.42	.43	.41
17	.72	.45	.44	.53
18	.61	.45	.42	.44
19	.57	.37	.25	.57
20	.65	.52	.44	.46

*6.4   IMAGE ANALYSIS

Image analysis is also a principal factor variant in its usual application. As in the case of the principal axes with estimated communalities procedure, it is a principal factor variant in the sense that, after appropriate alterations are made to the correlation matrix, that matrix can be submitted to a principal factor program to find the desired factors. The program will then minimize the residuals of the particular matrix submitted. The differences in image analysis and other principal factor variants lie primarily in the alterations of the correlation matrix before the factors are extracted. Image factors can also be extracted by maximum likelihood procedures (Jöreskog, 1969b).

Section 6.4.1, The Concept of Image Analysis, contains the basic theoretical background and concepts of image analysis. Section 6.4.2 indicates how the correlation matrix is altered to produce image factors. Differences between image analysis and principal axes are discussed in Section 6.4.3.

6.4.1 The Concept of Image Analysis

The **image** of a variable is that part of it that can be estimated from other variables in the same substantive domain. The estimation procedure is that of multiple regression; each variable is predicted from the other $v - 1$ variables by using the appropriate beta weights calculated by multiple regression formulas. Therefore:

$$\hat{Z}_{vi} = \sum_{j=1}^{k} b_{vj} Z_{ji} \tag{6.4.1}$$

where $\hat{Z}_{vi}$ is individual i's score on the image of Z_v, b_{vj} are the standardized multiple regression weights for variable v on each of the k variables (where $k = v - 1$) and Z_{ji} are individual i's scores on the other $v - 1$ variables. All variables are assumed to be in standard score form. The $\hat{Z}$ is that portion of Z that is predictable from the set of variables. Image factor analysis utilizes each and every variable's image. Because the scores therefore include only that variance that overlaps with at least one other variable, only common factor variance is included in the analysis.

The **antiimage** of the variable is that part that cannot be predicted from the other variables (i.e., its residual portion). Thus:

$$U_v = Z_v - \hat{Z}_v. \tag{6.4.2}$$

And:

$$Z_v = \hat{Z}_v + U_v \tag{6.4.3}$$

where U_v represents the antiimage scores for variable V.

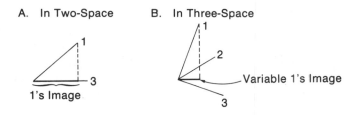

FIG. 6.1. The image of variable 1.

The term *image* derives from the geometric representation of the predicted part of each variable. In Fig. 6.1, variables 1 and 3 are plotted in two-dimensional space, while 1, 2 and 3 are in three-dimensional space. Each vector is unit length with each defining its own dimension. The variables are not at right angles and therefore they are correlated with each other. That part of variable 1 that is predictable from the other variables is the same as that part of variable 1 that would exist if variable 1's dimension were eliminated. In *A*, variable 1's image is that part predicted from the only other variable, 3. In *B*, that portion of variable 1 that overlaps with variables 2 and 3 would be represented in a two-space. The portion of 1 predictable from 2 and 3 is found by dropping a line perpendicular to the other dimensions. Note that variable 1 is considerably shorter as an image than it was originally. The variance of variable 1 is reduced by that section of it that is not predictable from variables 2 and 3 when it is represented only in the space defined by variables 2 and 3.

The image factors are those factors that best reproduce the relationships among the images of the variables. Because these variables have lengths less than 1.0, their relationships are represented by covariances rather than correlations.

6.4.2 Solving for the Image Solution

Image analysis proceeds conceptually by solving for the principal factors of the variance–covariance matrix formed from the image scores calculated from the original standard scores. In such a case, the variances are the squared multiple correlations of each variable with the other $v - 1$ variables. The covariances are similar to adjusted correlations (i.e., they are the standard score correlations adjusted for the reduction in the variance of each variable). They are not then actually correlations but are covariances instead. Rather than computing all of the image scores and then calculating the variance–covariance matrix—a perfectly legitimate but awkward procedure—the image variance–covariance matrix can be computed directly from the correlation matrix itself. The formula is:

$$G_{vv} = R_{vv} + D_{vv}R_{vv}^{-1}D_{vv} - 2D_{vv} \tag{6.4.4}$$

where G_{vv} is the image variance–covariance matrix and D_{vv} is a diagonal matrix where the elements are the reciprocals of the diagonal elements in R_{vv}^{-1}. This means that D_{vv} contains $1 - R^2$ which is, by definition, the antiimage variance. (In publications on image analysis, D is sometimes symbolized as S^2).

Equation (6.4.4) uses the inverse of the correlation matrix. If one or more variables have a multiple correlation of 1.0 with the other variables, the correlation matrix will not have an inverse (i.e., it will be singular). The first approach to this problem is to examine the data closely for any variables that are experimentally dependent upon other variables, as, for example, the sum of a set of variables already in the analysis. Experimental dependency among variables should be eliminated. If there are no experimentally dependent variables and the correlation matrix still is singular, then procedures suggested by Kaiser (1976a) and Kaiser and Cerny (1978) can be followed.

Because covariances rather than correlations are being factored, a legitimate question is whether or not the formulas for the common factor model must now involve the variances of the images. They would, were it not for the fact that the interest is not in how the image scores correlate with the derived factors, but with how the original scores correlate with and are predicted from the factors defined by the images. The original scores are, in this discussion, assumed to be in standard score form.

Note that the image analysis pattern and correlations among factors are used to reproduce the image variance–covariance matrix and not the original correlations.

Example

Three image factors were extracted from the box variables. The squared multiple correlations were calculated by inverting the correlation matrix. These were then used to define D, and G was calculated. The principal factors of G were then extracted. These factors are given in Table 6.4.1. Because the communality estimates are quite high, the factors are quite similar to the principal components.

The factors do not, of course, give the three dimensions of space because they have not yet been rotated. It is doubtful that anyone would ever hypothesize that the three dimensions would appear directly in the principal factors.

6.4.3 Relationship of Image Analysis to Common Factor Analysis

The similarity of the equation (6.4.3) to that used to define the common factor model means that image analysis is a variant of it. As the number of variables included in the analysis approaches the entire universe of the variables or infinity, the image analysis model and the traditional common factor model become identical. This follows intuitively by noting that as the number of variables becomes infinitely large, some other variable is bound to exist that is essentially

TABLE 6.4.1
Image Factors from the Box Data

	A	B	C	R^2
1. Length squared	.85	−.44	−.09	.96
2. Height squared	.86	.17	.39	.93
3. Width squared	.86	.42	−.21	.98
4. Length plus width	.95	−.08	−.22	.97
5. Length plus height	.95	−.21	.17	.99
6. Width plus height	.96	.22	.08	.99
7. Longest inner diagonal	.93	−.17	−.06	.94
8. Shortest inner diagonal	.92	−.01	.04	.92
9. Space inner diagonal	.96	−.18	−.02	.97
10. Thickness of edge	.76	.35	−.09	.82

a parallel form of the variable under consideration. In that case, all of the reliable variance of the variable would enter into the common factors under both approaches.

Images from the universe of variables are, however, never factored. Only that part of the image of the variable is used in any given analysis that comes from the sample of variables included in the analysis. Because the initial theory considered only a population of variables and individuals to define the variable's image, this more restricted concept is called a **partial image.** With the number of variables usually included in a factor analysis, there is a distinct difference between partial image analysis and traditional common factor procedures such as principal axes. The traditional approach to common factor analysis defines the correlation between the variable and factor as including all of the overlap between the variable and that factor in addition to the overlap with the other variables. In the partial image approach, only that part of the variable that overlaps with other variables influences the correlation of the variable with the factor. Variance that overlaps with the factor but not with the other variables would be excluded from the correlation between the variable and the factor in the partial image approach but not in principal axes.

*6.5   OTHER RELATED PROCEDURES

6.5.1 Minimum Residual Analysis (Minres)

The standard principal factor solutions seek to minimize all the elements in the total correlation matrix. In principal axes, the importance of the diagonal elements is decreased, not by ignoring them but by altering the elements in the diagonal. Once communality estimates have been accepted, the principal factor solution is used to minimize each of these diagonal elements as well as each of the off-diagonal elements. The minimum residual approach contrasts with both of these principal factor variants by simply ignoring the diagonal of the correlation matrix. Thus, **minimum residual analysis** maximally accounts for the variance in the off-diagonal elements and thereby minimizes each off-diagonal residual. Communalities result from the analysis. The result could be considered almost an ideal principal factor solution because all the residual elements are minimized. By ignoring the diagonal, a very close fit to the off-diagonal elements can be achieved. No harm is done to the diagonal elements because they are calculated so that their residuals are always zero. Minimizing all the elements of the correlation matrix satisfies the purpose of the principal factor approach.

Minres is a principal factor variant for several reasons. First, the usual procedure for solving for it utilizes characteristic roots and vectors. Second, a principal factor analysis will give the identical results from a correlation matrix containing the communality resulting from a minimum residual analysis as does minres itself. The intimate relationship between minimum residual analysis and principal factor analysis is such that the former could be conceptualized as a communality estimation procedure for principal axes analysis and the result would be the same.

The derivations of minimum residual analysis (Comrey, 1962; Harman & Jones, 1966) do not involve specific factors, error variances, or uniquenesses. Instead, the authors simply note that one is interested in analyzing the overlap between variables and that such overlap is represented solely by the off-diagonal elements. The diagonal elements represent the overlap of the variable with itself and are therefore of no interest. However, minres is functionally part of the common factor model as defined here and can be used to solve for it.

Minimum residual analysis is iterative and begins with the characteristic roots and vectors of the correlation matrix. The procedure then checks the efficiency with which the factor pattern so generated reproduces the off-diagonal elements. This gives rise to new estimates of factor loadings that more adequately reproduce the off-diagonal elements. The communalities are calculated after the solution has stabilized. If a Heywood case arises, the offending communality can be arbitrarily reset to 1.0 (Harman & Jones, 1966) or resolved by more sophisticated procedures (Harman & Fukuda, 1966).

Desk calculator and computer program procedures for minres analysis are given by Comrey and Ahumada (1965) for the successive extraction of factors, and by Harman and Jones (1966), Harman (1967), and Nosal (1977) for simultaneous factor extraction. The Comrey and Harman solutions differ slightly (Lee & Comrey, 1978).

6.5.2 Alpha Factor Analysis

Alpha factor analysis (Kaiser & Caffrey, 1965) maximizes the alpha (Cronbach, 1951), or Kuder–Richardson, reliabilities of the common factors. The first common factor extracted is that factor that has the highest correlation with the same factor in the universe of variables (i.e., it is the best parallel form for the universe common factor). The alpha reliability of the factor extracted could be considered as the validity coefficient of this factor with reference to the common factor from the universe of variables [although McDonald (1970) has raised questions about this interpretation of alpha]. The procedure is frankly psychometric rather than statistical; it is assumed that the correlation coefficients are from the population. Analysis begins with communality estimates that are used to adjust the correlation matrix. Principal factors are then extracted from the adjusted matrix. Glass (1966) points out that the similarity of the observed P_{vf} in a sample to the population P is a function of the reliabilities of the variables.

Bentler (1968) presents another variant on alpha factor analysis where the alpha reliability is also maximized. However, in this case, the alpha reliability is that of the observed score composite. The procedure is within the common factor model and maximizes the alpha, or internal consistency, reliability of factor scores.

Note that these procedures produce, as the first factor, the factor that has the highest reliability, then the factor with the second highest reliability, and so forth. This characteristic is not maintained when the factors are rotated.

6.5.3 Maximum Likelihood Factor Analysis

Principal factors as normally extracted are based on equations for which it is assumed that the population correlation matrix is being factored. In maximum likelihood procedures it is explicitly recognized that a sample is being analyzed. Maximum likelihood procedures are defined as those that best reproduce the population values (the meaning of "best reproduce" is further discussed in Chapter 7). Any factor solution that best reproduces the population values is a maximum likelihood analysis.

The maximum likelihood concept by itself is insufficient to establish a unique factor solution, and can be used with an infinite number of solutions for a factor analytic problem. This allows both exploratory and confirmatory maximum likelihood factor analysis, a distinction discussed further in Chapter 7. Because an infinite number of solutions are possible, limits in addition to the maximum likelihood criterion per se are necessary to provide a unique solution. In exploratory maximum likelihood analysis, those further limits are set mathematically in the principal factor tradition of accounting for as much variance as possible in each successive, orthogonal factor, but with the new restriction that they be within the maximum likelihood specifications. Thus maximum likelihood factor analysis is also a variant of the principal factor solutions because one criterion for each factor is the same as in other principal factor procedures.

The relationship of maximum likelihood to principal factors can be further identified by examining the limiting assumption in an exploratory maximum likelihood analysis that uniquely determines the factors. For example, Lawley and Maxwell (1963) give their limiting assumption as:

$$J_{ff} = L'_{fv} \, U_{vv}^{-1} \, L_{vf} \tag{6.5.1}$$

where J is a diagonal matrix with its elements arranged in order of magnitude. The result of this assumption is that the factors have similar characteristics to principal factors (e.g., they minimize the residuals within the restriction of being maximum likelihood estimates). However, the early computational procedures often produced diverse results. Harman (1967) gives examples of maximum likelihood solutions calculated by different procedures where differences of loadings across the procedures were as great as .3 or .4. It appears that such differences arose from different criteria for stopping iterations and also because different procedures reached different solutions that produced the same residual matrices. Procedures used to calculate the maximum likelihood factor solutions iterate for appropriate communalities.

Recent developments (Jennrich & Robinson, 1969; Jöreskog, 1967; Jöreskog & Lawley, 1968; Jöreskog & Sörbom, 1982) have included algorithms that lead to numerically stable solutions under conditions commonly encountered in practice and that are faster than the older procedures—but maximum likelihood procedure is slower than the principal factor solutions, may not converge without using exorbitant time from even the fastest computers, and may lead to difficulties in communalities in over 50% of the runs (Kaiser, 1976b). If problems are encountered in the calculations, consult Van Driel (1978).

Rao (1955) provides the basis for another solution for the maximum likelihood factors. This variant seeks factors that have the maximum canonical correlations with the variables (i.e., the first factor is that which correlates highest with a linear function of the observed variables); the second is maximally correlated with the variables under the restriction that it is uncorrelated with the first factor, and so forth. This **canonical factor analysis** involves communality estimates; it does give maximum likelihood factors. The maximum likelihood test of significance for whether or not a residual matrix contains significant variance applies to canonical factor analysis. Algorithms for the efficient solution of the canonical maximum likelihood problem have not been as thoroughly investigated as have those for the Lawley maximum likelihood factors.

*6.6 NONLINEAR AND NONMETRIC FACTOR ANALYSIS

In Chapter 2, it was noted that the component and common factor models were both defined as linear models. Factor analysis is linear because the models show each variable being reproduced by a weighted linear combination of the components or a weighted linear combination of the common and unique factors. The models may, of course, be wrong and the factors may be curvilinearly related to the variables. The possibility of curvilinear relationships between the factors and the variables has led to several suggestions for nonlinear factor analysis. Lingoes, Roskam, and Borg (1979) contains useful papers in this area.

McDonald (1962) discusses the problem from within a standard factor-analytic approach. If there are curvilinear relationships between a given factor and the variables, the variables could be estimated by a linear formula using, for example, the factor and the factor squared if the relationship is quadratic. Therefore, a factor analysis may produce two factors: one for the factor itself and one for the factor squared. The problem then lies in finding the proper interpretation of the second factor. Hicks (1981) approaches the problem by factoring cross products with the original variables. Unfortunately, analytic methods for detecting such cases are not currently available.

Shepard and his associates (Shepard & Carroll, 1966; Shepard & Kruskal, 1964) have suggested alternative techniques for summarizing data when the relationships may be nonlinear. The first method, proximity analysis, begins with a distance measure in non-Euclidean space. In the second approach, the "factors" are sought so that they can be related to the observed variables by a function that is as smooth or continuous as possible. The smallest number of factors that will provide sufficient continuity is assumed to be the minimum number needed. Continuity is defined as a function of the squared distances among the observed variables in relationship to the same measures among the factors, an empirical defnition that has been developed further by Kruskal and Carroll (1969).

When developed, nonlinear factor analysis will undoubtedly prove useful in special cases. However, it is doubtful that the linear cases will be supplanted except by a procedure that will allow both linear and curvilinear relationships and give reference to the former. The reason is quite simple: the correlation between a variable and that same variable squared is generally between .9 and 1.0. This means that minor curvilinear relationships are represented fairly well by a linear approximation. It is only when the sign of the factor is, for example, positive and the sign of the factor squared is negative that the curvilinear relationships would be important. The same line of reasoning follows for higher polynomial equations. Thus, when Thurstone analyzed the original box problem (Thurstone, 1947), the variables were nonlinear functions of the factors—but the factors were still recognizable.

Because factor analysis is based on linear relationships, interval or ratio measurement is expected. Attempts to generalize factor analytic techniques to nominal or ordinal data have been made by Guttman and Lingoes (Guttman, 1968; Lingoes & Guttman, 1967). Rather than seeking to reproduce the correlation matrix directly, as factor analysis always does, the Guttman–Lingoes procedures reproduce another matrix, T_{vv}, where the pattern of elements is the same as in the original matrix of indices of association.

In the examples given (Lingoes & Guttman, 1967), the analyses were of matrices where correlation coefficients were adequate to summarize the data.

The results were much the same as those arising from standard factor-analytic procedures. Although the authors argue that their procedure is more adequate for identifying simplexes, circumplexes, and other such data structures, one suspects that the identification is more a function of how the results were looked at rather than the nonmetric procedure actually used. It should be noted that Kelly's nonparametric factor analysis also seems to result in essentially the same factors as found in the standard parametric analysis (Arthur, 1965).

The reason the results from the nonmetric approach are not more impressive may arise from the versatility of the correlation coefficient. Although it is often thought that at least interval data are needed for correlation coefficients to be calculated, this is not true. The primary influence on correlation coefficients in the usual study appears to be the rank order of individuals rather than the intervals between the points on the scale. Indeed, Spearman's rank correlation coefficient is a special case of the Pearson product-moment correlation coefficient that has been used throughout this discussion; if rank data are submitted to a standard computer program for Pearson product-moment correlations, the results will be Spearman rank correlation coefficients (Nunnally, 1978). Weeks and Bentler (1979) report that factoring ranked data by the usual linear analysis is preferred to special monotone models because it gives the same results and avoids known problems of monotone methods.

The correlation coefficient will always be the best linear representation between two variables. The necessity for interval and normally distributed data lies more in the significance tests than in the correlation coefficient. Therefore, the only place in standard factor analysis where normally distributed, equal interval data are necessary is where statistical tests making these assumptions are utilized—and such situations are not yet common in factor analysis. The investigation of nonmetric factor analysis for nominal data rather than ordinal data would be of greater interest.

6.7   APPLICATIONS FOR PRINCIPAL FACTORS

The first situation where principal factors are appropriate is when an efficient condensation of the variables is desired. The first principal factor is the best single condensation, as previously noted. For example, one may have multiple measures of performance in a learning experiment on which analyses of variance are to be computed. Because the dependent variables are correlated, independent analyses of variance cannot be run. However, if the dependent variables are multiple representatives of one construct, then the first principal factor can be extracted, scores computed, and these scores used in a single analysis of variance. The scores will be that composite of the variables that covers the maximum amount of variance of the set of variables.

Another situation for principal factors is as a first step to orthogonalizing the variables. The purpose of orthogonalizing the variables is to reduce the correlations among the variables to zero. Uncorrelated variables allow an independent test of significance between each of the variables and another set of variables or experimental treatments. The principal components are extracted and then rotated so that one factor is identified with each variable but with the restriction that the factors are uncorrelated. Other variables can be correlated with the orthogonalized variables by extension analysis (cf. Section 10.5), or uncorrelated factor scores can be computed for use in other statistical routines (cf. Chapter 12). Principal factor orthogonalization splits the overlap among variables (Gorsuch, 1973b).

The most frequent situation where principal factor solutions are used is exploratory factor analysis. The purpose is to examine the structure of a given domain as represented by the sample of variables. The long-term interest is to identify basic conceptual dimensions that can be examined in future research. The appeal of principal factors is that they represent the greatest proportion of the variance of the variables in the fewest possible dimensions. Although the factors are usually rotated to a more "meaningful" position (cf. Chapter 9), the rotation does not alter the total amount of variance extracted or the number of dimensions.

6.8   A COMPARISON OF FACTOR EXTRACTION PROCEDURES

The research investigator has a number of factor extraction procedures from which to choose. Each has its possibilities and its advocates. To aid in comparing the procedures Table 6.8.1 has been prepared. The comparisons are only for the techniques of this chapter. Diagonal, multiple-group, and confirmatory analyses serve distinctively different purposes, and hence are not comparable with these procedures for exploratory factor extraction.

The first column of Table 6.8.1 indicates which procedure is being considered. In the second column the principle of extraction is summarized; the third indicates the nature of the model assumed in the procedure. The second and third columns provide the major information by which procedures are compared in Section 6.8.1, whereas other aspects of a solution that may influence the selection of a procedure are discussed in Section 6.8.2.

6.8.1 Impact of the Extraction Procedure on the Results

The communalities of the variables may be such that the differences among most component and common factor procedures become trivial. For example, all the exploratory common factor procedures merge toward principal component analysis as the communalities approach 1.0. **When the communalities are 1.0, the principal component, axis, minimum residual, alpha, and maximum likeli-**

TABLE 6.8.1
Comparison of Exploratory Factor Extraction Procedures

Type of Analysis	Principle of Extraction	Definition of Uniqueness	Communality Estimates	Factor Scores
Principal Components	Maximizes variance accounted for	None	None needed	Calculated
Principal Axes	Maximizes variance accounted for	Specific factors, random error	Numerous estimation procedures	Estimated
Minimum Residual	Minimizes off diagonal residuals	Specific factors, random error	Iterates to appropriate estimates	Estimated
Image	Minimizes residual images	That part of each variable not correlated with any other variable in the analysis	Squared multiple correlation	Calculated
Alpha	Maximizes generalizability to factors underlying domain of variables	Psychometric error	Iterative	Calculated
Maximum Likelihood- Lawley and Jöreskog	Best estimate of reproduced correlation matrix in the population	Specific factors, random error	Iterative	Estimated
Maximum Likelihood- Rao	Factors maximally correlated with variables while giving best estimate of population reproduced correlation matrix	Specific factors, random error	Iterative	Estimated scores have highest possible R^2 with factors

Notes: All of the above are principal factor variants. Maximum likelihood procedures often result in problematic solutions.

hood solutions are virtually identical. In cases where the communalities are generally low or where there is wide variation expected among the variables as to their communalities, the principal component solution becomes a more distinctive procedure.

A similar conclusion can be drawn with regard to the number of variables. As the number of variables increases, the proportion of the elements of the correlation matrix that are in the diagonal decreases, and the diagonal elements take on less importance. Hence the principal component procedure tends to merge with the principal axes and minres approaches. In addition, as the number of variables increases, the likelihood of image analysis giving the same results as, for example, minres analysis increases. With more variables, any given variable's R^2 is more likely to approach its communality. **As the number of variables increase, communality estimates and the method by which exploratory factors are extracted both become less important.**

The few empirical studies that compare the various extraction procedures generally bear out the theoretical conclusions. Tucker, Koopman, and Linn (1969), for example, found principal components and principal axes (using R^2) to produce the same factors when the communalities were high for all 20 variables. Harris and Harris (1971) found most ability factors to appear when truncated principal component, alpha, and several other common factor procedures were used. Velicer (1974, 1977; Velicer, Peacock, & Jackson, 1982) found maximum likelihood, principal component, and image factors to be alike both for patterns of loadings and for stability upon dropping some variables before and after rotation. Kallina and Hartman (1976) found no interpretable difference between component and common factors. When Browne (1968a) compared several different procedures for the accuracy with which they reproduced known population factor loadings, the results were much the same across several common factor procedures. Maximum likelihood analysis was slightly more accurate, but this increase in accuracy was so minor as to be negligible. Only in the case of large sample sizes ($n = 1500$) did the maximum likelihood procedure give distinctively more accurate estimates of the factor loadings than the other procedures. Principal components were not included; it would probably have given somewhat different results because only twelve variables and four factors were involved.

Some evidence (Dziuban & Harris, 1973; Velicer, 1977) suggests that the last few principal components factors may differ when many factors are extracted. Because component analysis is designed to reproduce all the variance of all variables, the last factor or two sometimes becomes virtually a ''singlet,'' that is, has a single high loading. A singlet does reproduce the 1.0 in the diagonal for that variable, but reflects none of the overlap with other variables. Common factor procedures are not reproducing a 1.0 in the diagonal, and so their equivalent factor does not have the high single loading. Lee and Comrey (1979) document this result further and also conclude that truncated principal components inflate factor loadings.

The general conclusion is that when the number of variables is moderately large, for example, greater than 30, and the analysis contains virtually no variables expected to have low communalities (e.g., .4), practically any of the exploratory procedures other than diagonal or multiple-group analysis will lead to the same interpretations. The investigator can therefore select the procedure that is readily available.

What procedure is best when the number of variables is not large? In the components case, the selection is straightforward. Each of the three possible procedures is sufficiently unique so that the only question is whether or not the situation warrants them. There is no real alternative. Diagonal and multiple-group factors can be used either for statistical control or hypothesis testing, whereas principal components are used for exploratory work. But a component model can only be accepted if the resulting communalities do turn out to be high. Real differences can be expected between the results of a component analysis and a common factor analysis when the number of variables is not great (e.g., less than 20) and some communalities are low.

When a common factor model is used with only a few variables, the method of extracting the factors is probably less critical than the method of estimating the communalities. If the communality estimates are similar—as they generally are if a careful estimate is made—the results will probably be sufficiently similar so that the same interpretations would result. If there are doubts, the best procedure is probably to factor with each of the several appropriate communalities and only interpret results occurring across all solutions.

This writer's personal preference is to begin with a common factor extraction procedure. The common factor model has three characteristics to recommend it. First, there are few studies where the variables are thought to be error-free and where all of the variances of the variables can be expected to be predicted from the factors. This is particularly true in the social sciences and at the growing edge of other sciences where factor analysis is often used. Hence, our concepts fit the common factor model.

Second, component analysis produces higher loadings than common factor analysis. As was shown in the example of Table 6.3.3, the loadings may be sufficiently inflated so as to be misleading. Kazelskis (1978), in providing a procedure for correcting component loadings for spuriousness due to the variable overlapping with the factor, gives an illustration where the average squared loading before correction is one-third higher than after correction. A common factor analysis produces more conservative loadings.

The third advantage of common factor analysis is that it produces a component analysis if the latter is truly appropriate. If the communalities are actually unities, then the communality estimates will be unities inasmuch as they are accurate and the common factor analysis automatically becomes a component analysis. Component procedures, such as truncated principal components, do produce solutions where the communalities are less than one, but these communalities are seldom as low as would be given by a common factor analysis. Therefore, a common factor analysis is more likely to result in an actual component analysis when that is the best model than vice versa.

Examples

Without knowing the theoretical approach of the particular investigator, it is not possible to specify which solution is the best one for any of our examples. Different investigators would wish to test different hypotheses and so might use different approaches. Naturally, the results would confirm some and disconfirm other hypotheses.

We can, however, suggest some possible procedures that would be appropriate for each of our basic examples.

In the box problem, a hypothesis testing approach is appropriate. The example was constructed with the three dimensions of space in mind. Therefore, confirmatory maximum likelihood or diagonal analysis with each of the major dimensions being a hypothesized factor would be an appropriate solution. Inasmuch as the factors did not predict all the variance, the error designed into the example is obscurring the results.

Rees approached his physique data with an exploratory factor analysis. As noted in Chapter 5, it is possible to also test some hypotheses with the same data. that is, to explore the practice of determining clothing fit by only two dimensions. This hypothesis can also be tested by confirmatory maximum likelihood analysis.

In an exploratory analysis of the physique data, one could opt for a component or common factor model. It would depend upon what was deemed important (i.e., whether or not a factor that was virtually a specific would be of any importance). Principal components would be used if the component model were chosen. If a common factor model were chosen, then maximum likelihold, minres, or image analysis would probably be chosen. Although the results would vary from the component analysis because the number of variables is not great, the common factors would not be expected to vary much within themselves. The correlations between variables and the communalities are both sufficiently high so that any reasonable estimate can be expected to lead to much the same result.

It is apparent from the reliabilities that a component model is not appropriate for the ability variables. Within the common factor model, they could be factored from a number of different perspectives to test different hypotheses. Naturally, many of these can be tested by multiple group and confirmatory maximum likelihood procedures. The ability problem includes a sufficient number of variables with sufficiently high correlations so that exploratory maximum likelihood, principal axes, minres, and image analysis would all lead to similar results. The image analysis solution would be more discrepant from the other solutions in a matrix where the overlap between variables was less. If the purpose of the exploratory procedure were, however, to select a few variables for a new study, then the diagonal analysis procedure of Section 5.3.3 would be appropriate.

Note, however, that even these general conclusions could be overthrown in the presence of a new theory. Such a theory could demand a reexamination of the data with a different procedure, and the new analysis might lead to better estimation that is more consistent with other data. Such reanalysis of data did occur when a relativity perspective challenged the Newtonian perspective. Such is the nature of science.

6.8.2 Other Considerations

Communality Estimation.   In Table 6.8.1, the last three columns can be used to decide what procedure to use when the principle of extraction still leaves some choice. The communality estimation procedure, summarized in the fourth column, follows principally from the assumptions made about the unextracted variance. It appears that reasonable estimates of the communalities can generally be made in all cases, but the more accurate procedures might be necessary when only a few variables are being factored.

Factor Scores.   In a factor-analytic study, factor scores are seldom needed. Instead, the interest lies in the relationship among variables and factors, a relationship that is calculated without need for the factor scores. Even if the interest is in relating the factors to variables not in the factor analysis but collected on the same subjects, more efficient procedures are available than correlating with factor scores (cf. Section *10.5). Factor scores will be needed only if chi-squares and other such noncorrelational analyses are to be run. The fifth column indicates which procedures give factor scores that can be directly computed and the procedures where factor scores can only be estimated. **All procedures give only estimates of the factor scores when generalized to a new sample (cf. Chapter 12);** there is no current evidence on the relative generalizability of factor scores produced by the different factor extraction procedures.

Scale Invariance.   The factor-analytic solutions of Table 6.8.1 could also be compared on whether they are "scale-invariant." Scale invariance occurs if the factor structure and factor scores are unchanged even though variables are multipled by a nonzero constant and covariances are factored (McDonald, 1970). It has been shown that principal components, principal axes, alpha analysis, and maximum likelihood solutions all have this property (Kaiser & Caffrey, 1965; McDonald, 1970), as well as diagonal factor analysis. All correlational analyses can be considered scale invariant regardless of whether or not the solution is rotated. Scale invariance does not appear to be an important consideration in selecting among factor extraction procedures.

7

Confirmatory Maximum Likelihood Solutions

Confirmatory factor analysis tests hypotheses that a specified subset of variables legitimately define a prespecified factor. Confirmatory multiple-group factor analysis was presented in Chapter 5. The concept underlying maximum likelihood factoring and the procedure itself are described in Sections 7.1 and 7.2. This procedure differs from exploratory factor analysis because explicit hypotheses are tested. Rotation is not used and the confirmatory factor analysis gives a solution directly. An introduction to several of the applications for confirmatory maximum likelihood factor analysis is in Section 7.3.

7.1. THE MAXIMUM LIKELIHOOD CONCEPT

In the maximum likelihood approach, estimating the population parameters from sample statistics is the central concern. A procedure is sought for generalizing from a sample of individuals to the population of individuals. (This is, it should be noted, a definite departure from principal factors where most derivations assume that population parameters were involved.) There are numerous ways in which estimates of the population parameters could be made. For the procedure derived to maximize the likelihood function, the method of estimating the population parameters must have two valuable characteristics. First, a maximum likelihood estimate will have the highest probability of converging to the population parameter as the size of the sample increases toward that of the population. Second, the estimated parameters will be the most consistent with the smallest variance across samples. Even though maximum likelihood estimates may occasionally lead to biased solutions, their other advantages often outweigh this disadvantage.

In maximum likelihood factor analysis, the information provided by R_{vv} is used to obtain the best estimates of the factor loadings and uniquenesses needed to reproduce the population R_{vv}. The procedure is basically concerned with estimating the population correlation matrix under the assumption that the variables came from the designated number of factors. The maximum likelihood procedure itself does not uniquely locate the factors. Given a specified number of factors, there are an infinite number of positions to which the factors could be rotated that would satisfy the likelihood function. All these solutions would give the same estimated reproduced correlation matrix. The calculation procedures make further assumptions in order to determine unique factors, but these assumptions are not a part of the maximum likelihood concept.

Derivation of the appropriate equations begins with the following definition of concern as a typical starting point:

$$C_{vv} = L_{vf} C_{ff} L'_{fv} + U_{vv} \qquad (7.1.1)$$

where the C's are covariance matrices, L_{vf} is the factor pattern of maximum likelihood weights, and U is a diagonal matrix if the factors account for all of the covariances among the variables. The correlation matrix is simply a standardized covariance matrix and is included as a special case of maximum likelihood analysis. To simplify equations, C_{ff} is often assumed to be a diagonal matrix (i.e., the factors are assumed to be uncorrelated). Also note that because a covariance matrix is analyzed, the technique can be readily applied to a partial image covariance matrix for maximum likelihood image analysis. The presence of U_{vv} in the equation indicates that the procedure is in the common factor tradition.

The assumptions underlying Eq. (7.1.1) are that the correlations between the factors and the unique factors and the correlations among the unique factors are all zero. The maximum likelihood approach goes on to assume that the common factor and unique scores are both normally distributed so that, as a result, each variable would have a normal distribution. The variables are also assumed to have a multivariate normal distribution.

Because of these assumptions, it is usually recommended that the distributions of variables included in a factor analysis be examined for normality. If a variable's distribution departs widely from normality, that variable is to be dropped from the analysis. However, Fuller and Hemmerle (1966) utilized uniform, normal, truncated normal, Student's t, triangular, and bimodal distributions in a Monte Carlo study of the robustness of the maximum likelihood estimation procedure. With large n's (200), only a few variables (five), and with two common factors, they concluded that the maximum likelihood procedure was relatively insensitive to departures from normality. The large n used in the study is important because the maximum likelihood statistical procedure has been developed only in terms of large sample estimates. Unfortunately, no one seems to know exactly where a large n begins and a small n leaves off. If the number of individuals is less than 50, it would probably be safe to assume that the sample size is in the small category. On the other hand, sample sizes of 200 or so would be definitely in the large sample category. The area between 50 and 200 would, in this author's rough estimation, probably fall in the large sample category, but there may be interactions with, for example, the number of variables being analyzed.

An important characteristic of the maximum likelihood procedure is that statistical tests of significance have been derived (Lawley, 1940, 1941). The test of significance gives a chi-square statistic with the null hypothesis being that all the population covariance has been extracted by the hypothesized number of factors. If the chi-square is significant at the designated probability level, then the residual matrix still has significant covariance in it. The significance test is discussed more fully in Chapter 8, but it should be noted that even minute, trivial factors will usually be significant when a large sample is used.

7.2   CONFIRMATORY MAXIMUM LIKELIHOOD FACTOR ANALYSIS

Jöreskog (Jöreskog, 1966, 1969a; Jöreskog & Gruvaeus, 1967; Jöreskog, Gruvaeus, & Van Thillo, 1970; Jöreskog and Lawley, 1968) has differentiated between exploratory maximum likelihood factor analysis and confirmatory maximum likelihood factor analysis. Whereas the former simply finds those factors that best reproduce the variables under the maximum likelihood conditions, the latter tests specific hypotheses regarding the nature of the factors. Confirmatory maximum likelihood factor analysis extracts factors with predefined characteristics and then tests to determine if the residual matrix still contains significant variance. The predefined parameters can be in the P_{vf}, R_{ff}, or in the unique variances, U_{vv}. In addition, the loadings and correlations for which there are hypotheses can be tested for significance by the use of large sample approximations to the standard errors. Examples of confirmatory factor analysis are given by Gebhardt (1971), Jöreskog (1971), and Boruch and Wolins (1970), as well as in the references mentioned previously and in the next section.

Parameter Definition.   Parameters can be predefined by being set equal to a specified value. This is particularly useful in R_{ff} where the diagonals are set equal to 1.0 and some off-diagonals may be set to zero. Setting all off-diagonals to zero means that the factors will be uncorrelated. Setting part of the off-diagonals to zero will make some of the factors uncorrelated with the other factors. Setting some factor correlations to zero may be particularly useful where overlapping variances need to be partialed out in an unambiguous way. For example, if one factor is expected to be from the content and another from the method by which different contents were measured, theory and practice might require that these be uncorrelated to maximize interpretability.

Setting elements of P_{vf} equal to certain values is also useful. One element of a particular column may be set equal to unity so that a diagonal factor is extracted, or a set of elements may be set to zero so that the factor is defined independently of these variables. Values intermediate between zero and one may also be used.

Parameters may also be specified by being set equal to each other. In this case, no particular value is given for the elements that must be equal. These parameters are free to vary so long as they maintain their equality.

Restricted and Unique Solutions. In confirmatory maximum likelihood analysis, it is necessary to distinguish between unrestricted and restricted solutions, on the one hand, and unique and nonunique solutions on the other hand. An **unrestricted** solution can be identified by the fact that the solution can be obtained by rotating from another maximum likelihood solution. An infinite number of solutions will fulfill the same minimum conditions that it does. Several unrestricted solutions from the same data will have the same communalities. Exploratory factor analyses are unrestricted solutions.

A **restricted** solution does limit the whole factor space and cannot be obtained by rotation from unrestricted factors. Restricted solutions from the same data will have different communalities and uniquenesses from unrestricted solutions of the same data. More than f^2 parameters in the factor loadings and correlations between the factors must be specified for it to be a restricted solution, and those specified parameters must be properly placed. Most confirmatory factor analyses would specify a sufficient number of parameters (i.e., more than f^2) so that they would produce restricted solutions, but partially restricted solutions with less than f^2 restrictions are also legitimate.

Both restricted and unrestricted solutions may be such that there is only one factor position that will satisfy the fixed elements for parameters. If so, the solution is **unique.** To be unique, at least f^2 elements in the factor loading matrix and in the matrix of correlations among factors must be specified. In addition, each column of P_{vf} must have a sufficient number of fixed parameters so that it too is specified. For example, even though more than f^2 elements were specified in a factor matrix where the last two factors had no elements specified, it is apparent that this solution would not be unique because the last two factors could be rotated independently of the others.

Generally speaking, confirmatory factor analysis is most useful when the hypotheses establish a restricted, unique factor space. However, confirmatory factor analysis can be used when only one or two loadings are specified and all other elements are unrestricted. If, for example, a loading on variable one was specified as 1.0 and it was further specified that this factor be uncorrelated with all the other factors, then the confirmatory factor analysis machinery could be used to extract a diagonal factor from one's data as well as exploratory factors for the rest of the data.

Regardless of the mode of analysis, competing theories can always exist to explain the same observed data. Therefore, more than one restricted, unique confirmatory maximum likelihood factor analysis can be found that would adequately account for the data. The arguments between the theories can only be resolved on the basis of new data that one can explain and the other cannot, or other evidence outside that particular research study.

Significance Testing. Several types of significance tests are available in confirmatory maximum likelihood analysis. First, standard errors are available for elements that are left free to vary, and they can be used to compute the significance level. Generally this is done by computing the large-sample Z test. The probability for that Z is found in a normal curve table. Second, an overall test of the adequacy of the hypothesized factors to reproduce all the data is provided by a chi-square test. The chi-square test may be used directly to establish if more factors are necessary; this use is discussed further in Chapter 8. Note that it tests only if *more* factors are needed.

A highly useful significance testing procedure is to compare the chi-square from one factor-analytic model with another. The confirmatory maximum likelihood analysis is run for the first factor model, and the chi-square computed. A second factor model is then established by expanding the first model to contain further specifications. For example, the second model may have several extra factors over and above what the first model hypothesized. The second model is then used to compute a chi-square also. If the expanded, second model better reproduces the data, the chi-square will be *smaller*. If the second model adds nothing to reproducing the data, the chi-squares from the first and second models will be the same.

Note that the chi-square statistic is additive as are its degrees of freedom. Hence the chi-square from the second model can be subtracted from the chi-square of the first model to provide a chi-square test of whether the further specification of the second adds significantly to the reproduction of the data over and above the first model. The degrees of freedom for this chi-square test are the differences between the two degrees of freedom from the first and second model.

One useful test for a confirmatory factor analysis is to allow the first model to be that of no common factors at all or from Monte Carlo-determined factor structures (Heeler & Whipple, 1976). The second model is the set of proposed factors being tested. The chi-square from the first model will be quite large because, hopefully, it fits the data very poorly indeed. The chi-square from the second model should be small if the hypothesized factors are indeed major ones necessary to reproduce the data. Subtracting these two chi-squares should therefore give a difference chi-square that is reasonably large and statistically significant if the hypothesized factors do aid in reproducing the data. A significant difference chi-square between the second model and the first model, in this case, indicates that those factors are indeed appropriate for the data set, although they may not be the only factors necessary. Use of the difference between two models gives a significance test of the relevance of the hypothesized factors to the factor solution.

These are significance tests. Use of significance tests introduces assumptions that the factor-analytic model itself does not require. For example, multivariate normality as well as independence of errors are assumptions for multivariate tests for significance. The robustness of the confirmatory maximum likelihood procedures to violations of assumptions is currently unknown. Do note that the statistical theories have only been developed for large samples.

As in any statistical procedure where a hypothesis is tested for significance, the hypothesized factor model is specified *prior* to an examination of the data. The significance levels found hold only for models that are so prespecified. If the models are not completely prespecified, the other major option is to base part of the model upon the data themselves. But then the model is sure to fit the data even if the data are only chance. This type step-wise model building by the confirmatory factor analytic method could be used but *only if* the probability levels are neither taken seriously nor reported.

Computation.   Jöreskog and Sörbom (1982) have presented a program for confirmatory factor analysis. The program is based upon the same procedure used by Jöreskog's program for exploratory maximum likelihood factor analysis, but evaluates an even more general model that includes factor analysis as presently described. In processing the data, any elements in the factor loading matrix, correlations among factors, or uniqueness matrix can be specified, and the maximum likelihood factors will be found which best produce those elements. The hypotheses can mix uncorrelated and correlated factors. The only unfortunate characteristic about the confirmatory maximum likelihood program is that it requires an extensive amount of computer storage space and will therefore process only 40 or so variables on the larger of contemporary computers. Further developments in the programs are occurring.

Example

Confirmatory maximum likelihood analysis is appropriate for the personality problem. Not only are verbal comprehension and anxiety factors hypothesized, but it is thought that they are the only factors that are needed to account for the data. It is this latter hypothesis—that no additional factors are needed—that can be tested by maximum likelihood analysis with only one model.

Six parameters were specified as zero; these were loadings 4 to 6 for the first factor and 1 to 3 for the second factor. The correlation of each factor with itself was specified as unity but the correlation between the two factors was left free to vary. The communalities were also left free to vary; the reliabilities were used as the initial communality estimates for the iterative communality estimation. Therefore, more than f^2 parameters were set and so a unique, restricted solution would result.

TABLE 7.2.1
Confirmatory Maximum
Likelihood Factor Pattern for
Psychological Data

	Verbal Comprehension	Anxiety
1. Information	.77	.00
2. Verbal Ability	.86	.00
3. Verbal Analogies	.57	.00
4. Ego Strength	.00	−.70
5. Guilt Proneness	.00	.58
6. Tension	.00	.70

Note: $r_{AB} = -.21$.

The factor pattern is given in Table 7.2.1 along with the correlation between the factors. All specified parameters are set exactly at the specified value and the other parameters solved within those restrictions. The chi-square of the residuals after these two factors had been extracted was 5.53 with eight degrees of freedom. This is not significant at even the .10 level. The null hypothesis that these two factors accounted for all the common variance among these six variables was accepted.

7.3 APPLICATIONS

The applications for confirmatory maximum likelihood factor analysis are primarily limited by our ingenuity in developing appropriate hypotheses. Testing for a Hypothesized Factor Structure (Section 7.4.1), Scale Validity Analyses (Section 7.4.2), and Causal Path Analysis (Section 7.4.3) are three of the possible uses most widely discussed. A concluding perspective comment is then given (Section 7.4.4).

7.3.1 Testing for a Hypothesized Factor Solution

Confirmatory factor analysis provides a series of possible tests for a hypothesized factor structure. The hypothesized factor structure would be a result of a strong theory or past data that allow for specification of a unique factor resolution. This means that a number of variables need to be identified, for example, which should have factor pattern weights of zero with this particular factor. Further information needs to be available so as to specify the size of each variable's uniqueness (and thus its communality because the uniqueness is one minus the communality). Reliability information is often used for such specification (as in Chapter 6) but they are overestimates and so some specific factor variance would also be included in the solution. Correlations among factors may also be set to zero if the theory or past data strongly suggest that it is an appropriate hypothesis.

One or two variables that are hypothesized to load very high on the factor are also identified so that the proper factor is hypothesized. If one variable in particular has consistently loaded the factor in the past or is theoretically seen as intrinsic to its meaning, that variable may be set with a loading of 1.0. The other variables would then be left free to vary. The resulting solution would give the variable weighted 1.0 a prime emphasis in defining the factor given the restrictions of the zero loadings as well. Those values left free to vary would be given appropriate loadings depending upon the data, and the standard errors reported. The comparison of the observed loading with the standard errors allows for a significance test of whether a particular variable is related to a particular factor, a useful subhypothesis.

If one particular variable is not seen as critical or intrinsic to the factor, two or three variables might be seen as equally identifying the factor. In that case each of these several variables may be required to have equal loadings, although one runs a slight chance of the program setting them all equal to zero under this condition.

The model testing outlined previously compares the model with more specification against a model with less specification where the latter is a subset of the former. If two radically different models are specified—as when two alternative factor theories exist—there is currently no direct way to test which better fits the data by the confirmatory factor-analytic method. It may well be that both produce a significant decrease in the chi-square compared to that found when no model whatsoever is specified. Each could also have a nonsignificant chi-square at the same time. What this would show would be that both models could legitimately represent the data. Such a result is not uncommon in scientific endeavors where several mathematical models are often equally able to reproduce the data. In factor-analytic terms this is demonstrating that several alternative rotational positions exist for the same set of data, each of which is associated with a different theory. The resolution to this problem is always one of design: a new set of data needs to be collected so that these two theories lead to differential prediction.

Confirmatory factor analysis is powerful because it provides explicit hypothesis testing for factor analytic problems. Exploratory factor analysis should be reserved only for those areas that are truly exploratory, that is, areas where no prior analyses have been conducted. If prior analyses have been conducted, then either those results or a strong theory challenging those results should be used as a hypothesized structure in the new study. **Although the next three chapters are primarily concerned with exploratory factor analyses, the space and time given to that technique is a function of complexity of resolving its problems, not of its theoretical importance. On the contrary, confirmatory factor analysis is the more theoretically important—and should be the much more widely used—of the two major factor analytic approaches.**

7.3.2 Scale Validity Analysis

Confirmatory maximum likelihood analysis can be used for examining the hypothesized validity of a battery of tests. Convergent and discriminant validity can be tested for significance by comparing appropriate hypothesized factor structures.

Convergent validity occurs when several variables deemed to measure the same construct correlate with each other. To test convergent validity, a factor is hypothesized for each of the characteristics being measured by a subset of variables in the analysis. The chi-square resulting from this analysis is subtracted from the chi-square found under the hypothesis of no factors to evaluate whether the hypothesized factor structure representing convergent validity does reproduce the data significantly. This analysis can be further sharpened by running it separately for each of the several constructs that are represented in the subset of tests, either by running that single factor alone to see if it significantly reduces the chi-square as compared to no factors or, perhaps better, by determining whether that factor significantly reduces the chi-square when compared to a model that contains all the other constructs except it. Factor loadings of several variables hypothesized to relate to the construct can also be tested for significance. They could be specified as equal for the one model and the chi-square for that model subtracted from another hypothesized factor structure where they are allowed to vary. If the two differ significantly from each other, then one or more of the variables is more related to the construct than one or more of the other variables. Other variable-factor tests are also possible.

Discriminant validity can also be tested through confirmatory factor analysis. In testing for convergent validity it was assumed that the correlations among the constructs—that is, the factors defined by the variables hypothesized to be related to the constructs—were allowed to be free to vary. Another hypothesized factor structure can be computed but with the qualification that the correlations between one or more of the constructs being tested for discriminant validity is one. The difference between chi-squares from these two models tests whether the constructs have a correlation significantly less than 1.0. If the correlation between the factors for the two constructs is not significantly different from 1.0, the difference chi-square will be insignificant. This means the null hypothesis of no discriminatory validity would be accepted. If the difference chi-square is significant, then the null hypothesis is rejected and the model that assumes discriminatory validity by allowing the correlation to be less than one is the more appropriate one.

The problem of discriminant and convergent validity is more complex if each construct is measured by multiple methods. For example, the degree to which a person holds to certain values may be evaluated by several different methods. The first method could be a self-rating, the second method could be the admiration technique of Scott (1965), and the third could be a rating by friends of the degree to which each person shows the values. Ideally all measures for a particular value would correlate highly regardless of whether people were rating themselves or taking Scott's scales or being rated by others. In practice it often occurs that a set of ratings, for example, may correlate highly among themselves rather than correlating with the other value measures. The classical article on the multitrait multimethod problem is by Campbell and Fiske (1959) but the problem was recognized long before. Cattell, for example, had been conducting analyses of this general type for a decade (Cattell, 1946). He factored for personality characteristics in answers to questionnaires, ratings of a person's behavior by others, and objective tests. The approach used at that time was one of factoring separately within each of the three methods to establish trait factors within methods, and then interrelating those factors across methods. Exploratory factor analyses including data across several methods have not been recommended because factors mixing both trait and method variance were common.

Confirmatory maximum likelihood factor analysis allows new approaches to this continuing problem of multitrait multimethod data. One approach to testing both for factors representing constructs and factors representing methods is to hypothesize a matrix such as that illustrated in Table 7.3.1. In this example there are three constructs being measured, with each construct measured through method A and through method B. Multiple forms are used for each construct for each method to allow an ample number of data points for unique model specification. If all construct factors exist, then the pattern of factor loading should be as given in the first three columns of the table. Ideally, the factor loadings for the three constructs should reproduce the data without methods factors, but methods factors may also be necessary, and are shown as the last two columns in Table 7.3.1. Confirmatory maximum likelihood tests would be as follows:

1. To test if the hypothesized construct factors do reproduce the data, a confirmatory maximum likelihood factor analysis would be computed with only the construct factors and the resulting chi-square subtracted from the chi-square for a model with no factors. If this difference chi-square is significant, then the constructs as hypothesized are appropriate for the data.

2. If the chi-square from the construct factors model is significant, then method factors may exist. Add the method factors to the construct factors for a total of five hypothesized factors, compute the confirmatory maximum likelihood solution, and subtract this chi-square from the chi-square for the hypothesized construct factors only. A significant difference chi-square at this point indicates the method factors are also necessary. If the chi-square test for the hypothesized factors shows no additional significant variance, then there is no methods variance over and above the construct variance and the analysis is complete.

3. Note that methods factors or construct factors could be alternative constructions appropriate for the same set of data. That could be identified by

TABLE 7.3.1
Example of Multitrait Multimethod Factor Matrix

	Factors				
	Content			Methods	
Scales (by methods)	Anxiety	Extra-version	Conscien-tiousness	Question-naires	Ratings
A. *Questionnaires*					
Anxiety, form A	a.	0	0	a.	0
Anxiety, form B	a.	0	0	a.	0
Anxiety, form C	a.	0	0	a.	0
Extroversion, form A	0	a.	0	a.	0
Extroversion, form B	0	a.	0	a.	0
Extroversion, form C	0	a.	0	a.	0
Conscientiousness, form A	0	0	a.	a.	0
Conscientiousness, form B	0	0	a.	a.	0
Conscientiousness, form C	0	0	a.	a.	0
B. *Ratings by Others*					
Anxiety, form A	a.	0	0	0	a.
Anxiety, form B	a.	0	0	0	a.
Anxiety, form C	a.	0	0	0	a.
Extroversion, form A	0	a.	0	0	a.
Extroversion, form B	0	a.	0	0	a.
Extroversion, form C	0	a.	0	0	a.
Conscientiousness, form A	0	0	a.	0	a.
Conscientiousness, form B	0	0	a.	0	a.
Conscientiousness, form C	0	0	a.	0	a.

Notes: Correlations among factors are, in this example, set equal to an identity matrix. "a " identifies loadings left free to vary.

running the confirmatory maximum likelihood solution for only the methods factors and subtracting the resulting chi-square from the chi-square for no factors. If this difference chi-square is significant whereas the chi-square for the methods factors over and above the construct factors is not significant, that suggests the method and construct factors are alternative theoretical positions appropriate to these data.

4. The tests can be expanded to determine if the construct factors add significantly over and above the method factors. This would be the most stringent test of whether the construct factors were indeed necessary to adequately represent the data.

If both construct and method factors, as illustrated in Table 7.3.1, are appropriate, an examination of the loadings in the matrix will suggest whether method factors or construct factors are more important for any particular variable, given this sample. Such an analysis may allow for selecting the least biased variables or for building corrective factors into new versions of the variables.

Example

Kenny (1976) applied confirmatory factor analysis to a multitrait multimethod matrix. The data included four methods of measuring attitudes towards cigarette smoking and towards capital punishment. Several questions were raised, including whether the four attitude methods were measuring the same construct (convergent validity) and whether the two constructs were independent (discriminant validity). The multitrait multimethod question was also raised because four types of instruments were used to measure the two attitudes.

A hypothesized factor matrix was established and can be seen by noting the zeros in Table 7.3.2. All correlations between factors except those reported in the table were set equal to zero.

The construct factors were defined by setting the variables for the other constructs equal to zero. The method factors were defined in a fairly unique manner. Because multiple forms were not indicated, identifying methods factors as in Table 7.3.1 was not possible. Instead, Kenny established a unique factor for each of the variables and then allowed the unique factors to be free to correlate. If the two unique factors from variables using the same method correlated together, then that would be evidence of a method factor. Allowing the unique factors in the solution means that a less-exacting communality estimate is needed.

The results indicate excellent convergent validity because the correlations on the construct factors are quite high and because the chi-square test was not statistically significant, thus suggesting the factors in Table 7.3.2 account for all the significant

TABLE 7.3.2
Multitrait Multimethod Factor Structure: Methods
Factor as Correlations Among Unique Variances

Variables Construct–Method		Trait Factors		Unique Factors							
		Cigarette Smoking	Capital Punishment	U_1	U_5	U_2	U_6	U_3	U_7	U_4	U_8
1. Cigarette	A	.89	0	.45	0	0	0	0	0	0	0
2. Cigarette	B	.85	0	0	0	.53	0	0	0	0	0
3. Cigarette	C	.91	0	0	0	0	0	.40	0	0	0
4. Cigarette	D	.86	0	0	0	0	0	0	0	.51	0
5. Punishment	A	0	.87	0	.48	0	0	0	0	0	0
6. Punishment	B	0	.96	0	0	0	.24	0	0	0	0
7. Punishment	C	0	.72	0	0	0	0	0	.41	0	0
8. Punishment	D	0	.96	0	0	0	0	0	0	0	.33
Factor Correlation		.25		.18		.29		.21		.27	

Note: Zeros indicate a parameter specified as zero in the model. All other intercorrelations among factors were specified as zero. The unusual ordering of the unique factors allows ready presentation of the correlations among unique factors for variables using the same method of measurement. Adapted from Kenny (1976).

variance among the variables (chi-square = 10.35, df = 15). The equality of the factor loadings was tested separately for each of the constructs. First the loadings for the cigarette attitude construct were constrained to be equal, but the difference between chi-squares for this model and the prior model allowing them to be free to vary was not significant so that they can indeed be assumed to be equal (chi-square for the second model = 10.76, df = 18, difference between this and the earlier chi-square = 10.76 − 10.35 = .41, df = 18 − 15 = 3). A similar method was used for the capital punishment factor with the same result.

To test for discriminant validity, the correlation between the two construct factors was set equal to one. The chi-square from this solution was 117.48 (df = 16); subtracting this chi-square from the earlier one gives a resulting chi-square difference of 107.13 (and subtracting their df gives a resulting difference df of 1). This difference chi-square is significant (p < .001), thus leading to rejection of the null hypothesis that the correlation between the two constructs is one. Some discriminant validation is indicated and, because the observed correlation was only .25, it seems reasonably good.

As Kenny notes, the sample size for this analysis was small. This means that it would be difficult to find any chi-square significant. With a greater number of subjects, other factors might have been needed to account for all the significant variance.

7.3.3 Causal Path Analysis

Confirmatory factor analysis relies heavily upon the investigator's theory of how one variable influences or affects another (the term *cause* is used in a very loose and intuitive sense). It is based upon the fact that although correlation does not imply causation any more than an ANOVA significance test implies causation, causation does imply significant correlation. If variable A causes variable B, variables A and B must be correlated in appropriate data. Likewise if variable A causes variable B which in turn causes variable C, then A must correlate with B and B must correlate with C. Interestingly, path analysis shows that variable A must also correlate with variable C, but that partialing B out of the correlation would drop the A–C correlation to zero if the data are consistent with the model. Causal analysis is discussed in detail in Bentler (1980), Bentler and Woodward (1979), and Kenny (1979).

When path analysis proceeds with the observed variables as each being a separate theoretical construct, then regression techniques are sufficient to provide the statistical solution. Often, however, a theoretical construct cannot be uniquely identified with any particular measured variable because measured variables may be biased by method variance or another contaminating factor. Hence investigators often wish to include several measures of the construct and relate these jointly to the other variables. The construct itself is therefore a latent variable rather than an observed, or measured, variable. In this situation confirmatory maximum likelihood factor analysis establishes a factor from the set of measured variables to represent the latent variable. It also establishes factors for other latent variables. The models include measurement error and specific factors as well as common factors (Rock, Werts, Linn, & Jöreskog, 1977). The factors are hypothesized to relate in the appropriate manner as set out by the theoretical model for the paths.

A causal path analysis may become quite complex, and can only be generated when there is a strong theory that defines the relationships quite well. Once latent variables and paths are hypothesized, however, they imply a particular factor structure that can then be tested through confirmatory factor analysis. Again several models are usually compared against each other to determine which is the most effective.

Example

Bentler and Woodward (1978) evaluated Head Start data to determine the effectiveness of the program. The problem in analyzing the effectiveness arose from the fact that children in the comparison group systematically differed from those in the Head Start group on family indices (e.g., mother's education, father's occupation, family income) which are generally associated with more success on the outcome variables (the Illinois Test of Psycholinguistic Abilities and the Metropolitan Readiness Tests).

Two alternative factor models were established. Both models included three factors for the variables reflecting familial indices and one factor for the two dependent variables (to test the overall Head Start effects). The first model contained a further factor defined by a variable scored one if the child was in the Head Start program or zero if not, and the second model left this variable out. If Head Start influenced the scores in addition to influences from family differences, the second model should better reproduce the data and produce a smaller chi-square than the first model. The first model had a chi-square of 8.38 (df =9), the second model had a chi-square of 9.06 (df = 10), for a difference in chi squares of .68 (df = 1) which has a probability level of .5. No Head Start effects could be confirmed in this analysis. Because the chi-square for the first model was also insignificant, all the differences in outcome are explained by the family indices factors.

The advantage of approaching path analysis factor analytically is that it allows for multiple independent variables that overlap conceptually and more than one dependent variable. Use of confirmatory factor analysis in such situations is still new, but it appears quite encouraging. Note that once again factor analysis is blending over into other methods of analysis. In this case it is a strong contender for a hypothesis testing approach for the same data that might be analyzed in an exploratory manner by canonical correlations. Both of these techniques are part of the multivariate general linear model, and such "merging along the edges" is to be expected.

7.4 HYPOTHESIS TESTING BY MAXIMUM LIKELIHOOD AND MULTIPLE-GROUP PROCEDURES

Confirmatory maximum likelihood factor analysis still remains a complex, expensive procedure to use. It is appropriate for complex and difficult problems. For simple problems, however, numerous other procedures are available that provide tests readily understood by a broad audience and hence may be preferred (Gerbing & Hunter, 1980). For example, hypotheses specifying several correlations as equal can be tested (Neill & Dunn, 1975; Steiger, 1979). This can be illustrated by pointing out the relevancy and appropriateness of multiple-group factor analysis for hypothesis testing.

Multiple-group factor analysis (Chapter 5) allows several significance tests of direct interest and importance. First, those variables that are not used to define a particular factor can be tested to determine if they are significantly related to the factor. If it is hypothesized that factor Exvia in one lab is the same as factor Extroversion in another lab, the marker variables for the former are used as the defining variables for a factor and the Extroversion scale of the latter also included; if that scale correlates significantly with the Exvia factor, a relationship is established. The test is the simple two-tailed *t* test for correlations, which is applied to the appropriate element of the factor structure. There are no difficulties or complexities in doing so (the test cannot be applied, however, to those variables used in defining a factor because they are part of the factor score, unless part–whole corrections are made).

If the null hypothesis is that correlations among factor scores are zero, then multiple-group significance testing would be a more elegant procedure than confirmatory factor analysis. One computes correlated multiple-group factors, and tests the correlations among the factors for significance by the ordinary formulas. (Note that *correlated* multiple-group factors is only so named because it allows the factors to be correlated; it does not demand that they be correlated. Uncorrelated factors will occur, on the average, if the factors are uncorrelated in the population.) Further, the matrix of correlations among the factors can also be tested for significance (Chapter 8). The correlation matrix also can be subdivided and the significance test computed on a subset of the variables as well.

The multiple correlation of several multiple-group factors with a variable not used to define any of those factors can be tested, and the multiple correlation of one set of factors with another factor can also be tested. The latter allows the possibility of causal path analysis with multiple dependent variables if the factor structure of those dependent variables is hypothesized in advance. Forms of canonical correlations can be computed for significance testing if the dependent variable factors are extracted as orthogonal (Kerlinger & Pedhazur, 1973, pp. 382–386).

Maximum likelihood confirmatory factor analysis has the advantage of being able to test one full factor-analytic model against another, thus providing broad multivariate tests. It also allows for tests of whether a particular factor is needed in addition to a set of other factors.

If the purpose of the project is to identify where "the factors have gone astray," there is no substitute for examination of the residual matrix in either of the two procedures. Because the residual matrix is more readily computed by the multiple group procedure than by confirmatory maximum likelihood, there is no need to use the complex maximum likelihood analysis unless one of its unique advantages for testing the significance of a residual matrix or for comparing alternative models is needed (Gerbing & Hunter, 1980).

8

Determining the Number of Factors

In the previous chapters, factors have been extracted to a predesignated number. When this number was reached, the analysis was assumed to be complete and further factors were not extracted. Preknowledge of the number of factors desired means the area has either been thoroughly investigated or that one is testing for a hypothesized number of factors. In the latter case of hypothesis testing, it was noted that the probability that significant variance was left after the hypothesized number of factors were extracted is evaluated in maximum likelihood analysis (Chapters 6 and 7).

Most factor analyses reported in the literature appear to have been concerned with exploration rather than hypothesis testing. Not hypothesizing a specific number of factors gives rise to the question of the ''proper'' number of factors to be extracted from a correlation matrix. In the search for new ways to conceptualize a domain, investigators have used objective procedures to determine the number of factors that they should extract. These procedures are based upon the characteristics of the data itself rather than upon knowledge of the area or a set of hypotheses.

This chapter begins with a discussion of how the adequacy of a given number of factors is evaluated in the component and common factor models (Section 8.1). The discussion then proceeds into three categories of methods used to estimate the correct number of factors. First, a statistical approach is recommended and the resulting procedures are summarized in Section 8.2. Second, in Section 8.3 procedures developed from a mathematical approach are summarized. In theory, the correlation coefficients are assumed to be population parameters and the minimum number of factors that could be used to reproduce the data are sought. In practice, all factors of interest are assumed to be statistically

142

significant. The procedures of Section 8.3 should therefore be used after the factors have been found to be statistically significant.

Third, the procedures of Section 8.4 are attempts to extract those factors that account for nontrivial variance and eliminate factors accounting for such small portions of the variance as to be uninteresting in a particular research setting. The concluding comments, Section 8.5, contain an overall perspective on the number-of-factors problem with suggestions on how the three approaches to the number of factors can be most effectively utilized in a particular situation.

8.1   ADEQUACY OF THE FIT OF THE MODEL TO THE DATA

The accuracy with which the data matrix can be reproduced from the factor pattern and factor scores is primarily a function of the number of factors extracted. If there is insufficient accuracy with a certain number of factors, another factor can be extracted and the accuracy must increase. As will be shown in Section 8.3, perfect reproduction of the original variables and their correlations can always be obtained by extracting enough factors. However, such cases are usually trivial because they require extracting as many factors as there are variables in the analysis. The major use of factor analysis is to find a limited number of factors that will contain the maximum amount of information.

To determine how closely the goal of perfect reproduction has been approximated, the adequacy of reproducing the correlations from a given number of factors is evaluated (Section 8.1.1). If there is too much inaccuracy in the solution, another factor is extracted and the accuracy is reevaluated. The accuracy of reproducing the correlations is related to the factor-analytical model being used (Section 8.1.2).

8.1.1 Evaluating the Adequacy of the Factors

Regardless of whether a hypothesized number of factors or an arbitrary number has been extracted as a first guess in searching for the proper number of factors, the adequacy of the reproduction of the correlations can be evaluated to determine if one or more additional factors should be extracted. Checking the adequacy of the reproduced correlations is easier than checking the adequacy of reproducing the variable scores, and both checks are closely related. The factors already extracted are first used to reproduce the correlation matrix by the appropriate formula [e.g., Eq. (3.4.5)]. The reproduced correlation matrix is then subtracted from the original correlation matrix to give the residual matrix.

An error often made is to interpret the elements of the residual matrix as correlations. Despite the fact that the off-diagonal elements look like correlations, they are actually covariances. Residual covariances usually appear small (e.g., .1) but often represent partial correlations that are quite high (e.g., the previous .1 could be a partial correlation of .7) and therefore cannot be interpreted as one would a correlation.

The covariances in the residual matrix are examined. If they are sufficiently small, then that set of factors is adequate and another factor is not needed. If there are numerous moderate covariances or if a subsection of the matrix has several high covariances, at least one more factor is extracted.

Example

After the extraction of principal components from the box correlations, the residuals were calculated. These are given in Table 8.1.1 with the first component's residuals in the lower half of the matrix and the residuals after three components had been extracted in the upper half. The residual covariances were calculated by subtracting the reproduced correlations from the original matrix with unities in the diagonal. An examination of the lower half shows some covariance remaining. The residuals range from $-.18$ to $.40$. Comparing the larger elements with their counterparts in the upper half of the matrix after the extraction of the additional components shows a reduction in their magnitude. The residuals now range from $-.08$ to $.13$. The covariance left after three components have been extracted is probably not worth further analysis.

The residuals after the first factor do not appear large because they are covariances. Several partial correlations for this residual matrix are actually over .8.

One simple statistic for the adequacy of reproducing the correlations is the mean of the absolute values of the residuals. As the accuracy of reproduction of the correlation coefficients increases, this mean decreases. Also, the standard deviation of the absolute values of the residuals provides useful information. If the standard deviation is relatively high, even though the mean is low, this suggests the residuals are not uniformly low. Instead, a subset of variables still warrants another factor. Actual examination of the residuals, their means, and standard deviations has been replaced by procedures that do not require the actual computation of residuals.

8.1.2 Evaluating Adequacy for Component and Common Factor Models[1]

In the component model each variable is to be reproduced in its totality and all its variance accounted for. **Thus, the diagonal elements of the correlation matrix, which are the variances of the variables, are as important in determining the adequacy of the fit of the component model as are the off-diagonal**

---

[1]The correlated and uncorrelated versions of each model reproduce the correlation matrix with the same accuracy. (The equality of reproduction by correlated and uncorrelated models becomes more apparent in Chapter 9, where rotation is discussed.) Therefore, only the distinctions between the component and common factor models is discussed here.

TABLE 8.1.1
Residual Covariance Matrices after Principal
Components Have Been Extracted From the Box
Correlations

	1	2	3	4	5	6	7	8	9	10
1	05 26	03	−03	−03	02	−02	−03	−02	−02	05
2	−11	04 25	−03	−02	02	−02	01	−06	−01	05
3	−18	−01	07 25	03	−04	02	01	03	01	−08
4	05	−12	02	04 09	−02	01	−01	03	01	−05
5	08	03	−14	−03	03 09	−01	−01	−02	−01	05
6	−13	07	09	−03	−04	02 08	02	−00	01	−03
7	07	−06	−07	03	02	−03	09 14	−07	00	−02
8	−02	−01	−01	01	00	01	−07	13 15	00	−04
9	06	−05	−07	02	03	−03	04	01	02 06	−02
10	−10	02	15	−04	−08	03	−10	−10	−11	10 40

Note: The lower half gives the residual variance–covariances after one component had been extracted; the upper half gives the residuals after three components were removed. Decimals have been omitted.

elements. But the concept of an exact fit in the component model is a concept referring to the underlying population. In actual data, the investigator would not be discouraged by some error in reproducing the correlations because he has access only to a sample from the population. Usually, fewer factors than variables are extracted, and the resulting inaccuracies in the reproduced correlation matrix are allowed as error in the model.

In the common factor model no attempt is made to reproduce the total variance of the original variables. Instead, it is assumed that the original variables contain some unique variance that could be either from variance that does not overlap with the other variables or from random error such as that introduced by fallible measurement. As was noted in Eq. (3.5.7), unique variance affects only the diagonal elements of the population correlation matrix. **The adequacy of the fit of the common factor model is a function of the reproduction of the off-diagonal elements; the diagonal elements are adjusted as necessary to maximize the accuracy of the off-diagonal reproduction.** All communality estimation procedures are in this category. The proper residual matrix for a common factor solution is found by subtracting the reproduced correlation matrix from the correlation matrix after communality estimates have replaced the unities in the diagonal.

Example

The difference in how the component and common factor models reproduce the correlation matrix can be illustrated by the residual covariances given in Table 8.1.2. The upper half of the matrix gives the residuals after two principal components have been extracted from the matrix. The lower half of the matrix gives the residuals after two principal axis factors have been extracted from a matrix where the squared multiple correlations were used as the initial communality estimates with the solution then being iterated twice. The principal axis diagonal residuals are not included because they are a function of the number of times a solution is iterated; they can be reduced to almost any desired value by iterating more.

TABLE 8.1.2
Component and Common Factor Residual
Covariance Matrix for Six Personality Variables

	1	2	3	4	5	6
1	.27	−.09	−.21	.00	.02	−.00
2	.04	.22	−.17	.04	.03	.01
3	−.01	.02	.43	−.04	−.08	.03
4	.00	.04	−.04	.34	.20	.16
5	.02	.03	−.08	−.01	.43	−.20
6	−.02	−.00	.01	−.04	.01	.36

Note: The residuals after two principal component factors have been extracted are given above the diagonal; the residuals after two common factors have been extracted are given below the diagonals.

An examination of Table 8.1.2 shows that the principal component solution allows off-diagonal residuals of .2 so as to better reproduce the diagonal unities. The common factor solution is better able to reproduce the off-diagonal elements with the same number of factors because it is not concerned with the diagonal unities.

It should be noted that this case was picked for its illustrative value. Not only are the number of variables quite limited—which gives more importance to the diagonal elements as compared to the off-diagonals—but the off-diagonal elements were only moderate. If there had been a larger number of variables or if the communalities had been high, the residuals from the two procedures would have been more alike.

The common factor approach differs from the component model in another aspect vital to evaluating the accuracy with which the correlations are reproduced. Noncommon factor variance was explicitly included in the common factor model. In deriving the relationship between the correlated common factors and the correlation matrix, (3.5.6) was used as an intermediate step. This equation is as follows:

$$R_{vv} = P_{vf}\, R_{ff}\, P'_{fv} + D_{vv}\, R_{uf}\, P'_{fv} + P_{vf}\, R'_{fu}\, D'_{vv} + D_{vv}\, R_{uu}\, D'_{vv} \qquad (8.1.1)$$

The derivation then proceeded by assuming the correlations between the unique and common factors, R_{uf}, were all zero and that the correlations among the unique factors, R_{uu}, formed an identity matrix. As a result of these assumptions, the original correlation matrix with unities in the diagonal could be reproduced from the factor pattern, correlations among factors, and a diagonal matrix of the uniquenesses for each variable (U_{vv}).

The assumptions for simplifying Eq. (8.1.1) concern the population; they will never be true in any given sample. Instead, the elements of R_{uf} and the off-diagonal elements of R_{uu} will depart from zero by chance. The more they depart from zero, the less likely the model will fit the data. Because the standard error of a correlation is a function of the sample size, **larger samples will usually lead to clearer indications of the number of factors when the common factor model is appropriate** and the number of factors is actually less than the number of variables. With smaller samples, sampling errors will be more influential and thus limit the clarity of a solution.

However, the reduction of R_{uf} to a zero matrix and R_{uu} to an identity matrix interacts with the unique factors. Each matrix that is assumed to have zero correlations is multiplied by the diagonal matrix of unique weights, D_{vv}, and so the error introduced varies with the height of communalities regardless of the sample size. Where the communalities are low, the random correlations are given more weight. If communalities are high, however, R_{uf} and R_{uu} are multiplied by a virtually null matrix and their effect is less. Naturally, if the uniquenesses are all 0, the result would be the same as if one had originally started with the component model. **Therefore, high communality situations can be expected to contain less error not included in the model and the number of factors may be easier to estimate accurately.**

8.2   STATISTICAL APPROACHES TO THE NUMBER OF FACTORS

In the statistical procedure for determining the number of factors to extract, the following question is asked: Is the residual matrix after f factors have been extracted statistically significant? If there is statistically significant variance left, then at least one more factor could be extracted with some assurance that non-chance variance is being processed. If there is no significant variance, then the correct number of factors has already been extracted. The number of factors is found in exploratory analyses by sequentially testing the residuals until one is found to be insignificant. Note that when the significance is determined by testing the residual matrix, the probability procedures are reversed from the usual interpretation; that is, if the statistic is significant at beyond the .05 level, then the number of factors is insufficient to totally explain the reliable variance. If the statistic is nonsignificant, then the hypothesized number of factors is correct.

In statistical tests of the number of factors, the variables are assumed to have a multivariate normal distribution. Although moderate departures will probably leave the test relatively unaffected, large departures from multivariate normal distributions restrict the use of statistical tests.

Aside from advocates of the maximum likelihood procedures, the significance testing approach is not widely used. Several criticisms of it can be made. One serious objection is that it is too dependent upon sample size. If thousands of subjects were included, even the most trivial and uninterpretable factors would be highly significant. Another problem is that a line cannot be simply drawn designating all factors on one side of it as nonerror and those on the other as error. Occasionally, an error factor may occur in the midst of moderate-size substantive factors. At other times, a small but valuable substantive factor may occur over the line into the nonsignificant categories. Still another problem with statistical tests for the number of factors is that research hypotheses generally say that the predicted factors will occur but do not exclude the possibility of un-known factors also being present, a condition that these tests do not cover. Finally, some of the significance tests are not accurate. For these reasons, psy-chometrically oriented factor analysts prefer to have a large number of subjects and then to assume statistical significance of the resulting factors. A "large number" is usually defined as five or ten times the number of variables but not less than several hundred. If fewer individuals are used, statistical tests are absolutely necessary.

The discussion is begun by considering whether or not any factors should be extracted by any method from the original correlation matrix (Section 8.2.1). Procedures available for principal component (Section 8.2.2), maximum likeli-hood (Section 8.2.3), and common factor (Section 8.2.4) methods of extraction are then discussed.

8.2.1 Testing the Correlation Matrix for Significance

As several studies illustrate (Armstrong & Soelberg, 1968; Horn, 1967; Humphreys & Ilgen, 1969), random data often give results that can be interpreted. They generally factored correlations among random variables with randomly assigned labels and found interpretable factors. For this reason, the correlation matrix should always be tested for significance. Computer programs should include this check automatically; if it is not included, then the investigator should run it whenever there is *any* doubt about the possible significance of his matrix.

Bartlett (1950) has presented a chi-square test of the significance of a correlation matrix with unities as diagonal elements that is widely recommended. The equation is:

$$\chi^2 = -\left(n - 1 - \frac{2v + 5}{6} \right) \text{Log}_e \, | \, R_{vv} \, | \qquad (8.2.1)$$

where $|R_{vv}|$ is the determinant of the correlation matrix. The degrees of freedom are:

$$df = v \, \frac{v - 1}{2} \, . \qquad (8.2.2)$$

The determinant of a correlation matrix is the most difficult part of the equation to evaluate. If the characteristic roots of the correlation matrix with unities as diagonal elements are available from the factoring process, the determinant can be calculated by multiplying all the characteristic roots together:

$$|R_{vv}| = c_1 c_2 c_3 \ldots c_v \qquad (8.2.3)$$

where c_v is the last characteristic root of the matrix. Note that the test is not appropriate if any characteristic root is zero or negative.

Example

The ability correlations can be tested for significance. The necessary characteristic roots are given later in Table 8.3.1. The first step in applying Bartlett's test is to evaluate the determinant by Eq. (8.2.3). The result is 0.00001043. Such small determinants are to be expected from real data; the smaller the determinant, the more likely the matrix will prove to be significant. The $\log_e$ of the determinant is then -11.4137, and the chi-square can be computed by Eq. (8.2.1):

$$\chi^2 = -\left(145 - 1 - \frac{2(24) + 5}{6} \right)(-11.4137)$$

$$= -\left(144 - \frac{53}{6} \right)(-11.4137)$$

$$= (144 - 8.8333)\,(11.4137)$$

$$= 135.1667 \ (11.4137)$$

$$= 1543.$$

The degrees of freedom are given by (8.2.2):

$$df = 24 \ \frac{(24 - 1)}{2}$$

$$= 12 \cdot 23$$

$$= 276.$$

Because chi-square tables seldom list this large a df, the chi-square can be transformed to a t (Guilford, 1965a, p. 582). The t is 31 and is highly significant. The matrix can be legitimately factored.

Two empirical studies (Knapp & Swoyer, 1967; Tobias & Carlson, 1969) have examined the efficacy of Bartlett's test for the significance of a correlation matrix. Both agree that it appears to function as expected with empirical data. Indeed, the results suggest it is a relatively powerful test. For example, with only 20 individuals and 10 variables, the average population intercorrelation need only be .36 for virtually all sample correlation matrices to produce a significant chi-square by this test. With large samples, even trivial correlations could produce a significant result.

8.2.2 The Significance of Principal Components

In addition to providing a test of significance for the correlation matrix based on the characteristic roots, Bartlett (1950) also gave a significance test of the residuals after a given number of factors had been extracted. Like the former test, this test can be calculated solely from the characteristic roots of the correlation matrix with unities as the diagonal elements. It does require that the roots removed correspond to well-determined characteristic roots.

Bartlett's chi-square is given by:

$$\chi^2 = - \left(n - 1 - \frac{2v + 5}{6} - \frac{2f}{3} \right) \ \mathrm{Log}_e \ r_f \tag{8.2.4}$$

where n is the number of individuals and r_f is defined as follows:

$$r_f = | \, R_{vv} \, | \Bigg/ \left[c_1 \, c_2 \cdots c_f \left(\frac{v - c_1 - c_2 \cdots - c_f}{v - f} \right)^{v-f} \right]. \tag{8.2.5}$$

In both of the preceding equations, f refers to the number of factors already extracted. The number of degrees of freedom for this test of significance (Bartlett, 1951) is:

$$df = (v - f - 1) \ (v - f + 2)/2 \tag{8.2.6}$$

Because Bartlett's test of significance involves only the characteristc roots, it is easily included in a principal component computer program. The chi-square value is definitely influenced by the number of significant digits used; both correlations and roots need to be entered with at least four significant digits beyond the decimal place, and the calculations should be programed as "double precision."

Example

Table 8.2.1 contains the results of applying Bartlett's significance test for the number of factors to both the box and the physique data. Chi-squares are used when the df is 30 or less, but these are converted to t's when the df is greater than 30.

To illustrate the calculation of the entries in the Table, we shall consider the third residual matrix of the box problem more carefully. Note that the question asked is whether the residual matrix contains significant variance.

First, r_f is calculated by Eq. (8.2.5):

$$r_3 = .000000000303 \Big/ \left[8.224 \cdot 0.776 \cdot 0.392 \left(\frac{10 - 8.224 - .776 - .392}{10 - 3} \right)^{10-3} \right]$$

$$= .000000000303 \Big/ \left[2.502 \left(\frac{.608}{7} \right)^7 \right]$$

$$= .000000000303 \ / \ [2.502 \ (.0000000373)]$$

$$= \frac{.000000000303}{.00000000933} = .00325.$$

TABLE 8.2.1
Bartlett's Significance Test of Box and Physique Data

No. of Factors Already Extracted	Box Data		Physique Data	
	df^a	t or Chi-Square	df^a	t or Chi-Square
0	45	55.0	66	51.2
1	44	32.8	65	39.3
2	35^a	28.2	54	36.6
3	27	531.8	44	35.4
4	20	343.9	35^a	33.7
5	14	115.6	27	758.1
6	9	65.2	20	643.9
7	5	48.7	14	536.4
8	2	37.1	9	352.5
9	0	—	5	197.0
10	—	—	2	79.9
11	—	—	0	—
12	—	—	—	—

[a] t is used whenever the $df > 30$ by the formula $t = \sqrt{2\chi^2} - \sqrt{2\,df} - 1$. df's for the first line are calculated by Eq. (8.2.2). All tests are significant ($p < .001$).

Note: These results were calculated with 6 digit precision.

The $\log_e$ of r_3 is -5.73 and is substituted into Eq. (8.2.4):

$$\chi^2 = -\left(99 - \frac{2.10 + 5}{6} - \frac{2 \cdot 3}{3}\right)(-5.73)$$

$$\chi^2 = -(99 - 4.167 - 2)(-5.73)$$

$$\chi^2 = 92.833 \cdot 5.73$$

$$\chi^2 = 532.$$

with $df = \dfrac{(10 - 3 - 1)(10 - 3 + 2)}{2}$, or 27, by Eq. (8.2.6).

An examination of Table 8.2.1 suggests that the data are extremely good; as many factors as desired could be extracted and they all would be from matrices with significant variance. A complete component solution would need virtually as many factors as variables.

With so many factors significant in the box and physique data, one could question the value of the test as an aid in determining the number of factors. Certainly factor 8 of the box problem, for example, would be trivial and impossible to adequately interpret. Fortunately, the test does not always indicate that all possible factors are significant. For example, the second factor from the personality variables is extracted from significant variance, but the residual matrix after that factor has a probability greater than .05 of occurring by chance.

The traditional Bartlett's significance test is a test only of the residuals, not of the factor extracted. Using the fact that chi-squares and their degrees of freedom are both additive allows a more direct test of each factor: subtract the chi-square of the residual after the factor is extracted from the chi-square immediately before that factor is extracted and look up the resulting chi-square difference in the chi-square table with the degrees of freedom being the difference between the two degrees of freedom. Applying the test of individual roots for significance to Table 8.2.1 indicates, again, that all factors are significant in these rather strong data, but the significance level is only .01 for the last two factors for the box problem. Zak (1979) gives an example of this test with personality data.

Bartlett (1950) reported that the principal component solution can produce a factor with only one variable loading it when that variable correlates virtually zero with all the other variables in the matrix. Also, in an analysis of several hundred variables, Bartlett's test can artifactually show all factors to be significant. All factors will be reported significant when the estimate of the determinant is near zero, an estimate that may occur falsely if the calculation is not sufficiently precise and the last 50 or so roots are all less than .5.

8.2.3 Test of Significance in Maximum Likelihood Analysis

Lawley (1940) derived the formula for testing the significance of the residuals in the maximum likelihood procedure. He assumed that the variables have a multivariate normal distribution and that maximum likelihood estimates of the factor loadings have been used. These estimates must be from data where no two factors have the identical root and where the number of iterations is adequate; otherwise, negative chi-squares may result. His derivation is based on the fact that the elements of the sample covariance matrix follow a Wishart distribution because the variables are normally distributed. Although the discussion of his test usually centers on the correlation matrix, the derivations are actually for the more general case of covariance matrices.

The formula used to calculate the approximate chi-square is given in many varieties. Lawley and Maxwell [1963, Eq. (7.15)] give the following:

$$\chi^2 = n - 1 \left(\text{Log}_e \frac{|\hat{C}_{vv}|}{|C_{vv}|} \right)$$
(8.2.7)

where C_{vv} refers to the observed correlation or covariance matrix that is being analyzed and $\hat{C}_{vv}$ is the reproduced covariance/correlation matrix after the hypothesized number of factors has been extracted. The number of degrees of freedom for the chi-square is:

$$\text{df} = \frac{(v - f)(v - f + 1)}{2}$$
(8.2.8)

The test can be used in either confirmatory or exploratory analyses. In the former case, it is hypothesized that a given set of factors exhausts all of the significant variance in the matrix. The hypothesized factors are then extracted and their residuals tested for significance. In the latter case, each residual is tested after each additional factor is extracted. The process of extracting a factor and testing the next residual continues until a nonsignificant residual is noted. The number of factors already extracted is then designated as the proper number.

The application of maximum likelihood significance tests to exploratory factor analyses can be considered only an approximation procedure. The significance test logic was established for the case where a given number of factors is hypothesized and one significance test computed, not for the case where a series of significance tests is computed. The latter is rather like computing multiple t tests and allows one to capitalize on chance. Use of maximum likelihood significance tests in exploratory factor analysis can therefore be expected to label some insignificant factors significant, but not vice versa.

Whether or not the maximum likelihood test indicates the correct number of factors is a matter of some debate. For example, Browne (1968a) found that it generally produced the correct number of factors, although with small sample sizes it would occasionally underestimate the number of factors. As the sample size increased, the test became more accurate and the small latent roots became very small indeed. This does point out that an increase in the number of subjects may not simply give more significant factors; it may also give more accurate estimates of very small roots that continue to be nonsignificant as the sample size increases. Linn's (1968) Monte Carlo study gave results that were not as favorable for the maximum likelihood test of significance. With 20 variables and 100 to 500 subjects, the maximum likelihood procedure underestimated the number of factors in two samples, estimated it correctly in one, and overestimated in the remaining five. When Harris and Harris (1971) compared the maximum likelihood estimates of the number of factors with other procedures, they found it occasionally gave an exceptionally large estimate of the number of factors (e.g., twice as many), as found by Schönemann and Wang (1972). In the component case it does have reasonable power to identify a factor (Geweke & Singleton, 1980) but not with the lower communalities associated with truncated components and common factor models (Schönemann, 1981).

Nevertheless, the maximum likelihood test of significance for the number of factors to extract is the best statistical procedure currently available. It would appear to give an *upper* bound to the number of factors that could legitimately be extracted from any matrix.

8.2.4 Other Common Factor Tests of Significance

Because Bartlett's test of residuals is easily computed, the question arises as to its possible usefulness for determining the number of common factors to extract. It would be calculated from the characteristic roots of the correlation matrix with unities as the diagonal elements. However, because the test finds both common factors and specifics significant, it gives too many factors (Gorsuch, 1973a). For common factor analysis, the test could only be used to establish an upper bound. If the next residual matrix is nonsignificant by Bartlett's test, it would certainly be nonsignificant by any test that checked only for common factors. Zwick and Velicer (1980) found it accurate with a clear number of factors so long as N was definitely greater than v.

Lawley (1955) has generalized his maximum likelihood test of significance to the case of centroid factors and arrived at the same formula as Rippe (1953). However, Browne (1968a) tested this statistic for both the principal axes with iterated communalities and centroid solutions. His results indicated that it usually grossly overestimates the chi-square that would be given if the maximum likelihood procedure were to be used with the same data, as does Jöreskog's (1962) test of a matrix with squared multiple correlations in the diagonal (Browne, 1968b).

In summary, the empirical studies suggest that **any of the common factor statistical tests can be used provided one remembers that they are unidirectional indicators. If the residuals are insignificant, they will be insignificant by any better test as well. If the residuals are significant, they could still be nonsignificant by a more accurate test.**

A relatively untried procedure for estimating the significance of the residual matrix after a number of common factors has been extracted has been given by Sokal (1959). His procedure is a conceptually simple one. The residual matrix has its elements converted to partial correlations (i.e., each residual is converted so that it represents the correlation between any two variables under consideration with the factors already extracted partialed out). Using tables of the significance level of ordinary partial correlation coefficients, the number of significant residuals in the off-diagonals of the matrix are then counted. If the number appears to be more than could happen by chance—where, unfortunately, the number that could happen by chance cannot yet be computed exactly—it is assumed that at least one more factor is significant. Sokal presents some simplified procedures for calculating this test when a computer is not available. It does have the disadvantages that the residual matrices must actually be calculated at each step and that empirical analyses of its usefulness have yet to be done.

Sokal's procedure could be applied to any procedure for extracting factors and would be particularly appropriate in the case of diagonal and multiple group factors defined by hypotheses. In these two cases, the test of any given residual converted to a partial correlation coefficient is an exact one. In the several cases on which Sokal tried this procedure, including two plasmodes, the results were encouraging.

Another relatively untried procedure based upon converting the residuals to partial correlations is given by Velicer (1976). He creates an index based on squared partial correlations of the residual matrix. The value of this index is computed after each factor is extracted, and the number of factors is that value that minimizes the index. The rationale is based upon the fact that when one moves from a common factor with most variables loaded on it to a specific with only one or two variables loaded on it, some partial correlations actually begin increasing in the residual matrix. The index is computed from a components analysis, but may have some relevance for common factor analysis as well. It needs to be tested closely in a variety of situations because these same arguments suggesting the partial correlation will increase for a specific component also suggest that the index may increase for factors that are still common factors but only have a few loadings on them; thus the index may underestimate the number of factors commonly deemed acceptable, except in cases of very clear data for which it has worked appropriately (Zwick & Velicer, personal communications).

Another promising approach is to compare the observed characteristic roots with characteristic roots found by factoring randomly based matrices of the same order. The average roots from random data show the distribution of roots where no factors existed (Horn, 1965b; Humphreys & Ilgen, 1969). The recommended decision rule for the number of factors that can be deemed significant is to accept any factor with a root that accounts for more variance than the same root does in the random data. If the average roots from random data are plotted on the same graph as roots from the observed data and the observed data are based upon significant variance, the first roots of the real data will be considerably larger than the initial roots from random data. The graphs of roots will eventually cross. The crossing point determines the number of factors. Humphreys and Ilgen

(1969) report that the procedure gives a result similar to maximum likelihood significance tests.

Montanelli and Humphreys (1976) present an equation by which the average roots from factoring a large number of random matrices can be predicted with multiple correlations greater than .99. Use of their equation means it is unnecessary to generate a hundred or so random matrices to find the average roots. Use of their equation does require factoring the correlation matrix with squared multiple correlations as the diagonals, and hence it is solely a common factor procedure. As with any statistical procedure, it can be considered an upper bound for the number of factors to extract; applying their procedure to the physique data indicated that all factors that could possibly be tested by this procedure would be deemed significant even though few investigators would extract so many.

The Montanelli and Humphreys equation should only be applied after Bartlett's significance test has been computed on the correlation matrix itself. For if the correlation matrix is truly random, then the odds are 50/50 that the first root will be higher than the root given by the equation.

8.3   MATHEMATICAL APPROACHES TO THE NUMBER OF FACTORS

The mathematical approach to the number of factors is concerned with the number of factors for a particular sample of variables in the population and not concerned with samples of individuals. The theories are all based on a population correlation matrix, but the resulting procedures can be applied to an observed correlation matrix. The estimate of the number of factors for that particular matrix is used as an estimation of the number of factors in the underlying population. The upper bound to the number of factors that could be accepted would be given by tests of statistical significance.

Mathematically, the number of factors underlying any given correlation matrix is a function of its rank (Section *8.3.1). **Estimating the minimum rank of the correlation matrix is the same as estimating the number of factors.** Estimation procedures are discussed in Section 8.3.2.

*8.3.1 Rank of a Matrix

The matrix algebra concept of the rank of a matrix is a generalized concept that can be applied to any matrix. When it is applied to a correlation matrix, the question becomes identical to that of the number of factors necessary to reproduce the matrix. However, a consideration of the more general case provides useful background.

Any matrix can be expressed as the product of two other matrices. In factor-analytic research, the following are examples of such matrices:

$$Z_{nv} = F_{nf} P'_{fv};$$
$$R_{vv} = P_{vf} P'_{fv};$$
$$R_{vv} = S_{vf} P'_{fv}.$$

(8.3.1)

The first equation simply expresses the fact that the reproduced scores are a function of the factor scores and the factor pattern. The other two equations give two ways of computing the correlation matrix, with the first applicable to uncorrelated factors and the second applicable to correlated factors. Both Z_{nv} and R_{vv} are the product of two other matrices.

Are there exceptions to the rule that any matrix can be expressed as the product of two other matrices? No, when it is realized that one of these matrices can be the identity matrix. The following equation is a general one that shows that every matrix can be considered to be the product of two matrices:

$$A_{jj} = A_{jj} I_{jj}$$

(8.3.2)

Although this is a trivial case, it does point out the generality of the statement.

The **rank** of the matrix is the *smallest common order* of any of the possible pairs of matrices that will yield the original matrix when multiplied together. (The "common order" is the subscript that two matrices being multiplied together have in common.) The common order in each of the three equations given in Eq. (8.3.1) is f. In Eq. (8.3.2), the common order is j. Assuming that no other matrices with a smaller common order can be found to reproduce Z, R, or A, the rank of both Z and R is f and the rank of matrix A is j. Because the number of factors is the common order in the equations [Eq. (8.3.1)], the number of factors is the same as the rank. This is fitting: the search for the number of factors is a search for the smallest number of dimensions that can reproduce the data.

The rank of the matrix may be defined in many ways. It is often defined as the largest order of a nonvanishing minor determinant of the matrix, or it can be defined as the minimum number of dimensions needed to portray the matrix in hyperspace. Still another possible approach to defining the rank of a matrix is to call it the number of positive, nonzero characteristic roots of the correlation matrix. The variety of ways in which the rank of a matrix could be defined underscores the mathematical importance of the concept. For the present purpose, the simple equivalence of the rank of the matrix to the smallest common order of any of the possible factor matrices of the original matrix is useful because the rank is then obviously identical to the number of factors.

The maximum possible rank of a matrix is always its smallest order. This can be shown by utilizing an identity matrix. Assume that a given set of variables cannot be reduced to a smaller number of factors. The set of variables can, however, be expressed as a product of a "factor score" matrix, which is identical to the original score matrix, and an identity matrix used for the factor pattern. The result is:

$$Z_{nv} = F_{nv} I_{vv} \tag{8.3.3}$$

In Eq. (8.3.3) n is greater than v. If it were not, then the following equation would be used:

$$Z_{nv} = I_{nn} F_{nv} \tag{8.3.4}$$

Because the rank is defined as the smallest common order of any of the possible factor matrices, one would choose Eq. (8.3.4) over Eq. (8.3.3) whenever n is less than v. The maximum number of factors underlying the data matrix is the number of individuals or variables, whichever is less.

The rank of a matrix may be smaller than its smallest order. One such case occurs whenever some of the variables are linear functions of other variables. Then, the variables that are linearly dependent can be expressed in the following form:

$$Z_{nv} = Z_{ng} W_{gv} \tag{8.3.5}$$

where Z_{nv} is the total data matrix with linearly dependent variables, Z_{ng} is a matrix of nonlinearly dependent variables with g less than v, and W_{gv} is the weight (or transformation) matrix necessary to change Z_{ng} into Z_{nv}. Note that some columns of W would probably be composed of a single element with 1.0 in it and with all other elements 0 (i.e., some of the variables in Z_{ng} may not necessarily be altered).

With linearly dependent variables, Z_{nv} is a function of two matrices. The rank of Z_{nv} must therefore be equal to or less than the smallest common order of those two matrices, g. Because it was assumed that g was less than v, and that g is the number of nonlinearly dependent variables, the maximum rank is g.

If variable C is defined as $A + B$ or $.5A + 36B$ and is added to an analysis, the number of variables will be increased but not the number of factors. Indeed, because the resulting correlation matrix will have a rank less than its order, its determinant will necessarily be zero and it will have at least one nonpositive characteristic root. Although linearly dependent variables and factors may occasionally be of interest, the usual concern is only for the linearly independent variables. In many calculation procedures it is assumed that all variables are linearly independent.

Example

In the physique data Rees originally collected, several variables were redundant. One or two were defined in a linearly dependent manner. For example, suprasternal height is the height of a person at his shoulder and is composed of symphysis height (measured from the floor to the pelvis) and trunk length (measured from the pelvis to the shoulder).

All three height measures were included in the original analysis. In addition, several variables were so closely related to a set of other variables that they were perfectly predictable. Chest circumference at inspiration was such a variable because, in this female sample, it correlated highly with other statistics.

When these two linearly dependent variables were added to the original dozen analyzed in this book, the factor solution was affected. The rotated principal components were still recognizable but the factor that was defined by, for example, symphysis height shifted from the impact of adding suprasternal height so that it became the definition of that latter variable. After the addition of these two redundant variables, the correlations between the factors were reduced in the promax rotated solution. The reduction was sufficient to reduce the possibility that the higher order general factor (cf. Chapter 11) would be noticed.

The correlation matrix had nonpositive roots and its inverse did not exist. Therefore, some calculation procedures produced ridiculous results. For example, loadings over 2.0 were obtained for the image factors because of the linearly dependent variables.

The rank of a correlation matrix is the same as the rank of the data matrix underlying it. This can be illustrated by the following decomposition of the correlation matrix:

$$R_{vv} = Z'_{vn} Z_{nv} \, n^{-1} \qquad (8.3.6)$$

where the data matrices are in standard score form. The scalar does not affect the rank since it is another way of expressing a v by v diagonal matrix. If the rank of the data matrix is f, which is defined as being equal to or less than v or n, then the data matrix can be expressed as the product of the factor score and factor pattern matrices:

$$Z_{nv} = F_{nf} P'_{fv} \qquad (8.3.7)$$

The rank of the data matrix is therefore f. From the derivations given previously, it then follows that:

$$R_{vv} = S_{vf} P'_{fv} \qquad (8.3.8)$$

Because the smallest common order of Eq. (8.3.8) is the same as the rank of the raw data matrix, the rank of the correlation matrix is the same as that of the data matrix.

The rank of the data or covariance or correlation matrix is almost always equal to the number of variables when linear composites are avoided. Almost every variable has variance that does not overlap with the other variables; if they did completely overlap, some of the variables would probably be dropped. In addition, each variable is usually measured imperfectly and therefore has a component of random error. The random error component will guarantee that each variable adds to the rank of the matrix. In mathematical terms, the correlation matrix is therefore *real* (i.e., all the elements are real numbers), *Gramian* (i.e., it can be expressed as the product-moment of another matrix), and *non-*

singular (i.e., it has a rank equal to its order). Such a matrix has the following properties: (1) its determinant is greater than zero; (2) an inverse exists; (3) all its characteristic roots are positive; and (4) a real nonsingular matrix P exists such that $R = P P'$.

Because a correlation matrix can be assumed to be nonsingular until proven otherwise, a component analysis is generally of a matrix whose rank is equal to its order. Therefore, full component analysis is technically incomplete until it has extracted as many factors as there are variables.

Common factor analysis, however, alters the diagonals. With the alteration of the diagonals, the rank of the matrix may be reduced. If this is so, then the number of factors is necessarily less than the number of variables. The resulting solution will be more parsimonious because it has fewer factors accounting for the important elements of the correlation matrix (i.e., the correlations among the variables). Because proper diagonals in the correlation matrix can lower the number of factors needed, the communality problem has been viewed as a search for elements consistent with the reduced rank of the correlation matrix.

To be proper, the correlation matrix with communality estimates should preserve the real, Gramian nature of the correlation matrix. Image analysis adjusts the off-diagonal elements to preserve this property. Although the other communality estimation procedures are not known to preserve the Gramian nature of the correlation matrix, the results are not noticeably affected. The degree to which one can violate basic mathematical foundations and yet achieve sensible results is sometimes surprising.

8.3.2 Estimation of the Rank of a Correlation Matrix

To the extent that the full component model fits the data, the rank is not estimated. The rank is calculated. However, models seldom give a perfect fit and therefore the minimum rank that seems appropriate for the data is estimated. The minimum rank is the smallest rank that will lead to "adequate" reproduction of the observed correlations when sampling error and the inaccuracies of the model that can be tolerated are taken into account. The smallest possible rank is selected for reasons of parsimony.

In common factor analysis, the rank of the matrix being factored is indeterminate because the diagonal elements are unknown. Therefore, the smallest rank that would not require inappropriate communalities is sought. Although the procedures for estimating the rank of a matrix have usually been developed for the common factor model, they have also been widely applied to component analysis.

Guttman's Lower Bounds for the Rank.   In one of the classic papers in factor analysis, Guttman (1954) provided three procedures for estimating the lower bound for the number of factors. In these procedures it is assumed that population correlations are being considered. The results are lower bounds in the sense that the minimum rank of the matrix with the true communalities in the diagonal must be equal to or greater than the number provided by the estimate. In this case true communalities are those that lead to the fewest factors being extracted, but which are still legitimate elements. These lower bounds are as follows:

1. Roots ≥ 1 with unities. Guttman proved that the minimum rank of the matrix with communalities in the diagonal is equal to or greater than the number of characteristic roots that are ≥ 1.0. This holds true only when the roots are extracted from the matrix with unities in the diagonal.
2. Roots ≥ 0 with r^2. This procedure uses the square of the highest correlation of a column for the communality estimate in the matrix from which the criterion roots are extracted. The highest correlation is selected without regard to sign. In this case, the number of nonnegative roots is a mathematically stronger or more accurate lower bound for the minimum rank than the roots ≥ 1 criterion.
3. Roots ≥ 0 with R^2. With squared multiple correlations in the diagonal of the correlation matrix, Guttman proved that the number of nonnegative characteristic roots is also a lower bound for the number of factors. It is the most accurate or strongest of the three lower bounds for the rank of the matrix with proper communalities in the diagonal. If the universe of variables is in the analysis, this is quite a close estimate.

The three criteria are related in the order in which they are given. Roots ≥ 1 with unities give the fewest factors, whereas roots ≥ 0 with R^2 give the largest number of factors. Roots ≥ 0 with r^2 give an intermediate estimate.

Example

The characteristic roots for the box, physique, and ability problems are given in Table 8.3.1. The first set is for the correlation matrix with unities, the next for the correlation matrix with the square of each variable's highest correlation, and the third for the matrix with R^2s in the diagonal. A line has been drawn in each case to indicate the decision reached from using Guttman's criterion. The minimum number of factors moves progressively up as the diagonal elements are altered from 1.0 to r^2 and then to R^2.

The zero and negative roots appear because the alteration of the diagonal elements has reduced the rank of the matrix. Summing all the roots gives the sum of the diagonal values in the matrix. When unities are not used in the diagonal, the last roots are zero or negative. With negative roots, the sum of only the positive roots will necessarily be greater than the sum of the diagonal elements.

When applied to the box data, Guttman's three criteria gave 1, 5. and 6 as the minimum rank to which the matrix could be reduced by altering the communalities. The criteria gave 4, 6, and 9 factors for the physique data, and 5, 9, and 13 factors for the ability variables. Because the roots with R^2 have been calculated, the others are technically not needed because they are poorer estimates of the lower bound. In every case, however, roots ≥ 0 give more factors than anyone extracts from these problems.

Roots ≥ 1.0 give a closer fit to the number of factors usually extracted. This is fortunate because, being the easiest to calculate, it is the one in general use.

TABLE 8.3.1
Latent Roots for Use with Guttman's Criteria
for the Minimum Rank

Diagonal Elements:	1.0	Box r_{XY}^2	R^2	1.0	Physique r_{XY}^2	R^2	1.0	Ability r_{XY}^2	R^2
1	8.22	8.07	8.18	5.09	4.59	4.91	8.16	7.48	7.68
2	.78	.57	.71	1.73	1.39	1.61	2.07	1.44	1.62
3	.39	.22	.33	1.16	.52	.88	1.70	.99	1.20
4	.31	.08	.21	1.03	.28	.71	1.52	.73	.90
5	.18	.00	.11	.87	.26	.62	1.01	.19	.42
6	.05	−.08	.00	.68	.08	.46	.92	.17	.40
7	.03	−.11	−.01	.52	−.05	.25	.89	.13	.33
8	.02	−.11	−.01	.46	−.11	.23	.84	.08	.29
9	.02	−.15	−.02	.26	−.25	.06	.77	.01	.24
10	.01	−.16	−.03	.13	−.30	−.03	.73	−.03	.19
11				.04	−.42	−.09	.64	−.08	.11
12				.02	−.54	−.15	.54	−.16	.04
13							.54	−.18	.03
14							.50	−.23	−.02
15							.46	−.25	−.04
16							.41	−.29	−.07
17							.40	−.31	−.09
18							.34	−.33	−.12
19							.33	−.37	−.14
20							.32	−.39	−.17
21							.29	−.43	−.23
22							.26	−.45	−.23
23							.20	−.48	−.25
24							.17	−.49	−.26

Use of Guttman's Lower Bounds.   When a sample correlation matrix is being factored rather than a population correlation matrix, both roots ≥ 0 criteria produce an exorbitant number of factors. The analyses comparing the root criteria with other methods for determining the number of factors report that both of these criteria are gross overestimates (Linn, 1968; Tucker, Koopman & Linn, 1969). These analyses include situations where the number of actual factors is known. The stronger lower bounds overestimate the number of factors because any sample correlation is influenced by essentially random and irrelevant factors that, although technically there, are of no interest and are impossible to replicate. For example, measurement error within a particular sample will be correlated at chance levels and lead to minor factors, but these factors are of no interest.[2]

---

[2]The roots ≥ 1 criterion has been suggested by several theoretical rationales in addition to Guttman's (Kaiser, 1970; Kaiser & Caffrey, 1965). Horn (1969b) has, for example, noted that the proof for the reliability of the factor scores becoming zero or negative when factors with roots less than 1 are extracted (Kaiser & Caffrey, 1965) assumes component scoring. In component scoring, all

The major criticism of the root ≥ 1 criterion is that Guttman proved it to be a poor estimate for *the* number of factors. As noted above, Guttman proved that it was a lower bound for the number of factors, but many investigators have used it as both a lower and an upper bound because they have assumed it to be *the* number of factors for the matrix. That it cannot be considered in this light can be illustrated by several studies. For example, Mote (1970) found the extraction of six factors, instead of four, led to more adequate interpretations. Humphreys (1964) factored 21 psychological variables collected from 8158 subjects where the variables had all been included in previous analyses. Only five factors had roots greater than unity but, from an examination of the distribution of the residuals, Humphreys chose to extract and rotate 11 factors. Ten of these eleven factors—twice the number indicated by the root ≥ 1 criterion—were interpretable and consistent with the earlier factor-analytic findings.

It is the common experience of investigators using the root ≥ 1 criterion that it gives a fairly consistent number of factors as a function of the number of variables. The number of factors ranges from the number of variables divided by five to the number of variables divided by three. The criterion gives generally appropriate results providing that the data are such that the number of factors can be expected to fall within this range. In some cases, however, it appears more reasonable to assume that the number of factors is somewhat less than the characteristic root criterion gives. This is particularly true of item analyses where, when the root criterion is followed, the number of factors is so great that many factors have only one or two major loadings. Although these may be factors in a technical sense, they are not of interest in the average investigation of items.

Evaluation of the Root ≥ 1 Criterion.   In some studies the accuracy of the root ≥ 1 criterion has been investigated. In each case, the author generated matrices from a known number of factors and then computed the root ≥ 1 criterion. The problems investigated by Cattell and Jaspers (1967) involved 10 to 30 variables; the correlations were based on n's of 50, 300, and the population. Root ≥ 1 underestimated the correct number of factors in six cases and correctly estimated it in two. Browne (1968b) had matrices with 12 and 16 variables based on n's of 100 and 1,500. With the smaller n, the root ≥ 1 criterion gave the correct number of factors in 20 samples and overestimated the number of factors in 10 samples; with the large n, it gave the correct result in all 10 samples. Linn

---

variables are used to estimate factor scores. However, if the factor were estimated by using only those variables that defined it, then the reliability could be adequate even though the latent root was less than 1.0. (Gorsuch, 1980). For example, if two out of 100 variables define an orthogonal factor by each loading it .7 while all other variables load it exactly zero, then the latent root for that factor would be .98. However, the internal consistency reliability can be .66 for those two variables considered alone. Admittedly, this reliability is not high, but it is certainly not zero. Only occasionally is the component scoring upon which Kaiser bases his alpha reliability considerations relevant to the situations where factor analysis is most commonly used.

(1968) used samples of 100 or 500 and had 20 to 40 variables. He also varied the communalities in his problems. The latent root ≥ 1 criterion underestimated the known number of factors five times, correctly estimated the number of factors in six cases and overestimated it five times. Four of the overestimations were grossly inaccurate with the estimated number of factors being given as twice as many as were known to be in the matrix. All of these four cases occurred with the larger number of variables and low communalities.

Zwick and Velicer (1980) found it accurate for $v = 36$ and 3 to 12 factors, but a gross overestimate when v was 72 but the number of factors was still the same unless the N and communalities were high. Zwick and Velicer (1980) found it to give $v/3$ to $v/5$ factors for low communality situations and to overestimate the number of factors for high communality situations. These results are discrepant from Hakstian, Rogers, and Cattell (1982) whose analyses showed this rule to perform well with high communalities, particularly for v of 26 with 8 factors (and to underestimate for v of 32 with 20 factors). Schönemann (1981) and Lee and Comrey (1979) also express serious reservations about it, as did Anderson, Acito, and Lee (1982) who found the number of factors ranging from $v/4$ to $v/10$.

Assuming that these plasmodes are accurate portrayals of the situations usually faced when factor analyzing, it is apparent that the latent root ≥ 1 criterion is approximately—but only approximately—correct. Depending upon the situation, it will often underestimate or overestimate the number of factors. It is not truly a mathematical criterion, but a rule of thumb of some use with less than 40 variables where the number of factors is expected to be between $v/5$ and $v/3$ and the N is large.

8.4   EXTRACTING THE NONTRIVIAL FACTORS

Most factor analysts are aware that the statistical approach to the number of factors is available only for certain procedures and may lead to extracting factors of trivial importance. The mathematical approach may also lead to trivial factors from some perspectives. This follows from the fact that in real data the rank of the matrix is almost always equal to its order. Reducing the rank by communality estimation procedures may help but, unfortunately, the procedures for determining the minimum rank may still lead to trivial factors.

Several methods have been suggested for estimating the number of nontrivial factors. The methods do not develop from the sophisticated rationales of either the statistical or the psychometric varieties. Instead, a method usually develops from the investigator's experience with a series of factor analyses. She or he happens to notice a common characteristic across these studies that appears to give the best number of factors and therefore suggests the use of this procedure in future research.

The more important methods are based on computing the percentage of variance extracted (Section 8.4.1), plotting the roots (Section 8.4.2), or examining different numbers of factors (Section 8.4.3).

8.4.1 Computing Percentage of Variance Extracted

Perhaps the oldest method that is of even limited current interest is the percentage of variance extracted. The **percentage of total variance extracted** is computed by dividing the sum of the characteristic roots for the factors extracted by the total sum of all the variances; this is the same as the number of variables when correlations are being factored. Or the **percentage of common variance extracted** is computed by using the sum of the communality estimates in the division. Usually, investigators compute the cumulative percentage of variance extracted after each factor is removed from the matrix and then stop the factoring process when 75, 80 or 85% of the variance is accounted for. The component model seeks to reproduce all the variance and would therefore use the percentage of total variance extracted, whereas the percentage of common variance extracted would be appropriate when the common factor model is used.

A predetermined level of variance to be extracted may not be set; a table of the percentages may be examined instead. Usually factor extraction is stopped after a large portion of the variance has been extracted and when the next factor would add only a very small percentage to the total variance extracted. The procedure is an informal analysis of the information gained relative to the costs incurred. The information gained is reflected in the increased variance that is accounted for when an additional factor is extracted. The costs of that additional factor consist of increased complexity, more computational time, and greater difficulties in replicating such small factors. If a new factor does not add very much to the information already extracted, it would not be worth extracting and interpreting.

8.4.2 Plotting Roots

In accounting for an adequate amount of the variance while minimizing the number of factors, the percentage of variance extracted need not be computed. Because the divisor remains the same, only the cumulative roots need to be examined to obtain the same information. An even simpler procedure is to look at the raw roots themselves. When the roots drop dramatically in size, an additional factor would add relatively little to the information already extracted. Thus, the percentage of variance method has become a "break-in-the-roots" method.

The most detailed discussion of this procedure, along with additional theoretical rationale, has been given by Cattell (1966d). He refers to the procedure as the **scree** test because the term denotes the rubble at the bottom of a cliff. From an examination of a graph of characteristic roots (e.g., Fig. 8.1 and Fig. 8.2), the analogy is obvious; the first few roots show the cliff and the rest show the rubble.

A basic rationale for the scree test is that the battery of variables is measuring a limited number of factors well and a larger number of trivial, specific, and error factors much less well. Therefore, the predominant factors account for most of the variance and are large, whereas the other factors are quite numerous but small. Because the principal factor solution extracts factors by size, the substantive factors will be extracted first and the smaller trivial factors will be removed later. Because the smaller factors are so numerous and are taken out in order of size, it would be expected that plotting them on a graph would result in a straight line sloping downward. The dominant factors should not fall on this line because some of them will be much more dominant than others and they will be stronger than the trivial factors.

One complication that can occur is the presence of several breaks and several straight lines. For example, it is often apparent that the last few roots drop off rather sharply. Because no one is interested in extracting almost the same number of factors as variables, this drop is ignored and the straight line is based upon all the roots except those in that last drop.

A more serious problem occurs when there are two breaks among the first half of the roots. It is then difficult to decide which break reflects the ''proper'' number of factors, and other evidence may be needed to resolve the issue.

A problem also exists when there is no obvious break. Although the scree test can still provide a solution by noting where the last roots no longer form a straight line, the exact number of factors would not be conclusive. One should be sure that such a correlation matrix is significant because random roots often have no major breaks in their curve.

Horn and Engstrom (1979) have noted an interesting parallel between the scree test and Bartlett's significance test. As they show, the major element in Bartlett's significance test is a check of when the last roots are approximately equal. Based on a single example, they suggest that using Bartlett's significance test with an alpha level of .0002 to .0005 for samples with N's of 100 to 150 will give the same result as a scree test on a larger sample. (As their example demonstrates, a scree from a larger sample is more stable and allows for a clear decision on the number of factors as shown earlier in this chapter; hence if there is argument about the scree for a particular problem, that argument might be resolved by collecting more data.)

Subjective Scree.   Cattell (Cattell 1978; Cattell & Vogelmann, 1977) has detailed how one can apply the scree test to a set of data used in the investigation by subjective judgement. Anyone planning to use this test needs to examine the Cattell references closely and practice applying the scree test to the data published therein before actually using it.

Applying the test is relatively simple. All the roots are plotted with the value of the root along the ordinate and the root's factor number as the abscissa. A clear plastic ruler or straight edge is laid across the bottom portion of the roots to see where they form an approximately straight line. That point where the factors curve above the straight line formed by the smaller roots gives the number of factors. Cattell originally suggested taking the first factor on the straight line as the number of factors to be sure that sufficient factors were extracted; he has since (Cattell & Jaspers, 1967) suggested that the number of factors be taken as the number immediately before the straight line begins, the procedure followed here. The scree procedure does provide a solution with the minimum number of factors accounting for the maximum amount of variance.

Example

In Fig. 8.1 the roots of the physique correlation matrix are presented in graphic form. The straight line was drawn to identify the scree. The test clearly indicates that two factors maximize the ratio of the amount of information extracted to the number of factors.

The roots from the correlation matrix of ability variables and from that problem's correlation matrix where R^2s have replaced the unities in the diagonals are both plotted in Fig. 8.2. Here again a straight edge was laid on the lower roots to determine where the scree stopped. Four factors are indicated by both sets of roots.

The scree criterion gives the same number of factors as are commonly extracted from these two examples.

CNG Scree Test. The subjective score test does involve human judgment, and therefore has two major limitations. First, the degree of training necessary to establish high reliability is unknown and some judges have been shown to have a

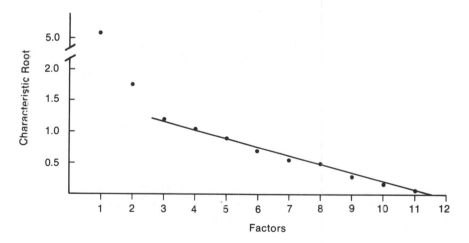

FIG. 8.1.   Plot of the physique characteristic roots.

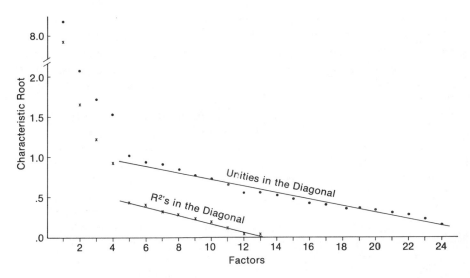

FIG. 8.2.   Plot of the ability characteristic roots.

lower than desired reliability (Crawford & Koopman, 1979). Second, because it involves subjective judgement, it cannot be programmed into the computer run. Both of these problems do not occur with an objective test.

Gorsuch and Nelson (1981) have translated the procedures for the subjective scree into an objective scree test labeled the CNG Scree Test (for Cattell–Nelson–Gorsuch). Mathematically the slope of, for example, the first three roots is determined and compared against the slope of the next three roots. The slopes of all sets of three factors are computed. A major difference between the slopes occurs at the number-of-factors point. The procedure can be utilized by proceeding either from the largest to the smallest roots, or from the smallest to the largest roots. Using the objective scree test on the Cattell and Vogelmann (1977) plasmodes indicated that it was more accurate then the subjective scree test (Gorsuch & Nelson, 1981).

A CNG scree test computer program can be added to any factor analysis program so that the number of factors can be determined in the computer run. The CNG scree test is appropriate regardless of what is in the diagonal of the correlation matrix.

Evaluation of the Scree Test.   Cattell and Jaspers (1967) found the scree test to be correct in six out of eight cases. The other two cases indicated more factors than the model actually had. Zwick and Velicer (1980) found it reasonably accurate.

These results suggest that the scree test is in the correct general area. The scree test does have an additional advantage over the root ≥ 1 criterion in that it can be run with communality estimates in the diagonal instead of unities. Tucker, Koopman, and Linn (1969) plotted roots for components and common factors extracted from the same four correlation matrices. They found the breaks to occur at the same point in both sets of curves.

It should also be noted that Hamburger (Cliff & Hamburger, 1967) found the roots for samples of 400 subjects to have more definite breaks than those where the number of subjects was only 100. Linn (1968) concurs in this conclusion and also suggests that the test is more accurate when the communalities are higher and where the ratio of variables to factors is higher. These results are consistent with theoretical expectations (cf. Section 8.1.2).

The scree test works best where the major influences in the matrix are considerably stronger than the minor influences. This usually means that there is a fairly large number of variables for every factor extracted. The more variables defining each factor, the larger the associated roots will necessarily be.

The situation where the correlation matrix is dominated by a few factors that are considerably larger than any irrelevant factors is the one where prior knowledge exists. That is, the domain is sufficiently investigated that the variables can be selected that are highly related to the factors of interest. Therefore, the scree test should give the most positive results in confirmatory factor analysis where the hypotheses are based upon extensive prior research. In using factor analysis as an aid to exploring a new area, it can be expected to be more ambiguous.

Empirical studies of factor analysis have evaluated the scree test. The results are encouraging. Tucker, Koopman, and Linn (1969) found it to be correct in 12 of their 18 cases. In four of the analyses, it indicated slightly fewer factors than those that had been programmed in; in the other two cases the number of factors was indeterminant with the two screes occurring; one of the two screes indicated too few factors and the other indicated too many. Cliff (1970) also found it generally correct when factoring Monte Carlo data, particularly if all borderline factors were considered to be in the scree. Linn (1968) found the scree test to be correct in seven cases, gave fewer factors than were known to be there in two cases, and overextracted in one case. Linn also reports four instances in which he felt the scree test to be indeterminant and two cases in which the scree test had two breaks, one of which was correct whereas the other indicated too many factors.

8.4.3 Examining Varying Numbers of Factors

In addition to the scree test, another method has been used in determining the number of factors to extract. Wrigley (1960; Howard & Gordon, 1963) suggested that several more factors be extracted than will probably be retained. All factors are then rotated, if that is desired, and the number of trivial factors noted. Trivial factors are usually defined as all factors that do not have at least two or three loadings above a certain specified level (for example, an absolute value of .3), but it might better be defined as those factors without a unique set of defining variables. If the factor has no variables that load it and it alone, it has not yet been sufficiently clarified for theory development. At best, one can only suggest new variables that might load such a factor in a future factor analysis. The number of trivial factors is subtracted from the number extracted and this new number of factors is examined. If any factors are still trivial, the number of factors can be adjusted once more. Crawford (1975) has explored indexes of interpretability, but they need further development. Anderson, Acito, and Lee's (1982) data show that this rule is, as expected, accurate with many variables per factor (e.g., $f = v/3$, although they reference Veldman rather than the earlier work noted above).

Example

In the physique problem, the concern is with establishing major dimensions by which women can be classified. Historically, the concerns centered on the use of these classifications for investigating the relationships between physical characteristics and medical histories, personality, and behavior. For that reason, a specific factor—or even a doublet—would be of little interest. Only common factors would be of concern.

Four principal component physique factors were extracted and rotated by the promax procedure (cf. Chapter 10). The fourth factor had one pattern element of .9 whereas the next highest one was $-.3$. Since this factor appeared to be a specific, the final solution would need to include three or less factors by this criterion.

Revelle and Rocklin (1979) have suggested that the proper number of factors are those factors that maximize "simple structure." Simple structure, discussed in Chapter 9, is often used as a rotation criterion for the final position for the factors. Their suggestion is that different numbers of factors be extracted and rotated to, for example, the Varimax position (as detailed in Chapter 9) and that the proper number is that which maximizes their very simple structure (or VSS) index. The VSS index is based upon the degree to which the original correlations are reproduced by a factor matrix where all the smallest elements in the factor pattern have been replaced by zeros. Although the article applies to both orthogonal and oblique solutions, it has only been tested on the orthogonal solution. The authors report that it provides better resolution for the number of factors to be extracted in simulations that they ran than the root greater than 1, Montanelli and Humphreys, and maximum likelihood tests. It can be programmed into computers and certainly should be examined in future Monte Carlo studies.

The concern with factors that are useful for a particular theoretical purpose, as opposed to determining the "proper" number of factors, is probably the basis for the feeling that statistical and mathematical approaches are not always accurate. When a small number of variables is factored, even factors with one major loading and two or three minor loadings are of great interest. In this case, the mathematical approaches often indicate two few factors. But when factoring a hundred or so items, any factor with only one or two major loadings and several minor loadings is usually uninteresting. In this case, mathematical approaches to the number of factors generally overestimate the number of factors needed. This suggests that the number of factors and the associated method of determining that number may legitimately vary with the research design.

8.5 THE SEARCH FOR THE PROPER NUMBER OF FACTORS

By this time, the reader may possibly feel that there is no single way to determine the number of factors to extract. Although it is a matter for reflection and will differ from study to study depending upon the purpose of the study, some recommendations can be made. **Certainly any extracted factor should be highly significant in the statistical sense.** Because the factor can be expected to be more stable as the sample size increases, any factor extracted should be based on a sample sufficiently large so as to be highly significant.

Bartlett's test for the significance of the correlation matrix should be written into factor-analytic programs so that the results are always available. Because this test, as well as Lawley's, can now be readily run on computers, rules of thumb such as ten individuals for every variable are less necessary. This is fortunate because they never were very accurate.

The statistical test for the number of factors that is used in a particular situation depends upon the method of extraction being used. Maximum likelihood tests would naturally be used with a maximum likelihood extraction procedure, a procedure that should be used whenever there is any doubt about the significance of the common factors. In those cases where a principal component procedure is used, Bartlett's significance test for residuals can be incorporated in the computer program provided that it is remembered that this test gives only an upper bound to the number that might be significant.

A second step in determining the number of factors is to carry out a CNG scree test. The recent literature supports the scree test as being reasonably accurate under varying conditions. Hakstian, Rogers, and Cattell (1982) report the scree as good with high communalities (e.g., averaging above .6) and with a v/f ratio of at least 3 to 1, as was the root ≥ 1. However, the subjective scree gave overestimates with lower communalities (this is consistent with Cattell's—who applied the scree—overall recommendation: extract a few extra factors when error is high and drop them when they fail to replicate, but never underfactor). Virtually all of the recent studies (e.g., Anderson, Acito, & Lee, 1982; Hakstian, Rogers, & Cattell, 1982; Schönemann, 1981; Zwick & Velicer, 1980) have found sufficient inappropriate results so that the root ≥ 1 criterion should only be used by those who have examined the research studies sufficiently to know its limits. Wrigley's criterion is useful when the number of variables per factor is expected to be high.

TABLE 8.5.1
Promax Factor Patterns for the Box Problem, f = 2, 3, 4, 5, and 6

Number of Factors Rotated

Variables	2		3			4				5					6					
	A	B	A	B	C	A	B	C	D	A	B	C	D	E	A	B	C	D	E	F
1. Length squared	1.1	-.2	1.2	-.1	-.2	1.2	-.2	-.1	.1	1.2	-.2	-.1	.1	.1	1.1	.0	.1	.0	-.1	-.2
2. Height squared	.3	.6	-.1	.0	1.0	-.0	.0	1.0	.1	-.0	.0	1.0	.1	.0	.1	.1	1.0	-.0	-.1	-.0
3. Width squared	-.0	1.0	-.0	.8	.2	-.2	1.0	-.0	.3	-.1	1.0	-.0	.2	.1	.0	.9	.1	.1	-.0	-.0
4. Length plus width	.7	.3	.8	.3	-.1	.6	.6	-.2	.1	.6	.5	-.2	.0	.1	.6	.4	-.2	.0	.2	.1
5. Length plus height	.9	.1	.7	-.1	.4	.7	-.1	.4	.0	.7	-.1	.4	.0	.1	.5	-.2	.3	.1	.2	.1
6. Width plus height	.3	.7	.1	.4	.6	.0	.6	.4	.1	.0	.5	.4	.0	.1	.0	.3	.3	.1	.2	.2
7. Longest inner diagonal	.9	.1	.8	.1	.1	.7	.2	.0	.0	.8	.3	.1	-.1	-.2	.6	.1	.0	.0	-.3	.7
8. Shortest inner diagonal	.6	.3	.4	.0	.5	.3	.6	.2	-.2	.3	.4	.2	-.1	.5	.1	.1	.0	-.0	1.0	-.2
9. Space inner diagonal	.9	.1	.8	.0	.2	.7	.3	.1	-.1	.7	.3	.1	-.1	.1	.5	.1	.0	-.0	.2	.3
10. Thickness of edge	-.2	1.0	-.0	1.0	-.1	.1	.1	.1	.8	.1	.2	.1	.8	-.1	.0	.1	-.0	1.0	-.0	-.0

172

How critical is it if the estimated number of factors is wrong? Some light has been shed on this question by examining the effect of the number of factors on the rotated solution. Although the influence affecting the stability of a rotated solution is discussed in later chapters, it can be noted here that rotation does redistribute the extracted variance across the factors. With additional factors, more variance is extracted for each variable and more dimensions exist in which to work than was originally the case. Therefore, the nature of the factors after rotation may shift somewhat depending upon the number of factors extracted.

Several investigators have reported analyzing their data to determine the stability of the rotated factors as more factors are extracted (Dingman, Miller, & Eyman, 1964; Howard & Gordon, 1963; Keil & Wrigley, 1960; Levonian & Comrey, 1966; Mosier, 1939b; Shaycoft, 1970). Although the number of correlation matrices analyzed in this way is small, the results are consistent. As the number of factors increases, there is first some shift in the nature of the common factors. However, the common factors tend to stabilize around the root ≥ 1 or the scree test point. After that point, the common factors are relatively stable with the addition of more factors leading to more specific factors appearing in the rotated solution. With even more factors, the common factors will break down; when there are as many factors as variables, each factor is generally a specific. This suggests that one or two extra factors do little harm but too many may cause a common factor to be missed.

Examples

To determine the robustness of the solutions when varying numbers of factors were extracted, box principal components were rotated by the promax (cf. Chapter 10) procedure. The promax factor patterns for three to six components are summarized in Table 8.5.1.

Factor A has some changes across the rotations. These changes primarily occurred in those measurements less intrinsically related to length. Length squared itself remained virtually unchanged. In all the solutions, this factor is recognizable as length.

Factor B had a change when four factors were rotated as opposed to three. When two or three were rotated, thickness was predicted from this factor as well as width squared. When four were rotated, however, thickness rotated off to its own factor. As a fifth and sixth factor were added, another variable likewise moved towards loading a specific factor.

Factor C's major loading, height squared, is stable as three, four, five, and six factors were rotated. Some minor loadings became less; by factor six, the variables length plus height and width plus height appear to be too low. This suggests that the solution has begun degenerating.

Factor D is stable after it begins to appear but is a specific.

On the basis of the scree test, two or five factors could be extracted from the box problem (the root ≥ 1 criterion indicated only one factor). The rotated factors are stable in meaning across this range except for one change in the width factor. Although the factor was initially a cross between width squared and thickness, width became its own factor when thickness broke off to form the fourth factor. By the six-factor solution, several factors have started to shift to pure specific factors. When 12 factors were also rotated, virtually every factor was a specific and the correlations among the factors approximated the correlations among the original variables.

Whether three or four factors can be considered to give a better solution depends on the perspective adopted. A common factor approach would stop at three factors because the fourth is obviously a specific. A components approach would not necessarily stop with three factors because a specific factor would be of interest. Although the three-factor solution does approximate the three dimensions of space, it could be suggested that thickness is an independent parameter. Although it is measured within the three-space, it could be measured in any of the three and the same score would result. Unlike the other variables, it is therefore not uniquely related to any particular space and could be considered independent. Box manufacturers appear to base thickness on the width of the box more than its length or height, a conclusion reached from its tendency to load the width factor.

These rotations suggest that either three or four factors would be appropriate and relatively stable even if one or two extra factors were extracted. More than six factors would lead to what most analysts would consider a degenerate solution.

Various numbers of factors for the physique problem were also rotated. An examination of the factor for the several rotations supported the previous studies that an extra factor does little harm.

It is interesting to note that Cattell has recommended for years that an extra factor or two be extracted (Cattell, 1952). Upon rotation, he expected to be able to sort out the unique factors from common factors. In addition to the examples just quoted that suggest that this does occur, Shaycoft (1970) also included some random variables in his factor analysis. When he extracted and rotated a large number of factors, these random variables defined error factors with one random variable to each factor. This is the same result that Gorsuch (1967) found when he also extracted a large number of factors from a correlation matrix that contained a few random variables. Therefore, if one is in doubt concerning extracting the proper number of factors, the error should probably be slightly on the side of too many factors provided that the common factors do not degenerate. However, the probability of replicating the small, extra factors is not high (cf. Chapter 16).

Is there any check that, in a given problem, the number-of-factors decision had a critical influence on the final solution? Here again we can turn to the suggestion of extracting varying numbers of factors. An examination of the several solutions will at least give a feel for the importance of the number-of-factors decision for that particular problem. In the final report, interpretation could be limited to those factors that were well stabilized over the range that the number of factors could reasonably take. The other factors can be reported as less clear and interpreted accordingly, unless they are supported by evidence external to the factor analysis.

9 Rotation and Interpretation of Factors[1]

In Chapter 3, factor analysis was defined as solving the equation $Z = F P'$ for both F and P with only the Z known. Without knowledge of either the F or the P, the problem is mathematically indeterminate because an infinite number of F's and P's could exist to satisfy the equation. All of the F and P combinations reproduce Z with the same number of factors and the same degree of accuracy. Chapters 5, 6, and 7 gave methods of extracting the factors to meet certain specifications. The specifications were generally sufficient so that F and P were uniquely defined. For example, for the principal factor variants, the solution was restricted so that each factor maximally reproduced the elements of the matrix from which it was extracted, a restriction that generally leads to a unique solution. After the factors have been extracted, it is not necessary to retain the initial restrictions. In the principal factor solution, for example, the requirement that each successive factor must account for the maximum variance possible can be relaxed and other solutions found by rotation. Although the size of each factor may shift, the *set* of new factors will retain the same ability to reproduce the original data matrix as was found for the set of principal factors. Hence, both the rotated and the unrotated factors will reproduce the same correlations with the same degree of accuracy.

Research studies can be designed so that the factors are directly interpretable without further rotation. Diagonal, multiple group, and confirmatory maximum likelihood are all analyses that are guided by prior theory and give directly

---

[1]By this point in a study of factor analysis some students feel confused and are groping for a total view of factor analysis. An overall perspective develops naturally after the completion of a few more chapters.

interpreted results. Occasionally, this is true of the other solutions, particularly the first principal factor. If the variables have been sampled appropriately to hypothesize that the underlying dimension of interest is the factor determined by that weighted composite of the variables that accounts for the most possible variance, then the first principal factor is the solution. In Spearman's theory of general intelligence, the first principal factor often is an appropriate solution for a battery of psychological tests of ability.

However, in exploratory factor analysis the factor analyst seldom selects the variables so that the principal factors—or any other factors given by the initial solutions—are of theoretical interest. It is generally assumed that the initial factors will be rotated so that the factors meet criteria that make them more relevant to the purpose of the study. The variables are therefore selected so that the rotated factors have a greater likelihood of being meaningful.

To rotate factors requires that a principle be utilized to determine the position of the factors. Suggested principles for rotating factors are set out in Section 9.1, Principles for Guiding the Rotation of Factors. Most rotations are to analytic criteria and are carried out by computers. They may assume the factors will be orthogonal (i.e., uncorrelated) as in Section 9.2 or may allow them to be oblique as well (Section 9.3). Section 9.4 summarizes the distinctiveness characteristic of the major analytic procedures. The concluding section, 9.5, Interpreting Factors, contains some basic principles that underlie the use of a factorial solution.

Example

If the variables are not appropriately sampled, the first principal factor will not be useful as a final solution. In the six personality variable problem, three variables from two discrete areas were included. The variable vectors in a two principal axis (iterated communalities) space are given in Fig. 9.1 with the principal factors. In the attempt to account for the most variance, the first principal factor is a composite of high verbal comprehension and low anxiety. The second factor pits verbal comprehension against anxiety. Neither factor passes close to any variable. Neither of the two clusters of variables is identified with either factor, although the clusters are obvious in the correlation matrix.

The factors need to be rotated to a more meaningful position. Figure 9.2 presents the two factors after a simple structure rotation by Varimax (Section 9.2.2). After rotation, the factors can be easily labeled because no variable has a major loading on more than one factor.

9.1   PRINCIPLES FOR GUIDING THE ROTATION OF FACTORS

If the data are to determine the position of the factors, a principle for guiding the rotation is needed. The one that is generally accepted is that of simple structure (i.e., rotating to the most parsimonious position; Section 9.1.1). Criteria for simple structure have been suggested (Section 9.1.2). Several other criteria for

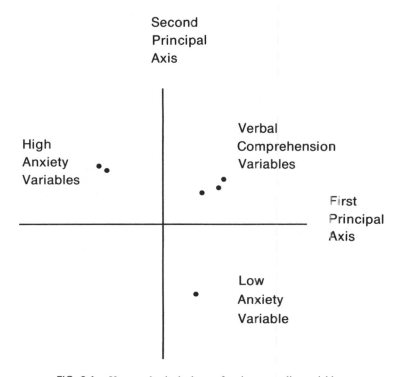

FIG. 9.1.   Unrotated principal axes for six personality variables.

rotation have been suggested but have never come into wide use (Section *9.1.3).

9.1.1 Simple Structure

The criteria of simple structure were used by Thurstone (1935) to provide a psychologically meaningful solution to the problem of the indeterminacy of the factors. Thurstone hoped that the factor pattern of any given variable would be constant when the variable was included in another factor analysis containing the same common factors. To achieve this goal, he suggested that the factors be rotated so that each variable loaded on as few factors as possible. Thurstone showed that such rotation leads to a position being identified for each factor that would be independent of the number of variables defining it. Therefore, a simple structure factor should be relatively invariant across studies. This invariance is not true of a principal factor because it shifts with the addition or deletion of a few variables.

Another argument is to simply ask the question, "Why should a more complex solution be chosen arbitrarily over a simpler solution?". If there is no other

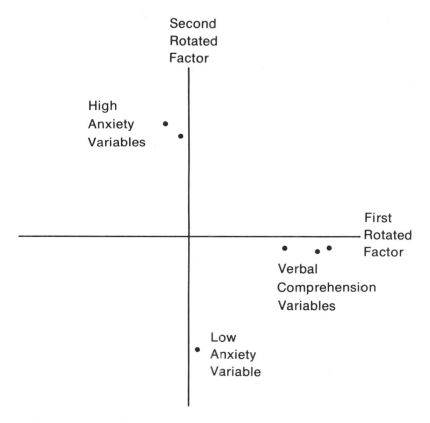

FIG. 9.2. Simple structure factors for six personality variables.

guide to defining the factor, then the simplest way is the best. Figure 9.3 contains initial factors *A* and *B* as they are often extracted from the data. *A'* and *B'* then indicate the approximate simple structure positions of the rotated factors. The latter positions lead to a cleaner definition of each factor. It is "simple" because each variable loads on as few factors as possible.

9.1.2. Criteria for Simple Structure

The use of visual simple structure as well as its logic led Thurstone to suggest several criteria (Thurstone, 1947; p. 335) for evaluating a solution. These are:

1. Each variable should have at least one zero loading.
2. Each factor should have a set of linearly independent variables whose factor loadings are zero.
3. For every pair of factors, there should be several variables whose loadings are zero for one factor but not for the other.

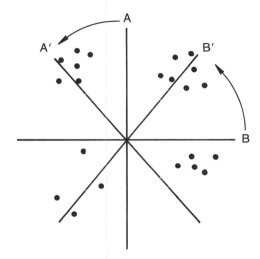

FIG. 9.3.   Rotating initial factors, *A* and *B,* to simple structure positions, *A'* and *B'.*

4. For every pair of factors, a large proportion of the variables should have zero loadings on both factors whenever more than about four factors are extracted.
5. For every pair of factors, there should be only a small number of variables with nonzero loadings on both.

All these criteria were, however, derived from the appearance of the diagrams. It was these factor plots that actually determined whether or not the simple structure was simple structure for Thurstone.

Example

The factor matrices for the orthogonal solutions plotted in Figs. 9.1 and 9.2 are given in Tables 9.1.1 and 9.1.2. The former presents the unrotated principal axis solution (R^2 used as communality estimates with two iterations) and shows none of the five charac-

TABLE 9.1.1
Unrotated Principal Axis Loadings for
Personality Variables Problem

Variables	Factors	
	A	*B*
1. Information	.70	.31
2. Verbal Ability	.73	.36
3. Verbal Analogies	.53	.24
4. Ego Strength	.39	−.55
5. Guilt Proneness	−.34	.48
6. Tension	−.44	.50

TABLE 9.1.2
Simple Structure Factor
Loadings for Personality Variables

	Factors	
	A	B
1. Information	.76	−.09
2. Verbal Ability	.81	−.07
3. Verbal Analogies	.58	−.07
4. Ego Strength	.06	−.67
5. Guilt Proneness	−.05	.59
6. Tension	−.12	.66

Note: $r_{AB} = 0.00$.

teristics Thurstone identified with simple structure. The latter table presents the Varimax rotation to simple structure. If loadings up to ±.10 are assumed to be random variations from zero, an assumption usually made, then the second table does meet Thurstone's criteria.

Cattell has been a major exponent of the concept of parsimony in the Thurstone tradition. In addition to stressing the visual compellingness of a simple structure rotation, he has stressed hyperplane count as an analytical criterion to be reached (Cattell, 1952; 1966b, pp. 184–189). The **hyperplane count** consists of the number of essentially zero loadings on a factor or set of factors. The hyperplane count is always determined by the factor pattern. Maximizing the hyperplane count therefore minimizes the number of factors necessary to reproduce any given variable. To allow for some randomness of loadings around zero, the hyperplane count usually includes the number of variables with loadings on the factor between +.10 and −.10. Theoretically, this limit should be varied as a function of parameters such as sample size, but the +.10 and −.10 levels are generally used. This may be just as well because no one really knows how to determine the standard error of a zero loading.

Cattell uses the percentage of the elements in the factor loading matrix that are in the hyperplane as his analytic criterion. Although Cattell generally finds that the percentage of loadings in the hyperplane reaches about 65 or 70% after a thorough rotation, it should be noted that the percentage reached is a function of the characteristics of the study. One characteristic influencing the hyperplane count is the number of variables relative to the number of factors. Many factors relative to the number of variables allow for more zero loadings, particularly if many variables load only one factor. Generally the ideal maximum percentage in the hyperplane would occur when each variable loaded only one factor (i.e., $1 - v/fv$ which then becomes $1 - 1/f$). Maximum hyperplane percentages are then a direct function of the number of factors extracted. Low communalities likewise produce higher hyperplane counts. (Communalities of zero would, naturally, produce a solution with 100% of the loadings in the hyperplane.)

An additional influence is the degree of correlation between the factors in an oblique solution. When the factors are highly correlated, then the factor pattern weights are systematically lower for the overlapping factors. The weights drop because the weight given to one factor is indirectly applied to all other factors correlated with it. Hence, a high hyperplane count can be obtained by extracting many factors from few variables with low reliability and rotating to a highly oblique position. No level of hyperplane count can be set as that defining "good simple structure" unless the characteristics of the study are known in detail.

Hofmann (1978) has suggested a further index of simple structure. Unlike percentage in the hyperplane, it is an index that is reasonably independent of the number of factors. Basically he computes the number of factors that have major loadings for that variable, and calls this the "index of variable complexity." It ranges from one when the variable is loaded by only one factor to f when all extracted factors load the variable. Because it is an index, it will often be a number such as 1.3, thus indicating that the variable is definitely influenced by more than one factor but is not highly influenced by two factors. It can be averaged across variables for an overall index of complexity for the study.

In rotation, an additional criterion is usually introduced: positive loadings. Positive loadings are obviously appropriate in the abilities domain because negative correlations almost never exist in the correlation matrix. Other correlation matrices are also unlikely to be generally negative (this is partly due to our conceptual patterns and partly to the ability to reverse the direction of scoring of many variables). For this reason, most data sets can be rotated so that most major loadings are positive.

Note that the direction of a factor is always arbitrary. Any factor with a preponderance of negative salient loadings can always be reversed. One simply multiplies the factor (i.e., its loadings and correlations with other factors) by -1 to reverse the factor's direction if that is necessary to achieve more positive loadings.

There is nothing in the simple structure principle to guarantee that one and only one position can be found. Two separate investigators could both rotate visually and find different solutions. Analytic programs can also find more than one position meeting their criteria (Cattell & Gorsuch, 1963). However, a simple structure solution will invariably be found even if the variables are only randomly related. The data-based simple structure positions do tend to be fewer and of better quality than those found in random data (Cattell & Gorsuch, 1963), but the simple structures in random data are similar to those observed in real data (Humphreys, Ilgen, McGrath & Montanelli, 1969).

When a particular criterion for simple structure has been reached, it is still meaningful to ask if this is a statistically significant simple structure. Bargmann (1954) has outlined the procedure for conducting such a test. The test compares the number of loadings within the hyperplane with the number to be expected if the variables are randomly distributed throughout the hyperspace defined by the given number of factors. Cattell (1978) gives the details of this test with tables ranging from 5 variables and 2 factors up to 28 factors and 140 variables. The procedure seems to assume that the factors are equal in size after rotation, which means that the test will only be applicable when variables are carefully sampled for the study to meet this criterion. An additional limitation is that the problem of differing communalities is not discussed (it is easier to get a large number of variables in the hyperplane when the communalities are low then when they are high, even though the latter are more desirable). It should also be noted that the test is a psychometric one and that it asks about the relationship of the observed distribution of loadings to the distribution if the variables were randomly distributed, and so does not take into account the size of the sample.

*9.1.3 Other Rotational Criteria

Simple structure is the most widely used principle for rotation, but the selection of this principle is mathematically arbitrary. Other procedures would be equally appropriate if one's philosophy of science supported them for a particular problem.

Cattell (Cattell & Cattell, 1955) has suggested that **proportional profiles** would be a better criterion than simple structure. To meet the proportional profiles criterion, two factor solutions of the same variables but from different individuals must give proportional factor patterns. To achieve this, both studies would be rotated jointly until a position was found where the loadings on factor A, for example, of the first study would equal the loadings on the same factor of the second study if the latter were all multiplied by a constant. A practical solution for achieving this criterion has not yet been achieved, although progress has been made (Evans, 1971; Meredith, 1964b) and is discussed in the next chapter.

Eysenck (1947) has used criterion rotation in his research. Criterion rotation involves correlating all the variables in the analysis with a dichotomous variable representing membership or nonmembership in a particular subcategory. The factor is then rotated until the pattern of loadings is proportional to the pattern of correlations with the criterion. A diagonal factor, where a vector is placed through the variable of group membership, is a more efficient procedure for achieving the same goal.

9.2   ORTHOGONAL ROTATION FOR SIMPLE
STRUCTURE

Several procedures have been recommended for analytical orthogonal rotation. The procedures include, in order of their historical introduction, quartimax (Section 9.1.1) and varimax (Section 9.1.2). Other procedures have also been proposed (Jennrich, 1970) but have not gained wide acceptance. Quartimax and varimax were developed from a consideration of the parsimony implied by simple structure. All of the orthogonal criteria restrict the transformation matrix so that the factors are uncorrelated. (Section *10.1.1 details the restrictions.) These are redefinitions of simple structure.

9.2.1 Quartimax

In an attempt to identify what is meant by parsimony in rotation, Ferguson (1954) pointed out that Thurstone's simple structure is extremely complex mathematically and cannot, apparently, be represented in any equation for the purpose of manipulation. He also criticized Thurstone's approach for utilizing discrete concepts rather than continuous ones. Thus, Thurstone talks about the number of zeros in a column even though zero loadings in the population are seldom zero in samples. In addition, significant but trivially low loadings are also useful in establishing the simple structure but are ignored in Thurstone's discrete approach.

Ferguson's explanation of the parsimony concept is developed from a one-variable and two-orthogonal factor case and then generalized to other situations. In the two-orthogonal factor case, the most parsimonious description of one variable is where one factor passes through the variable and the other factor is placed at right angles to it. A reduction in parsimony occurs inasmuch as the factors are rotated away from this position. Maximum nonparsimony occurs when the variable has equal loadings on both factors. Note that the cross product of the two squared loadings is zero when parsimony occurs and is highest at the nonparsimonious position. This can be generalized to more than one variable and more than two factors. If the loadings are all squared to avoid problems with sign, the crossproducts between any two columns of the factor matrix will be greatest where variables have mutual loadings on those two factors and least where those variables that load one factor do not load another. Therefore, seeking to minimize the crossproducts between squared loadings for a given variable will maximize its loadings on the smallest number of factors and minimize all other loadings.

When a criterion for the total factor matrix—rather than just two factors—is desired, it is convenient to consider the communality of the variables. These communalities are defined as:

$$h_v^2 = p_{v1}^2 + p_{v2}^2 + p_{v3}^2 + \ldots + p_{vf}^2 \tag{9.2.1}$$

If Eq. (9.2.1) is squared, then:

$$h_v^4 = \sum_f p_{vf}^4 + \sum_f \sum_{f'} p_{vf}^2 p_{vf'}^2 \text{ (where } f' \neq f). \tag{9.2.2}$$

The importance of this equation is that it attributes the square of the communality to separate components with the latter component being a direct function of crossproducts between columns. By either maximizing the fourth powers to the right of the equal sign or minimizing the crossproducts, Ferguson's parsimonious solution will be found. From the fourth-power maximization approach has come the term **quartimax.**

Although Ferguson developed a rationale for quartimax, the criterion had been previously proposed by Carroll (1953). He derived it directly from Thurstone's recommendation that each variable's factor loadings contain a large number of zeros and that the columns of the factor pattern matrix should have zeros for one factor where the other factor has salient loadings. Saunders (1953) proposed the same criterion when he sought to maximize the number of large and small loadings while minimizing the number of intermediate-sized loadings. To do so was, he pointed out, to maximize the kurtosis of the squared loadings, that is, to maximize the variance of their fourth powers. The squared loadings were used so that the sign of the loading would not effect the rotation. Neuhaus and Wrigley (1954) independently proposed the same criterion in order to increase the high loadings and decrease the low loadings for a variable.

Quartimax has not been widely accepted owing to one shortcoming. A quartimax solution tends to include one factor with all major loadings and no other major loadings in the rest of the matrix, or have the moderate loadings all retained on the same factor. The general factor is teamed with other factors that have a few major loadings and numerous small loadings. The result fits the definition of simple structure: Each variable should have only one high loading with all other loadings small. Although each variable's complexity is kept near the minimum, the complexity of the first factor is maximized rather than minimized.

Computer programs for the quartimax procedure are generally available.

9.2.2 Varimax

Kaiser (1958) noted the tendency of quartimax to produce a general factor. He also noted that the purpose of the quartimax criterion is to simplify the factor pattern of a variable, an approach consistent with the traditional factor-analytic model that is developed from the perspective of reproducing the variables. However, the problem in exploratory factor analysis is to simplify a factor rather than a particular variable because the interest invariably lies in learning more about the factors rather than about the variables. Kaiser therefore suggested that the variance of the squared loadings across a factor be maximized rather than the variance of the squared loadings for the variables. The resulting criterion to be maximized is:

$$V_f = \left[v \sum_v (p_{vf}^2)^2 - \left(\sum_v p_{vf}^2 \right)^2 \right] \Big/ v^2 \qquad (9.2.3)$$

where V_f is the variance of the squared loadings for factor f, the p_{vf}'s are the loadings, and v is the number of variables. That rotation position is sought where the variance is maximized across all factors in the matrix and is called the **varimax** solution.

When the variance of a factor is maximal, there must be numerous high loadings and small loadings. The extreme case would be where half the variables have loadings of $+1.0$ or -1.0 and the other half have loadings of zero. If loadings were either zero or one, the factor would be most interpretable because the numerous small loadings that cause difficulties would be completely eliminated.

Maximizing the varimax function means that any tendency toward a general factor in the solution will be minimized. **Varimax is inappropriate if the theoretical expectation suggests a general factor may occur.** To apply varimax, for example, to items of a test with high internal consistency is inappropriate because high internal consistency means there is a general factor underlying most of the items in the test. Data that may give a general factor should either be obliquely rotated and higher-order factors extracted (cf. Chapter 11) or explored by some other rotation procedure. Tenopyr and Michael (1964) have made suggestions on modifying the normal varimax procedure for use when the correlation matrix contains a general factor.

Kaiser (1958) noted that the application of Eq. (9.2.3) did not lead to maximum interpretability. From his examination of trial matrices, the problem appeared to be that some variables had much higher communalities than others. Because these variables necessarily had higher average loadings than those with low communalities, they overly influenced the final solution. To equalize the impact of variables with varying communalities, Kaiser reformulated his criterion to follow a suggestion by Saunders. Each variable's squared loadings were divided by its communality and the variable's sign restored. This row normalization brings all variables to unit length and thus gives them equal weight. It is the normalized varimax criterion that is the standard varimax used in contemporary analysis.

For the special case of two factors, Kaiser was able to show that changes in the composition of the set of variables being analyzed did not affect the rotated position. The stability of the rotated position was proved for the case where the variables were from two pure clusters each of which formed a perfect factor and where the correlation matrix had a rank of two. He also was able to demonstrate that, in the case of the 24 ability variables, dropping several variables from the analysis did not greatly alter the factor patterns of the other variables so long as there were a sufficient number of variables to produce each factor in some form. Kaiser attributes part of the tendency toward invariance to the normalizing feature, an argument that is compatible with Thurstone's (1947) discussion of the results of sampling variables (cf. Chapter 16 for a further definition and discussion of invariance).

However, others have not always found varimax to give invariant factors. Butler (1969), for example, found that the normal varimax factors were not particularly invariant when Thurstone's original box problem was analyzed in the same manner that Kaiser used to analyze the 24 ability variables. In a comparison of several rotation procedures, varimax has been found to be no more invariant than the several oblique procedures against which it was tested (Gorsuch, 1970) or slightly more invariant (Dielman, Cattell, & Wagner, 1972). The conditions under which varimax is relatively invariant across a sampling of variables are therefore not completely identified.

Varimax is available on virtually every computer that has any programs for factor analysis. A variety of programs for achieving the varimax criterion under several conditions are given in Horst (1965) and Sherin (1966). Several modifications to process special cases have been recommended (Cureton & Mulaik, 1975; Jackson & Skinner, 1975).

Examples

The box components, physique, and ability principal axes (with highest correlations as communality estimates) were rotated to the normalized varimax criterion. The results are presented in Tables 9.2.1, 9.2.2, and 9.2.3. The box solution is reasonable but not as good as one might hope for. Not only are the three defining variables lower on their factors than expected, but no loadings are below .2. Thurstone's concept of simple structure is not met here, probably because varimax gives uncorrelated factors, whereas the length, height, and width of a box are highly correlated in practice.

The simple structure for the physique data (Table 9.2.2) is better than varimax simple structure for the box factors. If the loadings less than .2 are disregarded, most variables load only one factor. If only salient variables are considered (e.g., loadings above .3, a figure that is both twice the minimum significant correlation for the n of 200 and interpretable), then only a few variables load on both factors. The same is true of Table 9.2.3.

The first physique factor is most closely related to the circumference measures and would be so labeled. It seems to reflect the thickness of the body, but the thickness

TABLE 9.2.1
Varimax Solution for the Box Components

Variables	Factors		
	A	*B*	*C*
1. Length squared	.92	.23	.22
2. Height squared	.35	.40	.82
3. Width squared	.35	.81	.38
4. Length plus width	.77	.52	.31
5. Length plus height	.75	.30	.56
6. Width plus height	.48	.60	.63
7. Longest inner diagonal	.79	.37	.39
8. Shortest inner diagonal	.62	.39	.58
9. Space inner diagonal	.79	.37	.47
10. Thickness of edge	.28	.87	.23

TABLE 9.2.2
Varimax Solution for Physique Factors

	Factors	
Variables	A	B
1. Stature	.22	.90
2. Symphysis height	.03	.94
3. Breadth of skull	.23	.14
4. Length of skull	.17	.45
5. Biacromial diameter	.45	.43
6. Transverse chest diameter	.63	.13
7. Sagittal chest diameter	.67	.28
8. Bicristal diameter	.61	.18
9. Length of sternum	.36	.47
10. Chest circumference (at expiration)	.85	.11
11. Hip circumference	.84	.13
12. Weight	.79	.31

TABLE 9.2.3
Varimax Solution for the Ability Factors

	Factors			
Variables	A	B	C	D
1. Visual Perception	.17	.21	.65	.15
2. Cubes	.10	.10	.48	.06
5. General Information	.75	.22	.18	.13
6. Paragraph Comprehension	.76	.08	.20	.23
7. Sentence Completion	.80	.16	.19	.09
8. Word Classification	.59	.25	.33	.12
9. Word Meaning	.80	.06	.19	.21
10. Add	.17	.76	−.10	.16
11. Code	.19	.55	.08	.36
12. Counting Groups of Dots	.03	.73	.19	.08
13. Straight and Curved Capitals	.19	.57	.40	.06
14. Word Recognition	.19	.07	.05	.57
15. Number Recognition	.10	.07	.11	.54
16. Figure Recognition	.08	.09	.43	.48
17. Object-Number	.15	.23	.06	.61
18. Number-Figure	.02	.36	.30	.45
19. Figure-Word	.15	.18	.23	.38
20. Deduction	.39	.09	.44	.30
21. Numerical Puzzles	.18	.44	.39	.21
22. Problem Reasoning	.38	.13	.41	.31
23. Series Completion	.38	.23	.50	.23
24. Woody-McCall Mixed Fundamentals, Form I	.36	.49	.17	.30
25. Paper Form Board	.15	−.01	.56	.11
26. Flags	.23	.10	.56	.06

interpretation would need to be confirmed in another study because no thickness measure was included here. The second factor is clearly a height measure. Perhaps a width factor would also have occurred if measures such as the width of the shoulders had been included.

From Table 9.2.3, ability factors can be identified. The first factor is related to variables concerned with verbal ability. The second factor appears to be numerical ability, whereas the third is related to visual ability. However, the interpretation of factors B and C seem less clear than factor A and therefore would need to be closely checked in a future study. Factor *D* appears to be based on the ability to recognize words, numbers, and so forth. The numerous minor, positive correlations in the matrix suggest that it would be difficult to actually measure the factors while keeping them uncorrelated even though an uncorrelated model is being used.

9.3. OBLIQUE ANALYTIC ROTATION FOR SIMPLE STRUCTURE

To rotate orthogonally it must be *assumed* that the factors are uncorrelated. Many investigators would prefer either to test this assumption or to allow some minor correlations among the factors. Such solutions are referred to as **oblique** because the angles between factors are no longer orthogonal when represented geometrically. The degree of correlation allowed among factors in an oblique rotation is always minor to moderate and can be influenced by a user-defined parameter in several procedures. No one allows the factors to become highly correlated; if two factors ever did become highly correlated, most investigators would redo the analysis with one less factor.

Numerous procedures are available for oblique rotation. Some, such as the traditional visual rotation by which the factors are rotated to a position that matches the investigator's judgment of simple structure, are discussed in the next chapter. In this section a sampling of the analytic procedures are presented in detail (most major analytic rotation procedures are tabled in Section 9.4). Discussed in Section 9.3.1 is direct oblimin, a procedure widely available in statistical packages at major computer centers. Promax (Section 9.3.2) is included as a somewhat different technique that is known for its demonstrated quality (as checked by empirical studies). Maxplane (Section 9.3.3) is a uniquely different approach to solving for simple structure.

All of the analytic procedures are used to simplify the structure of a factor analytic matrix. Simple structure as defined by the computational algorithm is sought in one of two matrices. First it may be sought in the traditional factor pattern, and thus be an approach to simplifying the weights that reproduce the variables from the factors. Second, simple structure may be sought in the *reference vector structure,* which is a variable by factor matrix containing the partial correlation of each variable with each factor after the other factors are statistically held constant (cf. Sections 9.5 and 10.2 for further details). Direct oblim-in simplifies the structure of the factor pattern whereas promax and maxplane simplify the reference vector structure.

Throughout the literature on oblique solutions, comments are made that "the intercorrelations seem "too high" or "too low." Evaluations of the proper level of correlations among factors are seldom supported by reference to data. The present position (cf. Section 9.4.1) is that factors should correlate as highly as one would expect representative measures of the factors to correlate in future research. An estimate of the appropriate level of intercorrelation between two factors is given by the correlations between those variables that are salient on the first factor and those variables that are salient on the second factor.

9.3.1 Direct Oblimin

Carroll (1957) noted that two early attempts to generalize the principles for orthogonal rotation to the oblique case had proved only partially successful. First, in Carroll's generalization of his quartimax approach, **quartimin,** he mini-mized the sum of the crossproducts of the squared variable loadings. But quar-timin produced solutions where the factors intercorrelated at an objectionably high level. Second, in Kaiser's (1958) generalization of varimax for the oblique case, he required that the sum of the covariances of the squared factor loadings be minimized, a procedure called **covarimin.** Unfortunately, covarimin gener-ally produced an orthogonal solution.

Carroll suggested that quartimin and covarimin be given equal weight in the rotated solution. To do so, the following expression is minimized where b is the **biquartimin** criterion:

$$b = \sum_{f} \sum_{f'} \left[v \sum_{v} a_{vf}^2 a_{vf'}^2 - k \left(\sum_{v} a_{vf}^2 \right) \left(\sum_{v} a_{vf'}^2 \right) \right] \qquad \text{(where } f' \neq f\text{)}$$

where a_{vf} is the vf element from the reference vector structure. A user-set param-eter, k, varies the emphasis between the two criteria. In practice the rows of the matrix are often normalized, as has been found effective with varimax.

The user-set parameter k produces solutions ranging from highly correlated factors to almost uncorrelated factors, depending on its value. Values of k be-tween 0 and 1 produce more highly correlated solutions. A value of 0, which gives both criteria equal weight, produces a solution with factors that are not correlated quite so highly as a positive value. When k is negative, the correla-tions decrease more; when k is minus 4 or so, the factors are orthogonal.

Unfortunately the setting of k is generally left exclusively to the user so that k is a guess. It seems that the most sophisticated way to use this parameter is to vary it systematically from 1 to -4 and select the solution that maximizes the observed simple structure (as, for example, seen in the hyperplane count) and that produces correlations among the factors that are similar to the correlations among the highest loading variables for each of the factors.

Jennrich and Sampson (1966) suggested using Eq. 9.3.1 for the factor pattern instead of the reference vector structure. They were able to show mathematically that the procedure will not rotate a factor to be a linear function of the other factors and that some factor matrix minimizes the function.

9.3.2 Promax

For **promax** Hendrickson and White (1964) recommend altering an orthogonal rotation so that it gives an oblique solution. The orthogonal solution is used as a basis for creating an ideal oblique solution. The unrotated factor matrix is then rotated to the best least-squares fit to the ideal solution by the Procrustes procedure (Section *10.4.1). Although promax can use any orthogonal rotation as a basis for the ideal solution, either varimax or quartimax has been the usual initial solution.

To create a solution better than that given by the orthogonal rotation, the moderate and low loadings need to be lower than in the orthogonal solution while the high loadings remain relatively high. Such an improved solution may be possible if the factors are allowed to be oblique.

Mathematically, all factor loadings become lower when they are raised to a higher power. For example, the square of .4 is .16 and its cube is .064. However, high and low squared factor loadings have a greater relative difference than they did before squaring. If the original loadings are .9 and .3, .3 is one-third as large as .9. But the squared loading for the second variable, .09, is one-ninth as large as the squared loading for the first variable, .81. In this case, the absolute difference also increases. The relative discrepancy between the large loadings and the moderate to small loadings can be increased further by raising the factor loading to a power greater than 2. The higher the power, referred to as k in promax literature, the closer the moderate loadings come to zero. Because increasing the number of zero elements will bring the matrix closer to several of Thurstone's criteria, the procedure has as sophisticated a rationale as any other analytic criterion.

Naturally, the resulting idealized matrix has even the highest loadings lowered somewhat. This is no great problem when the idealized matrix is considered to be the reference vector structure. As the factors become correlated, the factors overlap more. Partialing out the other factors from the elements for any given factor in the reference vector structure means the correlations with the reference vectors will average lower than the equivalent orthogonal factor loadings.

Because higher powers reduce the loadings more, higher powers necessarily lead to greater correlations among the factors. By varying the power, the degree of obliquity can be varied as well as the simplicity of the structure. The proper power is that giving the simplest structure with the least correlation among factors. The usual procedure is to simply raise the factor loadings of the orthogonal matrix to the fourth power and restore the sign of each loading. Then the closest fit of the data to this hypothesized matrix is found by applying the Procrustes solution. If the correlations increase more than the quality of the structure, then the power of 2 is tried. If the $k = 4$ solution is good, a $k = 6$ solution might also be tried.

Hendrickson and White (1964) present several illustrations showing that the simple structure reached is of as high a quality as that of any other analytic procedure. A good solution is generally achieved by raising the loadings to a power of four, but they occasionally used the power of two where that seemed to give better simple structure.

Because the procedure gives good simple structure, is easily programmed, and is extremely fast, its popularity is spreading rapidly. Section 9.4.3 shows that the solution is a quality one.

Examples

The promax solutions for the box components and for the ability factors were both computed from the varimax solutions. The former is in Table 9.3.1 and the latter in Table 9.3.2. The fourth power was used for both of these tables. The tables include the correlations of the variables with each factor with other factors partialed out (reference vector structure), the weights by which the factors reproduce the variables (factor pattern), the variable–factor correlations (factor structure), and the correlations among factors. The box promax components are as expected: the correlations place major emphasis on the three basic dimensions with one exception already discussed in Chapter 8. The reference vector structure elements are much lower than the other loadings because the factors intercorrelate, but each dimension does make its own unique contribution. Due to the extensive overlap among the factors, all elements in the factor structure are quite high. The correlations among the factors are slightly higher than the correlations among the three best variables, suggesting that a $k = 2$ solution might be tried.

The ability factors reach a good simple structure solution upon promax rotation. Some 50% of the elements are between .10 and −.10; although the hyperplane count is not as good as a visual rotation would probably give, it is better than varimax's 23%. There are definite correlations among the factors but, even so, the interpretations from S and P would be quite similar for all factors except C. The pattern is helpful for interpreting C because it indicates which variables overlap with this factor and not with the other factors. Variables 2 and 6 both correlate .5 with C, but the pattern shows that variable 6 does so only because it correlates quite high with A, which, in turn, correlates with C.

The shifts in correlations among the factors as a function of the power to which the varimax loadings are raised can be illustrated with the ability factors. Table 9.3.3 presents the correlations among the factors for the first, second, fourth and sixth powers. They increase as the power increases. Because the correlations among the salient variables for one factor and those for another factor range from about .35 to .50 in the ability correlation matrix, the fourth power intercorrelations are as high as one would want to go.

TABLE 9.3.1
Promax Rotation (k = 4) of Box Components

Variables	A. Reference Vector Structure			B. Factor Pattern			C. Factor Structure			D. Correlations Among Factors		
	Length	Width	Height	Length	Width	Height	Length	Width	Height	1. Length	2. Width	3. Height
1. Length squared	.71	−.06	−.11	1.18	−.09	−.20	.96	.58	.66	1. 1.00		
2. Height squared	−.06	.01	.58	−.11	.02	1.05	.73	.72	.98	2. .69	1.00	
3. Width squared	.00	.53	.10	.00	.83	.17	.71	.96	.79	3. .78	.74	1.00
4. Length plus width	.48	.22	−.05	.80	.34	−.09	.96	.82	.78			
5. Length plus height	.41	−.07	.24	.69	−.10	.43	.95	.69	.89			
6. Width plus height	.08	.23	.32	.13	.36	.58	.83	.88	.95			
7. Longest inner diagonal	.50	.05	.05	.83	.07	.09	.95	.71	.79			
8. Shortest inner diagonal	.27	.03	.27	.45	.05	.50	.87	.73	.88			
9. Space inner diagonal	.45	.01	.12	.79	.02	.22	.98	.73	.86			
10. Thickness of edge	−.02	.66	−.05	−.03	1.02	−.08	.62	.94	.66			

TABLE 9.3.2
Promax Rotation ($k = 4$) of Ability Factors

A. *Reference Vector Structure*

	Factors			
	A	B	C	D
	Verbal	Numerical	Visual	Recognition
Variables	Ability	Ability	Ability	Ability
1. Visual Perception	−.06	.02	.55	−.03
2. Cubes	−.05	−.02	.43	−.06
5. General Information	.62	.08	−.00	−.04
6. Paragraph Comprehension	.62	−.08	.01	−.07
7. Sentence Completion	.67	.03	.01	−.08
8. Word Classification	.42	.10	.16	−.06
9. Word Meaning	.67	−.09	−.01	.05
10. Add	.06	.70	−.22	.04
11. Code	.02	.43	−.06	.22
12. Counting Groups of Dots	−.13	.64	.10	−.07
13. Straight and Curved Capitals	−.01	.44	.30	−.12
14. Word Recognition	.07	−.07	−.09	.50
15. Number Recognition	−.03	−.07	−.01	.48
16. Figure Recognition	−.12	−.10	.31	.36
17. Object-Number	.00	.07	−.10	.52
18. Number-Figure	−.17	.19	.18	.32
19. Figure-Word	−.00	.04	.11	.28
20. Deduction	.19	−.09	.29	.15
21. Numerical Puzzles	−.02	.28	.27	.04
22. Problem Reasoning	.18	−.05	.26	.16
23. Series Completion	.16	.04	.36	.05
24. Woody-McCall Mixed Fundamentals, Form I	.19	.35	.00	.13
25. Paper Form Board	−.02	−.15	.49	−.01
26. Flags	.05	−.05	.48	−.09

B. *Factor Pattern*

	Factors			
	A	B	C	D
	Verbal	Numerical	Visual	Recognition
Variables	Ability	Ability	Ability	Ability
1. Visual Perception	−.08	.03	.77	−.04
2. Cubes	−.07	−.02	.59	−.08
5. General Information	.80	.10	−.01	−.06
6. Paragraph Comprehension	.81	−.10	.02	.09
7. Sentence Completion	.87	.04	.01	−.10
8. Word Classification	.55	.12	.23	−.08

(continued)

TABLE 9.3.2—(*Continued*)

B. Factor Pattern (continued)

	Factors			
Variables	A Verbal Ability	B Numerical Ability	C Visual Ability	D Recognition Ability
9. Word Meaning	.87	−.11	−.01	.07
10. Add	.08	.86	−.30	.05
11. Code	.03	.52	−.09	.29
12. Counting Groups of Dots	−.16	.79	.14	−.09
13. Straight and Curved Capitals	−.01	.54	.41	−.16
14. Word Recognition	.09	−.08	−.13	.66
15. Number Recognition	−.04	−.09	−.02	.64
16. Figure Recognition	−.16	−.13	.43	.47
17. Object-Number	.00	.09	−.13	.69
18. Number-Figure	−.22	.23	.25	.42
19. Figure-Word	−.00	.05	.15	.37
20. Deduction	.25	−.11	.40	.20
21. Numerical Puzzles	−.03	.35	.37	.06
22. Problem Reasoning	.24	−.07	.36	.21
23. Series Completion	.21	.05	.49	.06
24. Woody-McCall Mixed Fundamentals, Form I	.24	.43	.00	.18
25. Paper Form Board	−.02	−.19	.68	−.02
26. Flags	.07	−.06	.66	−.12

C. Factor Structure

	Factors			
Variables	A Verbal Ability	B Numerical Ability	C Visual Ability	D Recognition Ability
1. Visual Perception	.37	.36	.71	.38
2. Cubes	.23	.20	.50	.22
5. General Information	.81	.42	.48	.40
6. Paragraph Comprehension	.82	.31	.50	.46
7. Sentence Completion	.84	.37	.48	.37
8. Word Classification	.70	.44	.57	.40
9. Word Meaning	.85	.30	.48	.45
10. Add	.30	.77	.21	.36
11. Code	.36	.65	.37	.53
12. Counting Groups of Dots	.22	.74	.39	.31
13. Straight and Curved Capitals	.38	.66	.58	.35
14. Word Recognition	.32	.23	.27	.59
15. Number Recognition	.24	.22	.28	.56

(*continued*)

TABLE 9.3.2—(*Continued*)

C. *Factor Structure* (continued)

	Factors			
	A	B	C	D
	Verbal	*Numerical*	*Visual*	*Recognition*
Variables	*Ability*	*Ability*	*Ability*	*Ability*
16. Figure Recognition	.28	.26	.54	.57
17. Object-Number	.31	.38	.31	.66
18. Number-Figure	.24	.48	.48	.57
19. Figure-Word	.30	.32	.39	.48
20. Deduction	.54	.30	.61	.50
21. Numerical Puzzles	.37	.56	.57	.44
22. Problem Reasoning	.53	.33	.59	.51
23. Series Completion	.55	.43	.68	.48
24. Woody-McCall Mixed Fundamentals, Form I	.52	.63	.47	.53
25. Paper Form Board	.29	.14	.56	.27
26. Flags	.37	.24	.60	.27

D. *Correlations Among Factors*

	Factors			
	A	B	C	D
	Verbal	*Numerical*	*Visual*	*Recognition*
Factors	*Ability*	*Ability*	*Ability*	*Ability*
A. Verbal Ability	1.00			
B. Numerical Ability	.44	1.00		
C. Visual Ability	.59	.50	1.00	
D. Recognition Ability	.51	.52	.58	1.00

The same solutions gave varying hyperplane counts for the ability data. Varimax (i.e., promax with $k = 1$) gave 23%, promax with a power of 2 gave 46%, 4 gave 50%, and a power of 6 gave 49%, as did a power of 8. The choice to be made among the k greater than 2 promax solutions is therefore to be made on the basis of the correlations among factors; the fourth power solution was chosen because it had moderate correlations that were consistent with the correlations among salient variables.

9.3.3 Maxplane

Cattell and Muerle (1960) departed from the usual approach of building an oblique program on a principle first operationalized in orthogonal rotation. Feeling that the analytic solutions had not been particularly successful in producing the kind of simple structure found by the visual rotator, they suggested that the computer be programmed to act as a visual rotator. Thus the heart of the **max-**

TABLE 9.3.3
Correlations among Promax Ability Factors as a
Function of the Power Used

A. First Power (same as varimax)

	A	B	C	D
A	1.0			
B	0	1.0		
C	0	0	1.0	
D	0	0	0	1.0

B. Second Power

	A	B	C	D
A	1.00			
B	.26	1.00		
C	.37	.26	1.00	
D	.32	.31	.33	1.00

C. Fourth Power

	A	B	C	D
A	1.00			
B	.44	1.00		
C	.59	.50	1.00	
D	.51	.52	.58	1.00

D. Sixth Power

	A	B	C	D
A	1.00			
B	.48	1.00		
C	.65	.58	1.00	
D	.56	.58	.67	1.00

E. Eighth Power

	A	B	C	D
A	1.00			
B	.50	1.00		
C	.67	.62	1.00	
D	.58	.60	.71	1.00

plane program is to plot a factor against another factor and then rotate one factor to see whether or not it increases or decreases the value of a criterion.

Although different criteria could be used, the primary criterion is that of hyperplane count. If rotating a factor to a position 10 degrees from the initial position results in increased hyperplane count, then that factor is rotated to that position. The search is then for that solution that gives the maximum hyperplane count. The width of the hyperplane for the criterion count is determined by the user in light of his particular problem and the number of individuals on which the correlations are based. Naturally, the factors are not allowed to approach each other to the point where the correlations are exceptionally high.

The maxplane procedure has been further programmed by Eber (1966). The program takes each pair of factors and shifts each factor on the other factor by a set number of degrees (e.g., 10 degrees). The shifts continue until the computer has tried all possible positions between the original one for that factor and one that is as close as 45 degrees to the other factor. It then examines the hyperplane count of each and selects that one position that maximizes the hyperplane count as the new position for the factor. The process is continued until all the factor pairs are examined in this manner. The procedure is iterative in the sense that the pairs of factors are then again examined several times. It iterates until the hyperplane count is no longer increased by another pass-through process.

Maxplane programs involve a distinctively different procedure than any other analytic approach to the rotation problem. As such, maxplane solutions have been included in some experimental work but have not yet become widely accepted. One of the procedure's limitations for practical use is that it often takes considerably more time than some of the other procedures.

9.4 COMPARING ALTERNATIVE SOLUTIONS

With several procedures for rotating the factors in exploratory factor analyses, evaluations are needed to determine which one is most appropriate for specified conditions. To evaluate the solutions, criteria need to be invoked. The criteria that can be suggested are presented in Sections 9.4.1 and 9.4.2. The former includes criteria that are internal in the sense that they are based on the characteristics of the solution itself. Some of the internal criteria could be used to decide, for example, which of three different solutions was best in the same study. The latter includes criteria that are external in the sense that evidence outside of a particular analysis is used to decide whether or not the procedure is a good one.

Studies have been made comparing several of the rotation procedures. The evaluative studies are summarized in Section 9.4.3 and appropriate conclusions drawn. Problems with the current comparative studies are also noted. Indices to evaluate the similarity of several solutions are given in Chapter 13.

9.4.1 Internal Criteria

When several rotation procedures have been applied to the same data, they can be compared on a series of dimensions. Such comparisons will often eliminate poor solutions.

Examination of the Results.   The most primitive procedure is to examine the factor loadings for the "ease of interpretation." This procedure has been widely used as a prime basis for judging the quality of the solutions. Although the investigator is often familiar with Thurstone's requirements for simple structures and may even apply some of them, the overall conclusions are actually drawn from the feel that he or she gets for the solution.

Using interpretability to choose the best solution has obvious problems. First, there can be legitimate arguments about choosing solution *X* over solution *Y,* or solution *Y* over solution *X,* for the same data. Second, the investigator may unknowingly be biased toward his own "pet" procedures or accept that solution which capitalizes on chance to support his theoretical position. Third, it appears that many individuals using this procedure have allowed nonsignificant differences between solutions to influence their conclusions. So long as there are minor differences in the second place after the decimal, it seems that the conclusion is always that there are some "important" differences between the two solutions. But differences in the second digit are probably not replicable if, for example, another random sample of individuals from the same population is chosen.

This procedure should be used only at the most preliminary stages of evaluating a rotational technique—and then used with considerable discretion.

Comparison with Visual Rotation.   An improvement upon simple examination of the results is to compare the rotated solution with a visually rotated solution of the same data. The visual rotation is assumed to be closer to the definitions of simple structure as originally promulgated.

A customary procedure has been to compare the analytic rotation against a visual rotation already published in the literature. Although this procedure may have arisen for sake of convenience, it has the obvious advantage of reducing bias, because the person doing the rotation was unacquainted with the analytic technique to be applied. Whether or not one rotation procedure reproduces a particular visual rotation better than another can be empirically verified.

Comparing an analytical procedure with a visual rotation does have the problem of the fallible criterion. Visual rotators occasionally err in their judgment and therefore produce erroneous results. In such a case, the analytic solution matching better with the visual rotation may actually be the poorer solution. Naturally, there is also the problem that different visual rotators will probably produce somewhat different solutions, and who is to say which is best? Although the investigators who originally rotated the classical studies to visual simple structure were bright, innovative scientists, it is difficult to assume that the rule of apostolic succession will be any more appropriate here than elsewhere.

This criterion is further complicated when the analytic procedure has parameters that are systematically varied to produce the best match with one visual rotation. Not only may the criterion be fallible, but selecting a particular parameter from among several may well capitalize on chance and not generalize to any other studies.

Hyperplane Count.   The number of variables in the hyperplane is an objective criterion for rotation. Because zero loadings do greatly simplify the solution, it is obviously relevant. However, it cannot be applied alone. On the one hand, it is somewhat gross because it ignores many elements that load between the hyperplane and the definition of the salient loading for that study. Two solutions that produce essentially the same hyperplane count could vary in the degree to which they produce these intermediate loadings, but the solution producing the fewest intermediate loadings would be a more desirable one. The other problem is that it does not take into account other aspects of the solution, such as the correlations among the factors (cf. Section 9.1.1). Therefore, hyperplane count can be used only in the context of other considerations.

Examination of the Iteration Sequence. The analytic procedures are applied by iterative methods. The programs are generally written so that the factors are rotated pair by pair and the varimax, biquartimin, or other criterion value computed. The iteration continues so long as the changes affect the factor loadings. Usually, the iteration sequence is stopped when the rotation is such as to leave the first two decimal places unaffected (Kaiser, 1958). However, some programs also stop when a certain number of iteration cycles have been completed (e.g., 100) under the dubious assumption that further accuracy is not worth the computer time that would be required.

An examination of the criterion values computed across the iteration sequence may provide suggestive evidence of the quality of the solution. If the iterations continue until the solution is iterated for the maximum number of times allowed in the program, then the simple structure is still unclear. If, on the other hand, the procedure quickly converges, then a simple structure has been found.

Invariance Across Random Transformations of the Unrotated Factors. Even if the cycling is stopped because the criterion has been reached, that does not mean that a unique simple structure has been found. As Cattell and Gorsuch (1963) demonstrate, the same analytical programs can give two different solutions that both meet the same criterion for the same data if the data do not have a clear simple structure. In that case, alternative simple structures exist that equally meet the analytical criterion. If it is suspected that alternative simple structures exist, this hypothesis should be checked by randomly transforming the unrotated factors and submitting these for analytical rotation. If the simple structure is clear, the solution resulting from rotating the randomly transormed factors should be the same as the solution from rotating the unrotated factors without the random transformation.

Ease of Measurement. The degree to which the resulting factors can be easily measured will be a prime criterion for studies that are principally oriented toward measuring the factor in further research. To be easily measured, the factors should rotate to a solution where each variable is correlated with only one factor so that the salient variables can simply be added together to give a meaningful and valid measure of that factor. Alternatively, those procedures that result in measurement techniques with the highest multiple correlation between the factor estimate and the factor score may be the most preferred. Analytic rotation procedures can be compared against each other as to the degree to which they give factors that can be easily measured.

Intercorrelation of Variable Clusters.   One debate in the oblique rotation area is the extent to which the factors should correlate. Present criteria appear simple: If a procedure has factors that correlate too high, then it should be rejected; but if the factors correlate too low, then it should also be rejected. However, the definition of "too high" and "too low" is often a subjective one and varies depending upon who is examining the solution. Only in the case of rotation to singularity is the criterion an explicit one. Whenever the squared multiple correlation of one factor with the other factors is 1, the factors obviously have excess correlations.

In some cases, however, there is evidence as to how high the factors should correlate. If the factor solution is one where obvious clusters of variables are uniquely identified, then the factors should intercorrelate at approximately the same level as the groups of variables intercorrelate or as multiple-group factors passed through the clusters of those variables intercorrelate. The multiple-group method can be easily used to determine what are reasonable correlations among factors.

In a few other cases, the factors are uniquely identified by one variable that has a loading close to unity. The raw correlation among the variables defining such factors should be approximated by the correlations among factors. For example, Thurstone's box problem produces factors of length, height and width; these three variables are in the matrix and all produce loadings above .95 on their respective factors. The correlations among the factors should therefore be at the same level as the correlations among these variables.

This criterion could be particularly important where, again, ease of use in future research is a prime consideration. In that case, the future factors will probably be measured by clusters of variables and the rotation solution will hopefully predict how those clusters will intercorrelate. To the extent that it does not, it is an unacceptable rotational procedure.

Cost/Performance Ratio.   When there is no other way to decide between two different analytical procedures, cost becomes the deciding factor. **Any procedure that is convenient to calculate is the accepted one unless another procedure can be shown to have definite advantages over it.** *Definite advantages* are those that are demonstrated with data, not subjective opinion. This principle is used in borderline cases. In actuality, "borderline" becomes a very broad area when the investigator has a large number of variables and a small budget but a relatively narrow area with a large budget and a small number of variables.

9.4.2 External Criteria

In the case of external criteria, there is objective evidence independent of the rotated solutions themselves as to which solution is the better one. Such data may arise because the underlying factors can be assumed to be known and may come from a well-researched factor-analytic area or a problem especially designed to test given assumptions. Another major area of external criteria is the long-term parsimony of the solution. Factors that will appear under a wide variety of conditions are obviously more desirable than factors that appear only under highly specialized conditions. The extent to which an analytic rotation procedure encourages the appearance of such robust factors would be a deciding factor. It should be noted that Thurstone's reason for turning to simple structure was his feeling that simplicity would lead to better replicability and invariance of the factor (Thurstone, 1947, p. 362).

External criteria are obviously of greater importance than internal criteria. Only when the analytic solutions produce factors that are essentially the same in terms of the external criteria would one wish to examine the internal criteria.

Plasmodes.   The use of empirical data where the factors in the area are well understood, or the use of Monte Carlo studies for evaluating rotation techniques, is of great importance. In plasmodes, it is assumed that the basic factors are known and that the factor solution should produce those same factors. Empirical measures of the extent to which a solution does so can be easily developed.

The only problem in the plasmode approach lies in the assumptions made in drawing up the plasmode. It should obviously match the area being researched as closely as possible. Some plasmodes have not been completely appropriate. Thurstone's classical box problem, for example, has virtually no variables that are linear combinations of the factors being sought: length, height, and width. Instead, they are multiplicative and interactive functions of those factors. It is perhaps surprising that any rotation solutions find the box factors—and very encouraging.

Replication Across Individuals.   A prime criterion for any rotation solution is that it should produce the same factors when random sets of individuals are drawn from the same underlying population. If it cannot, the solution is of no value. Naturally, most solutions will give some replicability and the question then becomes that of which solution has the factors that are most likely to replicate.

In most studies, the number of individuals will be sufficient for dividing the sample in half. The best solution would then be the one that produced the most similar results across the two sample halves.

When a new sample is drawn from a different population, a better solution would give more of the same factors. The production of factors that are robust across populations would be a strong point for any procedure.

Invariance Across Variables. Even as populations of individuals can be sampled, populations of variables can, in theory, also be sampled. The same arguments for choosing factor solutions that replicate across subjects apply to choosing those that replicate across variables. It should, however, be noted that it is much more difficult to define a population of variables than it is a population of subjects. This makes the criterion hard to apply, but special situations may still be identified where some of the factors should appear even though the set of variables is altered (cf. Chapter 16).

9.4.3 Comparisons Between the Rotation Procedures

Numerous analytical procedures have been developed for rotating to simple structure. Table 9.4.1 gives a sample of such procedures. They employ a number of different techniques attempting to arrive at the most appropriate simple structure. Almost all have compared their solutions against data previously rotated visually to simple structure, and the authors claim their procedure is one of the best.

Comparative studies of rotational procedures have often been conducted. Recent studies include Crawford and Ferguson (1970), Dielman, Cattell, and Wagner (1972), Eyman, Dingman and Meyers (1962), Gorsuch (1970), Hakstian (1971), Hakstian and Boyd (1972), Hofmann (1978), Horn (1963), and Tenopyr and Michael (1963). Dielman, Cattell, and Wagner (1972) present a table summarizing the earlier studies. Unfortunately, the studies are not as conclusive as might be expected. Most studies have considered only one or two of the possible criteria given previously, and the criteria have usually been the less interesting ones concerned with the internal characteristics of the solution. Examples of using a poor criterion are the recent studies that compared the analytic solutions to rotated solutions. In the long run, analytical simple structure is sought not because an expert "likes how it plots," but because it is parsimonious, and parsimonious solutions should be more stable. The stability of the solution across samples of variables and individuals is of greater importance than agreement with visual solutions or other internal characteristics of the solution.[2]

From comparisons of orthogonal analytic procedures with visual rotation procedures, it is generally agreed that varimax presents a solution closer to the visual rotation solutions than quartimax (Baehr, 1963; Eyman, Dingman, & Myers, 1962; Hakstian & Boyd, 1972). Although this conclusion is not unanimous—Tenopyr and Michael (1963) factored a situation where they expected a fairly broad general factor and concluded that varimax removed too much vari-

---

[2]Additional problems include the reliance upon a limited sample of studies and the lack of significance tests.

TABLE 9.4.1
Sample Analytic Simple Structure Rotation
Procedures

Name	Oblique?	Principle	Comments
Binormamin (Kaiser & Dickman, 1959)	Yes	Combines quartimin and covarimin criteria.	
Biquartimin (Carroll, 1957)	Yes	Equally weights quartimin and covarimin criteria.	Usually good, but occasional .8 correlation between two factors.
Covarimin (Kaiser, 1958)	Yes	Minimizes sum of covariances of squared factor loadings.	Gives almost uncorrelated factors.
Direct oblimin (Section 9.3.1)	Yes	Minimizes a function of factor pattern varying from covarimin to biquartimin to quartimin by user-set parameter.	Available in many statistical packages.
Equamax (Saunders, 1962)	No	Combines quartimax and varimax criteria.	Spreads variance more equally across factors
Indirect oblimin (Carroll, 1960)	Yes	Same as direct oblimin except uses reference vector instead of factor pattern.	
Maxplane (Section 9.3.3)	Yes	Maximizes hyperplane count by simulating visual rotation.	Solution often differs from other programs.
Oblinorm (Bentler & Wingard, 1977)	Yes	Scale-free version of binormamin.	
Oblimax (Pinzka & Saunders, 1954)	Yes	Maximizes kurtosis of all loadings.	Gives highly correlated factors.
Obliquimax (Hofmann, 1970)	Yes	Early version of orthotran.	
Optres (Hakstian, 1972)	Yes	Uses a promax-type rotation with a salient variable target matrix.	Also see Cureton, 1976.
Orthoblique (Section 10.3)	Yes	Generalizes an orthogonal solution to oblique; a class of rotations.	Less similar to orthogonal starting solution than Promax.

(continued)

TABLE 9.4.1—(*Continued*)

Name	Oblique?	Principle	Comments
Orthomax (Harman, 1960)	No	Combines both quartimax and varimax criteria.	Gives quartimax, equamax, or varimax depending on user-set weighting of the criteria.
Orthotran (Section 10.3)	Yes	Heuristic search for simplest orthoblique solution.	
Promax (Section 9.3.2)	Yes	Generalizes any orthogonal solution to an oblique one with same high loadings. Factor correlations vary with user set parameter.	Efficient procedure giving good solution.
Quartimin (Carroll, 1957)	Yes	Minimizes sum of cross-products of squared loadings.	Gives highly correlated factors.
Quartimax (Section 9.2.1)	No	Simplified loadings for a variable.	General plus group factors.
Tandem Criteria (Comrey, 1967)	Yes	Uses jointly the criteria that correlated variables should be loaded by same factors and uncorrelated variables loaded by different factors.	
Varimax	No	Maximizes variance of squared loadings of a factor.	THE orthogonal procedure.

ance from this first factor and quartimax removed too little from it—the weight of the evidence is certainly in favor of varimax.

Gorsuch (1970) used several objective measures to evaluate rotation procedures. He counted the number of elements in the hyperplane, calculated the squared multiple correlation of a scale resulting from each factor with the factor itself, determined the replication of the factors across two samples of subjects and determined the replication of the factors across three samples of variables. **The basic conclusion in this study was that biquartimin, maxplane, promax, and varimax all produced the same factors.** On the numerous criteria evaluated, the only major difference was found in calculation times; varimax–promax as a unit was five to thirty times faster than other oblique procedures. The study did conclude that an oblique rotation for that data might be more appropriate because the factors were then somewhat easier to measure and the oblique solutions indicated a slightly greater invariance of the factors across sampling of variables. Horn (1963) and Dielman, Cattell, and Wagner (1972) also concluded that the rotation procedure used did not greatly affect the replicable factors when comparing varimax, oblimin, binomimin, maxplane and Harris–Kaiser solutions. Inasmuch as differences did occur, promax based on varimax or quartimax and the Harris–Kaiser solutions tended to be better in these and other studies (Hakstian, 1971).

The Harris–Kaiser orthoblique solutions are a set of solutions. Hofmann's (1978) version, orthotran, may be the best. In rotating 17 sets of data, it produced better hyperplane count, lower variable complexity, and higher congruence with visual rotations than did the independent cluster and "A'A" technique for Harris–Kaiser factors. In this study oblimin was almost as good. (Despite wide availability, few empirical comparisons have been made with direct oblimin rotations.)

Some data do suggest that the analytic criterion is important. When variables were sampled, varimax gave more invariant solutions than maxplane and biquartimin (Bailey & Guertin, 1970). In sampling across individuals, varimax gave more invariant factors than quartimin or biquartimin (Smith, 1962). Although promax and the Harris–Kaiser procedures were not included in either study, they should function more like the solution upon which they are based—varimax—than like, for example, the oblique biquartimin, a conclusion supported by studies such as Gorsuch (1970) and Dielman et al. (1972), which included varimax with the oblique procedure in their comparisons.

If the simple structure is clear, any of the more popular procedures can be expected to lead to the same interpretations. Rotating to the varimax and promax or Harris–Kaiser criteria is currently a recommended procedure. Both give factors that are similar to those found by a visual rotation, both are as invariant as any of the solutions, and the calculations are easier than for other procedures. Biquartimin, oblimax and maxplane should probably be avoided, unless maxplane is used for a distinctive solution.

Another advantage of the varimax–promax or varimax-Harris–Kaiser sequence is that they provide a basis for determining whether orthogonal or oblique factors are more acceptable. If the correlations among the oblique factors are negligible, then the varimax solution would be accepted as a reasonable solution. If the correlations seem significant, the oblique solution would be the choice. Comparing orthogonal and oblique solutions encourages selection of the simpler uncorrelated factor model if that is actually relevant. Assuming that the factors are either uncorrelated or correlated is avoided. An examination of rotational use in clinical research found that most studies assuming orthogonality were unjustified (Loo, 1979). Even Guilford, long an advocate of orthogonal rotation, has been reanalyzing his past studies for oblique factors (Guilford, 1981).

In the analysis of a particular study, it could be wise to apply several rotational procedures to each of two random halves of the total pool of individuals. A comparison of the results (cf. Chapter 13) would quickly indicate which factors should be interpreted. If a factor appeared in one solution but not in another on the same individuals, then its simple structure is not very clear. It should be clarified in future research before being taken too seriously. A factor occurring across several simple structure solutions and across both sample halves would need to be taken very seriously indeed. If varimax, promax, and Harris–Kaiser solutions are all computed and the interpretation is restricted to factors appearing in all solutions, the investigator can be assured that his factors have a high likelihood of replicating in a new sample, regardless of the type of analytical rotation.

In the previous discussion it was assumed that an exploratory factor analysis is being conducted. However, such analyses may be less profitable than hypothesis-testing approaches such as multiple-group factors and confirmatory factor analysis. Hopefully, a few exploratory analyses will suffice to move any area into a hypothesis-testing stage.

9.5   INTERPRETING FACTORS

The interpretation of a factor is based upon the variables that are and are not related to that factor. When the factors are uncorrelated, one matrix summarizes factor–variable relationships. When the factors are correlated, the contribution of each variable to the interpretation will differ depending upon which of several factor matrices is examined. The role of each matrix in interpretation is pointed out in Section 9.5.1.

A problem in interpreting the factors is deciding when a borderline loading should be considered significant or salient (Section 9.5.2). Using the salient loadings to cluster the variables (Section *9.5.3) may aid the interpretation. The final interpretation is made on the basis of the factor–variable relationships (Section 9.5.4).

In any given investigation, factors may occur that present problems for interpretation. Such problems arise when the variables are not sufficiently understood, when the factor includes such a wide range of variables that they cannot be readily integrated, or when the factor is poorly defined. Poorly defined factors are generally those that do not have several salient loadings by variables that load only the factor up for interpretation. Without a unique set of variables loading the factor, there is no real basis for interpreting the factor. There is, of course, no reason to interpret all factors; the following discussion assumes that only factors well defined by interpretable variables are being examined.

9.5.1 Interpretation of Factor Matrices

The relationship between variables and factors can be described in several ways. The more important of these are:

1. The weight matrix to calculate variable standard scores from factor standard scores: P_{vf}.
2. The correlations of the variables with the factors: S_{vf}.
3. The correlations of the variables with the reference vectors, V_{vf}, which are the correlations between the variables and the factors when the variance attributable to all the other factors has been removed. (Chapter 10 gives formulas for V.)

Cattell (1962) and White (1966) set forth other possible matrices that may be useful for the more sophisticated investigator.

There is no problem in choosing a matrix for interpreting uncorrelated factors because all three of these matrices are identical in that case. It was proved in Chapters 2 and 3 that P and S are the same. V is identical to P and S when the factors are uncorrelated (proved in Chapter 10).

The reference vector correlations have a distinctive interpretation in a correlated factors solution. Because the correlation with the reference vector is the correlation of the variable with a vector orthogonal to the other factors, **a reference vector correlation is the part correlation of the variable with the factor with the variance predictable from the other factors removed.** It therefore reflects the distinctive relationship of the factor to the variable, a relationship that is statistically independent of any of the other factors in the analysis. The correlation coefficients in S do not reflect the independent contribution because the correlation between a variable and a factor is a function not only of its distinctive variance but also of all of the variance of the factor that overlaps with the other factors.

Although P is basic to the theory of factor analysis, it does not show the relationship of variables to the factors but of the factors to the variables. To use P for interpretation, the meaning of the factors should already be known. Learning how a relatively unknown variable is reproduced from known factors may add substantially to the interpretation of that variable.

The basic matrix for interpreting the factors is the factor structure. By examining which variables correlate high with the factor and which correlate low, it is possible to draw some conclusions as to the nature of the factor. Factor structure interpretation has several advantages. First, investigators are practiced in interpreting correlation coefficients. The coefficients have a limited range and raters have a feel for what practical importance each part of the range has. Second, S shows the relationship of the variable to the full factor. The elements of P and V systematically exclude overlap among the factors and represent only their unique contributions even when the overlap is theoretically important.

Third, S gives the relationship of the variables to the factors even if the factors are taken out of this specific context. Regardless of what other factors occur in the next study, the variables should correlate at the same level with a particular factor. The factor pattern and reference vector structure shift with the context of factors in which they are included and therefore can be interpreted only in that context. If factors C and D are highly correlated and factor D does not occur in the next analysis, the pattern elements for C will shift across the analyses. The only exception is where all the factors affecting the variable are included in the particular analysis or can be assumed to be orthogonal to those included. One can be assured that this exception occurs only in a large, multivariate experimental study or in a quite well-investigated area. Even essentially random correlations between factors can occasionally affect the loadings of V and P (Gordon, 1968). V and P are, therefore, less stable than S.[3]

It cannot, however, be said that V and P have no place in the interpretation of factors. Through the use of these matrices, the unique contribution of each factor to each variable can be evaluated. That information is often highly useful, particularly when the other factors in the solution are well known. Investigators such as Thurstone have always used P in their interpretations. **Indeed, proper interpretation of a set of factors can probably only occur if at least S and P are both examined.** (In addition, one or more of the matrices described in Chapter 11 are usually needed to interpret correlated factors).

In reading research reports, it is necessary to know exactly which matrix is presented as a factorial solution. Often, and particularly in older reports, only V is presented. If only one matrix is presented, however, it should usually be S because readers could still understand it even if they were unacquainted with the characteristics of a P or V. Ideally, all three matrices would be presented so that the reader would have the greatest amount of information to guide conclusions.

9.5.2 Salient Loadings

"Salient" has been used previously on an intuitive basis to identify high loadings. More technically, a **salient loading** is one that is sufficiently high to assume that a relationship exists between the variable and the factor. In addition, it usually means that the relationship is high enough so that the variable can aid in interpreting the factor and vice versa. What is a salient level for S may not, of course, be a salient level for P. Unfortunately, there is no exact way to determine salient loadings in any of the three matrices used for interpreting factors. Only rough guidelines can be given.

One lower bound for the definition of a salient variable is its significance level. Standard statistical texts provide formulas for testing the significance of the correlation coefficients in S, the multiple regression weights in P, and the part correlations in V (Guilford, 1965a; Nunnally, 1967), if one assumes these are ordinary correlations, weights, and part correlations. Where the variables

---

[3]Brogden (1969), Darlington (1968), Gordon (1968), and White (1966) discuss the problems involved in interpreting weights (cf. Section 12.2.2 also).

defining all the factors are specified before the data are examined, as in diagonal and multiple-group factoring, no capitalization upon chance occurs and the formulas are appropriate. Other procedures for extracting and rotating the variables do involve capitalization upon chance so that the standard error of the loadings in S, P, and V are higher than given by the formulas. It is therefore apparent that if any loading is insignificant by these significance tests, it has no chance of being significant by a better test. On the other hand, even if a loading is significant by the formulas, it may not actually be significant if capitalization on chance has occurred. These formulas generally provide only a lower bound for identifying salient loadings. Horn (1967) and Humphreys et al. (1969) show that the loadings arising by chance can be impressive.

Some empirical research, as summarized by Cliff and Hamburger (1967), does suggest that the formulas may not be totally inappropriate. In the case of rotating to a hypothesized position, the empirically found standard errors are approximately those given by the appropriate formula. Pennell (1968) has extended this analysis to take into account the size of the communalities as well. He found that his Monte Carlo standard errors for S were slightly above those for raw correlations of zero when the communalities approached zero but were only two-thirds that for variables with high communalities. Again, Pennell's analysis was for rotations to hypothesized factors.

What happens when chance correlations can be capitalized upon? Fortunately, in the table of Hamburger's results (Cliff & Hamburger, 1967), the standard errors of orthogonally rotated solutions are also given. From that table, it is apparent that the nature of the structure influences the standard error of the correlations in the factor structure. As the simple structure becomes more poorly defined—and therefore more options are available for the position of the factors—the standard error increases. But in every case, **the standard error of elements of S reported by Hamburger was considerably greater than that for the standard error of an ordinary correlation coefficient.** For his 12-variable problem, the observed standard error was roughly 150%–200% greater than the standard error for the correlation coefficient. This was true across several different procedures which rotated to simple structure.

The general approach is to have a sufficiently large sample so that anything that would be of interest for interpretation would be significant. A rough check can be provided by doubling the appropriate standard error and assuring that the minimum salient loading is significant by that rough test. For example, the minimum significant correlation coefficient ($p < .05$) with an n of 100 is about .2; therefore, only elements of S greater than an absolute value of .4 would be interpreted if the analysis was based on 100 individuals. If it was expected that elements as low as .3 would be interpreted, then a minimum n of 175 would be needed. These figures are for problems with small to moderate size correlation matrices, and may be too conservative for problems with many variables.

There are three more exacting but computationally more difficult ways of checking the possible statistical significance of loadings. The first is to use the formulas of Archer & Jennrich, (1973), which later research (Archer, 1976) suggests are reasonably accurate for rotated loadings. The second is to use confirmatory maximum likelihood factor analysis (Jöreskog, 1978). After the exploratory analysis, Jöreskog sets forth a several-step procedure for ascertaining whether the salient loadings can be considered significant. Basically a confirmatory maximum likelihood solution is identified by finding one or two variables for each factor that are loaded by only that factor with all other loadings so small and trivial that there is no doubt that they are insignificant. These trivial, insignificant loadings are set to 0 for the confirmatory maximum likelihood factor analysis. Standard errors are then available for all of the loadings that were not preset to 0. Because the loadings set to 0 were picked on the basis of the data themselves, the procedure cannot be considered to give exact significance tests; however, any loading found insignificant by this procedure would certainly be found insignificant by a more exact procedure.

The third procedure for checking possible statistical significance of loadings uses the "jackknife" approach (Lindell & St. Clair, 1980). Jackknife approaches are general ones for use when exact significant tests are not available. Essentially the procedure is to divide the N cases into k subgroups of n observations apiece. Each of the k subgroups is separately subtracted from the total sample, and the remaining subjects factored. Hence there are k factor analyses, each based upon $N - n$ observations. The result of these factor analyses are then submitted to an appropriate computer program (Lindell & St. Clair, 1980) which reports back the jackknifed estimates of the factor coefficients with estimates for evaluating statistical significance.

With large n's, loadings so small as to be uninterpretable may still be statistically significant. No one could identify that part of the variance of the variable that was causing a loading of, for example, .12. Therefore, another lower bound for defining the salient variable is that of meaningfulness. This may be the reason for the popularity of an absolute value of .3 as the minimum loading for interpretation.

Another influence on the meaningfulness of a loading in addition to its absolute size is the distribution of that variable's loadings across all the factors. If the variable loads on one and only one factor, then the interpretation is simplifed. Unless the communality were considerably lower than the reliability, one would simply interpret the central thrust of the variable as being related to the factor. Because this characteristic makes the solution much easier to interpret, it is a strong argument for simple structure rotation. If, however, the variable has high loadings on several factors, then the variance of the variable must be subjectively divided for interpretative purposes. This can only be done by examining the pattern of other loadings on the factors. Therefore, what is an interpretable salient loading for one variable may not be an interpretable salient loading for another variable.

*9.5.3 Cluster Analysis of Variables as an Aid to Interpreting Factors

The purpose of a cluster analysis of variables is to group together those variables that are most alike. Such a grouping can aid in the interpretation of factors by bringing together variables of a similar composition. It can also aid in interpreting the variables (Bromley, 1966).

In a simple procedure for clustering, one first identifies those variables that are salient on one and only one factor. These variables then form a cluster that is identified with the name of the factor. If there is a clear simple structure in the data, then it would be expected that there would be as many of these clusters as there are factors.

Additional clusters of variables can be formed from variables that have salient loadings on the same set of factors. All of the variables with the same pattern of salient loadings are put into an appropriately named cluster. This procedure would then generate several clusters in addition to those that define the factors.

Numerous variables may not have a pattern of salient loadings that is identical with that of any other variable. Several procedures have been developed to aid in determining how such variables are to be clustered. For example, Bromley (1966). Cureton, Cureton, and Durfee (1970), Guertin and Bailey (1970), and Tryon and Bailey (1970) give procedures by which variables not forming a clear cluster can nevertheless be placed into groups. The writer feels that cluster analysis is valuable when the clusters are clear and that borderline variables should be simply placed in a miscellaneous category.

Cluster analysis often becomes an implicit multiple-group factor analysis. This occurs when each cluster of variables is, for example, scored as a single entity and the variables are correlated with that score. The difference between such a cluster analysis of variables and the usual multiple-group factor analysis is primarily one of terminology, although in multiple-group factor analysis the defining variables are usually given by a priori theoretical considerations whereas cluster analysis often proceeds on an empirical basis.

A cluster analysis generally gives more clusters than there are factors. For example, a cluster analysis of the 24 ability tests problem gives results that range from the four clusters of Tryon and Bailey (1970), which seem to be quite similar to the factors often found in this problem, to the six clusters of Cureton, Cureton and Durfee (1970).

The only real advantage of cluster analysis is in the interpretation. By grouping variables together, the solution is simplified and thus made more comprehensible to the finite human mind. The same result can be obtained by replacing nonsalient loadings of the factor matrix with dashes and salient loadings with capital X's. One then can easily identify pure clusters of variables because they have the identical patterns of salient loadings. The more elaborate cluster analysis procedures seem to add little to the interpretation over a simple clustering of the variables based on the factor matrices. Clusters also seem to have a less conceptually clear basis and to be less parsimonious than similarly based multiple-group factors.

9.5.4 Interpretations as Hypotheses

A factor can only be interpreted by an individual with extensive background in the substantive area. With such background, the patterns of loadings in all relevant matrices can be examined to build up an interpretation of the factor. The interpretation will be based in part upon the salient loadings but will also be dependent upon the nonsalient loadings. Whenever a particular interpretation is proposed, it must be systematically checked against the variables that are unrelated to the factors to assure that these nonrelationships are also theoretically consistent.

What are the interpretations concerned with? Anything in that area that might have caused the observed correlations. The sources of factors can vary considerably. For example, the way the individuals are selected for the analysis can lead several variables to vary and generate a factor, or several variables can be measured in a tautologous manner so that they will correlate sufficiently to generate a factor. Hopefully, the design will be adequate to eliminate these as plausible hypotheses so that the influences most important for the theoretical evaluations at hand will underlie the factors.

The summary of the interpretation is presented as the factor's name. The name may be only descriptive or it may suggest a causal explanation for the occurrence of the factor. Because the name of the factor is all most readers of the research report will remember, it should be carefully chosen.

Once a factor has been named, there is a tendency to reify it. It is assumed that the name is completely accurate and that the factor "explains" the variables. However, a factor is only one operational representative of the construct implicit in the factor's label—and it might not be the best one. Further research after the exploratory factor analysis is almost always necessary to assure that the factor is a legitimate operational representative of the construct. Manipulative experimental or quasi-experimental studies involving scores on the factor are usually necessary before the factor can be interpreted causally.

It must be stressed that interpretations of factors are post hoc unless a hypothesis testing procedure is used. In any *post hoc* situation, no interpreation is regarded as final but only as a lead for further research. The interpretation leads to including new variables that, under the interpretation, should load this factor and only this factor in a new analysis. When such variables do load upon the hypothesized factor, then the interpretation would be confirmed. The widely followed practice of regarding interpretation of a factor as confirmed solely because the post hoc analysis "makes sense" is to be deplored. Factor interpretations can only be considered hypotheses for another study.

*10 Rotation

There are occasions when more detail is necessary regarding particular aspects of rotation, detail that was not presented in the last chapter. For example, Chapter 9 assumed computer programs were available and did not provide detail on the algebra by which rotation is calculated. Further details may be needed if simple structure rotation in the traditional sense is judged inappropriate. Further detail also may be needed for procedures currently in development.

The first section, 10.1, contains the basic algebraic principles of rotation. A description of the use of the principles for visual rotation, that is, rotating to simple structure when the simple structure criterion is the gestalt seen by viewing the plotted factors, is next (Section 10.2). Visual rotation was the original method and is still used as a criterion that many analytic approaches attempt to duplicate; with appropriate programming for time-sharing computer systems, visual rotation can now compete with analytic rotation from an efficiency perspective.

There are other analytic procedures than those presented in Chapter 9. One of these, the Harris–Kaiser class of solutions, is intriguing in its derivation (Section 10.3). Further analytic procedures based upon principles other than simple structure per se are in Section 10.4. The chapter concludes with a technique, extension analysis, which allows factor loadings to be calculated for variables that were not included in the factor analysis (Section 10.5).

10.1 ALGEBRAIC PRINCIPLES OF ROTATION

In Chapter 9 we explained how rotation is carried out but did not present the mathematics behind the equations. Geometric or algebraic derivations could be presented. Harman (1976) gives geometric derivations and the algebraic derivations are presented in this section.

---

*May be considered optional reading.

Rotation of factors is a case of linear transformations of matrices. The basic principles of transforming factors where the factors may be correlated is given in Section 10.1.1. Because the factor extraction procedures usually extract uncorrelated factors, it is assumed that the rotation procedure always starts with a set of uncorrelated factors. The special case of rotating for uncorrelated factors is discussed in Section 10.1.2.

10.1.1 Transformation: The General Case

The basic factor equation is:

$$Z_{nv} = F_{nf} P'_{fv} \qquad (10.1.1)$$

in which, as in earlier chapters, F is the factor score, P is the factor pattern, and Z refers to the reproduced variables. If it is desired to change the factors, then a matrix of weights is needed. This matrix contains the weights to be given to each of the old factor scores to create the new factor scores. Defining this weight matrix as W gives the following basic equation:

$$F_{nf'} = F_{nf} W'_{ff'} \qquad (10.1.2)$$

where $F_{nf'}$ are the n individual scores on the f' new factors, F_{nf} are the n individual scores on the f original factors and $W'_{ff'}$ is the weight matrix for transforming the old factors, f, to the new factors, f'. It will be assumed throughout that $f = f'$ (i.e., there is no change in the number of factors). Note that each row of the standard weight matrix, $W_{f'f}$, gives the set of weights by which one new factor can be calculated from the original factors. Because a matrix multiplication is involved, the transformations are linear with the new factors being a weighted summation of the old factors. The W in Eq. (10.1.2) is a transposed matrix, as shown by the prime, because the usual form of it is with the new factors, f', as rows.

$W_{f'f}$ may not take any imaginable form. One restriction on $W_{f'f}$ is that the factors should maintain their variances of one no matter how they are rotated.

When F is transformed, P must also be shifted so that the reproduction of Z can be maintained. The transformation matrix, $T_{ff'}$, is defined as that matrix which shifts the original P into the new P, that is:

$$P_{vf'} = P_{vf} T_{ff'} \qquad (10.1.3)$$

where $P_{vf'}$ is the new factor pattern for the new set of factor scores. Naturally, the following condition must also hold true:

$$Z_{nv} = F_{nf'} P'_{f'v} \qquad (10.1.4)$$

The relationship between $W_{ff'}$ and $T_{ff'}$ can be derived. Substituting Eqs. (10.1.2) and (10.1.3) into Eq. (10.1.4) gives:

$$Z_{nv} = F_{nf} W'_{ff'} (P_{vf} T_{ff'})' \qquad (10.1.5)$$

Removing the parentheses:

$$Z_{nv} = F_{nf} W'_{ff'} T'_{f'f} P'_{fv} \tag{10.1.6}$$

Substituting in the definition of Z_{nv} from Eq. (10.1.1):

$$F_{nf} P'_{fv} = F_{nf} W'_{ff'} T'_{f'f} P'_{fv} \tag{10.1.7}$$

However, this equation can only hold true if:

$$I = T_{ff'} W_{f'f} \tag{10.1.8}$$

Postmultiplying each side of Eq. (10.1.8) by the inverse of W gives:

$$W_{f'f}^{-1} = T_{ff'} \tag{10.1.9}$$

or premultiplying by the inverse of T gives:

$$T_{ff'}^{-1} = W_{f'f} \tag{10.1.10}$$

In calculating T and W, or vice versa, note that the subscripts are in opposite order. Because these are square matrices, it is easy to make an error and accidentally transpose a matrix.

Although rotation can be viewed as concerned with shifts in the factor scores, it is more convenient to rotate in terms of the factor pattern. Not only are the calculations easier because one does not have the large F matrix involved, but P is used to understand and interpret the nature of the new factors. Most of the principles for rotation are based upon an examination of P. Hence, T is the matrix most utilized in rotation and W is only calculated on special occasions, as in visual rotation.

Once T is established, it is then possible to solve for other matrices of interest. In particular, the correlations among the new factors, f', are desired and the appropriate formulas can be derived. From the definition of correlations:

$$R_{f'f'} = F'_{f'n} F_{nf'} n^{-1} \tag{10.1.11}$$

Substituting from Eq. (10.1.2):

$$R_{f'f'} = (F_{nf} W'_{ff'})' (F_{nf} W'_{ff'})n^{-1} \tag{10.1.12}$$

Rearranging terms:

$$R_{f'f'} = W_{f'f} F'_{fn} F_{nf} n^{-1} W'_{ff'} \tag{10.1.13}$$

Because the original factors are defined as uncorrelated:

$$R_{f'f'} = W_{f'f} I W'_{ff'} = W_{f'f} W'_{ff'} \tag{10.1.14}$$

R can also be calculated from T; substituting from Eq. (10.1.10) into Eq. (10.1.14) gives:

$$R_{f'f'} = (T_{ff'}^{-1}) (T_{ff'}^{-1})' \tag{10.1.15}$$

$R_{f'f'}$ contains the correlations between the factors only if the factor scores are unit length. Because the extraction procedure invariably extracts factors of unit length, it is only necessary to preserve this characteristic. The diagonals of $R_{f'f'}$ will be unities if and only if the rows of $W_{f'f}$ or $T_{ff'}^{-1}$ are normalized (i.e., the sum of the squared elements must be 1.0).

10.1.2 Orthogonal Transformations

If the factors are to be transformed orthogonally, then there can be no correlation among the factors. In that case, $R_{f'f} = I$. From Eq. (10.1.15) it follows that:

$$(T_{ff'}^{-1})\,(T_{ff'}^{-1})' = I \tag{10.1.16}$$

and from Eq. (10.1.14):

$$W_{f'f}\,W_{ff'}' = I \tag{10.1.17}$$

Multiplying Eq. (10.1.17) by the inverse of W:

$$W_{ff'}' = W_{f'f}^{-1} \tag{10.1.18}$$

From Eqs. (10.1.9) and (10.1.18):

$$T_{ff'} = W_{ff'}' \tag{10.1.19}$$

And:

$$W_{f'f} = T_{f'f}' \tag{10.1.20}$$

Therefore, in the orthogonal case the weights necessary to rotate the factor scores are the identical weights used to transform the factor pattern as well. Note that the usual form of the weight matrix is the transpose of the usual form of the transformation matrix.

Multiplication of an orthogonal transformation matrix by another orthogonal matrix leaves the product an orthogonal matrix. This can be shown by defining A and B as two orthogonal transformation matrices. The product of these two matrices is then defined as T, the final transformation matrix. If T is an orthogonal matrix, then $T\,T'$ will equal an identity matrix. The proof that $T\,T'$ is an identity matrix, and therefore that T must be an orthogonal matrix, begins with the following definition of a new matrix, C:

$$T\,T' = C \tag{10.1.21}$$

Substituting the definition of T:

$$(AB)\,(AB)' = C \tag{10.1.22}$$

Then:

$$A\,B\,B'\,A' = C \tag{10.1.23}$$

Because B is orthogonal:

$$A I A' = C \qquad (10.1.24)$$

Because A is also orthogonal:

$$I = C \qquad (10.1.25)$$

So the product of multiplying one orthogonal transformation matrix by another is also an orthogonal matrix.

Orthogonal transformation matrices can be built from other orthogonal transformation matrices. To begin, a 2-by-2 orthogonal matrix is developed. Developing the matrix is simple: when one element is given, the other elements are defined so that the sums of the squares of the rows and columns equal 1.0. A minus sign is given to any of the elements—the one selected is your choice—so that the off-diagonal elements of the identity matrix will equal zero when the matrix is postmultiplied by its transpose. The 2-by-2 matrix can be imbedded in as large a matrix as desired because the other elements of the matrix can have ones for diagonal elements and zeros for off-diagonal elements with the result still multiplying out to an identity matrix. By multiplying together a series of such matrices, a final orthogonal transformation matrix can be established. This procedure is extensively used in visual rotation.

Example

Assume a_{11} is given as .6 and a 2×2 orthogonal transformation matrix is desired. Because $A_{2,2}$ must be orthogonal, $A A'$ is I. So $a_{11}^2 + a_{12}^2 = 1$ and $a_{12} = \sqrt{1 - a_{11}^2}$ or .8. Then $a_{11}^2 + a_{12}^2$ and $a_{21}^2 + a_{22}^2$ both equal one, while $a_{11} a_{12} + a_{21} a_{22}$ equals zero. Therefore, a_{21} and a_{22} are $-.8$ and .6.

In the same manner, we can draw up another such matrix:

$$B = \begin{bmatrix} .71 & .71 \\ -.71 & .71 \end{bmatrix}$$

Then:

$$= \overset{A}{\begin{bmatrix} .6 & .8 \\ -.8 & .6 \end{bmatrix}} \cdot \overset{B}{\begin{bmatrix} .71 & .71 \\ -.71 & .71 \end{bmatrix}} \overset{=}{} \overset{T}{\begin{bmatrix} -.14 & .99 \\ -.99 & -.14 \end{bmatrix}} \cdot$$

And:

$$TT' = \begin{bmatrix} 1.01 & .00 \\ .00 & 1.01 \end{bmatrix} \cdot$$

(The diagonal elements are not exactly 1.00 owing to rounding error.) This demonstrates both the construction of a 2-by-2 orthogonal transformation matrix and the fact that multiplying two orthogonal matrices gives an orthogonal transformation matrix.

10.2   ROTATING VISUALLY

Initially, analytic procedures for rotation were not available. Capitalizing upon the geometric representation of factors, investigators found it worthwhile to rotate the data by plotting the unrotated solution. The investigators then determined how the factors could be shifted to more intuitively compelling positions. Because the principles are simpler when rotating to orthogonal simple structure, that is discussed first (Section 10.2.1). The case of oblique visual rotation is then discussed (Section 10.2.2). Thurstone found it useful to introduce a new coordinate system for oblique rotations, and this procedure is widely used in analytical rotation. The use of the new vectors in rotation to oblique simple structure is discussed in Section 10.2.3. In this discussion simple structure is assumed to be the criterion of rotation, but the principles apply to rotating to any visually determined position.

It is generally agreed that some individuals are better rotators than others in that plots of their solutions are more intuitively compelling. The importance of the differences between rotators has never been investigated, nor has any criterion been developed for who is a good rotator and who is not, except that of hyperplane count. The possibility of rapid visual rotation from a terminal on a time-sharing computer means visual rotation is now feasible, and questions of the nature and replicability of intuitively compelling procedures now can be investigated. Chapter *4 is essential background for this section.

10.2.1 Orthogonal Visual Rotation

Visual rotation is begun with the factors provided by the extraction process. The unrotated factors are used as the coordinates for a plot. The endpoint of each variable vector is then determined by its factor pattern (cf. Chapter 4). Because it is difficult to "plot" four or five factors in hyperspace, the factors are plotted two by two. Factor one is plotted first against factor two and then against factor three and so on. After factor one has been plotted with all other factors, then factor two is plotted with factors three, four, etc. This process continues until all the factors have been plotted against each other.

For any one plot, there are only two factors and these two factors are used as the abscissa and ordinate for the plot. The variable's factor pattern loadings on only the two factors determine its position on that particular plot.

After all the variables have been plotted for a given pair of factors, the two-factor plot is examined to determine where shifts might be made to bring the factors closer to the variables. The examination ideally proceeds without any knowledge of the variables to avoid capitalizing on chance to favor a pet theory.

When the new position has been selected for a factor, that single factor is then entered on the plot. Once the first factor is rotated, then the second factor is drawn to form a right angle with the first. Naturally, one rotates that factor of the pair which will most improve the situation. If a rotation would force the other factor too far away from a desired position, then a compromise position is used.

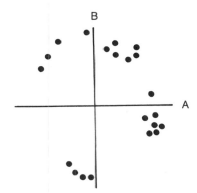

FIG. 10.1.   Unrotated factors.

Example

Figure 10.1 presents two unrotated factors. A glance at the plot suggests that both *A* and *B* should be shifted so that their vectors pass closer to the clusters of variables. In this case, Factor *A* was moved down to the fourth quadrant until it was just on the other side of the cluster of variables. The rotated solution is illustrated in Fig. 10.2.

Because the new factors are drawn in at unit length, their relationships to the original factors are given by their coordinates. The coordinates form a weight matrix, $W_{f'f}$ which is used with the original f factor scores to compute the rotated f' factor scores (cf. Eq. 10.1.2). The values of f' and f are the same; the prime is added to separate the rotated from the original factors. The elements of $W_{f'f}$ are read off the plot.

When the two factors are orthogonal, the reading of one weight element is sufficient. The other elements can be calculated from it because Eq. (10.1.17) shows that the weight matrix times its transpose must equal the identity matrix. The other weights can be calculated as follows:

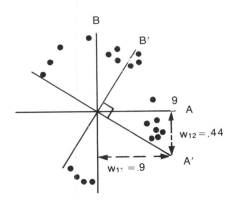

FIG. 10.2. Determining the weights for the orthogonal rotated factors.

$w_{11} = w_{11}$ as read from the plot

$$w_{21} = \sqrt{1 - w_{11}{}^2}$$

$$w_{12} = \sqrt{1 - w_{11}{}^2} \qquad\qquad (10.2.1)$$

$$w_{22} = \sqrt{1 - w_{12}{}^2} = \sqrt{w_{11}{}^2}$$

The signs are given by an examination of the plot.

Example

In Fig. 10.2 the coordinate of A' on A is .9. By the application of the formulas in Eq. (10.2.1), the total factor pattern for A' is $.90\ A - .44B$, whereas the factor pattern for B' is $.44\ A + .90\ B$.

It is best to read all four coordinates from the plot and then adjust them to give a matrix that will be consistent with the above equations. This reduces the error in interpreting the plot.

With the weights for transforming the old factor scores into the new factor scores, it is now possible to calculate the **transformation matrix** to transform the factor pattern to the new factor pattern. In the orthogonal case, the appropriate transformation matrix $T_{ff'}$ is shown by Eq. (10.1.19) to be the transpose of the weight matrix (i.e., $T = W'$). The old P is postmultiplied by T and the new P plotted. If the solution is satisfactory, then those are the rotated factors. If not, a new transformation matrix is developed from an analysis of this new plot.

The second transformation matrix would be applicable to the P just computed rather than to the original P. However, to avoid cumulative rounding errors, the next P is computed from the original P. This is possible because, as shown in Section 10.1.2, orthogonal matrices multiplied times each other remain orthogonal. The transformation matrix to take the unrotated P to the second rotated position is derived simply.

By definition:

$$P_{vf''} = P_{vf'}\, T_{f'f''} \qquad\qquad (10.2.2)$$

where f'' identifies the third solution. Then substituting a definition of $P_{vf'}$ into Eq. (10.2.2):

$$P_{vf''} = P_{vf}\, T_{ff'}\, T_{f'f''} \qquad\qquad (10.2.3)$$

This can be readily generalized to any number of transformation matrices. The same type of derivation for producing the second rotated position factor scores from the unrotated factor scores also holds and gives:

$$F_{nf''} = F_{nf}\, W'_{ff'}\, W'_{f'f''} \qquad\qquad (10.2.4)$$

The two factors being rotated may be only two of many. In that case, the total transformation matrix would contain a four-element subsection showing the relationships between the two factors being rotated. The rest of the transformation matrix contains unities in the diagonal elements and zeros in the off-diagonals. When the original P is postmultiplied by this transformation matrix, only the factors being rotated are altered. With the new P, two more factors are plotted for possible rotation. One of these factors may or may not be one of the factors already rotated. From this plot, a new transformation matrix is determined, Eq. (10.2.3) is used to develop a total transformation matrix, and the original P is postmultiplied by the total T for the next P. This procedure would be continued until the investigator was satisfied with all of the plots.

A procedure that many rotators find easier is to plot each of the unrotated factors against every other factor. On all of these plots, the appropriate shifts would be determined and an appropriate transformation matrix developed. All of these transformation matrices would be multiplied together to give a total transformation matrix. This one transformation matrix would then be premultiplied by the original P to give the first new P. All of the factors would then again be plotted against each other and another transformation matrix determined. The process is contined until either the solution is perfect or excessive weariness sets in. This procedure calculates a new P only when all of the factors have been examined and rotated against each other. It thus involves considerably less labor than recalculating P at each step.

With either procedure, the rotations made on one plot can interact in an unforeseen manner with those made on another plot. For this reason, the factors are always replotted after the first transformations are made to determine how accurately the total transformations produce the desired solution. In any major study, one plans to plot each pair of factors against each other many times. This allows experimentation with new positions and, if necessary, backing off from those new positions at a later point. In personality data with 15 to 20 factors, it has been the writer's experience that 15 to 20 overall rotations, where each such rotation entails examining $f(f - 1)/2$ plots between factors, are needed. The rotation is finished when all further transformations decrease the hyperplane count in V.

*10.2.2 Direct Visual Rotation for Oblique Simple Structure

Rotating directly to oblique simple structure was a procedure superseded by Thurstone's reference vector system (cf. Section 10.2.3) because the latter was easier. However, direct oblique rotation is again making an appearance in an occasional analytical procedure. The procedure is basically the same as that derived under orthogonal visual rotation, but, of course, allows factors to be correlated.

The unrotated, orthogonal factor pattern is plotted with the original factors as orthogonal coordinates and the variables as points that are plotted by their weights. In placing the new factors, both factors are drawn to ideal positions without regard for their relationship to each other. Such factors are shown in Fig. 10.3. The coordinates, or weights, of both new factors are then read off the plot, as is also shown in Fig. 10.3. The weights for one factor cannot be calculated from those of the other factors because the factors need not be orthogonal to each other. However, the weights for any given factor must have their sum of squares equal to 1.0 to maintain that factor's unit length. Therefore, after the weights are read from the graph, the weight matrix, $W_{f'f}$, is normalized by rows to reduce the impact from minor errors in reading the plots. (W is normalized by rows by dividing each element in the row by the sum of the squared elements for that row.)

The calculation of the new P from the old P is more difficult in the oblique case than in the orthogonal case because T is not the transpose of W. Instead, Eq. (10.1.9) indicates that $W_{f'f}$ needs to be inverted (i.e., $T = W^{-1}$). Although the coordinates are the weights to calculate the factor scores from the original factor scores, they are not the weights to calculate the new factor pattern.

When the original factor pattern has been postmultiplied by T, the rotated factors are plotted to determine whether or not further rotation is necessary. Although the correlated factors are often plotted as if they were uncorrelated, it is naturally better to plot them accurately. To plot correlated factors, it is necessary to first obtain $R_{f'f'}$ by multiplying the weight matrix by its transpose [cf. Section 10.1.1, particularly Eqs. (10.1.10) and (10.1.15)]. The correlations among the factors are, as noted in Chapter 4, the cosines of the angles among the factors and are used to plot the two factors. The factor pattern is then used to plot the variables (the procedure for plotting variables when the factors are correlated is given in Chapter 4).

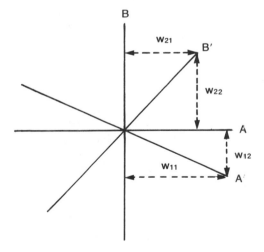

FIG. 10.3. Determining the weights for the oblique rotated factors.

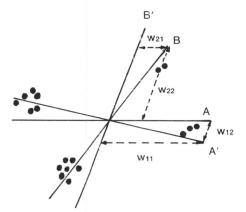

FIG. 10.4. Determining $W_{f'f}$ when rotating correlated factors.

Upon examination of the plot of the correlated factors, further rotation may be necessary. The new factors are drawn in where desired and their weight matrix determined. Figure 10.4 illustrates the determination of the weights. The new weight matrix is then inverted to obtain the new transformation matrix. The transformation matrix will shift the initial rotated factors into a new position. Because the maintenance of orthogonality is no concern, every factor can be plotted against every other factor and all of the weights entered into one large matrix, $W_{f''f'}$. However, the weight matrix determined by the oblique plot gives only the weights for computing the factor scores from those of the prior rotation. To minimize the accumulation of calculation error, this weight matrix needs to be replaced with one that can be used with the original, orthogonal factors. From Eq. (10.2.4) it is apparent that the desired weight matrix is:

$$W_{f''f} = W_{f''f'} \, W_{f'f} \tag{10.2.5}$$

Therefore the weight matrix estimated from the oblique plot is premultiplied by the weight matrix that transforms the factors from their unrotated form to the last oblique position. $W_{f''f}$ is then normalized by rows to assure the factors retaining their unit length, before being inverted.

A problem may arise when rotating factors without observing the factors simultaneously in hyperspace. Some rotations may be incompatible with other rotations. The result would be factors that are not unit length. Therefore, the transformation matrix, calculated as the inverse of the weight matrix, is normalized by columns to maintain unit-length factors.

As is true in the orthogonal case, the factors can be rotated pair by pair with a new pattern calculated after each shift or rotated simultaneously by one major weight matrix drawn up from all the plots. The calculation advantages obviously lie with the latter, but with either procedure a large number of rotations can be expected if a good simple structure is desired.

10.2.3 Oblique Visual Rotation by Reference Vectors

Visual rotation originated in the days before computers. Without a computer, constantly taking the inverse of $W_{f'f}$ requires an extensive amount of calculation. Thurstone avoided taking an inverse by setting up and rotating **reference vectors** (the term *reference* was used because they are solely for the purpose of plotting points, and using vectors indicates that they are *not* the factors). The reference vectors are such that the reference vector loadings are proportional to the factor pattern coefficients. When the number of zeros in the reference vector matrix is maximized, then the number of zeros in the factor pattern is maximized as well. This procedure allowed Thurstone to rotate without inverting the weight matrix at each step.

The stress on the number of zero elements in the reference vector loadings is characteristic of Thurstone. He was oriented toward basing the factors on, in essence, the variables that did not load them rather than the variables that did. However, because there are a limited number of degrees of freedom in any rotational solution, this approach is generally equivalent to basing the facor on the variables which define it.

Figure 10.5 shows the reference vectors, V_A and V_B, for factors A and B when the factors correlate .5. A *reference vector* is defined as that vector normal (i.e., orthogonal) to a factor's hyperplane. In a multidimensional space, the hyperplane is the intersection of all other factors with a given factor. In the two-dimensional situation, factor B defines factor A's hyperplane, and all factor pattern elements of A that lie on this line are exactly zero. This applies to oblique as well as orthogonal solutions because the weight on A is established by drawing a line parallel to B from the variable to A. Likewise, factor A defines factor B's

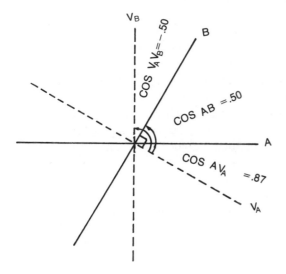

FIG. 10.5.   Reference vectors.

hyperplane. Because the reference vector is defined as orthogonal to its factor's hyperplane and the other factor defines that factor's hyperplane, the reference vector for A, V_A, has been drawn in Fig. 10.5 as orthogonal to factor B. The reference vector for factor B, V_B, has been drawn orthogonal to factor A. The figure also gives the cosines of the angles for the various relationships with factor A's reference vector.

It can be noted that the vector V_A correlates .87 with factor A and $-.50$ with vector V_B. This illustrates two principles: First, the reference vector is not identical with the factor but is only correlated with it. As the correlations between factors increase, the correlation of a reference vector with its own factor decreases. Second, the correlation between a factor's reference vector and another factor's reference vector is opposite in sign and approximately the same magnitude as the actual correlation of those two factors.

The **reference vector structure** gives the correlations of the variables with each factor's reference vector. This is illustrated in Fig. 10.6 where, for simplicity's sake, only the reference vector for factor A is entered. Because the reference vector is, like the factor, unit length, the correlation between V_A and 1 is the cosine of the angle formed by 1 and the vector. The factor pattern element for variable 1 is given by its coordinate; this coordinate is determined by drawing a line parallel to B from 1 and noting where it crosses factor A. In the illustration, the factor pattern loading $p_{1A} = .50$. The correlation of variable 1 with factor A is given by the cosine of the angle between 1 and A. The cosine is computed by noting where a line perpendicular to A from 1 crosses A and then solving for the cosine by the usual equation where the cosine equals the adjacent side divided by the hypotenuse; the correlation between 1 and A is, in the example, $.80/.95$, which equals .84.

The correlations with the reference vectors are determined in the same manner as with a factor. A line perpendicular to the reference vector is dropped from 1 to

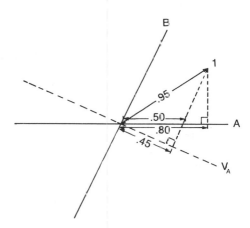

FIG. 10.6. Correlations with reference vectors.

form a right-angle triangle; the correlation then equals the adjacent side divided by the hypotenuse which, in this case, is .45/.95 or .47.

Because reference vector A is orthogonal to B and the line is drawn from 1 orthogonal to V_A, that line is parallel to B. Therefore, the same line is used to determine both p_{1A} and v_{1A}. Use of the same line demonstrates one reason why Thurstone introduced reference vectors: because the factor pattern coefficient is always proportional to the reference vector structure correlation, maximizing the number of zeros in the latter matrix is the same as maximizing the number of zeros in the former matrix. As the figure illustrates, the reference vector correlation will always be slightly less than the factor pattern weight.

The procedure for rotating reference vectors visually with the aid of a computer is set forth by Cattell and Foster (1963). Rotating the reference vectors involves the use of another transformation matrix, λ, which rotates the reference vectors. The rotation proceeds in the same manner as noted previously for oblique visual rotation. The relationships between the reference vector transformation matrix and other matrices of interest are as follows (see Harman (1976) for derivations):

$$V_{vf'} = P_{vf}\lambda_{ff'} \tag{10.2.6}$$

$$V_{vf''} = P_{vf}\lambda_{ff'}\lambda_{ff''} \tag{10.2.7}$$

$$R_{rr} = \lambda'_{f'f}\lambda_{ff} \tag{10.2.8}$$

where R_{rr} contains the correlations among the reference vectors. If D_{rr} is a diagonal matrix of reciprocals of the square roots of the diagonal element in R_{rr}^{-1}, then:

$$T_{ff'} = \lambda_{ff'} D_{rr}^{-1} \tag{10.2.9}$$

The correlations among reference vectors are checked after each shift to evaluate the degree of obliqueness. From the preceding formulas, it can be noted that orthogonal factors are again the initial position, and the λ is altered to reflect the desired shifts in the factors. No inverses are needed until the transformation matrix for the factors themselves is needed. Thus, there is a considerable savings of computational time when facilities for the rapid inverse of a matrix are not available.

With modern computing facilities, there is no reason why the factor pattern cannot be rotated directly. However, due to the historical precedent of Thurstone—and, perhaps, a lack of understanding that he went to reference vectors principally for ease of calculation—the oblique analytical rotation programs usually rotate the reference vector structure. Even oblique Procrustes is generally approached by assuming that the hypothesized matrix, H, is actually a reference vector structure.

Given the availability of computers, it now appears that both the reference vector and the primary factor approaches to rotation are practical. If the former is chosen, then the rotation will be based on equations and procedures such as are given in this section. Each of the resulting factors will be primarily defined by those variables with high communalities that do *not* load that particular factor, a solution that can be considered more scientifically elegant than basing the factor on the usually small set of variables that load it (Cattell, 1966c, pp. 184*ff*).

The results of primary factor and reference vector rotation will probably be highly similar only if a distinct simple structure exists in the data. Otherwise, the two approaches may produce somewhat different results. Little is currently known about the degree to which one can commonly expect the two approaches to converge.

10.3   ORTHOBLIQUE SOLUTIONS

Harris and Kaiser (1964) have developed a general procedure for direct oblique rotation that is based upon a series of orthogonal transformations. From the series of orthogonal transformations and their rescaling, an oblique solution results. It is the combination of orthogonal and oblique solutions that gives it its label, **orthoblique.**

Rotating obliquely by using orthogonal transformations appears to be a contradiction in terms. It is, if it is interpreted too narrowly. However, if it is understood that an oblique transformation matrix can be formed by appropriately combining several orthogonal transformation matrices, then oblique rotation by orthogonal transformations is a possibility. The procedure of this section rescales a transformation matrix developed from, for example, varimax by multiplying it by a diagonal matrix, D_2. Another diagonal matrix, D_1, is used to keep the factors at unit length.

From the definition of orthogonality, all orthogonal transformation matrices have the following characteristic (cf. Section 10.1.2):

$$T_{ff'}\, T'_{f'f} = I = T'_{f'f}\, T_{ff'} \tag{10.3.1}$$

Matrices can be inserted into any equation, including (10.3.1), so long as the total insertion is an identity matrix. An insertion that has this characteristic is a matrix multiplied by its inverse. For example, a diagonal matrix multiplied by its inverse can be added to Eq. (10.3.1). Inserting such a diagonal matrix, D, into Eq. (10.3.1) gives:

$$T_{ff'}\, D\, D^{-1}\, T'_{f'f} = I \tag{10.3.2}$$

The following equation consists of a transformation matrix and two diagonal matrices that still give an identity matrix when multiplied (the subscript on the diagonal matrix does not indicate its order but, in this section, which of two diagonal matrices it is):

$$I = (\{D_2[T_{ff'}(D_1 D_1^{-1})\, T'_{f'f}]D_2^{-1}\} \{D_2^{-1}\, [T_{ff'}\, (D_1^{-1}\, D_1)T'_{f'f}]D_2\})$$
$$\tag{10.3.3}$$

Because the elements on the right-hand side of Eq. (10.3.3) equal an identity matrix, they can be substituted into any equation as desired. Harris and Kaiser (1964) ingeniously substituted such an equation into the characteristic roots-and-vectors equation that reproduces the correlation matrix. The reproduced correlation matrix as a function of the characteristic roots and vectors, from Eq. (6.1.7), is:

$$\hat{R}_{vv} = A_{vf} S_{ff} A'_{fv} \tag{10.3.4}$$

where A has the characteristic vectors and S contains the roots. Substituting Eq. (10.3.3) into the middle of Eq. (10.3.4) and adding parentheses gives:

$$\hat{R}_{vv} = (A_{vf} S_{ff}^{.5} D_2 T_{ff'} D_1) (D_1^{-1} T'_{f'f} D_2^{-1} D_2^{-1} T_{ff'} D_1^{-1})$$

$$(D_1 T'_{f'f} D_2 S_{ff}^{.5} A'_{fv}) \tag{10.3.5}$$

Because

$$\hat{R}_{vv} = P_{vf'} R_{f'f'} P'_{f'v} \tag{10.3.6}$$

we can define:

$$P_{vf'} = A_{vf} S_{ff}^{.5} D_2 T_{ff'} D_1 \tag{10.3.7}$$

and also define:

$$R_{f'f'} = D_1^{-1} T'_{f'f} D_2^{-1} D_2^{-1} T_{ff'} D_1^{-1} \tag{10.3.8}$$

Because $A_{vf} S_{ff}^{.5}$ is the formula for the principal factors, $P_{vf'}$ in Eq. (10.3.7) is proportional by columns to an orthogonal transformation of the rescaled principal factors. D_2 is a matrix that indicates the proportionality; T gives the orthogonal transformation matrix, and D_1 is the rescaling matrix. Harris and Kaiser (1964) applied this approach to rotation to the primary factors and those following their approach have done likewise.

D_1 is included in Eq. (10.3.8) to guarantee that the diagonal elements of $R_{f'f'}$ are unities. It is therefore calculated simply as a function of the orthogonal transformation matrix, T, and the other scalar matrix, D_2. If D_2 is an identity matrix, then the rotation is orthogonal. This is considered Case I by Harris and Kaiser; the other solutions from these formulas are Case II (Harris and Kaiser also present a Case III that is not discussed here because it does not appear profitable for oblique rotation). Case II does have the restriction that any two factors being rotated cannot be in the same or nonadjacent quadrants, a restriction that limits the average correlation among the factors.

Nothing has been said about how T and D_2 are formed. However, because T is an orthogonal transformation matrix, any orthogonal analytic program could be used to calculate an appropriate T. Varimax is often used.

The most useful approach to defining D_2 appears to be setting it equal to some power, p, of S. In simple cases where the variables form completely independent clusters and each variable is loaded by one factor, Harris and Kaiser (1964) suggest that D_2 be set equal to $(S^{.5})^{-1}$. Using quartimax to produce T, they found good results with such a solution. On the other hand, when the variables can be expected to be loaded by several factors, this procedure produces difficulties.

In other solutions, D_2 is usually dropped from the equation and S^p replaces S. When p is set to 0, the solution is the same as if D_2 were set equal to $(S^{.5})^{-1}$. The other value for p suggested by Harris and Kaiser was .5. A value for p of 1.0 will give an orthogonal solution.

Hakstian (1970b) has systematically varied the values given to p for a series of four problems. He also systematically varied T by using combinations of the quartimax and varimax criteria. The criterion for a proper rotation for each matrix was the visually guided rotation which had appeared in the literature. He generally concluded that the power of p was more important than whether or not quartimax or varimax was used and that this power should be equal to or less than .5. Howarth (personal communication) has reported encouraging results with the Harris–Kaiser procedure even for analyses of several hundred variables.

Although developing a program specifically to perform Harris–Kaiser rotations would be profitable (Hakstian, 1970a), the rotation can be performed with ordinary programs. Varimax, for example, would be used to calculate T, D_2 computed from the characteristic roots and D_1 solved to maintain the unities in R_{ff}.

The uses of the orthoblique solutions described previously does require somewhat arbitrary decisions, particularly the power of p that is to be used. Hofmann has attempted to resolve this problem by developing an index of simple structure and then finding the power of p that thus meets the criterion. His index of simple structure (Hofmann, 1978) is to maximize the variance of the columns of loadings in a special matrix consisting of the absolute values of the direction cosines (see Chapter 4). The criterion resembles that of varimax because it is maximizing the variance of a column of loadings, but instead of using squared loadings the absolute value of the direction cosines are used, thus leading to the somewhat different weighting for simple structure. The level of p is varied and the criterion checked; a two-stage procedure is used to overcome some minor technical problems. The procedure is called **orthotran.**

To provide empirical data on the usefulness of the orthotran solution, 17 sets of data for which a subjective rotation was available in the literature were reanalyzed. Four procedures were used in the analysis: Oblimin, a ''proportional'' orthoblique, and an independent clusters orthoblique (two alternative solutions for the Case II orthoblique set of solutions), orthotran, and the original subjective solution. The criterion by which each solution was evaluated consisted of the mean absolute correlation among factors (averaged by the Z transformation procedure), the percentage in the ± 10 hyperplane, the average variable complexity showing the average number of factors having salient factor pattern loadings per variable, and the coefficient of congruence between the rotated

TABLE 10.3.1
Orthomax Rotations of Truncated Box Components

Orthogonal Solution:	Varimax			Quartimax			Equamax		
	Factors			*Factors*			*Factors*		
	1	*2*	*3*	*1*	*2*	*3*	*1*	*2*	*3*
Reference Vector Structure									
Length squared	.74	-.07	-.01	.91	-.19	-.30	.68	-.04	.01
Height squared	-.00	.60	.09	.79	-.13	.45	-.10	.60	.06
Width squared	.02	.12	.60	.61	.40	.00	-.01	.09	.58
Length plus width	.51	-.02	.27	.87	.07	-.22	.46	-.00	.28
Length plus height	.46	.28	-.00	.96	-.22	.06	.38	.30	.00
Width plus height	.12	.35	.31	.81	.08	.19	.05	.35	.29
Longest inner diagonal	.54	.09	.10	.91	-.10	-.12	.47	.11	.11
Shortest inner diagonal	.32	.31	.10	.88	-.12	.12	.24	.32	.09
Space inner diagonal	.51	.16	.08	.96	-.14	-.06	.44	.18	.08
Thickness of edge	-.01	-.03	.71	.48	.54	-.12	-.01	-.06	.70
Hyperplane Count		11			5			12	
Average Variable Complexity		1.41			1.33			1.44	
Correlations Among Factors									
1.	1.00			1.00			1.00		
2.	.68	1.00		.40	1.00		.72	1.00	
3.	.61	.65	1.00	.14	.42	1.00	.60	.72	1.00

solution and the subjective solutions which contains the lowest and highest observed value for each procedure. Orthotran appears better than the other orthoblique solutions because the correlations were moderate, the hyperplane count was higher, the complexity was reasonably low, and there was a high congruence with the subjective solutions both in terms of parallel outcome on the first three criteria and in terms of the coefficients of congruence. In these samples, oblimin also gave good results, as would be expected from the general research noted in Chapter 9 showing most analytical solutions to give similar results for the criteria generally used in such studies. The two orthoblique procedures occasionally give poor solutions. The hyperplane count may be as low as zero, and the congruence index may be lower than the other two analytic procedures.

Example

Truncated principal components were extracted from the correlations given in Table 1.3.1 and rotated by Hofmann (personal communication) to three orthotran solutions. The three rotations differed in the original orthogonal rotation. Varimax, quartimax, and equamax were used, and the orthoblique rotation giving the smallest variable complexity was found, thus meeting the orthotran criterion. The results of these three rotations are given in Table 10.3.1. Included in the results are the reference vector structures, hyperplane counts, average variable complexities, and correlations among factors.

When starting from either varimax or equamax the orthotran solution is appropriate and the factors of length, height, and width are apparent. The correlations among factors are also appropriate, and the hyperplane count, for this problem, is almost as good as that of promax of Table 9.3.1. Quartimax gives a general factor when possible, and the oblique solution based on it gives a gneral factor of volume.

10.4 NONSIMPLE STRUCTURE ROTATION

As noted in Chapter 9, simple structure is a mathematically arbitrary criterion concept that will hopefully lead to greater invariance, greater psychological meaningfulness, and greater parsimony than would leaving the factors unrotated. Other rotational principles are possible, and others might be invented in the future. Selection of one of these other procedures or traditional simple structure depends upon the research design of the study.

There are two major classes of alternative procedures for a rotation that are presented here. The first class, in Section 10.4.1, consists of solutions based upon rotating to a hypothesized factor pattern. The hypothesized factor pattern could be a simple structure one or could embody any other form of factor loadings that were theoretically appropriate to the particular problem. The second class of solutions, Section 10.4.2, rotates two factor matrices from two indpendent studies to maximum congruence with each other.

10.4.1 Rotating to a Hypothesis: Procrustes

Guilford has suggested that utilizing purely mathematical models for simple structure rotation is of only limited usefulness. The major problem is that the ultimate goal of simple structure, invariance, may not be met, as Guilford has demonstrated (Guilford, 1975, 1977; Guilford & Hoepfner, 1969, 1971; Guilford & Zimmerman, 1963). An additional limitation is that it is solely exploratory and does not include information that might already exist that would guide the rotation into a confirmation of a previously found solution, or at least into a solution more congruent with patterns of theorization in the area. Guilford's preferred solution is to establish a matrix of hypothesized factor loadings, and use that as a target towards which the observed data are rotated.

Assume that H_{vf} is a hypothesized factor pattern for a set of variables. If H_{vf} can be used to reproduce the correlation matrix as well as any other factor pattern, then the f hypothesized factors will have been confirmed. Naturally, a hypothesized H_{vf} will seldom reproduce the correlation matrix perfectly. The interst lies in finding the matrix that is as close to the hypothesized matrix as possible while still reproducing the correlation matrix as accurately as the extracted factors do. What is sought is a transformation matrix, T, which will transform the P_{vf} to the best least-squares fit to H_{vf}. The H thus found is then evaluated to determine if it gives a better than chance fit to the original H.

The solution for T is called a **Procrustes** solution after the innkeeper in Greek mythology who had a bed that would fit anyone. If the visitor was too short for the bed, Procrustes stretched the visitor on a rack. If the visitor was too long for the bed, he trimmed the visitor's legs. The title was given to this procedure by Hurley and Cattell (1962) to stress the fact that the resulting solution invariably *looks* like a fit to the hypothesized matrix. Horn (1967) factored correlations from random data, gave the variables names, rotated to a Procrustes solution, and found that the factors could be interpreted as confirming his substantive hypotheses. Such an excellent fit is achieved by extensive capitalization on chance, but unacceptable expenses may be involved in stretching and trimming the data to fit the hypotheses. For example, correlations among factors may turn out to be 1.0 and the factors may have no relationship to the distinctive features of the data.

Deriving the Procrustes solution starts with the following definition:

$$P_{vf} T_{ff'} = H_{vf'} \tag{10.4.1}$$

where f' equals f but separate symbols are used to identify the original and the rotated factors. Although a nonsquare matrix does not generally have an inverse, the following does hold true:

$$(P'_{fv} P_{vf})^{-1} (P'_{fv} P_{vf}) = I \tag{10.4.2}$$

Multiplying through by $(P'P)^{-1}P'$ to eliminate P from the left side of Eq. (9.1.1) gives:

$$(P'_{fv} P_{vf})^{-1} P'_{fv} P_{vf} T_{ff'} = (P'_{fv} P_{vf})^{-1} P'_{fv} H_{vf'} \qquad (10.4.3)$$

which simplifies to:

$$T_{ff'} = (P'_{fv} P_{vf})^{-1} P'_{fv} H_{vf'} \qquad (10.4.4)$$

To assure that the factors remain at unit length, T must be normalized by dividing each element in a column of T by the square root of the sum of squares for that column.

Normalizing T means that H is no longer exactly reproduced but is only reproduced by the closest position that the factors can take and still account for the same amount of the variance of the correlation matrix as before rotation. The correlations among factors and the factor structure can then be calculated by Eq. (10.1.15) and (3.4.8). Discussions of variations on Procrustes, including an orthogonal version and computer programs, are given elsewhere (Borg, 1978; Browne, 1967; Browne & Kristof, 1969; Digman, 1967; Evans, 1971; Gower, 1975; Green, 1952; Gruvaeus, 1970; Hakstian, 1970b; Kalimo, 1971; Kristof & Wingersky, 1971; Lissitz, Schönemann & Lingoes, 1976; Mosier, 1939a; Schönemann, 1966; ten Berge, 1977).

As already noted, the Procrustes solution often gives correlations among factors that are unacceptably high. Whenever the best fit to H is poor in the data, the possibility of a singular matrix of correlations among factors is greatly increased.

In the hypothesis testing situation where the Procrustes solution is generally used, the maximum degree of permissible overlap among the resulting factors can be specified in advance. If the solution produces factors that overlap too much, then it would be automatically rejected and the hypotheses assumed to be untenable. The easiest operational procedure is to specify the maximal multiple correlation of any factor with the set of other factors. This can be calculated from the inverse of the correlations between factors [cf. Eq. (6.3.1)].

With no exact significance test for when the hypothesis is supported by the data, it is crucial that the resulting P_{vf} be examined critically. The reason for the name for this solution should always be remembered before the conclusion is reached that the factors are as hypothesized. Horn (1967) and Guilford (1977) should be considered essential reading if the Procrustes procedure is being used.

Occasionally Procrustes rotations have been compared against a rotation to a random target matrix (Horn, 1967; Horn & Knapp, 1973; Van Hemmert, Van Hemmert, & Elshout, 1974) for a perspective on significance. A program was written that randomly generated a series of random target matrices and tabulated an index of the degree to which the observed data matched each target matrix after Procrustes rotation (Gorsuch, 1968). The program was withdrawn when it became apparent that the distribution of the index of fit was sorely influenced by minor changes and assumptions about the similarity of the matrices, that is, on parameters that could be considered relatively arbitrary. Only an extensive, major research task could establish the appropriate parameters and the conditions under which they were indeed appropriate. (With the appearance of confirmatory factor analysis, that work did not seem worth the effort and the attempt was abandoned.) Therefore, conclusions from such comparisons are questionable.

Because confirmatory maximum likelihood and multiple-group factor analyses enable hypotheses concerning the correlations among the factors and individual elements to be tested for significance, they should be used wherever appropriate. Procrustes solutions can be expected to be used less as maximum likelihood and multiple-group programs become more generally available.

10.4.2 Confactor Rotation

Thurstone's definition of simple structure was, as noted previously, from the desire to find a principle that would produce invariant solutions. Cattell (1944; Cattell & Brennan, 1977; Cattell & Cattell, 1955) has taken the invariance principle one step further by suggesting that the rotated position be defined as a function of invariance across two samples. The technique utilizes two simultaneous factor analyses that are then rotated in conjunction with each other to produce convergent factors (where "convergent" is defined as discussed later).

Although the problem of simultaneous rotation of two, or even more, factor matrices has been discussed from a mathematical perspective on several occasions (Korth & Tucker, 1976; Meredith, 1964b; ten Berge, 1979), simultaneous rotation of two matrices from random samples of the same population has, at best, only a slight advantage over rotating a factor matrix from the correlations across all subjects. The errors would be unrelated in the two samples, and so results occurring across both samples would be stable; however, factoring the total sample would directly give results more stable than factoring either sample alone. Simultaneous rotation of matrices from two random samples also has the major problem that several possible solutions could be found simultaneously in both factor matrices. The fact that chance would operate in an uncorrelated manner across the two situations does reduce the number of possible rotation positions but does not uniquely define a rotation position; hence a further principle would still be necessary for unique rotation.

If, however, the samples were not randomly drawn but differed in the degree to which the several factors in the studies contributed to the variables, then, Cattell suggests, there would be a unique relationship between the two matrices. The factor matrix from a sample in which a factor was weaker would have lower loadings for that factor than would be found in a matrix from a sample in which the factor was stronger.

The observation of a shift in size of loadings as a function of a shift in the input of a factor is supported by the attenuation of correlations that occurs when there is restriction of range in a sample. As discussed in more detail in Chapter 16, reduced variance of a factor reduces (or attenuates) correlations among variables that are influenced by that factor. In extreme cases where the selection is complete and no variability remains on the factor, the correlations produced by that factor are then zero. It is the same as if we selected only those people receiving a score of exactly 120 on an IQ test, and then attempted to correlate IQ with another variable. All the correlations with that IQ variable would be zero because there was no variability on it (technically undefined, but always set equal to zero in computer programs). If the IQ scores were in the range of 119 to 121, then there would be a slight correlation with intelligence but not the same correlation to be found if the IQs ranged from, for example, 50 to 150.

Theoretically the restriction of variance is assumed to be on the factor scores, and that reduced variance leads to attenuated correlations. However, it is impossible to determine the variance of factors by the usual factor-analytic techniques. Indeed, all the variances of the factors are arbitrarily but systematically set equal to 1.0. Because the variances of factor scores are set equal regardless of the reduction in variance in one of the samples, the observed differences among the variables in the two samples can only be reproduced if the P's vary (because X = FP' and F is predetermined, only P can shift). It can be shown that the P of the restricted sample is proportional to the original P of the unrestricted sample when covariance analysis is conducted (Cattell, 1945). This conclusion led to the original name for this technique, proportional profiles, because the profile of the factor from the restricted sample was proportional to the profile of loadings for the factor in the unrestricted situation. This led to the conclusion:

$$P_{vf_1} = P_{vf_2} D_{f_2 f_1} \qquad (10.4.5)$$

where P_{vf_1} and P_{vf_2} are for sample 1 and 2, and D is a diagonal matrix of proportionalities between equivalent factors. Cattell (1944) presents evidence for the uniqueness of a position satisfying Eq. (10.4.5).

The preceding discussion is for the rotated factor matrix. In factor analysis, however, unrotated factors are generally extracted first, and the point of confactor rotation is to produce two rotated solutions so that Eq. (10.4.5) is true. It involves simultaneously solving for two transformation matrices, one for each of the two solutions. The equations are worked out in Cattell's articles for the orthogonal case, and involve several matrix multiplications and then taking the characteristic roots and vectors of an intermediate matrix. These steps are readily programmed on contemporary computers.

The technique is theoretically for factor analysis of covariance matrices, but most analyses proceed from correlation matrices because variable scoring procedures are sufficiently arbitrary so that factoring covariance matrices is not meaningful. In that case, the relationship of factor loadings in one solution with loadings in another solution will have only approximately the same proportionality across all loadings. Confactor rotation procedures may still be used and two factor patterns with proportional columns sought, but the results will only be approximate. The degree to which the lack of complete proportionality for correlational solutions disrupts the rotations is currently unknown.

There are several important assumptions in use of confactor rotation. The first assumption is that the same variables and factors are in both studies.

Currently, a second assumption is that the factors are uncorrelated. Cattell has produced several examples of confactor rotation for uncorrelated factors, demonstrating that the procedure works with these example cases. He has also demonstrated that the procedure is a good approximation if there are only small correlations among factors and the same small correlations among factors occur in both studies (a condition that might be hard to meet if the factors are truly restricted in one of the samples). Attempts to develop oblique rotation have not yet met with complete success. (As an intermediate approach, it is probably possible to follow the orthogonal confactor rotation by promax for an approximate oblique solution.)

The third assumption is that the selection that reduces the factor variance in one sample as compared to the other is both *simple* and *moderate*. By "simple" is meant that there is no interaction between the selection and correlations, that is, that the relationship among variables within the restricted sample does follow the same trends as in the nonrestricted sample. (Some of the early attempts by Cattell's co-workers to develop plasmodes for confactor rotation failed at this point because there were interactions when selection did occur.) By "moderate" is meant that the selection cannot be complete—or else all the correlations become zero—or be so extreme that the correlations among the variables become too small for the factor to be identified. An additional problem of extreme selection is that such selection is often accompanied by skews in distributions of variables, which would further disrupt correlations and make a unique solution difficult to identify. It is not yet known how much difference in variance of a factor is needed between the two samples. It is possible—if we're lucky—that two moderate N random samples would have sufficient differences in variability by chance to be suitable for confactor rotation.

Confactor rotations are definitely different from simple structure. There is no requirement that the matrix be simple by any of the Thurstone criteria or by the analytic criteria approximations to Thurstone's simple structure. In one example Cattell does demonstrate that confactor rotation gives the same factor pattern matrices, within proportionality, whereas simple structure rotation gives radically different solutions because of the negative effects of the selection biases. The argument for confactor rotation is that it is a more direct approach to the invariance sought through simple structure, and that invariance across samples produces greater scientific parsimony than would, for example, two different simple structures for the same data.

10.5   EXTENSION ANALYSIS

It may not be desirable to carry all the variables of interest in the factor analysis itself. If, for example, maximum likelihood factors were extracted and rotated, all variables included in that analysis would influence the final rotation. It may be more desirable to allow the rotated position of the factors to be established by a subset of the variables. Then the solution can be extended to the variables not initially included. This approach does assume that the same individuals provide scores on both the variables being factored and the extension analysis variables.

Several situations can arise where extension analysis is particularly appropriate. First, the original variable set may contain linear dependences that cannot be included in the analysis itself (Chapter 8 contains a discussion of linearly dependent variables and their effects on a factor analysis). For example, the relationship of individual items to the factors that are partially defined by the total score from those items may be of some interest. Because the linearly dependent variables are often of great theoretical interest, it may be important to know how they correlate with the factors. Second, extension analysis may be needed to test a hypothesis regarding the nature of a particular factor. A well-replicated factor may be hypothesized to be that which is measured by variable Z. To include variable Z in an exploratory factor analysis would usually allow it to help define the factor. Because this includes the possibility of capitalizing on chance, it would be better to determine variable Z's relationship to the factor when the factor is based solely on the other variables. Then variable Z is correlated independently with the factor.

A third situation is when a linear model statistical analysis—e.g., an ANOVA—is desired with the factors. The extension variables would be derived (or "dummy") variables for the main effects and interactions (Cohen & Cohen, 1975). The correlations of the derived variables with the factors are used for significance tests by linear model methods. The same analyses could be computed from factor scores, but extension analysis saves the need of computing factor scores for each case in the study.

The problem is to determine the correlations of a set of z variables not in the factor analysis with those v variables that were factored. This correlation is defined as follows:

$$S_{zf} = Z'_{zn} F_{nf} n^{-1} \tag{10.5.1}$$

where S is the structure matrix of the z new variables, and both the factor scores and new variable scores are assumed to be in standard score form.

Equation (10.5.1) could actually be calculated by computing factor scores, but there is an easier way. Let W_{vf} be the weight matrix by which factor scores in standard score form can be calculated from the original set of v variables. Then the following is true:

$$F_{nf} = Z_{nv} W_{vf} \tag{10.5.2}$$

Substituting Eq. (10.5.2) into Eq. (10.5.1) gives:

$$S_{zf} = Z'_{zn} Z_{nv} W_{vf} n^{-1} \tag{10.5.3}$$

Then:

$$S_{zf} = R_{zv} W_{vf} \tag{10.5.4}$$

And:

$$P_{zf} = S_{zf} R_{ff}^{-1} \tag{10.5.5}$$

The calculation of W_{vf} is discussed at length in Chapter 12, Factor Scores. As is apparent from this development, the quality of the extension solution is dependent upon the quality of the factor weight matrix, W, which is, in turn, dependent upon the quality of the factor solution. Because many factor procedures produce only estimates, inconsistencies can develop. For example, the correlations among estimated factor scores resulting from a W will be a nonidentity matrix even though orthogonal rotation was used (see Chapter 12). In such a case, the R_{ff} of Eq. (10.5.5) needs to be the correlations among the factor estimates to avoid negative communalities for the extension variables. (Factor scores estimates are, as noted in Chapter 12, an implicit multiple-group refactoring of the data and should be treated as such by recalculating matrices such as R_{ff} if used in further equations.) The extension analysis procedures presented by Dwyer (1937) and Mosier (1938), and developed further by Horn (1973) and McDonald (1978), utilize only a few of the possible ways to calculate W. Coles and Stone (1974) give an example of an extension analysis.

In some situations, extension analysis is not necessary because even the oddest of variables can be included in the factor analysis. In particular, multiple-group factors will be unaffected by any variable that is not used as a defining variable. Variables normally saved for an extension analysis may be directly included in that analysis. This is also true of some cases of confirmatory maximum likelihood analysis. However, extension analysis is needed when exploratory procedures are being followed.

11 Higher-Order Factors

The factor-analytic solution deemed acceptable may have correlated factors. If so, there exists a matrix of the correlations among the factors, R_{ff}. Although it is seldom calculated from actual factor scores, this matrix is defined as follows:

$$R_{ff} = F'_{fn} F_{nf} n^{-1} \tag{11.0.1}$$

This means that R_{ff} is a correlation matrix in every sense of the word. And if one has a correlation matrix, we can factor it.

Factoring the correlations among the factors gives rise to **higher-order** factors. When the original correlation matrix, R_{vv}, is factored, the results are said to be **primary** or **first-order** factors. Factoring R_{ff} gives **secondary** or **second-order** factors. The second-order factors now have a P, S, V, T, etc. These matrices are interpreted in the same manner as they are for primary factors except, of course, the variables are now the factors from the lower-order factor analysis.

If there are several second-order factors and they are rotated obliquely, there is also a matrix of correlations among the second-order factors, and this correlation matrix can be factored. Factors from the correlations among the second-order factors give **third-order** factors. The process can be continued as long as a correlation matrix is produced in the rotation. Higher order analyses stop whenever only one factor or uncorrelated factors occur.

Interpretation of higher order factors is discussed in Section 11.1, Interpretation of Higher Order Factors. The procedures for higher-order factor analysis are discussed in Section 11.2, Extracting Higher-Order Factors. For both interpretation and practical purposes, it is often useful to relate the higher-order factors directly to the variables; such computations are set forth in Section 11.3, Relationship of Variables to Higher-Order Factors. This chapter concludes with a brief note on the general applicability of higher-order factors in Section 11.4.

11.1 INTERPRETATION OF HIGHER-ORDER FACTORS

When factoring a set of redundant variables, numerous factors may occur that are narrow in scope. The narrow factors may correlate with each other and the resulting higher-order factor will be broader in scope. For example, factoring an anxiety test produces narrow scales of anxiety that correlate with each other to form a higher-order factor (Gorsuch, 1966). The broader factor of anxiety that can be extracted from the correlations among the primary factors have been of more theoretical importance than the narrow subcomponents of anxiety.

Primary factors indicate areas of generalizability. More generalization can occur within a factor than across factors, but this does not eliminate generalization across factors. When factors are correlated, some generalization is possible. These areas of generalization across the primary factors form the higher-order factors.

The essential difference between the primary factors and the higher-order factors is that the primary factors are concerned with narrow areas of generalization where the accuracy is great. The higher-order factors reduce accuracy for an increase in the breadth of generalization. In some analyses, the reduction in accuracy when going from primary to second-order factors will be small; in other studies it may be quite great. It depends upon the data being analyzed.

Examples

Several illustrations of phenomena that can be arranged as in a higher-order factor analysis may be helpful. These examples are, of course, only analogies to any given study. The first illustration, given in Fig. 11.1, is a common-sense analysis involving four levels. The highest degree of generality and the lowest degree of accuracy are achieved by noting that something is part of an earth-type planet rather than a star, asteroid, or some other object. Planet is the highest-order factor resulting from the hypothetical data analysis. At a more specific level—where the degree of generalization is less but the accuracy

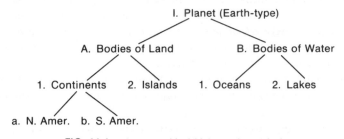

FIG. 11.1.   A geographical higher order analysis.

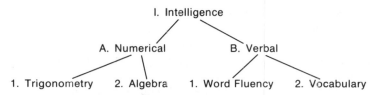

FIG. 11.2.   Some factors of intellect.

increases—one can divide the planet into areas of land and water. Another level divides the land into continents and islands, whereas the water is divided into oceans and lakes. Any of the categories at this level can be further subdivided; continents are so subdivided. A higher-order factor analysis is essentially concerned with organizing the data in a manner similar to the geographical example.

The next figure, 11.2, illustrates what might occur in a factor analysis of human ability variables. At the primary factor level, four factors might be found: trigonometry, algebra, word fluency, and vocabulary. The primary ability factors correlate together and one can identify second-order factors: numerical and verbal abilities. In this particular example, numerical and verbal abilities are assumed to correlate to form general intelligence. The highest degree of generalization is general intelligence. However, if a higher degree of accuracy is required and less generalization can be tolerated, the second-order factors could be used. Only in a few cases would the primary factors be needed for most applied purposes. Although the primary factors are highly accurate, they are also limited in the breadth of their application.

The total higher-order analysis can also be summarized in outline form because the interpretation of an outline is essentially the same as the different levels of factors. The most specific elements in the outline parallel the primary factors, the slightly broader divisions underneath which the most specific are organized are the secondary factors, and so on. In preparing such an outline, the highest order of factors forms the major headings (e.g., I, II). The next highest order of factors then forms the subdivisions of the major headings (e.g., A, B, C), and so forth. The subordination process continues until all the factors are included. An outline approach to reporting the analysis is particularly useful when many of the readers know little of factor analysis.

Example

The illustrations of the previous example can also be arranged in other ways to show the basic relationships. For example, the following outline can be developed:

    I. Planet (Earth-type)
        A. Land
            1. Continents
                a. N. America
                b. S. America
            2. Islands

    B. Water
       1. Oceans
       2. Lakes

The second example could be portrayed as follows:

    I. Intelligence
      A. Numerical ability
        1. Trigonometry
        2. Algebra
      B. Verbal ability
        1. Word Fluency
        2. Vocabulary

Outlines such as those given above are the bases of most textbooks and can be empirically derived by higher-order factor analysis.

In some senses, factors can be interpreted as more than just principles of organizing the data. For example, a factor may represent some form of influence at work. However, it is impossible to know from a factor-analytic study whether the primary factors are more basic in, for example, a causative sense or whether a higher-order factor might be the more basic. It is for this reason that Cattell (1966a) argues that higher-order factors are in no way "grander" or more important than lower-order factors. They all contribute to the understanding of the data.

It is sometimes implied that higher-order factors should be ignored because they are too "abstract" and "too far removed from the data." However, because higher-order factors can be measured with the same degree of accuracy as a primary factor, an attitude toward an object, or most other constructs, such criticisms are unfounded.

11.2 EXTRACTING HIGHER-ORDER FACTORS

Because R_{ff} is a legitimate correlation matrix, factors are extracted from it in the same manner as from the original correlation matrix. Any of the extraction and rotation procedures may be used. Some procedures will, however, have some special characteristics. For example, diagonal analysis would identify one of the higher-order factors with one of the primary factors. Such would only be desired when there were strong theoretical demands for doing so. Because few present theories specify characteristics of higher-order factors, it is expected that diagonal, multiple-group, and confirmatory maximum likelihood factor analyses would be of less current use than other procedures. As theories are further developed, hypothesis-testing factor analyses may come into their own in higher-order analyses.

The higher-order factors could be extracted on the basis of any of the four basic factor models: correlated components, uncorrelated components, correlated common factors, or uncorrelated common factors. The choice between the correlated and uncorrelated models will be made on a theoretical basis if a confirmatory procedure is being followed. In an exploratory analysis the decision is generally made by comparing an uncorrelated and a correlated solution. If the correlated solution definitely increases the quality of the result, it would be accepted over the uncorrelated solution.

The full component model is not entirely appropriate for higher-order analyses. This model says that the higher-order factors perfectly reproduce the primary factor scores, and that there is no other meaningful source of variance in those scores. Expressed in matrix algebra, the component model is:

$$F_{nf} = F_{nh} \, P'_{hf} \tag{11.2.1}$$

where F_{nh} and P_{fh} are, respectively, the higher-order factor scores and pattern. Because each primary factor is always independent, h equals f for Eq. (11.2.1) to be accurate. Equation (11.2.1) can be substituted into the basic component equation for the original variables:
Then:

$$Z_{nv} = F_{nf} \, P'_{fv} \tag{11.2.2}$$

$$Z_{nv} = F_{nh} \, P'_{hf} \, P'_{fv} \tag{11.2.3}$$

A new matrix can be defined:

$$P'_{hv} = P'_{hf} \, P'_{fv} \tag{11.2.4}$$

Substituting into Eq. (11.2.3) gives:

$$Z_{nv} = F_{nh} \, P'_{hv} \tag{11.2.5}$$

However, Eq. (11.2.5) is a primary factor equation. Therefore, the logic of the component model means that second-order components simply lead to the primary factors being rotated, and no higher-order analysis occurs.

The common factor model seems more appropriate. It holds that the variance of a common factor can be divided into two parts: that attributable to the higher-order factor and that which belongs to the primary factor alone. The common factor model gives the primaries a distinct role to play as well as allowing for the higher-order factors. Common factor analysis appears to be the generally appropriate model for a higher-order analysis.

In higher-order analyses, the number of primary factors being factored is generally small. Therefore, the best possible estimates of the communalities will be desired. The factor extraction procedure should be picked accordingly. For example, because iteration for communalities that began with unities as the diagonal elements has a greater likelihood of overestimating communalities, starting with a low estimate for iterating communalities is more appropriate. Minres and image analysis are also serious candidates because of their treatment of the communalities (cf. Chapter 6).

Determining the number of factors in a higher-order solution is decided without the aid of significance tests. The significance tests noted for primary factor analysis are not applicable to the higher-order analyses because the distribution characteristics of the correlation coefficients among the first-order factors are a function of the rotation procedure as well as a function of the sample size. It appears that the correlation coefficients, as noted in Chapter 9, will vary systematically depending upon the type of oblique rotation that is calculated. No formula exists to calculate standard errors under these conditions. Therefore, statistical tests of significance cannot be used.

The root ≥ 1 test, the scree test, and the examination of rotated solutions for different numbers of factors appear to be the best approaches to deciding the number of higher-order factors. Note, however, that the number of higher-order factors is quite small and one is generally interested in even doublets. Therefore, a nontrivial factor is generally defined as any that has more than two relatively small loadings after rotation.

Because of the similarity of procedures for higher-order analyses to those for primary factor analysis, the same programs can be used. One simply starts with a correlation matrix instead of raw data. Inappropriate output, such as the maximum likelihood chi-square, is ignored.

Examples

As noted in previous chapters, the box, physique, and ability problems all have definite correlations among the factors. Each is, therefore, a candidate for higher-order factoring. Because the number of factors is small, only one level of higher-order analysis will probably be needed in each case.

In the box problem, theory would suggest that a volume factor could occur. This factor would be a function of the three dimensions (or factors) of length, height, and width. It would occur because boxes empirically observed do not take on all the possible variations of length, height, and width. Instead, the carrying capacity is important and leads to building only those boxes where the three dimensions are correlated. The correlations among the factors suggest that this is so.

Two second-order factor analyses of the box problem are appropriate. First, if a second-order volume factor is hypothesized, then diagonal analysis is appropriate. It would start by correlating each of the three factors with a measure of volume (cf. *Section 10.5, Extension Analysis). These coefficients would be added to the R_{ff} as another row and column. The resulting four-by-four matrix of correlations would then have a diagonal factor extracted with volume as the defining variable. An examination of the residuals would determine whether this factor extracted all the common variance from that matrix.

A second approach to factoring the box problem would be to take out the common factors in the usual manner. By the loadings of the primary factors (or the original variables as discussed in later sections), the second-order factor would be interpreted as size, volume, or some other appropriate concept.

TABLE 11.2.1
Second-Order Factor of Ability
Variables

Primary Ability Factors	Second-Order Factor
A. Verbal Ability	.70
B. Numerical Ability	.65
C. Visual Ability	.78
D. Recognition Ability	.74

In the physique problem, a second-order factor can also be extracted. Because there are only two primaries, a second-order analysis is swift. We take the square root of the correlation between the factors, .55, to obtain the loadings for each factor: .74. They are minres loadings because the one off-diagonal element automatically becomes zero in the residual matrix and because the diagonal elements are ignored. With equal loadings on the two primaries of circumference and height, this appears to be a general size factor.

The correlations among the primary factors in the promax ($k = 4$) rotation from the 24 ability variables are sufficient to warrant factoring. On the basis of both Guttman's root $\geq$ 1 criterion and the scree test, one principal axis factor was extracted. Communality estimates were calculated by starting with the squared multiple correlations and iterating twice. The resulting factor pattern for the second-order factor is given in Table 11.2.1. The second-order factor is equally defined by each and every primary factor, and so represents general intellectual ability.

11.3 RELATIONSHIP OF VARIABLES TO HIGHER-ORDER FACTORS

Because most factor analyses are exploratory, the understanding of primary factors is based upon interpretations of their relationships with the original variables. The interpretations are post hoc and subject to considerable error. In the second-order analysis, P and S indicate the relationship of the second-order factors to the first-order factors. Interpretations of the second-order factors would need to be based upon the interpretations of the first-order factors that are, in turn, based upon the interpretations of the variables. Whereas it is hoped that the investigator knows the variables well enough to interpret them, the accuracy of interpretation will decrease with the first-order factors, will be less with the second-order factors, and still less with the third-order factors. If a fourth-order factor happens to be taken out, many possible inaccuracies in interpretation may occur when working from only the successive factor analyses.

To avoid basing interpretations upon interpretations of interpretations, the relationships of the original variables to each level of the higher-order factors are determined. Then the interpretations are based upon relationships with the variables as well as the relationships to the primary factors; for example, a higher-order factor may be found to have a higher relationship to a particular variable than it does with any of the primary factors. Interpreting from the variables should improve the theoretical understanding of the data and produce a better identification of each higher-order factor.

Example

In the illustration given in Fig. 11.2, a general intelligence test would be correlated with all the primaries and secondaries but would have its highest correlation with the third-order general intelligence factor. It would thus provide for a unique identification of that factor.

Another advantage of determining the relationships of the variables to each of the higher-order factors is that such matrices provide useful information if the higher-order factors will be used in further research. They indicate the extent to which the original set of correlations can be reproduced from a knowledge of only the higher-order factors. Such information might show, for example, that the primary factors are quite narrow and that the original correlation matrix can be reproduced almost as well from the higher-order factors. In that case, the higher-order factors might be considered those of greatest importance. In other cases, the higher-order factors may be of high generality but give poor accuracy in any applied situation. In such a case, the higher-order factors would seldom be used.

In Section 11.3.1 the weights given to the higher-order factors to reproduce the original variables are derived. A method for calculating the correlations between the variables and the higher-order factors is also given. The primary reference vectors can be paralleled in function across several levels of higher-order factors, as is shown in Section *11.3.2. Relationship of the Variables to Orthogonalized Primary and Higher-Order Factors. The analysis gives an understanding of what each factor contributes to each variable in addition to the contribution of all higher-order factors to each variable.

11.3.1 Factor Pattern and Structure

Finding the correlations of the variables with each higher-order factor is useful for interpreting those factors. The factor pattern is also important in many cases because it indicates the manner in which any original variable can be reproduced from only a set of higher-order factors.

We start with the basic equation:

$$\hat{R}_{vv} = P_{vf} R_{ff} P'_{fv} \tag{11.3.1}$$

From the second-order analysis, it is known that:

$$\hat{R}_{ff} = P_{fh} R_{hh} P'_{hf} \tag{11.3.2}$$

where the subscript h is used to denote the number of higher-order factors.

Substituting Eq. (11.3.2) into Eq. (11.3.1) and indicating that the correlation matrix is estimated only from the second-order factors by $\hat{R}_{vv}$ gives:

$$\hat{R}_{vv} = P_{vf} P_{fh} R_{hh} P'_{hf} P'_{fv} \tag{11.3.3}$$

Note, however, that the higher-order factor pattern for reproducing the original variables is defined as:

$$\hat{R}_{vv} = P_{vh} R_{hh} P'_{hv} \tag{11.3.4}$$

Hence:

$$P_{vh} = P_{vf} P_{fh} \tag{11.3.5}$$

The weights by which any variable is reproduced from the second-order factors are therefore sums of crossproducts of the original weights and the second-order weights.

The factor pattern derivation can be directly generalized to any number of higher-order factor sets:

$$P_{vh_k} = P_{vf} P_{fh_1} P_{h_1h_2} \cdots P_{h_{(k-1)}h_k} \tag{11.3.6}$$

where the number subscripted to h indicates the degree of higher-order analysis. For example, $P_{h_1h_2}$ is the pattern giving the loadings by which the correlations of the first set of higher-order factors can be reproduced by the second set of higher-order factors.

Example

From a promax ($k = 4$) rotation of the physique data using two principal axis factors (with the highest correlation in a column as the communality estimate), two factor patterns were calculated, P_{vf} and P_{fh}. Applying Eq. (11.3.5) gives the loadings presented in Table 11.3.1. From the table, it can be seen that no individual variable loads the second-order factor at a high level, but that it does have some power to reproduce most of the variables.

In Table 11.3.1, the greater generality characteristic of higher-order factors is seen because the factor predicts almost all of the variables. The characteristic of a decrease in accuracy is also seen because not one of the loadings is as high as the loading that variable has with one of the first-order factors.

Because stature and weight have the two highest loadings, the second-order factor can be labeled *size*. It is formed of equal parts of the two primary factors, circumference and height.

It is interesting to compare the higher-order solution with Eysenck's (1969) solution for similar data on men. He rotated the two primaries orthogonally and placed one vector through the middle of the set of variables. The factor was designated size and corresponds with the present second-order factor of the same name. His other primary factor, orthogonal to the first, places short, squat people at the opposite end of the factor from tall, thin people. Both Eysenck's and the present analysis may be adequate solutions for different purposes, but the one with a second-order size factor corresponds more closely both to our natural concepts and to the dimensions of physical space. It is thus consistent with well-known scientific principles and is the preferable solution.

TABLE 11.3.1
Physique Original Variable
Second-Order Loadings

Original Variables	Second-Order Factor Loadings
1. Stature	.56
2. Symphysis height	.50
3. Breadth of skull	.19
4. Length of skull	.31
5. Biacromial diameter	.44
6. Transverse chest diameter	.37
7. Sagittal chest diameter	.47
8. Bicristal diameter	.39
9. Length of sternum	.42
10. Chest circumference (at expiration)	.47
11. Hip circumference	.48
12. Weight	.55

Given the factor pattern and the correlations among the higher-order factors, the following equation holds true from prior proofs [Eq. (3.5.10)]:

$$S_{vh} = P_{vh} R_{hh} \tag{11.3.7}$$

With the results from the primary factor analysis and from each successive higher-order analysis, the correlations of the variables with the higher-order factors are readily calculated. These equations were first presented by Cattell and White (Cattell, 1966a).

*11.3.2 Relationship of the Variables to Orthogonalized Primary and Higher-Order Factors

In the primary factor solution, V gives the relationship of each variable to that component of each factor that is orthogonal to the other factors. The elements in V are part correlations and are often useful for interpreting factors. Part correlations may also be found at the higher-order level.

There are several ways all of the factors could be orthogonalized to produce part correlations. On the one hand, one could attempt to look at that part of the second-order factors that are orthogonal to the primaries—except that the higher-order factors would then no longer exist. On the other hand, the higher-order factors could be examined first and their relationships with the variables determined. That part of the variance of the variables not accounted for by the highest-order factors but which is accounted for by the primary factors could then be determined. The unique, nonoverlapping contribution of each primary could then be evaluated. With several levels of higher-order analysis, the process would start with the highest level of factors and continue down the order of analyses until the primary factors are reached. The relationships noted with the primary factors would be under the condition that all higher-order factors had been previously partialed out.

Not only is the latter orthogonalization a possible solution, it is also a desirable one. In science, the concern is with generalizing as far as possible and as accurately as possible. Only when the broad and not so broad generalities do not apply to a given situation does one move to the narrowest, most specific level of generality.

The solution has been provided by Schmid and Leiman (1957); another method is given by Wherry (1959). The result of the Schmid–Leiman procedure is a matrix, P_{vo}, which has v variables as rows and the "orthogonalized factors" as columns. The highest-order factors are listed first and the primaries are listed last. The elements are the correlations of each variable with the part of that factor that is orthogonal to all factors at a higher order. All of the variance predictable from a higher level of analysis has been partialed out of the correlation between a variable and a factor.

Because P_{vo} contains the weights to reproduce the variables from the "orthogonal" factors, and both the primary and higher-order factors are included, then it follows that:

$$\hat{R}_{vv} = P_{vo} P'_{ov} \qquad (11.3.8)$$

Deriving the solution of P_{vo} begins by noting the common factor definitional equation as applied to the second-order factors:

$$R_{ff} = P_{fh} P'_{hf} + U_{ff} \qquad (11.3.9)$$

where U is assumed to be a diagonal matrix with uniquenesses as the diagonal elements. Note that Schmid and Leiman assume the off-diagonals to be exactly zero. The off-diagonals are never exactly zero in a sample, and therefore the calculated solutions will always involve some error; the error can be reduced by using a minres solution because that procedure reduces the off-diagonals to near zero. Equation (11.3.9) assumes that the factors are orthogonal, which means that the highest order of analysis that is needed has been reached. Equation (11.3.9) can be illustrated as follows:

An equivalent way of illustrating this can also be given by adding the square root of each element of U to P:

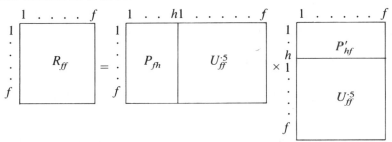

For sake of convenience, the following is defined from the second illustration:

$$A_{f(h + f)} = (P_{fh} | U_{ff}^{.5})$$ (11.3.10)

Then Eq. (11.3.9) can be rewritten as:

$$R_{ff} = A_{f(h + f)} A'_{(h + f)f}$$ (11.3.11)

Substituting Eq. (11.3.11) into the definition of the reproduced correlation matrix as calculated from the correlated primary factors gives:

$$\hat{R}_{vv} = P_{vf} A_{f(h + f)} A'_{(h + f)f} P'_{fv}$$ (11.3.12)

The desired matrix, P_{vo}, is defined as:

$$P_{vo} = P_{vf} A_{f(h + f)}$$ (11.3.13)

Then:

$$\hat{R}_{vv} = P_{vo} P'_{ov}$$ (11.3.14)

The derivation may be generalized to any number of higher-order factors. At each level, there would be an A that would contain the factor pattern loadings and the uniquenesses. A would be substituted into the next lower level's equation so that the variance represented in that lower-order factor pattern would be divided appropriately between the higher-order factors and the portions of the lower-order factors that appear as unique factors in that higher-order analysis. Note that the solution always begins with the highest order that is solved for and that this order must contain either one factor or uncorrelated factors. By substituting down through the equations, the relationships of the original variables to all of the higher-order factors are evaluated.

Example

For the second-order ability factor of Table 11.2.1, P_{vo} is formed by first determining $A_{f(h + f)}$. A is made up of P, which is already known, and U, which is not known. U is calculated by subtracting the communality of each variable from 1.0 and placing the results in the diagonals of a null matrix. The present U is:

$$U = \begin{bmatrix} .51 & 0 & 0 & 0 \\ 0 & .58 & 0 & 0 \\ 0 & 0 & .39 & 0 \\ 0 & 0 & 0 & .45 \end{bmatrix}$$

A is the factor pattern augmented by $U^{.5}$.

$$A = \begin{bmatrix} .70 & .72 & 0 & 0 & 0 \\ .65 & 0 & .76 & 0 & 0 \\ .78 & 0 & 0 & .63 & 0 \\ .74 & 0 & 0 & 0 & .67 \end{bmatrix}$$

P_{vo} can now be calculated by Eq. (11.3.13). The result is given in Table 11.3.2.

TABLE 11.3.2
Orthogonalized Higher Order Analysis of Ability
Variables

	Factors				
Variables	I General Intelligence	A Verbal Ability	B Numerical Ability	C Visual Ability	D Recognition Ability
1. Visual Perception	.54	−.05	.02	.48	−.03
2. Cubes	.34	−.05	−.02	.37	−.05
5. General Information	.58	.57	.08	−.00	−.04
6. Paragraph Comprehension	.58	.58	−.07	.01	.06
7. Sentence Completion	.57	.62	.03	.01	−.07
8. Word Classification	.59	.39	.09	.14	−.05
9. Word Meaning	.58	.62	−.08	−.01	.05
10. Add	.42	.06	.65	−.19	.04
11. Code	.51	.02	.40	−.05	.20
12. Counting Groups of Dots	.44	−.12	.60	.09	−.06
13. Straight and Curved Capitals	.54	−.01	.41	.26	−.11
14. Word Recognition	.40	.07	−.06	−.08	.44
15. Number Recognition	.37	−.03	−.07	−.01	.43
16. Figure Recognition	.49	−.11	−.10	.27	.32
17. Object-Number	.46	.00	.07	−.08	.46
18. Number-Figure	.50	−.16	.18	.16	.28
19. Figure-Word	.42	−.00	.04	.10	.25
20. Deduction	.56	.18	−.09	.25	.13
21. Numerical Puzzles	.54	−.02	.27	.23	.04
22. Problem Reasoning	.56	.17	−.05	.23	.14
23. Series Completion	.61	.15	.04	.31	.04
24. Woody-McCall Mixed Fundamentals, Form I	.58	.17	.33	.00	.12
25. Paper Form Board	.38	−.01	−.14	.43	−.01
26. Flags	.44	.05	−.05	.42	−.08

The power of the second-order factor can be observed in column one of Table 11.3.2. It is correlated with each and every variable and contributes more to most variables than does the nonoverlapping portion of the primary factors (given in columns two through five of the Table).

Orthogonalized?   The Schmid–Leiman solution is called "orthogonal" because Eq. (11.3.14) generally describes a truly orthogonal matrix. But this P_{vo} contains higher-order factors that are linear functions of the primaries and so P_{vo} cannot meet all the usual criteria for orthogonality. Further, the number of factors was already determined and that is the necessary number for R_{vv}; so having more than the primary factors in P_{vo} is redundant, and some of the factors must correlate with others. When factor scores are computed based on P_{vo}, they are correlated.

What then is the meaning of orthogonal in this solution? It is used to describe the relationships *between* the higher- and lower-order factors. The highest order is determined, and then the next highest order is based on the variance orthogonal to the highest order. This is true for each pair of levels. For example, if there are three levels, the second-order factors are orthogonal to the third order, and the primaries are orthogonal to the second order. Variance is separated sequencially or hierarchically moving from the highest order to the lowest order.

Checking the Solution.   An approximate check on the Schmid–Leiman solution is provided by the original reference vector structure. V gives the correlations of the variables with that part of each factor that is orthogonal to all of the other factors and therefore to all of the higher-order factors. The last f columns of P_{vo} give the correlations of the variables with the factors with all higher-order factors partialed out. V and the last f columns of P_{vo} should be quite similar; major discrepancies arise either from inaccuracies in reproducing the correlations among factors [e.g., U in Eq. (11.3.9) is not actually diagonal] or from inaccurate communality estimates.

If the higher-order communalities are overestimated, then variance is attributed to those higher-order factors at the expense of the lower-order factors. Therefore, it lowers the correlations between the variables and the orthogonalized parts of the primary factors. Underestimating the communalities leads to the opposite effect (i.e., the correlations with the orthogonal parts of the primary factors will be noticeably higher than the corresponding elements of V).

If all the correlations at the higher-order level were exactly reproduced by Eq. (11.3.9) and if the communalities were completely accurate, then the last f columns of P_{vo} will be slightly less than corresponding columns of V. The loadings in P_{vo} should be slightly lower than those in V because each factor has some overlap with higher-order factors that it does not have with the other primary factors. Partialing out the higher-order factors takes out more variance than just partialing out the other primary factors.

Because P_{vo} is an orthogonalized solution, the communalities of the variables equal the sum of the squared loadings in that matrix. The communalities provide another check on the accuracy of the solution.

Evaluating the Impact of the Higher-Order Factors. P_{vo} also provides a means by which the quality of the reproduction of the correlation matrix by any given level of factors can be estimated. First, the distinct impact of any particular factor is the sum of the squared loadings for that factor. Adding together the sums of squares for all of the highest-order factors gives the variance accounted for by those factors. The variance accounted for by higher-order factors can, for example, be compared with the total variance extracted to determine how well these factors alone would reproduce the correlation matrix.

Note that the degree of reproduction from the second-order factors alone in, for example, a three-level solution is a function of the variance attributed by *both* the second- and third-order factors. The impact of the primary factors alone would be calculated by adding the variance accounted for by the higher-order factors to the orthogonalized primaries. The original primaries account for all the extracted variance because the higher-order factors are simply linear combinations of them.

A comparison of the variance indices allows an evaluation of the payoff between generalizability and accuracy. The comparison is aided by converting each index to the percentage of extracted (or total) variance by dividing it by the sum of the communalities (or number of variables). If the highest-order factors contribute 40% to 50% to the extracted variance, then they are of definite interest. On the other hand, if the highest-order factors only count for 2% or 3% of the variance, then their impact is negligible and they will be of only limited interest. Alternatively, the variance indices can be converted to some other percentage form. One possibility would be to divide by the sum of the reliability coefficients under the assumption that they are adequate coefficients. The sum is divided into the variance accounted for by a particular factor to give the percentage of reliable variance accounted for by that factor.

Example

When the last four columns of Table 11.3.2 are compared with the reference vector structure from the promax rotation of Chapter 9, some differences can be seen. The P_{vo} elements are consistently lower than their counterparts. The differences are probably a function of the fact that each primary factor will have some variance in common with a higher-order factor in addition to its overlap with the other primaries. If the differences were much larger, overfactoring would be expected, and the second-order factor would be reextracted with more accurate communality estimates.

It is instructive to evaluate the degree to which the original variance can be accounted for by the higher-order factor alone or by any orthogonalized primary. Although not all of the ability reliability coefficients are adequate from the factor-analytic view, as noted in

TABLE 11.3.3
Variance Accounted for by Each Factor of the Ability
Higher-Order Analysis

Factors	Sum of Squared Loadings	Percentage of Extracted Variance	Percentage of Reliable Variance
Second-Order Factor I*	6.13	54	35
Total for Second Order*	6.13	54	35
Orthogonalized A	1.73	15	9
Primary Factors B	1.39	12	8
C	1.27	11	7
D	.92	8	5
Total for Orthogonalized Primaries	5.32	46	30
Total for Original Primaries and Orthogonalized Factors	11.44	100	65

*These two values are the same because there is only one second-order factor.

Chapter 6, they will be assumed to be adequate for illustrative purposes. The sum of the reliabilities given by Holzinger and Swineford (1939) is 17.69.

Table 11.1.3 gives several measures of the impact of the different factors. First, the sum of squared loadings for each of the orthogonalized factors is given. Next is the percentage of the extracted variance that each accounts for. Finally, the table gives the percentage of reliable variance that each factor and level accounts for. It is apparent that the general intelligence factor accounts for as much variance as all of the nonoverlapping or orthogonalized portions of the primary factors. The unorthogonalized primary factors do, it should be noted, account for all the variance accounted for by the second-order factor as well as the variance attributable to the orthogonalized primaries.

An estimate of the importance of the higher-order factors can be made without actually extracting them (Humphreys, Tucker, & Dachler, 1970). However, with the ease of factoring provided by modern computers, computing the factors may be the easier way of evaluating the importance of the higher-order factors.

11.4 USEFULNESS OF HIGHER-ORDER FACTORS

There is nothing sacred about either primary or higher-order factors. The importance of each lies in its relative merits for the theory under consideration. In some areas, it pays to concentrate on one level, whereas in others a different level may be desired. For example, if a set of items forming a test is factored, the higher-order factors may be of greatest interest because the primary factors would lead to narrow, two-item scales. However, in the examples used in this book, the interest would be in both primary and secondary factors. As the research in the area develops, the already researched levels will come to be part of the area's general paradigms. The appropriate level for research will probably shift so that the other levels are examined.

Example

The history of the area of human abilities reflects how the emphasis may shift from one level of factors to another. Spearman, an early scholar, was interested in the basic phenomena and investigated the highest-order factor in the area. Naturally, the development of the area led other investigators to break down the broad general intelligence factor into more specific ones. For example, Thurstone's primary mental abilities (1938) were seven to nine in number. The process of subdividing has continued. Guilford has been able to cut intelligence much more finely than Thurstone ever dreamed (Guilford, 1967).

In the process of examining the trees, some psychologists have forgotten the forest. McNemar in "Lost our Intelligence? Why?" (McNemar, 1964) has pointed out that general intelligence is a strong predictor and that the fine distinctions of interest to the serious scholar in the area are not necessary for many other purposes. Cattell (1963) and Horn (Horn, 1972; Horn & Cattell, 1967) have shown that intelligence has fairly specific factors that are organized together into higher-order factors.

Unfortunately, the general paradigm of intelligence has not yet solidified. Instead, one investigator may argue that a general intelligence test is meaningless because he can subdivide it into several factors, whereas another investigator finds the general score useful and so dismisses factor analysis as so much witchcraft. Both assume their factors are the only ones of interest. Both are right—but only for their own purposes. Both are also provincial and factor-analytically naive.

Rotating obliquely in factor analysis implies that the factors do overlap and that there are, therefore, broader areas of generalizability than just a primary factor. **Implicit in all oblique rotations are higher-order factors. It is recommended that these be extracted and examined so that the investigator may gain the fullest possible understanding of the data.**

For the higher-order factors to be most useful, it is recommended that each be related back to the original variables by the factor pattern, factor structure, and P_{vo} procedures. These are all easily calculated and provide special information to evaluate the relative usefulness of all of the factors.

The discussion of higher-order factors has been oriented towards traditional exploratory factor analysis, but it is readily integrated into a confirmatory factor-analytic approach (Bentler & Weeks, 1980). With the flexibility of confirmatory factor analysis, there are several ways in which such integration can occur. One way is to specify the primary factors in two models, one with the correlations left free to vary and another with the correlations set to zero. If the model with the correlations left free to vary reduces the chi-square significantly more—when tested by the difference between the two chi-squares approach—than the model with the correlations set equal to zero, then higher-order factors exist.

Another approach to testing for higher-order factors is the Schmid–Leiman procedure of Section 11.3.2. This approach gives an orthogonal version of the higher-order and primary factors with the loadings of each individual variable with each factor. A hypothesized structure such as Table 11.3.2 could be specified and tested against a model that had only the last four factors—that is, the primary factors—from the table without the general, higher-order factor. Both models would preset the intercorrelations among the factors to zero. If a general higher-order factor does exist, then the model containing all the primaries that is forced to be orthogonal should be less predictive than a model that contains the higher-order factor as well.

12   Factor Scores

In factor analysis the original matrix of observed variables is estimated or reproduced from two other matrices: the factor pattern and the factor scores.
Previous chapters have dealt with solving for factor patterns under various restrictions so that a unique solution may be found. Given the data and factor
pattern, it is possible to calculate or estimate the factor scores, that is, the scores
for each of the N individuals on the f factors.

Two situations often arise in which factor scores are desired. On the one hand,
it may be desirable to have factor scores to relate the factors to other variables,
principally nominal variables, that cannot be related to the factors by extension
analysis or by any other convenient method. On the other hand, a procedure of
scoring for the factors may be desired so that a formal factor analysis is not
necessary in future research. The latter situation arises when a limited subset of
the variables is to be carried in additional studies to measure the factor so that the
entire set of variables is not needed. It also occurs when the factor analysis is
used as an aid in item analysis and test construction. In most research situations,
a procedure for measuring the factors in future research is a prime product of the
study.

In both diagonal and multiple-group component analysis, the factors are readily scored. In the orthogonal versions, the first factor is either the variable or the
set of variables defining the factor. The succeeding factors are defined by other
variables after those variables have had that portion of their variance overlapping
with the previous factors removed. But only in diagonal and multiple-group
factor analysis are factor scores so easily defined and computed.

In principal component analysis, factor scores can be calculated, but there are
a number of formulas that can be used. The problem here is finding a formula

that is relatively efficient for the computing facilities at hand. The first two procedures for computing factor scores, given in Section *12.1, are appropriate for component scores; Kaiser (1962) gives other formulas. All procedures give the same factor scores.

The common factor model also has several equations for computing factor scores. The equations are given in Section *12.1 for the more exact procedures. Some choice is possible because the equations give common factor scores with varying characteristics. Section 12.2 contains some of the less elaborate methods for calculating factor scores, but which prove more valuable than the more exact procedures.

Section *12.3 contains another approach to factor scores, an approach concerned with clustering individuals into types. In Section 12.4 a procedure is suggested that can be readily utilized with any of the techniques of solving for factor scores to evaluate the characteristics of the scores. Considerations involved in selecting a method for scoring factors are discussed in Section 12.5.

*12.1 PROCEDURES FOR COMPUTING FACTOR SCORES

Determining the appropriate factor scores is inherently more difficult with common factors than when components are extracted. Common factor scores can seldom be computed because they are indeterminate, a phenomenon explained in Section 12.1.1. Therefore, estimation procedures have been suggested. Estimation procedures based on mathematical analyses—sometimes referred to as "complete" or "exact" estimation procedures—are presented and discussed in Section 12.1.2. The first two procedures are appropriate for computing component scores and are then no longer estimates. Less elegant approximation procedures applicable to either components or common factors are discussed in Section 12.2.

12.1.1 The Indeterminacy of Common Factor Scores

Common factor scores are indeterminate. **Indeterminacy** occurs when more than one set of factor scores can be constructed that satisfy all the necessary characteristics to be legitimate factor scores for a given factor pattern. With an infinite number of factor scores possible, any one set can only be considered estimates of the undefined theoretical scores. (See Schönemann & Steiger, 1978; Steiger, 1979; and McDonald & Mulaik, 1979, for recent discussion of this topic.)

The defining equation for the common factor model was given earlier as:

$$X_{vi} = w_{vi}F_{1i} + \ldots + w_{vf}F_{fi} + w_{vu} U_{vi} \qquad (12.1.1)$$

The unique factor scores for each variable are uncorrelated with any of the factors or any other unique factor scores. A result is that the original variables are only estimated from the common factors:

$$\hat{Z}_{nv} = F_{nf} P'_{fv} \qquad (12.1.2)$$

To calculate Z exactly, the unique factor scores and weights would also be needed in the equation.

When Eq. (12.1.2) is solved for the factor scores, a factor weight matrix needs to be premultiplied by the reproduced variable scores for the factor scores to be perfectly predictable. **The reproduced scores are, except in the case of image analysis, unknown as long as the factor scores are unknown.** Only the original scores are known. Inasmuch as the original scores are not perfectly correlated with the estimated scores, the factor scores will not be calculable. An implication of the indeterminacy of common factor scores is that the more the data depart from the component model, the more inaccuracy will be introduced into the factor scores. Another implication is that the inaccuracies in the factor scores increase with an increase in the uniquenesses, which is the same as saying that the inaccuracies increase as the communalities decrease.

The average *minimum* correlation between the two sets of factor scores, which both fit the data equally well under the common factor model, is a function of the ratio of variables to factors (Ledermann, 1938; Schönemann, 1971). Representative values are given in Table 12.1.1 for the uncorrelated factor case.

Table 12.1.1, however, gives only the smallest possible average correlations. Most correlations are well above these levels. Because the correlations *could* be low, the procedures of Section 12.4 are mandatory for factor scores. The factor scores are evaluated on the basis of the computed data, not on the basis of Table 12.1.1.

However, the indeterminacy of the factor scores is only a serious problem if one reifies the factors from a given study into ultimate realities. The present approach is to consider factors as constructs that will, hopefully, aid in theory

TABLE 12.1.1
Minimum Average Correlation Between Two Sets of
Factor Scores for the Same P
in an Uncorrelated
Common Factor Solution

Ratio of Factors to Variables	Minimum Average Correlation
1/20	.90
1/10	.82
1/5	.67
1/4	.60

development. Constructs are always abstractions from data and never observed. The best one can expect with any construct is that a psychometrically good operational representative will be found for it (Nunnally, 1978). If the estimates of the common factor scores correlate .8 or so with the theoretical factors (cf. Section 12.4 for calculating the correlation), the estimates are adequate for most scientific purposes. Few scientific measures have validities higher than .8.

Because of the indeterminacy of the factor scores, it has been suggested that component, canonical, or image analysis is more appropriate if factor scores are desirable. This is true for the original study but only for that study. **If a component weight matrix, for example, is used with a new sample, the computed scores will not correlate with the theoretical factor in the new sample much better than would estimated common factor scores because the component weight matrix will have capitalized on chance characteristics of the first sample.** So all factor scoring procedures only give operational representatives of the population factors when generalized to another sample. Empirically, Velicer (1976) found high correlations among the several solutions, so there is little practical difference between component, image, or common factor scores.

Note that this is currently an emotionally involved debate. Some referenced at the beginning of this section feel factor indeterminancy invalidates any and all common factor analyses. The arguments are always for that one study, however, with no consideration for generalizing to new samples. Hence factor indeterminancy is a major problem only if one is analyzing data solely for that sample; for scientific purposes it is the problem that few measures are perfect, a problem acknowledged as characteristic of most social scientific measures.

12.1.2 Exact Procedures

Four major procedures have been recommended for computing component and common factor scores. The results of each procedure are slightly different when used with common factors because of different theoretical bases and the indeterminacy of the scores.

The best procedure for computing common factor scores would have several characteristics. McDonald and Burr (1967) summarize the desired characteristics under four headings: First, the common factor scores should have high correlations with the factors that they are attempting to measure. Second, the common factor scores should be conditionally unbiased estimates of the true factor scores. Third, in the case of orthogonal factors, the factor scores estimated from one factor should have zero correlations with all other factors; if so, they are said to be **univocal.** Fourth, if the factors are orthogonal, the common factor scores should correlate zero with each other. If the factors are correlated, the correlations among factor scores should equal the correlations among factors. Because it is easier to work with orthogonal factors, several theoretical discussions of these procedures (Harris, 1967; McDonald & Burr, 1967) have restricted their discussions to uncorrelated factors. The following discussion will also consider correlated factors.

Idealized Variables. If the variables were perfectly measured and had no unique factor variance, then the following equation would hold true:

$$Z_{nv} = F_{nf}P'_{fv}$$ (12.1.3)

where Z is a matrix of idealized variable scores. In that case, F can be found by the following equation:

$$Z_{nv}P_{vf}(P'_{fv}P_{vf})^{-1} = F_{nf}$$ (12.1.4)

Then:

$$W_{vf} = P_{vf}(P'_{fv}P_{vf})^{-1}$$ (12.1.5)

where W is the weight matrix used to transform the standard scores on the variables to standard scores on the factors. The data are always available for solving Eq. (12.1.5) because the equation uses only the factor pattern. Note that the square matrix being inverted is only f by f and so presents no calculation problem. Equation (12.1.5) is an appropriate one to use for a full component analysis.

When used with common factors, Eq. (12.1.5) will generally give factor scores that correlate well with the desired factors. The correlations will be a function of the extent to which the Z in Eq. (12.1.3) is the observed Z. Only in the case of complete component analysis does the idealized data matrix equal the observed data matrix. (In image analysis, the idealized variable matrix is the image score matrix, which can be calculated.) Idealized variable estimates of common factor scores are univocal and are considered unbiased estimators. However, the common factor scores will often correlate among themselves even though the factors are uncorrelated.

Example

The factor weight matrix was calculated by the idealized variable method for the ability principal axes. The weight matrix from Eq. (12.1.5) is given in Table 12.1.2. The weights are small because of the large correlations among the variables and because there are several weights whose standard scores are used to compute one factor's standard scores. Of the problems commonly analyzed in this text, the ability data have the lowest communalities and so should have the greatest discrepancies between the actual and idealized variables. The quality of this solution will be evaluated in Section 12.4.

Regression Estimates. Regression estimates are from a multiple regression approach to estimating or calculating factor scores. Developing regression estimates begins with the following equation by which the weight matrix is defined:

$$Z_{nv}W_{vf} = F_{nf}$$ (12.1.6)

TABLE 12.1.2
Factor Score Weight Matrix for the Ability Variables
(Idealized Variable Method)

Variables	Factors			
	A	B	C	D
1. Visual Perception	−.03	.01	.24	−.03
2. Cubes	−.03	−.01	.19	−.04
5. General Information	.23	.04	−.01	−.03
6. Paragraph Comprehension	.23	−.04	−.01	.04
7. Sentence Completion	.25	.02	−.01	−.05
8. Word Classification	.16	.05	.07	−.04
9. Word Meaning	.25	−.04	−.02	.03
10. Add	.03	.35	−.10	.01
11. Code	.01	.21	−.03	.13
12. Counting Groups of Dots	−.05	.32	.05	−.06
13. Straight and Curved Capitals	−.01	.22	.13	−.09
14. Word Recognition	.03	−.04	−.05	.31
15. Number Recognition	−.01	−.05	−.01	.30
16. Figure Recognition	−.05	−.06	.13	.22
17. Object-Number	.00	.03	−.05	.32
18. Number-Figure	−.07	.09	.08	.19
19. Figure-Word	.00	.01	.04	.17
20. Deduction	.07	−.05	.12	.09
21. Numerical Puzzles	−.01	.14	.12	.02
22. Problem Reasoning	.06	−.03	.11	.09
23. Series Completion	.05	.02	.15	.02
24. Woody-McCall Mixed Fundamentals, Form I	.07	.17	.00	.08
25. Paper Form Board	−.02	−.08	.22	−.01
26. Flags	.01	−.02	.21	−.06

Being a nonsquare matrix, Z does not have an inverse. The usual procedure of premultiplying Z and F by $(Z'Z)^{-1}Z$ could be followed, but in this case a more meaningful multiplier—$(n^{-1}Z'Z)^{-1}(n^{-1}Z')$—can be used for the same effect:

$$(n^{-1}Z'_{vn}Z_{nv})^{-1}(n^{-1}Z'_{vn}Z_{nv})W_{vf} = (n^{-1}Z'_{vn}Z_{nv})^{-1}(n^{-1}Z'_{vn}F_{nf}) \qquad (12.1.7)$$

From the definition of correlation matrices, Eq. (12.1.7) simplifies to:

$$W_{vf} = R_{vv}^{-1}S_{vf} \qquad (12.1.8)$$

A minor limitation of Eq. (12.1.8) is that smaller computer facilities may not be able to invert a large R_{vv}. Hofmann (1978) gives formulas suitable when the inverse of R does not exist.

Equation (12.1.8) is a multiple regression solution and the common factor scores are those that have the highest correlations with the actual factors. Due to widespread familiarity with multiple regression approaches and the availability of programs, regression estimates are popular factor scores.

Regression estimates of common factor scores do, however, have their faults. In the case of uncorrelated factors, the estimated factor scores are often correlated with each other. The factor scores are neither univocal, because they do correlate with factors other than the factor that is being measured, nor are they unbiased. Heermann (1963) has provided procedures that overcome some of these difficulties but, it appears, which also slightly lower the multiple correlations with the factors being estimated.

Equation (12.1.8) will give an exact computation of full or truncated component scores. An examination of the equation reveals that the individual columns of the factor matrix are independent in the sense that they can be solved for one by one. S need *not* be the complete S but may contain only a limited subset of the total components. Therefore, the major components that are of interest in truncated component analysis can be solved without needing to include the trivial components as well; one need not have extracted the trivial components.

Example

The three box factors are truncated components. Assuming that we do not know the three basic dimensions or how to measure them, it might be desired to measure the empirically observed factors as a function of the variables. The correlation matrix is easily inverted and Eq. (12.1.8) is an appropriate method of computing the weight matrix.

The equations require the inverse of the correlation matrix to be postmultiplied by the factor structure. For the promax component solution, W was computed and is given in Table 12.1.3. The weight matrix generally gives the principal emphasis to the squares of length, height and width.

To calculate scores for individuals, the data matrix is postmultiplied by the weight matrix. The ten standard data scores for three individual boxes are given in Table 12.1.4. The factor scores are in Table 12.1.5.

TABLE 12.1.3
Box Factor Score Weight Matrix

| | *Factors* | | |
Variables	A	B	C
1. Length squared	.31	−.06	−.16
2. Height squared	−.08	−.06	.55
3. Width squared	−.02	.41	.04
4. Length plus width	.20	.16	−.11
5. Length plus height	.16	−.09	.19
6. Width plus height	−.01	.14	.27
7. Longest inner diagonal	.20	.01	.00
8. Shortest inner diagonal	.09	−.02	.23
9. Space inner diagonal	.19	−.02	.07
10. Thickness of edge	−.02	.53	−.10

TABLE 12.1.4
Standardized Scores from Z_{vf} for Three Boxes

	Variables									
Boxes	1	2	3	4	5	6	7	8	9	10
1.	.09	−.53	−.37	.03	−.27	−.56	−.02	−.61	−.11	−.49
5.	−1.00	−.40	−.67	−1.46	−.93	−.82	−1.09	−1.04	−1.21	−.49
25.	.79	.51	−.57	.12	.99	.11	−.13	1.06	.53	.57

Regression estimates can be used where it is desired to calculate both primary and higher-order factor scores from the original variables. The S would be the correlations of the variables with both the primary and higher-order factors from P_{vo}.

Minimizing Unique Factors.   Bartlett (1937) suggested a least-squares procedure to minimize the sum of squares of the unique factors over the range of the variables. Bartlett's procedure is intended to keep the noncommon factors "in their place" so that they are used only to explain the discrepancies between the observed scores and those reproduced from the common factors. The calculation formula is:

$$W_{vf} = U_{vv}^{-2}P_{vf}(P'_{fv}U_{vv}^{-2}P_{vf})^{-1} \qquad (12.1.9)$$

where U_{vv}^{-2} is a diagonal matrix of the reciprocals of the squared unique factor weights. Note the similarity of this equation to Eq. (12.1.5).

Bartlett's procedure leads to high correlations between the factor scores and the factors that are being estimated. It has the additional advantage of being univocal because the factor estimate correlates only with its own factor and not with other factors in the orthogonal case. It is an unbiased estimate. However, the factor estimates may correlate some with each other even if the factors are uncorrelated. Factor scores that minimize the unique factors seem to have considerable qualifications for possible use even though they have seldom been used.

TABLE 12.1.5
Factor Scores for Three Boxes

	Factors		
Boxes	A. Length	B. Width	C. Height
1.	−.00	−.43	−.62
5.	−1.23	−.70	−.60
25.	.55	−.09	.56

Uncorrelated Scores Minimizing Unique Factors. Anderson and Rubin (1956) proceeded in the same manner as Bartlett except they added the condition that the factor scores were required to be orthogonal. The resulting equation is more complex than Bartlett's:

$$W_{uf} = U_{vv}^{-2} P_{vf} (P_{fv}' U_{vv}^{-2} R_{vv} U_{vv}^{-2} P_{vf})^{-1/2} \qquad (12.1.10)$$

Equation (12.1.10) produces factor estimates whose correlations form an identity matrix. The estimates do have reasonably high correlations with the factors but the factor estimates are neither univocal nor unbiased estimators.

Comments on Estimates of Common Factor Scores. The characteristics of the best set of common factor scores are such that they cannot all be maximized at the same time. Univocal estimates have some intercorrelations among the factor estimates themselves. Minimizing the correlations among the estimates or with the factors with which an estimate is theoretically uncorrelated tends to decrease the correlation between that estimate and its factor.

There are several reasons why estimates of uncorrelated factors may be correlated. First, as writers in this area have assumed, the estimates are inappropriate. The second reason is that the uncorrelated model is inappropriate for the data. If a factor estimate is relatively good in other respects but gives moderate correlations among the factors, the data should be examined with the view that the factors may be better characterized as correlated than as uncorrelated. If it is necessary for research purposes that the factors be uncorrelated, then the Anderson and Rubin procedure can be used.

Third, the factors may be correlated in the sample in which the estimates are being calculated even though the factors are not correlated in the population. If the factors are uncorrelated in the population, they can be expected to be randomly correlated in any sample randomly drawn from that population. This statement is true if the "population" is broadly defined in the usual manner as, for example, "all the male adolescents in the United States," or if the population is defined as "the 154 adolescent males tested in July 20 at the Scout ranch" with the sample being one-half of the 154 males randomly selected and the other half held out for cross-validation purposes.

The correlations among factors uncorrelated in the population may be significant if a nonrepresentative sample is drawn from a population. "The 154 adolescent males tested on July 20 at the Scout ranch" are not representative of "all the male adolescents in the United States" and the selection procedure may well lead to factors being correlated with each other in the sample even though they are not correlated in the population. It is this phenomenon that accounts for the high correlations found among uncorrelated dimensions in the box problem. The dimensions of length, height, and width are uncorrelated "in reality" but are highly correlated when measured in a sample of boxes owning to the way box manufacturers "sample" the dimensions. Therefore, the best factor score estimates of factors uncorrelated in a population may be significantly correlated when evaluated in a sample.

When factors are allowed to be correlated, **the correlations among factor scores should reproduce those correlations.** The factor score correlations can be checked in two ways: first, the estimate should correlate with other factors at the same level as does the factor that it estimates. If factor A correlates .3 with B, the estimate of A should also correlate .3 with B. Second, correlations among the factor estimates should be the same as the correlations of the factors themselves. If A and B correlate .3, the estimates of A and B should correlate .3. Good reproduction of the correlations among factors is more likely when the factor scores can be shown to portray uncorrelated factors as uncorrelated or close to it.

12.2   APPROXIMATION PROCEDURES FOR FACTOR SCORES

The approximation procedures can be used for component, common factor, or higher-order factor scoring but give slightly different estimates of the factor scores than the equations in Section 12.1. *Approximation procedures* are those that have been developed on a common sense basis. They differ from those of Section 12.1 because there was originally no exact derivation and they correlate with the factors less than 1.0 even with component analysis. They can be excellent procedures; Wackwitz and Horn (1971) note that approximation procedures give less opportunity for capitalizing on chance. Bentler and Woodard (1979) provide statistical theory for the linear composite model of which these procedures are special cases.

This section begins with a discussion of approximation procedures occasionally used that either should never have been introduced or are no longer necessary (Section *12.2.1). A class of approximation procedures is presented next (Section 12.2.2) which is important for many research settings and is more accurate than the procedures of Section 12.1.

*12.2.1 Less Defensible Approximations

Several indefensible approximation procedures developed because of the difficulties of inverting matrices in the early days of factor analysis. A widely used procedure simply assumed that P_{vf} gives the weights by which the factor scores can be estimated, W_{vf}, instead of the weights to reproduce the variables. The unreasonableness of this procedure is apparent when Table 12.1.2 is compared with Table 9.3.2. The only rationale for using P is that it does allow each variable to contribute to the factor score. However, it fails to take into account the intercorrelations among the variables and among the factors. Mathematically it is on shaky grounds and is not recommended. Halperin (1976) demonstrates its inappropriateness.

A more mathematically legitimate procedure for approximating factor scores was developed by Ledermann (1939) and extended to oblique factors by Harman (1941). It simplifies the calculation procedure necessary to use the regression method by applying that approach to the reproduced correlations rather than the observed correlations. Inasmuch as the residuals vanished, the results of this procedure will be the same as those of the regression method that involves the inversion of the correlation matrix. It does involve inverting an f-by-f matrix.

The principle claim made for these approximation procedures is that they are calculable, whereas more exact procedures are not. However, the advantages in using P do not seem sufficient to offset the complete lack of elegance involved. Ledermann's procedure does require that only a small matrix be inverted. However, three of the four estimation procedures given previously in 12.1.2 also involve inverting the same size matrix and so there are no computational savings. It seems better to use one of the estimation techniques rather than the short approach to the regression method.

12.2.2 Multiple Group Approximations

Whenever factor scores are needed for the sample on which the factor analysis is calculated, they are computed by the equations given in Section 12.1. However, conditions may arise in research where approximation procedures are more appropriate than the more exact procedures.[1]

If the principal use of factor scores will be with another sample of individuals and with a reduced sample of variables, the procedures of Section 12.1 may not be appropriate for several reasons. First, the more exact procedures use all the variables to calculate a single factor; but including all the variables in a future study may not be possible and would often negate the purpose of the first factor analysis. The main reason for computing factor scores is to put the results of a factor analysis to work by providing interesting new measures to be used in research without including all the original variables. Thus, only a limited number of salient variables may be selected to be the basis of the factor scores. Second, because the exact procedures capitalize on chance in the initial analysis, part of the solution is based on nonsignificant differences. Generalizations of complex weighting procedures are seldom as stable as one might generally assume (Guilford, 1965a; Schmidt, 1971; Wackwitz & Horn, 1971).

Instead of computing a complex weight matrix where every variable is used in estimating each factor, a subset of variables can be given simple weights to estimate a factor. The procedure allows for a reduced variable set to be used in the next study and reduces the capitalization on chance. Where exceptionally good data are available, a study might even use a single variable to measure each factor; Adams (1975) shows that the data must be of very high quality.

---

[1]The use of factor estimates to compare factor scores of different populations is discussed by Cattell (1970a).

When a subset of variables is selected to be scored for a factor, an implicit multiple-group factor analysis is being conducted. The new factors are those defined by a linear composite of the variables. The linear composite has weights for each variable being used to measure the factor, and zero weights for all other variables; these weights form the W of Chapter 5. The equations of Chapter 5 give the P, R_{ff}, and S for these multiple-group factors. A comparison of these matrices with the original ones and a comparison of how well the multiple-group factors reproduce the original correlation matrix indicates what has been lost in moving to the multiple-group factors for ease of measurement. In some senses this solves the indeterminancy issue; multiple-group factor scores are technically calculated, not estimated. (But they remain estimates of the scientific construct giving rise to the factor in this study.)

The first step in building an appropriate weight matrix is to distinguish between salient elements and trivial or insignificant elements in S_{vf} or in a W_{vf} calculated by one of the more elegant procedures. The nonsalient elements either are excluded from the score calculations or have zeros entered into W_{vf} for their weights. If the analysis contains many high values, the minimum salient element might be placed at a quite high level (e.g., .6).

The weights of the salient variables are determined by one of two methods:

1. For each variable, examine all of its salient loadings on all factors to find that factor with which the variable has its strongest relationship. The variable is then used to measure only that factor; it is treated as a nonsalient variable on all other factors. A variable with two or more almost equal high loadings is not used to measure any factor.
2. For any given factor, all of the salient variables of interest are identified. These salient variables are then used to measure the factor.

The first option places the variables according to each variable's highest salient loading. When the variable obviously correlates with another factor even though the two factors do not correlate, the variable is best eliminated from measuring any factor. The major advantage of the highest loading option is that it results in a set of factor scores that are experimentally independent. Each variable will be used to measure one and only one factor. If the same variable is used to measure more than one factor—as can happen in the other procedure—the factor scores will be partially experimentally dependent. Such experimental dependency will produce spurious correlations among the factor scores. However, some factors may not be measurable because no variable will have its highest loading there.

The second procedure allows variables loading several factors to be used in measuring each. It may be appropriate if the research plan is to use only one factor at a time in further studies. Inasmuch as several factors in the same study are defined as a function of the same variables, experimental dependence will confound the results.

In either option, the nonzero weights could all be given a value of one or could vary from variable to variable. For example, each salient variable could be given a weight equal to its correlation with the factor. Varying the weights means that the factor score will be more dependent upon those variables that correlate highly with the factor and less dependent upon those that were just above the cutoff point for salient loadings. Differential weights assume there are significant differences between salients. Most research on differential weighting suggests that it is seldom worthwhile (Horn, 1965a; Moseley & Klett, 1964; Trites & Sells, 1955; Wackwitz & Horn, 1971) and requires large numbers of individuals (e.g., $n = 200$ for $v = 10$) for the weights to be generalizable (Schmidt, 1971). The scores calculated by fractional weights often correlate .95 with those from zero–one weights.

In both options the factor score weight matrix, W_{vf}, is based on an examination of the factor structure, a complete W, or on a W calculated for only those variables that could be included in the future analyses. The factor structure is examined rather than the factor pattern because it indicates the overall relationship between the variable and the factor. The approximate weight matrix, containing zeros for nonsalients and ones or varying weights for salients, would then be used with the original standardized variable scores to produce the factor scores.

When an experimenter builds up the W_{vf} by any of these options, the resulting multiple-group factors approximate the rotated factors. The approximation is warranted when a reduction in the number of variables is needed. Such a simplified weight matrix may also generalize to other samples as well as a more complex one, particularly if the original sample size is small and some salient variables fit neatly into groups with little overlap.

When multiple procedures are used, the relationships of the factor estimates to the original factors in the initial sample need to be carefully examined. The results could include some surprises. One may, for example, find that a particular measurement approach measures other factors as well as the factor that it was intended to measure. The quality of the factor scores can be evaluated by procedures given in Section 12.4.

All approximation procedures are implicit multiple-group refactorings of the data. The factors are technically no longer image factors, principal components, or whatever else was extracted. Rather the factor scores are multiple-group factors where W gives the weights for defining the factors. In this sense the factors are not estimated but calculated exactly. The characteristics of the multiple-group factors can be investigated by use of the multiple-group procedure (Chapter 5) using the W found here to define the factors.

Recognizing the approximations as implicit multiple-group factors sheds light on a criticism of these approximations. Writers such as Moseley and Klett (1964) and Glass and Maguire (1966) note that the resulting factor scores were correlated even though a varimax rotation had been used, but may this not simply indicate that the *assumption* of uncorrelated factors was unwarranted for their data? If the factors are uncorrelated, the variables clustering around one factor will be uncorrelated with those clustering around another and so would the multiple-group factors.

Examples

Multiple-group weights can be easily drawn for both the box and the ability data. In the former case a weight of one was given to each of the first three variables to define the factors.

In the second case the factor structure was examined by the first method given in this section. For factor A, variables 5, 6, 7, 8, and 9 were given weights of one. Factor B was formed by adding the standard scores of variables 10, 11, and 12. Variables 1, 2, 20, 25, and 26 were declared the defining variables for factor C. Factor D was estimated by including variables 14, 15, and 17. Variables 13, 18, 19, 20, 21, 22, 23, and 24 were not used to define any factor because their second highest correlations were within .10 of their highest ones. This system of weights would give approximate factor scores for all factors while reducing the total number of ability variables by one-third. It would also give three to five variables that could be used to measure a given factor if only one of the four factors were to be used in a research study. (The quality of the approximation is evaluated in Section 12.4).

*12.3   CLUSTER ANALYSIS OF INDIVIDUALS: TYPOLOGICAL SCORING

It is often useful to identify types of individuals (i.e., to establish categories where the individual is either completely in or completely out of each category). Not only may types be useful for theory, but they are often necessary in applied settings. In clinical areas, for example, the decision must be made to place a particular individual under a particular treatment condition, and it is seldom possible to give him .3 of one treatment and .4 of another, owing either to possible interactions between the treatments or to administrative difficulties. In such situations, it is useful to say that an individual is of a particular type and hence should be placed under a particular treatment.

Theoretically, types can be formed in two ways. First, one can place together those subjects whose scores fall within the same general area in hyperspace. For example, in Fig. 12.1 the factor scores for 10 individuals are plotted in a two-dimensional space. It is obvious that these individuals form three separate types because the individuals within any one of the three groups are more alike on these two factors than are two individuals from separate clusters.

Empirical analyses for clusters generally start by calculating the distance between each of the individuals for whom factor scores are available. Tryon and Bailey (1970) then use these distance measures as a basis for correlations among individuals that can be, in essence, factor analyzed. This procedure is closely akin to Q-technique factor analysis, which is discussed in Section 15.1.2, but it

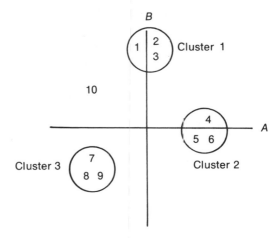

FIG. 12.1.   Factor scores of ten individuals.

:s more cumbersome than a direct Q-technique factor analysis. Other procedures (McQuitty, 1963) also use either factor scores or the original data matrix for clustering individuals. Factoring before clustering allows one to clarify the basis on which the individuals are clustered. These procedures provide empirical methods of producing typologies.

A second approach to clustering individuals builds from the fact that a typology is basically a nominal scoring system. In a nominal scoring system, each type is defined by a vector where all those within the type receive one score (usually a one) and all those who are not of that type receive a different score (usually a zero). Table 12.3.1 provides a typological score matrix for the ten

TABLE 12.3.1
Typological Standard Scores

	Types*		
Individuals	1	2	3
1	1.52	−.66	−.66
2	1.52	−.66	−.66
3	1.52	−.66	−.66
4	−.66	1.52	−.66
5	−.66	1.52	−.66
6	−.66	1.52	−.66
7	−.66	−.66	1.52
8	−.66	−.66	1.52
9	−.66	−.66	1.52
10	−.66	−.66	−.66

*A high score indicates that the individual is a member of the typological group or cluster. A negative score indicates that she or he is not a member of that group.

individuals plotted in Fig. 12.1; the zero–one scores were transformed to standard scores. The fact that the typological score matrix requires three columns instead of the two in the solution's factor score matrix is typical.[2]

The goal of a typological analysis in a factor-analytic context would be to find a set of factor scores that resemble the form in Table 12.3.1. One would begin with the factor scores as produced by a particular analysis and then transform those scores to create a typology. After the factor scores had been transformed to a typological pattern, factor pattern, structure, and correlation matrices could be computed. However, the details of this second approach to clustering individuals have not yet been developed.

In both cases, cluster analysis usually has more types than factors. Parsimony is slightly reduced for interpretability and usefulness.

12.4 EVALUATING THE FACTOR SCORES

Regardless of whether the scores are calculated, estimated, or approximated, the quality of the resulting factor scores needs to be checked. In the component model, the correlation of the factor scores with the factor itself should be unity and any departures from unity indicate an error in the procedure. In the estimation and approximation approaches, the check is crucial because some factors may be estimated quite well and others estimated or approximated poorly. The information also suggests which factors can be interpreted because a factor with poorly defined estimates is not as likely to replicate.

The quality of the factor scores is determined by calculating R_{fs}, the correlation of the f factors with the s scores for those factors. The main diagonal of R_{fs} contains the correlations of the factor scores with the factor that they measure. The rest of the matrix contains correlations of each factor with the other factor scores. For example, r_{21} is the correlation of factor 2 with the scores for factor 1; r_{12} is the correlation of factor 1 with the scores for factor 2.

If the factor scores are calculable, as in component analysis, then the following holds true:

$$R_{fs} = R_{ff} = R_{ss} \qquad (12.4.1)$$

That is, the factor scores should have the same relationship with the factors as the factors have among themselves, and the factor scores should have the same intercorrelations as do the factors. If the components are calculated properly, this equation will hold true. The relationships will only be approximated by common factor procedures and the comparison of the three matrices will be instructive as to the quality of the estimation.

---

[2]The columns of the typological score matrix are not independent and correlate negatively. If all individuals appear in one and only one of the clusters, each column of the typological score matrix will have a multiple correlation of 1.0 with the other columns.

To derive R_{fs} we begin with the definition:

$$R_{fs} = S_{ff}^{-1}F'_{fn}F_{ns}n^{-1}S_{ss}^{-1} \qquad (12.4.2)$$

where F_{ns} are the estimated factor scores and S_{ss} is a diagonal matrix of the standard derivations of the estimated factor scores. Assuming the factors are unit length and substituting the definition of factor scores gives:

$$R_{fs} = F'_{fn}Z_{nv}n^{-1}W_{vf}S_{ss}^{-1} \qquad (12.4.3)$$

where W_{vf} is the weight matrix used in calculating the factor scores under consideration. Substituting from the definition of the transposed factor structure gives:

$$R_{fs} = S'_{fv}W_{vf}S_{ss}^{-1} \qquad (12.4.4)$$

However, we now need S, the diagonal matrix of factor score standard deviations. The elements of S can be taken from the appropriate covariance matrix by calculating the square roots of the diagonal elements. The covariance matrix is defined by:

$$C_{ss} = F'_{sn}F_{ns}n^{-1} \qquad (12.4.5)$$

Substituting and rearranging terms:

$$C_{ss} = W'_{fv}Z'_{vn}Z_{nv}n^{-1}W_{vf} \qquad (12.4.6)$$

Because Z is in standard score form:

$$C_{ss} = W'_{fv}R_{vv}W_{vf} \qquad (12.4.7)$$

The diagonals of C are the factor score variances. From C_{ss}, S_{ss} and R_{ss} can be readily calculated. R_{fs} is basic and should be calculated whenever factor scores are used in the original study or whenever a W is computed for a future study.

Examples

The weight matrix for the box components was given in Table 12.1.3. The correlations between the factor scores and the original factors would indicate whether or not the calculations were correct. To obtain the standard deviations of the factor scores, C_{ss} was computed by Eq. (12.4.7) and is given in Table 12.4.1. Note that the factor scores are calculated exactly and are therefore standard scores with variances of one. The covariance matrix is also the factor score correlation matrix because the factor scores have unit length. The correlations among the factor scores are identical to the correlations among factors. R_{fs} was calculated by Eq. (12.4.4) and is identical to the C given in Table 12.4.1. The check shows the weight matrix was calculated correctly.

If the approximation weight matrix based solely on the squared measures of length, width, and height is used instead, R_{fs} will change. Using Eqs. (12.4.7) and (12.4.4) gives the R of Table 12.4.2. It shows that each factor is not calculated exactly. The scores for factor A correlate with the other two factors slightly lower than factor A did, but the scores for factor B correlate with factors A and C slightly more than did factor B. However, they

TABLE 12.4.1
Covariances Among Box Factor Scores

		Factor Scores		
		A'	B'	C'
Factor Scores	A	1.00	.69	.78
	B	.69	1.00	.74
	C	.78	.74	1.00

Note: These are the same as the correlations between the components and the scores, and the same as the correlations among the components.

TABLE 12.4.2
Correlations Between Approximate Factor Scores and Box Components

		Factor Scores		
		A'	B'	C'
	A	.96	.71	.72
Factors	B	.58	.96	.72
	C	.65	.79	.98

TABLE 12.4.3
Correlations Between Idealized Variable Factor Scores and Ability Factors

		Factor Scores			
		A'	B'	C'	D'
	A	.96	.34	.55	.46
Factors	B	.42	.90	.47	.46
	C	.56	.36	.92	.51
	D	.49	.44	.53	.89

TABLE 12.4.4
Correlations Between Approximate Factor Scores and Ability Factors

		Factor Scores			
		A'	B'	C'	D'
	A	.95	.37	.53	.38
Factors	B	.44	.90	.36	.36
	C	.60	.40	.87	.38
	D	.50	.50	.48	.79

TABLE 12.4.5
Correlations Between Single Variable Factor Scores
and Ability Factors

	Factor Scores			
	9	10	1	17
A	.85	.30	.37	.31
Factors B	.30	.77	.36	.38
C	.48	.21	.71	.31
D	.45	.36	.38	.66

are quite close. Given the quality of the scores and the ease with which only three variables, compared with ten, could be measured in a future study, few would opt for the complete computation method.

The correlations between the factor scores and the factors themselves were calculated for the ability data. The correlations for the idealized variable factor scores are in Table 12.4.3 and those for the approximation scores in Table 12.4.4. In neither case were the diagonal elements of C unities because common factors were not calculated exactly. The idealized variable factor scores do not correlate perfectly with the factors but they are adequate. The correlations with the factors are close to those found among the factors by the promax solution. The approximations also show correlations that would be usable for most purposes. For the first two factors, they are as good as the estimates, but for the last two factors, the approximations are slightly poorer than the estimates.

The correlations of the approximations based on several variables can be compared with the results of using only one variable per factor. The R_{fs} for that case is simply the appropriate rows of the factor structure entered into R, which is given in Table 12.4.5 for the ability data. The table shows that one variable measurement of A is good but that one variable measurement for factor D leaves something to be desired. The correlations between the factor scores and the factors the scores are not measuring are reasonable.

It should be remembered that R_{fs} is being calculated on the original sample; generalization to the same factors as found in another sample would involve some shrinkage. The diagonal of R_{fs} contains maximum values for the correlations of the factor scores with the factors in a new sample; the values would shrink more for the estimates than for the approximation scores because the former involve capitalization on chance.

12.5   SELECTING AMONG PROCEDURES

A crucial question is the similarity of factor scores estimated or approximated by various procedures. Several empirical studies have been conducted on this question (Glass & Maguire, 1966; Horn, 1965a; Horn & Miller, 1966; Moseley & Klett, 1964; Trites & Sells, 1955; Tucker, 1971; Velicer, 1976; Wackwitz &

Horn, 1971), all of which give essentially the same results. The common factor procedures of Section 12.1 produce factor scores that intercorrelate about .95. Laux and Tucker (1979) found all techniques produced the same degree of statistical significance when used as dependent variables in both univariate and multivariate analysis. In the case of uncorrelated factors, the orthogonality is reasonably well maintained in the original sample with the complete estimation procedures. The findings suggest that calculation ease may be used as the prime determinant of choice among the estimation procedures. The multiple-group procedures correlate about .8 with the more complete procedures and are also good choices for computing factor scores for the original sample of individuals.

Regardless of whether the rotation was orthogonal or oblique, approximation procedures are the only choice if future studies will not carry the full set of variables. It is important to know if the factors can be measured by the proposed approach before the scores are assumed to be adequate in future studies, and so the approximation procedures should be checked in the original sample by computing R_{fs}.

The effect of generalizing to a new sample has been investigated by Wackwitz and Horn (1971). In Monte Carlo studies of 12 samples, weight matrices were computed by Eqs. (12.1.5) and (12.1.8) as well as by two multiple-group methods. The criterion was the quality of the factor scores when generalized to a new sample. A simple approximation akin to option 2 in Section 12.2.2 gave better results than either of two more exact computational procedures. Morris (1979) has extended this work and again found multiple-group option 2 to give the highest cross-validated validities, higher even than the methods of Section 12.1. Bentler and Woodward (1979) provide both theory and illustrative examples supporting the implicit multiple group procedures, and Cotter and Raju (1982) demonstrate that multiple group factor scores give more generalizable factor scores than do the original variables or full factor score methods.

The multiple-group approach produced factor scores that, in a new sample, correlated better with the true scores, were more orthogonal when based on a varimax rotation, were more univocal, and had a more accurate pattern of interrelationships than the idealized variable or multiple regression approaches to estimating factor scores. The multiple-group methods are more accurate when generalizing to a new sample because they involve fewer opportunities to capitalize on the chance characteristics of one sample. The fact that the analysis is of a sample and not of the population has not been given adequate treatment in the development of the more exact procedures. Because in science one is always concerned with generalizing to new samples, the multiple-group methods are recommended for computing factor scores.

13

Relating Factors Across Studies

When several factor-analytic studies are conducted in the same substantive area, how similar are the several factors? The question of the similarity between two sets of factors also arises when two dissimilar factor-analytic procedures are used with the same data. It could be that the same factors occur or that the factors are all different, but usually empirical data are not clear. Some factors will replicate, others will not reappear, and still others will shift their character across studies. Evaluating the replication of factors is particularly important because there are so few significance tests for factor-analytic procedures.

To determine when a factor has been replicated, it is necessary to have objective means for relating factors from one study to those from another study. The methods of relating factors provide an objective basis by which the results of several factor-analytic studies from the same or different samples can be compared.

The information on a factor that could be used to relate factors is noted in Section 13.1. The possible procedures vary depending on whether the factors are extracted from the same individuals and whether they are based on the same variables. The combinations of variable and individual samples of prime interest are: same individuals and variables with different factor-analytic procedures (Section 13.2), same individuals but different variables (Section 13.3), same variables but different individuals when basic matrices such as R_{vv} or S_{vf} are available (Section 13.4), same variables but different individuals when R_{vv} or S_{vf} is unavailable (Section 13.5), and different variables and different individuals (Section 13.6). The procedures discussed give rise to indices of relationship from which a decision is made as to which factors are the same (Section 13.7) and hence "match."

The present chapter does not include all procedures for relating factors. Hundleby, Pawlik, and Cattell (1965) discuss several additional indices in detail. For example, in parallel profiles rotation (cf. Section *10.4.2) the factors from several studies are rotated simultaneously to the same simple structure. This rotation is used to maximize the similarity of the factors in the two studies but is not within the focus of this chapter. Instead, it is assumed that the factors have been independently extracted and rotated.

In the present chapter it is assumed that factor hypothesis-testing procedures are not appropriate. If confirmatory multiple-group or maximum likelihood factor analysis can be computed, then it would be preferred over procedures for relating factors. Confirmatory factor analyses can be used not only to test past findings in a new sample but also to factor several samples simultaneously (Jöreskog, 1971) to obtain the hypothesized structures. The procedures of the present chapter are generally used when, for example, a survey of the literature is being conducted or if one is evaluating whether the previously found factors are also the simple structure factors for a new study.

13.1   INFORMATION USEFUL IN RELATING FACTORS

Two factors are related to the degree that they correlate together when scored for an appropriate set of individuals. In some situations, product-moment coefficients are actually computed between the two sets of factor scores. In other situations, the correlations between the factor sets can be evaluated without actually calculating factor scores. Although the latter approach may be used because it is convenient, it is required whenever both sets of factor scores are not available on the same individuals.

Outside of the factor scores, the prime sources of information regarding the nature of a factor are the factor matrices. The reference vector structure, factor pattern, factor structure, and factor score weight matrices all provide useful information on the interrelationships between factors and variables. Inasmuch as the two factors have the same relationships to the same variables, they can be considered related. In some situations, a subjective examination of the factor loadings of several studies may lead to conclusions as to the nature of the factors. For example, based upon the factors replicated in previous studies, marker variables may have been included in each of the new studies. (**Marker variables** have high weights and correlations with the factors, and so should load the same factor if it appears in the new study.) If the marker variables again form the same pattern as previously found, then the factor could be considered replicated.

Examination of factor loadings to relate factors has several problems, however. First, it is only if the variable loads .9 or so in both analyses that one can be absolutely certain that it is the same factor. A variable with exceptionally high reliability can load two uncorrelated factors at the .6 to .7 level. This is illustrated in Fig. 13.1 where variables 1, 2, and 3 have high loadings on both factors. If factor A is identified by variable one, then factor B may be assumed to be A in another study because variable one also loads it at a high level. Complementary factors that are formed by the same variables but utilize different components of their variance do occasionally appear, although, fortunately, their appearance is rare. The other major problem with examining loadings is the subjectivity of the procedure. "Eyeball" analyses are prone to errors of expectation. The subjectivity can be overcome by indices given in later sections.

In addition to the factor matrices themselves, other evidence on the similarity of the factors may be available. The degree of certainty of the match could be heightened through use of such indirect evidence. The additional information available may include the following (Cattell, 1957, 1962):

1. The correlations of the factor with other factors and other variables is useful. Within the analysis itself, the correlations of a particular factor with other well-known, easily replicable factors may be available. Such a pattern of correlations should match across the two studies to the extent that the factors being related are the same. The factors should correlate with other variables outside the factor analysis itself in the same manner across the several studies. The more such correlations are available, the easier it is to evaluate whether the factors are functionally related.
2. The size of the factor in a given sample of variables is also an indication as to whether or not it could possibly be the same as another one in another analysis. If the factor is actually the same, then the proportion of variance accounted for by it in the total matrix should be approximately the same in the two studies where the samples of variables and of individuals have been drawn in the same manner.
3. The behavior of the factor as an independent or dependent variable in experimental research could also be examined. If the same conclusions are

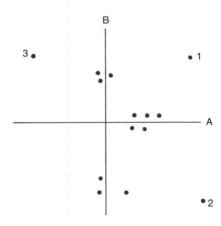

FIG. 13.1. Uncorrelated factors loaded by the same variables.

always reached with factors defined from two different studies, then it seems worthwhile to identify these factors as the same ones. Naturally, when the factors being related are taken to a new area, it will be worthwhile to run further checks. If they no longer give similar conclusions, a more comprehensive theory, including the fact that they function the same in the first area but not in the next one, would need to be developed.

But the supplemental pieces of information should be considered just that—supplementary. The basic criterion is whether or not the results from the various studies lead to the same factors, that is, whether or not the factor scores defined by the two studies correlate highly.

13.2   SAME INDIVIDUALS AND VARIABLES BUT DIFFERENT PROCEDURES

Occasionally, several factor-analytic procedures are applied to the same data and the question arises as to whether the same factors are identified by all the procedures used. The most general answer to this question is provided by correlating the factor scores that result from the several factor-analytic procedures being tested. The following procedure can be utilized regardless of how alike or how different the methods are.

Factor scores could be directly calculated by applying a factor score weight matrix from each of the different procedures to the same data and correlating the results, but a simpler procedure can be derived. By definition:

$$R_{fg} = S_{ff}^{-1} F'_{fn} F_{ng} n^{-1} S_{gg}^{-1} \tag{13.2.1}$$

where f refers to one set of factors, g to the other set, and R_{fg} is the matrix of correlations between the two sets of factor scores. The inclusion of the matrices of standard deviations, S_{ff} and S_{gg}, is necessary because the factor scores are standard scores only when the scores are computed exactly, as in a component analysis. The two solutions need not have the same number of factors.

The factor scores used in Eq. (13.2.1) may be those that result from *any* of the procedures discussed in Chapter 12. The scores may be based on only a limited subset of the salient variables in the analysis and have an associated weight matrix that contains a large number of zeros, or the factor scores may be estimated by one of the more complex methods. **Any set of factor scores computed through the use of any weight matrix may be used in the equations of this chapter,** provided that the mean of the factor scores is zero.

Substituting the definition of the factor scores into Eq. (13.2.1) gives:

$$R_{fg} = S_{ff}^{-1} W'_{fv} Z'_{vn} Z_{nv} W_{vg} n^{-1} S_{gg}^{-1} \tag{13.2.2}$$

where W and Z are defined as the factor score weight matrix and the standard score data matrix, respectively. The subscripts f and g on the W's refer to the weight matrices derived by the two different procedures. Shifting the scalar and substituting the definition of the correlation matrix gives:

$$R_{fg} = S_{ff}^{-1} W'_{fv} R_{vv} W_{vg} S_{gg}^{-1} \tag{13.2.3}$$

The S's are calculated by Eq. (12.4.7); the variances equal 1.0 for component or image scores in the original sample, but each is less than 1.0 for a common factor analysis. Even though Eq. (13.2.3) involves the full correlation matrix, it is easily computed.

Other solutions that might be more easily calculated can be derived. For example, factor scores might be correlated with another set of factors rather than another set of factor scores. Then only one definition of factor scores is substituted into Eq. (13.2.1):

$$R_{fg} = S_{ff}^{-1} F'_{fn} Z_{nv} W_{vg} n^{-1} S_{gg}^{-1} \tag{13.2.4}$$

From the definition of the factor structure and assuming the variables and factors are standard scores with the factors perfectly measured:

$$R_{fg} = S'_{fv} W_{vg} S_{gg}^{-1} \tag{13.2.5}$$

Equation (13.2.5) may be easier to compute than Eq. (13.2.3), but it can only be used to relate factors and factor scores, not two sets of factor scores or two sets of factors. It is generally better to relate factor scores because the scores are what would be used in future studies, and so Eq. (13.2.3) is the recommended approach. Morris and Guertin (1976) have programmed this solution, using regression-based factor scores.

13.3 SAME INDIVIDUALS BUT DIFFERENT VARIABLES

Including all the data available on a single sample of individuals in the analysis may not be desirable. It is often more useful to factor several domains separately and then relate the factors. Separate factor analyses are particularly appropriate if prediction or causation can be assumed from one domain to another on the basis of external information.

All of the standard statistical procedures available for analyzing the relationships between two sets of variables apply here and should be used according to the theory of the expected interrelationships. These procedures would begin with the calculation of factor scores from all the factor analyses. Multiple regression, chi-square, analysis of variance, or other procedures would be used as needed to interrelate the factor scores.

If the question is one of determining if the same factors occurred in the two domains, then correlations between the factor scores form an appropriate method of relating factors. Although factor scores could be calculated and correlated, there is, again, an easier way for computing the correlations between the sets of factor scores. Substituting into the definitional Eq. (13.2.1) gives:

$$R_{fg} = S_{ff}^{-1} W'_{fv_1} Z'_{v_1 n} Z_{n v_2} W_{v_2 g} n^{-1} S_{gg}^{-1} \tag{13.3.1}$$

where v_1 refers to the first variable set, v_2 refers to the second variable set, and the weight matrices are derived by any of the procedures of Chapter 12, including those that base the factor scores only on a limited subset of salient variables. Note that the data matrices, Z_{nv_1} and Z_{nv_2}, are two different standard score matrices, although the individuals are the same. Rearranging terms and substituting the definition of the correlations between two sets of variables gives:

$$R_{fg} = S_{ff}^{-1} W'_{fv_1} R_{v_1 v_2} W_{v_2 g} S_{gg}^{-1} \tag{13.3.2}$$

R_{fg} then contains the desired correlations between the two sets of factor scores.

Pinneau and Newhouse (1964) point out an important limitation on all methods for relating factors from separate analyses on the same individuals. Whenever the two sets of variables are factored independently because the data were collected at two points in time, then factors can correlate perfectly across the two data sets *only if both the factors and the individuals remain unchanged over that time period*. If the individuals' factor scores do shift in the time interval between the first and second data collection, then the shift will lower the correlations between the two sets of factors.

13.4   SAME VARIABLES BUT DIFFERENT INDIVIDUALS (R_{vv}, S_{vf}, AND W_{vf} AVAILABLE)

In the following discussion the variables are assumed to be the same and are ordered in the identical manner for each of the two studies. The ordering is no problem, but the identification of "identical" variables may not be as easy as it sounds. For example, the size of a city has a given value, but the meaning of that value shifts from era to era; what was defined as a huge city in 1776 is only a minor town in 1976. Moreover, significant variations may occur when the analysis is made in one laboratory under one observer as compared to another laboratory under another observer. Deciding which variables are equivalent is not possible mathematically; the decision must be based upon the investigator's thorough knowledge of his area and of his variables. (The problem in deciding which variables are equivalent underscores the points that (1) variables going into a factor analysis need to be thoroughly understood to produce profitable results; and (2) only investigators with a good substantive background in their area should be involved in factor analyses.)

Correlations Between Sets of Factor Scores.   Because the individuals are different, factor scores cannot be directly correlated. However, correlations between the factors can be computed in a new sample. The factor score weight matrices from both the previous analyses would be applied to the correlations for the new sample by Eq. (13.2.3) to give the correlation between the two sets of factor scores. The standard deviations of the factor scores would also be calculated on the new sample; they cannot be assumed to be unities even for weights from a component analysis. The new sample is desired because the factors from any given R capitalize on the chance fluctuations in it. A new R is used so that the random variations are unrelated to either of the sets of factors.

If it is not possible to collect a third set of data before relating the factors, other procedures are needed. If the correlations among the variables are available from one sample, the matrix can be used as an estimate of the correlations among the variables in both samples. The two weight matrices from the two studies and the R_{vv} would be used in Eq. (13.2.3). If R_{vv} is not available but the factor structure is, then Eq. (13.2.5) could be used to estimate what R_{fg} would be in a new sample. Variations on this solution for relating factors across individuals have been proposed by Ahmavaara (1954; Hamilton, 1967; Hundleby, Pawlik & Cattell, 1965), Hurley and Cattell (1962; Hundleby, Pawlik & Cattell, 1965) and Mosier (1938, 1939a). These are all basically the same as the present one; the differences are in the method of derivation and the way the weight matrix is defined. In the derivations in the literature, it has been assumed that $S_{ff} = S_{gg} = I$ (i.e., the weights were assumed to give standard scores in both samples), an assumption that may need to be made where R_{vv}s are not available but that is unlikely to be true and is not assumed in the present discussion.

Replication of the factors by the Ahmavaara–Cattell–Hurley–Mosier approach or by using Eq. (13.2.3) or Eq. (13.2.5) with one of the original samples is not as convincing as the use of a third sample. Using one of the original samples means that a different index of relationship would have resulted if the other sample's R_{vv} had been used instead. Different indices occur because the correlation matrix will shift somewhat from sample to sample, particularly if the samples are small. If the samples are truly random samples from the same population, these correlation matrices should not, of course, differ significantly and neither should the two R_{fg}s. If a new sample is used, all significance tests applicable to correlations in general are also applicable to R_{fg} because no capitalization on chance has occurred for the new sample.

If the correlation matrices from both studies are available, then the correlations between the two sets of factors can be calculated for each of the R's for Eq. (13.2.3) or each of the S_{vf}'s for Eq. (13.2.5). The two R_{fg}s should give equivalent results; the variations between them will give a feel for the sampling error involved in estimating the relationship between the factors.

Projecting the Variables Into the Same Space.   Another procedure has been suggested when basic matrices are available from two studies. The variables common between the two studies can be projected into the same space. Because the factor positions can be identified as a function of the variables, each set of factors can also be projected into the common variable space. The cosines of the angles among the factors are the correlations among the factors. The procedure was originally suggested by Kaiser (personal communication; Kaiser, Hunka & Bianchini, 1971).

To compute the correlations between the sets of factors, the study with the greater number of factors is taken and all operations occur within the space defined by those factors. The variables of the space-defining study are located by their factor loadings. The variables of the other study are then projected into this space and rotated so that the cosine between each variable's vector in one study and the same variable's vector in the other study is maximized. Usually, the mean cosine between variable vectors is also computed. If the mean cosine is low, it is not possible to relate factors at all because the relationships among the variables are different.

The factors from the second study are then projected into this space, a step that is possible because the relationships of the factors to the variables are known. At this point, both sets of factors from both studies are projected into the same space and therefore the cosines of the angles between the two sets of factors can be computed. The cosines represent the correlations between two sets of factors. The procedure gives an approximation to the correlations given by Eq. (13.2.5), but may give estimates greater than 1.0 (Kenney, Vaughan, & Cromwell, 1977).

The computational procedures are somewhat more difficult for Kaiser's method of relating factors than the other procedures. The procedure generally uses the unrotated orthogonal factors initially extracted from the correlation matrix and their transformation matrices for rotating to the reference vectors. Veldman (1967) presents a program for relating orthogonal factors by this method.

13.5   SAME VARIABLES BUT DIFFERENT INDIVIDUALS (R_{vv}, S_{vf}, AND W_{vf} UNAVAILABLE)

When relating the results of one study to previous ones, R, S, and W are often unavailable and the matrices necessary for Kaiser's technique may also be missing. Usually, sufficient data is available for a zero–one weight matrix to be developed and Eq. (13.2.3) solved using the current R_{vv}. If R_{vv} is not available, then other procedures must be sought.

Several procedures have been suggested that can be used to relate factors in almost any situation. Use of these procedures are often desirable only when the matrices needed for the solutions of Section 13.4 are not available. The procedures can be applied to any of the factor matrices available—reference vector structures, factor patterns, or factor structures—provided the same matrix is used across all studies and the comparison makes theoretical sense. Usually the factor patterns are the basis of comparison. A complete matrix may not even be needed.

The **coefficient of congruence** (Burt, 1948; Tucker, 1951; Wrigley & Neuhaus, 1955) was developed to relate factors when only factor loadings are available. The definitional formula is as follows:

$$c_{12} = \frac{\Sigma \, p_{v1} \, p_{v2}}{\sqrt{\Sigma \, p_{v1}^2} \, \sqrt{\Sigma \, p_{v2}^2}} \qquad (13.5.1)$$

where c_{12} is the coefficient of congruence between factor 1 and factor 2, p_{v1} are the factor loadings for the first factor, and p_{v2} are the factor loadings for the second factor. The formula has been generally applied to the factor pattern. **In the case of orthogonal components where the factor scores have means of zero and variances of one, the result of calculating coefficients of congruence on the factor pattern is identical to correlating the exact factor scores and is, indeed, a simplified formula for that correlation.** If the factor scores are only estimated rather than calculated, as in the case of common factor analysis or generalizing a component analysis to a new sample, then the results will not be correlation coefficients. Because correlation coefficients are more widely known and more easily interpreted, calculating correlations between factor scores is preferable to coefficients of congruence. (See Cattell, 1978, for significance levels.)

Occasionally, coefficients of congruence can give ridiculous results. Pinneau and Newhouse (1964) have pointed out that the index is highly influenced by the level and by the sign of the loadings. Factors whose loadings are the same size will, of necessity, have a high coefficient of congruence even if the patterns are unrelated. It would seem that this index should only be used when the information required for other procedures is not available.

The **salient variable similarity index, s,** (Cattell, 1949) is a test of significance for determining whether or not two factors match in the sense that they have the same salient variables. Several variables could load the same factor by chance, so the question arises as to whether or not a sufficient number of the identical variables load the two factors for it to be assumed that such parallel loadings could not have occurred by chance. Initial procedures for calculating s and tables of significance were given by Cattell and Baggaley (1960); Cattell, Balcar, Horn, and Nesselroade (1969) and Cattell (1978) present an expanded discussion and new tables.

Confirmatory factor-analytic procedures are a recent innovation that provide more elegant solutions for the problem of relating factors when the complete data are available for one set of individuals. The factor pattern or other information from the first study would be used to set up the hypotheses for the second study that would then be tested by confirmatory maximum likelihood factor analysis. Filsinger (1981) provides an example of one of the uses for this approach.

In every case it is preferable to attempt to gain the information sufficient to use the procedures of Section 13.4 rather than those of Section 13.5. All the procedures in this section are only approximations to those of Section 13.4, and

TABLE 13.5.1
Promax ($k = 4$) Solution for Grant-White Principal
Axes

A. *Factor Structure*

	Factors			
	A	B	C	D
	Verbal	Numerical	Visual	Recognition
Variables	Ability	Ability	Ability	Ability
1. Visual Perception	.38	.34	.71	.42
2. Cubes	.24	.18	.51	.23
3. Paper Form Board	.31	.27	.50	.31
4. Lozenges	.40	.26	.68	.34
5. General Information	.80	.40	.52	.41
6. Paragraph Comprehension	.81	.30	.48	.48
7. Sentence Completion	.84	.37	.46	.40
8. Word Classification	.69	.43	.54	.44
9. Word Meaning	.85	.28	.49	.47
10. Add	.30	.79	.25	.37
11. Code	.36	.62	.42	.53
12. Counting Groups of Dots	.22	.73	.42	.33
13. Straight and Curved Capitals	.39	.66	.61	.37
14. Word Recognition	.32	.23	.29	.57
15. Number Recognition	.24	.19	.33	.53
16. Figure Recognition	.29	.24	.54	.60
17. Object-Number	.32	.38	.27	.67
18. Number-Figure	.25	.46	.51	.58
19. Figure-Word	.31	.31	.35	.47
20. Deduction	.54	.28	.56	.52
21. Numerical Puzzles	.38	.53	.62	.46
22. Problem Reasoning	.54	.31	.56	.52
23. Series Completion	.57	.41	.67	.51
24. Woody-McCall Mixed Fundamentals, Form I	.53	.63	.44	.55

B. *Factor Correlations*

	A	B	C	D
A	1.00			
B	.43	1.00		
C	.59	.52	1.00	
D	.55	.51	.62	1.00

TABLE 13.5.2
Promax (k = 4) Solution for Pasteur Principal Axes

A. Factor Structure

	Factors			
	A	B	C	D
	Verbal	*Recognition*	*Visual*	*Numerical*
Variables	*Ability*	*Ability*	*Ability*	*Ability*
1. Visual Perception	.43	.21	.67	.28
2. Cubes	.10	.02	.47	.03
3. Paper Form Board	.17	−.11	.42	.10
4. Lozenges	.13	.26	.66	.24
5. General Information	.82	−.01	.30	.36
6. Paragraph Comprehension	.82	.15	.43	.41
7. Sentence Completion	.88	.04	.34	.32
8. Word Classification	.72	.20	.41	.35
9. Word Meaning	.82	.12	.50	.43
10. Add	.25	.22	.10	.71
11. Code	.44	.34	.35	.68
12. Counting Groups of Dots	.17	.12	.26	.56
13. Straight and Curved Capitals	.11	.24	.33	.48
14. Word Recognition	.03	.65	.15	.21
15. Number Recognition	−.08	.60	.19	.09
16. Figure Recognition	.21	.52	.52	.41
17. Object-Number	.13	.56	.14	.41
18. Number-Figure	.15	.51	.12	.21
19. Figure-Word	.15	.44	.34	.33
20. Deduction	.21	.25	.56	.20
21. Numerical Puzzles	.40	.24	.58	.54
22. Problem Reasoning	.55	.10	.60	.35
23. Series Completion	.49	.23	.72	.43
24. Woody-McCall Mixed Fundamentals, Form I	.36	.30	.49	.60

B. Factor Correlations

	A	B	C	D
A	1.00			
B	.12	1.00		
C	.47	.30	1.00	
D	.45	.41	.47	1.00

should be avoided. For example, the coefficient of congruents is an approximation of the correlations among factor scores, but it is obvious that approximations are less desirable than the actual correlations among factor scores—which can usually be calculated by the formulas as previously given.

Example

Holzinger and Swineford (1939) collected ability data at two schools. The Grant-White School has been used in prior analyses to illustrate factoring procedures. The data from Pasteur School can also be factored and both data sets used to illustrate factor relating.

Factors were extracted from the two samples in the same manner: principal axes with communalities iterated twice from squared multiple correlations. Rotations were to promax ($k=4$). Because students in the second school had been given variables 1 to 24 but not 25 and 26, all analyses were for variables 1 to 24 only. The resulting factor structures and correlations are given in Tables 13.5.1 and 13.5.2.

Zero–one weight matrices were determined for both samples by using each variable's highest loading to place it on a factor. However, the analysis stopped there: each factor was defined by the identical set of variables. Therefore, the factor scores of one analysis correlate 1.0 with the factor scores from the second analysis.

Both solutions were compared by Kaiser's procedure. The cosines between the variables ranged from .68 (poor) to .99 with a mean of .94 (excellent). Table 13.5.3 gives the cosines between the two sets of factors.

The s index was also calculated. From the Grant-White solution, the highest variable from each factor was selected as the marker: variable 9 from A, 10 for B, 1 for C, and 17 for D. The markers were used solely to identify the factors with which A, B, C, and D from the first study were to be matched in the second school's analysis. From the remaining 20 variables on each factor, one-sixth were selected as salients in each study. Because one-sixth of 20 is a fraction, 3.3, three salients were chosen. The number of matches was three for A with A, two for B with D, two for C with C and two for D with B. All of these values are significant at the .01 level or less by Cattell and Baggaley's (1960) table.

The ability data show an *exceptional* level of replicability. The strong relationships probably arise because of the investigators: they were well acquainted with a well-researched area and used tests with reasonable reliabilities.

TABLE 13.5.3
Cosines Between Grant-White and Pasteur Promax
Factors

Pasteur	Grant-White			
	A	*B*	*C*	*D*
A	.98	.40	.46	.43
B	.24	.34	.34	.93
C	.60	.46	1.00	.59
D	.49	.99	.53	.59

13.6 DIFFERENT VARIABLES AND DIFFERENT INDIVIDUALS

A situation may arise where one investigator has sampled a particular domain with one set of variables, whereas another investigator has sampled the same domain with another set of variables. The two studies are also assumed to have collected their data from different individuals. The question then arises as to whether or not the factors that they have both identified are the same.

There is no empirical way of solving this problem without collecting new data. When new data are collected from a new sample, the variables that clearly define the factors are included. Factor scores based on each prior analysis are then correlated in the new sample and the correlations are tested for significance.

If the area is relatively undeveloped so that the investigator does not have exact hypotheses as to which factors match, all of the marker variables from the two studies could be included in a further factor-analytic study. The factors from the resulting matrix would be related to the factors of each of the two prior studies by the methods previously given.

If the area is sufficiently researched, several factors may be hypothesized to be identical across the two studies. In that case, confirmatory multiple group or maximum likelihood would be the appropriate factor-analytic procedure to use to confirm or disconfirm the hypothesis.

13.7 MATCHING FACTORS

The indices developed in the preceding sections have been oriented toward determining the relationship between the factor scores. The usual result is a matrix of coefficients that gives the relationship of factor scores in one study to the factor scores in the other study. **Matching factors occurs when an investigator decides two factors are manifestations of the same construct.** Identifying factors as the same is a somewhat narrower problem than relating factors, although it is based upon the data from relating factors. It cannot substitute for relating factors because the factor-relating process may give new insight into the nature of the phenomena under investigation by the very way in which a factor from one study breaks up into several factors, or combines with other factors, in another study.

Matching generally proceeds by starting with the two factors that have the highest correlation. The two factors are considered a match. The next highest correlation is then sought and these two factors are considered a match. The process continues until all of the factors are matched or the correlations are too low to warrant matching.

Problems may arise in that the same factor may correlate quite well with two factors in the other study or may not correlate well with any factor in the other study. The matches may then be made so that the sum of the matching indices is maximized, or it can simply be reported that alternative matches exist or that no match exists. Except in unusual circumstances, the latter procedure is preferred because it would be less misleading for the purpose of interpretation.

The lower bound for matching two factors should be high because chance related factors can and do occur. The need for a high minimum correlation for matching factors is particularly acute if capitalization on chance can occur that would increase the match. For example, in confactor rotation (cf. Section 10.4.2), both studies are rotated to solutions that maximize the match and the resulting correlations are inflated. For example, Nesselroade and his associates (Nesselroade & Baltes, 1970; Nesselroade, Baltes, & LaBouvie, 1971) rotated pairs of solutions from random numbers to maximally similar positions. The congruence coefficients between pairs of solutions found some factors to be excellent matches (e.g., .9), particularly when a large number of factors was extracted from only a few variables.

If the correlations in R_{fg} are low, several possibilities exist. First, the two studies may simply have found alternative solutions—both equally good from a statistical point of view—which validly represent the phenomena at hand and reproduce the correlations among the variables equally. On the other hand, the low coefficients of relationship may be a function of actual differences across the studies. In the latter case, the nature of the measuring instruments might have shifted, or the samples were not actually drawn from the same population (it is assumed that similar factor-analytic methods have been used in both studies). The check for the alternative solution hypothesis consists of calculating the multiple correlation of the factors in one study with each factor in the other study. The multiple correlation can be computed by the usual multiple regression formula. If the correlations are high, then two rotation solutions for the same data have been found. If they are low, the nature of the phenomena is different and so the same factors cannot be identified. Conditions under which factors can be expected to replicate are discussed in Chapter 16.

*14 Data Transformations and Indices of Association

Factor analysis begins with a data matrix. Each variable in the data matrix has a particular mean, standard deviation, and distribution. Variations in the characteristics of the variables may have a definite effect on a factor analysis. One instance in which the distributions may distort the factor analysis is if the variables are dichotomous rather than approximations to continuous variables. The problems and possibilities of factor analysis with noncontinuous variables are discussed in Section 14.1.

Characteristics of the variables can be altered by both linear and nonlinear transformations. In Section 14.2 some of the transformations by which a set of scores might be altered and the probable impact of those procedures are presented.

Factor analysis generally begins with a summary of the relationships among the variables, such as a correlation matrix. Factor-analytic procedures are then applied to the summary as a convenient and efficient method for finding the factor pattern. Although the previous chapters dealt primarily with correlations, they are not the only statistics that can be factored. In Section 14.3 some indices of association that might be factored are discussed.

Nunnally (1978) gives more extensive discussions of many of the issues presented in this chapter.

14.1 NONCONTINUOUS DATA

When data are noncontinuous, it is possible for several individuals to receive exactly the same score on one variable. However, if these same individuals do not receive the same score on another variable, the two variables cannot correlate

---

*Optional.

perfectly even if the underlying relationship is perfect. The reduction in correlation occurs most often with dichotomous variables because a great number of individuals receive the same score. The effect is somewhat less important for trichotomies and is generally assumed to be negligible for variables where the score range across a dozen or so categories. Because the effect is most likely in dichotomous data and because dichotomous data are easy to work with theoretically, the discussions of this phenomena have centered on that case. It should be noted, however, that many of the principles extend to any variable where a large number of individuals receive the same score even though the other scores range across several points on a scale. Olsson (1979) has confirmed these effects for maximum likelihood analysis, where the greatest disruption is for the chi-squares (G. Huba, personal communication) if the kurtosis of the variables is only moderate (e.g., five to ten).

Section 14.1.1 is a discussion of the effects of discrete data with particular emphasis upon the possibility of creating spurious factors. In Section 14.1.2, the coefficients of association that have been suggested for dichotomous variables and their sensitivity to these effects are discussed.

14.1.1 Difficulty Factors

Variables that have the same split can receive a perfect positive correlation but not a correlation of -1. If the split is reversed for one of the two variables, the variable will then be able to receive a perfect negative correlation but not a perfect positive correlation. Table 14.1.1 gives samples of the maximum Pearson product-moment correlation that can occur between two dichotomous variables with different splits.

It is apparent that variables with similar marginal splits will correlate more with each other than they will with variables that do not have that same marginal split even when they all measure the same thing. Factoring data where the variables have different splits can lead to spurious factors. Two variables that have the same pattern of splits will correlate higher together than with another

TABLE 14.1.1
Maximum Product-Moment Correlations as a
Function of the Marginal Splits of Two Dichotomous
Variables

Split on Variable 1	Split on Variable 2				
	.10/.90	.20/.80	.50/.50	.70/.30	.90/.10
.10/.90	1.00				−1.00
.20/.80	.66	1.00			
.50/.50	.33	.50	1.00		
.70/.30	.22	.33	.66	1.00	
.90/.10	.11	.17	.33	.51	1.00

variable that is produced by the same factor but that does not have the same split, and produce a distinct factor. The spurious factors are referred to as **difficulty factors** because they were first noticed in the abilities realm where the several factors grouped items of similar difficulty together. The major effect is extra factors.

Difficulty factors in the abilities area are recognized by examining the mean scores on the variables. When a factor brings together only variables with similar mean scores, then it can be suspected to be a difficulty factor. Such factors generally occur when some tests are so easy that there is an end effect with numerous scores piling up in the high scores, and other tests are so difficult that there is an end effect at the low end of the scale. The easy tests then distinguish between the extremely low and moderately low ability individuals, whereas the difficult tests distinguish between the moderately high and high ability individuals. There is very little possibility of the variables correlating highly together because the poor ability people are not separated out by the hard test and the high ability people are not separated out by the easy test.

Example

A unidimensional scale whose items differ only in difficulty can be developed. Each item measures the same construct, but the dichotomous items are carefully selected so that each has a different difficulty level. Will such a scale give only one factor?

To find out, the responses of 105 hypothetical individuals to a 20-item scale were analyzed. The scale items were: "Is this person over 150 centimeters tall? Is he over 155 cm.? 160 cm.?" and so forth. Five individuals received each of the possible scores from zero through 20. Each item measured perfectly what it was to measure. The items were intercorrelated and factored.

Guttman's root ≥ 1 criterion indicated four factors and Bartlett's significance test did not indicate that any of these were insignificant. Communalities were iterated twice for four factors with the initial estimate being squared multiple correlations. Rotation was by varimax–promax ($k = 4$) from the principal axes. A second-order factor was indicated in the promax correlations among factors and extracted by the same principal axis procedure that had resulted in the primaries. The correlations between the second-order factor and the variables were computed.

The primary and second-order factor structures are given in Table 14.1.2 along with the mean of each variable and the correlations among the primary factors. An examination of the table shows the primaries are difficulty factors but that the unidimensional nature of the scale is recovered by the second-order factor.

The extent to which difficulty factors are important in empirical data is open to question until those data are thoroughly examined. Although examples can be built where difficulty factors occur, Borgatta's (1965) attempt to create difficulty factors by splitting his continuous variables in several different ways was unsuccessful. However, Gordon (1967) noted that changing the split of some variables did alter the results of the studies he reviewed.

TABLE 14.1.2
Results of Factoring a Perfect One-Factor Scale

A. *Factor Structure*

Variables	Percentage Passing	Promax Primary Factors				Second-Order Factor
		A	B	C	D	
1	95	.29	.09	.65	.17	.30
2	90	.44	.13	.87	.24	.42
3	86	.58	.17	.90	.29	.51
4	81	.71	.21	.85	.33	.59
5	76	.82	.24	.77	.38	.64
6	71	.89	.26	.68	.45	.68
7	67	.93	.28	.59	.52	.72
8	62	.93	.30	.50	.61	.75
9	57	.90	.32	.44	.69	.76
10	52	.85	.35	.39	.78	.77
11	48	.77	.39	.35	.85	.77
12	43	.69	.44	.32	.90	.76
13	38	.60	.51	.30	.93	.74
14	33	.52	.59	.28	.93	.72
15	29	.45	.68	.26	.89	.68
16	24	.38	.77	.24	.81	.64
17	19	.33	.85	.21	.71	.58
18	14	.28	.90	.17	.58	.52
19	10	.24	.87	.13	.43	.42
20	5	.17	.65	.09	.29	.29

B. *Factor Correlations*

	A	B	C	D
A	1.00			
B	.27	1.00		
C	.56	.18	1.00	
D	.57	.56	.27	1.00

The problems producing difficulty factors can be reduced by proper analytic procedures. The first appropriate procedure to use is that of higher-order factor analysis, as shown in the previous example. The primary factors do contain difficulty factors but higher-order factors generally do not. This procedure is particularly appropriate when factoring a set of items that may well reflect a single factor.

Gorsuch and Yagel (1981) found another procedure to also be effective in reducing problems of difficulty factors. They suggested grouping items into miniscales that are formed by adding together the scores of at least three items. All items are thus grouped into miniscales, and the miniscale scores are factored.

The problems associated with differential skew and mean differences are reduced by the manner in which the items are put into the miniscales. The miniscales are formed by grouping the two items with the most extreme positive skews, for example, together with the two items with the most extreme negative skews to form a four-item miniscale. The items with the next most extreme positive and negative skews are combined in like manner. If the items were selected from a very broad area and could well represent many factors, the items are first sorted by raters into homogeneous areas. This allows several miniscales for each of the possible constructs so that they can, if the data so warrant, relate to the same factors. The problems of extreme skews that produce difficulty factors are averaged out through the combining of several items. The results found at the second-order level in a problem such as that of the prior example then occur at the primary level, as demonstrated by Gorsuch and Yagel (1981).

Cattell (1956; Cattell & Burdsal, 1975) has suggested *radial parcels* to reduce the idiosyncratic characteristics of individual items. The purpose is to reduce the idiosyncratic characteristics of individual items by averaging several together that are quite similar to each other. The parcels are developed on the basis of a preliminary factor analysis of items and each parcel contains several items showing the same factor loadings across the unrotated factors. Each parcel is then scored as a miniscale, and scores from the miniscales formed by all the parcels are then factored. This procedure does reduce the problem with difficulty factors but does not eliminate it. Gorsuch and Yagel (1981) found that the only methods for actually eliminating difficulty factors were the higher-order factoring procedures shown in the prior example or the building of item parcels on the basis of both similarity of item content and difference in means.

The best present recommendation appears to be a *avoid variables with extreme skews*. In addition, results should be examined with the possibility of difficulty factors in mind. Appropriate research can be pursued to determine whether or not the factors are from difficulty levels or from substantive sources. Bentler (1970), DuBois (1960), Gibson (1963a, 1967), Horst (1965, Chapter 22), and McDonald (1969a, 1969b) have given tentative procedures to use if one has dichotomous variables with possible difficulty factors. Higher-order analyses should always be conducted because these appear to bring difficulty factors back together.

14.1.2 Coefficients of Association for Dichotomous Variables

The correlation coefficients that can be applied to dichotomous data are briefly summarized later. Although such coefficients have been derived for cases of two dichotomous variables and of a dichotomy being correlated with a continuous variable, no such coefficients have been derived for variables with three, four, and more splits. These noncontinuous variables can also produce spurious factors, although they are less likely to do so.

Phi and Point Biserial Correlations.   The phi and point biserial coefficients are simply the standard Pearson product-moment correlation applied to data containing dichotomies. A phi coefficient results if both variables are dichotomies, a point biserial if only one is a dichotomy. Separate formulas have been developed for these conditions because, if only two variables are being correlated, the calculation procedures can be simplified. Both are restricted in their maximum value by different splits in the variables being correlated. Because both are special cases of the Pearson product-moment correlation, they are generated by the ordinary correlation formula generally used in factor analysis programs. All of the factor-analytic derivations apply to both phi and point biserial correlations. Factoring such coefficients is quite legitimate. Both phis and point biserials can be intermixed with product-moment correlations of continuous variables with no major problems.

The maximum phi coefficient obtainable is a function of the splits on the two variables being correlated. It is possible to compute the maximum phi for any particular pair of splits (cf. Table 14.1.1). This has led to the suggestion that the observed phi be corrected by dividing it by the maximum phi possible given those splits, and the results factored. Hofmann (1980) examines this procedure in detail, giving several corrections to the factor analysis so as to make it more appropriate for this type coefficient. The problem with the coefficient is that it is no longer a true correlation coefficient, and so the "correlation matrix" may not have the mathematical properties necessary for most factor-analytic procedures. As Hofmann notes, use of a number of the factor-analytic constructs such as factor scores are questionable in this approach.

Tetrachoric and Biserial Correlation Coefficients.   If it is assumed that the dichotomies are actually representing variables that are basically continuous, then tetrachoric and biserial correlations can be calculated as estimates of the Pearson product-moment coefficient that would have occurred if the constructs had been measured with continuous variables. The former is for the case of two dichotomous variables and the latter refers to the case of one dichotomous and a continuous variable. Both assume that the variables are normally distributed in their underlying form. Because these coefficients are estimates of Pearson product-moment coefficients, they can be factored to give an estimated factor matrix.

In practice, problems often arise when tetrachoric and biserial correlation coefficients are factored. Because the assumption that the underlying variables are normally distributed is often inappropriate, the observed coefficients are often exceptionally large, for example, 1.32. In addition, the coefficients need not be consistent and non-Gramian matrices may result (Horn, 1973). Both situations are problematic when analyzing data.

The phi and point biserial correlation coefficients are better choices for factor-analytic purposes because they are always within normal ranges and give Gramian matrices. The product-moment coefficients also represent the relationships in the actual data rather than attempting to generalize to a theoretical variable that has not been observed. Difficulty factors can be avoided by using either higher-order factors or miniscales.

Correcting Coefficients.   Several iterative procedures are being explored to provide appropriate estimates of the correlations, assuming that the variables are distortions of underlying normal distributions (Christoffersson, 1975; Olsson, 1979; Young, Takane, & de Leeuw, 1978). They use iterative maximum likelihood and weighted least squares estimation. The programs are complex. Further testing may provide an appropriate corrective for skewed data, but the procedures are still insufficiently tested for general recommendation at this time.

14.2   EFFECTS OF TRANSFORMATIONS

The data as initially collected are often not in the most meaningful form. To increase the interpretability of the results, certain variables may be transformed. The simpler types of transformations are linear and are discussed in Sections 14.2.1, Transformations in Origin and Scale, 14.2.2, Normative, Ipsative, and Performative Linear Transformations, and 14.2.3, Transformations Producing Linear or Experimentally Dependent Variables. Such transformations occasionally cause spurious factors to appear or suppress other factors. Sections *14.2.4, Transformations of Shape, and *14.2.5, New Variables From Nonlinear Transformations, are discussions of transformations that alter the shape of the distributions as well as other characteristics. In the last section, 14.2.6, Transformations to Estimate Missing Data, the effects of missing data and how the missing elements may be transformed to be appropriate for factor analysis are considered.

14.2.1 Transformations in Origin and Scale

Both the mean and variance of a variable can be altered. The only transformation in origin widely used for factor-analytic purposes is where each variable's mean is set equal to a constant, usually zero. The result is referred to as a **column-centered** matrix because the point of origin, or zero, is placed at the central point of the scores given in a column of the data matrix. A matrix can also be **row centered** and would then have the mean of each row set to zero. Row centering occasionally has advantages for certain types of analyses and is discussed later. A matrix can be column centered and then row centered as well. When the rows or columns are centered, then the mean differences across rows or columns are removed. As Gollob notes (Gollob, 1968a, 1968b, 1968c; Tucker, 1968), such centering removes the main effect due to the variation in rows or columns just as main effects are removed in analyses of variance.

If the means of both rows and columns are all set equal to a constant, then the matrix is said to be **double centered.** Double centering a matrix is more difficult than it sounds. If the matrix is first column centered and then row centered, the column means will be disturbed by the centering of rows. Recentering of the columns would then disturb the centering of the rows. Whether or not columns are centered first or second can produce somewhat different results.

Variables are often rescaled so that the variances are brought to the same value. A data matrix is usually rescaled by columns but can also be rescaled by rows. If both rows and columns are rescaled, the order of rescaling will affect the results. Changing the point of origin and the variance interacts if one is on the rows and the other is on the columns.

The effect of rescaling the variances will vary depending upon how they are rescaled. As long as the rescaling process is in terms of columns, the correlations among those columns will not be affected. In this sense, the correlation matrix is scale free. The covariance matrix and its resulting factors will be altered depending upon how the matrix is rescaled. Variables with larger variances influence covariance analysis more than those with smaller variances. This permits the giving of differential weights to different variables if there is some theoretical basis for doing so.

It has been noted that a scale-free factor-analytic procedure is often desirable. Such a procedure would give the same factor scores regardless of whether or not the correlation matrix, a covariance matrix, or covariances from a rescaled data matrix were factored. A scale-free factor analysis would avoid some of the sample specificity introduced into the correlation matrix when the variables are standardized. Such standardization must, of necessity, proceed only on the basis of one sample and is therefore open to sampling error that the scale-free analysis would tend to avoid.

In some senses the factoring of the correlation matrix produces a scale-free solution. It is scale free in the sense that the impact of any arbitrary standard deviation is eliminated because standard deviations are all brought to the same value. It is also scale free in the sense that the factor matrices derived from the correlation matrix can also be used to reproduce the covariance matrix, providing the variances of the variables are known.

Nonscale-free techniques allow one to use factor analysis differentially. If the effects of both means and standard deviations are to be minimized, then the correlations can be factored. If, however, differences in variances are considered important pieces of information, then the covariance matrix can be factored and the results will be appropriately different (cf. Section 14.3). Intuitively, it seems that they should be different because the results are based upon more information in the covariance analysis than in the correlation analysis.

14.2.2 Normative, Ipsative, and Performative Linear Transformations

Several linear transformations of a single variable are widely used. Unless otherwise specified, the transformations are used independently. The common transformations are as follows:

Normative.   A normative transformation consists of bringing the means and standard deviations of all variables to the same values. Means of zero and standard deviations of 1 are the most common normative transformations. Nonnormalized T scores and stanines are other common examples of normative transformations. The purpose of the normative transformation is to bring each variable to some comparable unit. Note that in a normative transformation, the scores are not *normalized* because the distribution of scores remains unaltered.

The calculation of correlation coefficients implicitly normalizes the data matrix because the resulting index is that for standardized variables. Shifts in the normative scaling of variables will not affect the factor analysis if correlations are computed. Normative transformations would not generally be used with cross-product and covariance analysis because those analyses are used because the means of variances are meaningful.

Ipsative.   An ipsative transformation brings each *row* of the data matrix to the same mean (semiipsatization) or to the same mean and standard deviation (full ipsatization). Naturally, it must proceed from scores that can be meaningfully compared. If the statement that a particular individual is higher on one variable than on another is not meaningful, then ipsatization of the raw data is not appropriate. Scores are often normalized before ipsatization so that more meaningful comparisons can be made.

As in the case of normative scores, the actual means and standard deviations that result are less important than the fact that they are all brought to the same mean and standard deviation. The intent of ipsatization is to eliminate irrelevant differences among the individuals in the analysis. If the differences in mean level among individuals is a source of variation that confounds the analysis, then ipsatization is required. For example, in a decision theory approach to behavior, it is only necessary to know which of the possible choices is more valued. The absolute level is unimportant in a limited choice situation because the better choice—not the one above a specified level—is chosen. Ipsatized scores are needed to predict the behavior in a limited choice situation.

Some data collection procedures are self-ipsatizing. If a forced-choice format is used, then scores from the various elements of the forced choices will, of necessity, have the same mean and standard deviation for each variable. Such procedures are particularly valuable if, for example, one is more interested in the differences in the values that are held by individuals than in whether or not they hold to the general thrust of a culture's values.

Any ipsatization procedure does, however, influence the covariances and correlations among the variables. If an individual receives a high score on one of two variables being ipsatized, then he must receive a low score on the other variable. In the case of only two variables, ipsatization creates a perfect negative correlation, regardless of the original correlation between the unipsatized scores. With more variables, the average correlation among the variables will move closer to zero but still be negative. Any one ipsatized variable is perfectly predicted from the set of other ipsatized variables and thus is linearly dependent upon them. Because the correlations are an artifact of the ipsatization, variables ipsatized by either the test format or by later calculation should only be factored if the impact from ipsatizing is seen as desirable.

Performative. A performative transformation involves altering the origin and scale of first the columns and then the rows. It is not identical to the double-centered matrix where the means of rows and columns are all actually the same because only the rows have the same mean and standard deviation when the transformation is completed. The columns have approximately the same means and standard deviations.

The procedure arose because ipsatization can seldom be directly applied to the variables. When the means and standard deviations are arbitrary, ipsatizing gives a meaningless result. Transforming the variables makes the means and variances comparable. After the transformations of columns is completed, then ipsatization proceeds so that the rows are brought to the same mean and standard deviation. Appropriate analyses can then proceed, but the problems are the same as those of any other ipsatized scores.

14.2.3 Transformations Producing Linearly or Experimentally Dependent Variables

Several variables may be weighted and summed to create a new variable. The new variable is then **linearly dependent** on the old variables. Such derived variables can be legitimately included in the factor analysis provided that the variables from which they are derived are not included.

Inclusion of a derived variable with all the components on which it is based would have two undesirable effects in the analysis. First, the correlation matrix would have a rank less than its order because one of the variables could be predicted from the others. The derived variable would have a multiple correlation of 1.0 with the other variables. Most factor-analytic procedures are based on the assumption that the empirical rank of the correlation matrix is the same as its order.

Second, inclusion of a derived variable and some or all of its components can lead to spurious factors. The derived variable can form a doublet factor with each of the variables that form its components. Such doublets would provide no new information and therefore would be of little interest. Usually, the doublets do not appear clearly but the overlapping variance is partially scattered throughout the factor matrix. The effects can be complex and difficult to untangle. If it is desired to include the derived variable in the analysis, then the components can be excluded. If the components are of great interest and the derived variable is of less interest, the components can be included and the derived variable excluded. In either of these cases, the excluded variables can be related to the factors resulting from the factor analysis by extension procedures (cf. Section *10.5).

Experimentally dependent variables are those that are not based upon independent observations. For example, if the open-ended responses to a question are scored for two separate variables, then the given variables will be experimentally dependent because they are based upon the same material. Or, if the same closed-end questions are used in two or more scales—as happens in tests such as the MMPI and the Tennessee Self-Concept Scale—experimental dependence results.

The problem with experimental dependency is that the two variables then partake of the same error component. For example, if a person misunderstood one question and gave his response based upon that misunderstanding, that error would influence his score on two variables. Common error leads the two variables to spuriously correlate with each other and produces spurious factors. In statistical models error is assumed to be uncorrelated. (Linearly dependent variables are also experimentally dependent.)

A common violation of the need for linear and experimental independence is to include a total score along with the items in a factor analysis. The total score across a set of items is both linearly and experimentally dependent upon those items from which it is computed. Including the items and the score will generally alter the factorial solution, although the extent to which it affects the solution does vary from situation to situation.

*14.2.4 Transformations of Shape

In significance tests of correlations the variables are assumed to be normally distributed. Multivariate statistics generally are assumed to have multivariate normality, which is usually impossible to check. As a safeguard, it is often suggested that all data be normalized before factoring. Although normalizing variables will not guarantee multivariate normality, it will increase the possibility of such normality occurring.

Theoretically, normalizing the data would generally increase the correlations because the distributions would then be the same. Although the procedure will occasionally eliminate minor curvilinear relationships arising from differential skews, it appears that, in actuality, normalizing the data does not greatly increase many correlation coefficients. The lack of effect is probably because those points in the distribution of the data that are most widely separated are generally those most accurately measured, and yet they are the same ones that are often collapsed together in normalizing. On the other hand, where scores bunch together in the distribution, it can generally be assumed that the individuals are not noticeably different. Yet the "bunched" scores may be spread out under the assumption that they are actually different. Another reason correlations are not greatly affected by normalizing is that the correlation coefficient seems most sensitive to rank order, and yet rank order remains unaffected by normalizing.

Fuller and Hemmerle (1966) used a Monte Carlo approach with five variables and 200 individuals. They found uniform, normal, truncated normal, Student's t, triangular, and bi-model distributions to give essentially the same maximum likelihood factors. Brewer and Hills (1969) found the effects of even serious skewness to reduce the correlation only from, for example, .65 to .60. It appears that normalizing is not needed as a standard procedure for estimates of factor loadings.

Other transformations may also be of value in special cases. For example, if the individual is asked to report his income, a nonlinear transformation of that variable may eliminate the skew normally found with it. A log transformation is often used in such circumstances. Any transformation that increases the likelihood of finding a linear relationship with other variables is desirable.

*14.2.5 New Variables from Nonlinear Transformations

Some derived variables may be formed from the original variables by transformations that are not strictly linear in nature. Ratios are one such case. An analysis may include a series of percentages that are based on the same denominator and include the denominator as well. Because the ratios are not linear transformations of the denominator and the numerators, they may provide unique data and might not produce a specific factor.

Ratios, however, may also lead to a spurious factor. When a denominator or numerator is the same for all individuals, then the resulting derived variable correlates perfectly with the other component. A denominator with little variation compared to that of the numerator, or vice versa, will produce a high correlation between the ratio and the component that does change. Such correlations could lead to the appearance of a spurious factor.

In addition to ratios, nonlinear derived variables are commonly formed to investigate curvilinear relationships and interactions. The transformations involve multiplying two variables together or raising a variable to a power. Because the functions are multiplicative rather than additive, the problem is not as great as with linearly transformed variables. Even so, it may be fruitful to hold out ratios and other derived variables, or the components used to calculate them, for an extension analysis rather than allowing them to help define factors. The derived variables often correlate quite high (for example, .95) with the original variables and lead to specifics occurring as common factors. They are also experimentally dependent.

14.2.6 Transformations to Estimate Missing Data

In deriving the formulas for factor analysis, it was assumed that the observed data matrix is completely filled with meaningful data. In practice, however, some individuals may have scores on all variables except one or two. Several procedures for estimating the missing elements have been suggested.

First, the missing element can be replaced by calculating the mean for the variable from the individuals who do have scores on it. The mean is then used as the best estimate of the missing element. Or another individual can be selected at random and his score on the variables used to replace the missing element. The latter procedure will, on the average, leave both the mean and variance unaffected. The former procedure leaves only the mean unaffected. Both procedures reduce correlations with other variables.

To maintain the variable's correlations with other variables, a multiple regression analysis is used. The other variables are used to predict the variable with a missing element. The regression analysis is computed only with those individuals who have scores on all the variables to be used in the analysis. The regression weights are then applied to the known scores to estimate the missing score. A regression analysis is computed for every variable that has one or more missing scores.

The regression procedure has been found more effective for estimating what the correlation matrix would have been if all scores had been available (Timm, 1970). The other procedures against which it was compared included dropping the individuals who had a missing score, replacing the missing score with the mean, and a procedure based on principal components. The regression procedure was best whether 1% or 20% of the data were missing.

Computer programs are available that calculate each correlation coefficient from only the individuals who have the necessary scores. The resulting correlation matrices should be factored only if the number of individuals is quite similar for all elements. If the number of individuals varies widely from element to element, the coefficients may be sufficiently incompatible to prevent a factor analysis or distort the results.

14.3 INDICES OF ASSOCIATION

The prime differences between the indices of association that might be used for factor-analytic purposes are twofold. On the one hand, they vary in the extent to which the standard procedures for factor analysis discussed so far apply to them. The basic procedures were usually developed for correlation matrices, but generalization to other indices is often possible. On the other hand, the indices vary in the extent to which they are influenced by different aspects of the data. Some utilize more of the information, whereas others ignore certain aspects of the information available in the raw data.

Correlation analysis (Section 14.3.1) utilizes the information found regarding how the variables rank order the individuals and, to a lesser degree, also reflect the similarities of the distributions. Covariance analysis (Section 14.3.2) adds information on the variances of the variables. Cross-product and d^2 analyses (Section *14.3.3) are alike in that they are influenced by more of the information in the raw data matrix than the other procedures. The information utilized includes means, variances, and patterns of relationships. Other indices could also be used (Section *14.3.4).

Cattell (1972) has been expanding the traditional factor-analytic model to remove the assumptions of standardized variables and factors while maintaining meaningful analyses. However, the results are still tentative.

14.3.1 Correlations

In many cases where factor-analytic techniques have been used, both the mean and standard deviation of the variables are arbitrary. They are arbitrary because the nature of the area does not allow for ratio scales or because the variables cannot be measured in the same metric due to their widely differing characteristics. It would be difficult to conceptualize a metric that would be equally meaningful for measuring height and weight, but both variables may be included in the same analysis. Correlations resolve the problem by eliminating the influence of both means and variances. The resulting coefficient is therefore influenced only by the rank orders and shapes of the distributions. In this sense, the correlation coefficients are scale free.

Correlation coefficients are simply a measure of the linear relationships and will indicate whatever linear relationships are present. However, their interpretation is often facilitated by additional assumptions or knowledge. For example, normality of distributions are generally assumed when significance tests for individual correlation coefficients are derived. Interpreting the importance of a particular correlation coefficient can be aided by examining the extent to which variables have characteristics that prevent the correlation from being very large.

One characteristic of the data that will reduce a correlation coefficient is including variables with different distributions. For example, two perfectly correlated constructs may be operationalized by variables that differ in skewness, as noted in Section 14.1. Skewness will lower high correlations but leaves low correlations unaffected. Another factor that will attenuate the correlation coefficient is curvilinear relationships. These are not summarized by correlation coefficients except as linear approximations. Curvilinear relationships can often be found by examining a scatter plot between variables. Fortunately, both skewness and curvilinearity are not often so severe that the correlations are seriously distorted. An additional attenuating influence is restriction of range, which is discussed in Chapter 16.

The Pearson product-moment correlation coefficient is always assumed to be used unless stated otherwise. All the derivations given in previous chapters were in terms of it. Because rank correlation, phi, and point biserial coefficients are only special cases of the product-moment coefficient, they can also be used in factoring, provided the considerations in Section 14.1 are taken into account.

Correlation analysis need not proceed through the use of correlation coefficients. It can proceed directly from the data matrix and will produce the same results, provided that the "raw data" are actually standardized scores. Horst (1965, Chapter 12) presents procedures for factoring the data directly.

14.3.2 Covariances

In occasional situations, variables that have similar variances are more alike than those that do not. The deviation scores representing a person's height, circumference, etc., have the same metric, and comparisons of variances may be directly meaningful. Covariance analysis analyzes variables where the data matrix contains deviations from the mean. The measure of similarity is high when the variances are large and the rank order and shapes of the distributions are the same; it is small if the variances are small or the rank orders are dissimilar.

The covariance is defined as follows:

$$C_{vv} = X'_{vn}X_{nv}n^{-1} \tag{14.3.1}$$

where X_{nv} is a matrix of deviation scores where each score has been subtracted from its mean. Substituting from the basic equation of factor analysis gives:

$$C_{vv} = B_{vf}F'_{fn}F_{nf}n^{-1}B'_{fv} \tag{14.3.2}$$

where B gives the non-standardized weights. Then:

$$C_{vv} = B_{vf}C_{ff}B'_{fv} \tag{14.3.3}$$

However, it is not necessary to reproduce variable means and so the factors can be assumed to be in standard form. C_{ff} then becomes R_{ff}. B contains weights that adjust the factor scores to the appropriate variances as they reproduce the variables. With the exception of weights equal to zero, the weights will vary as a function both of the variable's variance and of its relationship to the factors. The largest weights will be those for variables with high variances and which are strongly related to a particular factor. The rows of B will have sums of squares that vary in keeping with the variable's variance and the extent to which the variance can be accounted for by the factors. For this reason, row-normalized rotation (cf. Section 9.2.2), which destroys the differences between rows of B, will give a distinctively different result from non row-normalized rotation. Weights can be compared within one variable, but the varying standard deviations need to be considered when comparing weights across variables.

The usual formula for computing the correlations between the variables and the factors is $S = PR$, but this formula is accurate only when P is for the standard scores, not the deviation scores. Each element of B needs to be divided by the variable's standard deviation to obtain the P used in computing the factor structure.

A principal factor extraction procedure will place the first factor as a function both of the variances of the variables and of the degree to which they overlap. It will seek to reduce the elements of C_{vv} and this can be best done by placing the factor closer to the variables with high variances than to those with low variances. In other words, if two variable clusters are of equal size in the matrix but one is based upon variables with slightly larger variances than the other, the principal factor will be placed closer to that cluster with the larger variances than to the other.

Covariance analysis can be performed by most computer programs oriented toward correlation matrices. However, the output format should be checked to be sure that there is sufficient room to print numbers in front of the decimal place. The results from the rotation programs will need to be interpreted with care because the labels for the matrices will no longer be appropriate. For example, the factor structure matrix normally printed contains correlations only if correlations are being factored. Covariance analysis is often used as the basic model from which factor analysis is developed (Bentler, 1976).

Example

The physique data can be analyzed by using covariances instead of correlations. The covariance matrix was constructed by using the correlations from Table 5.1.1 and the standard deviations from Appendix A. Weight was dropped because its scores were not directly comparable with the other variables. The covariance matrix was factored by the principal axis method and was iterated twice for communalities. The initial communality estimates were calculated by a procedure analogous to squared multiple correlations.

TABLE 14.3.1
Principal Axis Factors of Physique Covariances

Variables	A	B	C
1. Stature	3.83	3.00	−.00
2. Symphysis height	2.73	4.12	−.50
3. Breadth of skull	.16	−.00	.12
4. Length of skull	.23	.23	.11
5. Biacromial diameter	.81	.66	1.93
6. Transverse chest diameter	.89	−.27	.50
7. Sagittal chest diameter	.87	−.18	.27
8. Bicristal diameter	1.01	−.27	.19
9. Length of sternum	.59	.25	−.04
10. Chest circumference (at expiration)	5.79	−3.10	−.47
11. Hip circumference	4.18	−1.16	.40

Note: The twelfth variable, weight, was dropped because its scores were in a different unit.

The first three principal factors are given in Table 14.3.1. The first factor is again our friend of general size whereas the second one pits length against circumference. Factor 3 is a specific. The variables with low variances, 3 and 4, play a negligible part in the solution. In analyses of the correlation matrix, variable 4 definitely played a larger part in determining the first three factors.

The similarity of this solution to that from analyzing the correlations could be misleading. The results are often not much alike. If variables 3 and 4 had had the largest standard deviations and variables 1, 2, 10, and 11 the smallest, for example, the results would have shifted drastically.

*14.3.3 Cross Products and d^2

When two variables are compared, there are three ways in which they may be similar or dissimilar. First, the two variables may or may not have the same means. Second, the variables may or may not have the same variances. And third, the variables may or may not have the same high scores and low scores for the same individuals, that is, the same rank order, shape, or pattern. Both cross products and distance measures such as d^2 are influenced by all three of these sources of similarity.

d^2 is an index of the distance between any two variables when these variables are plotted in a space of individuals. Each individual represents an orthogonal axis in that space and the points are plotted as vectors therein. The coordinates of the vectors are given by the individual scores.

Figure 14.1 plots three variables in a space defined by two individuals. Both individuals have a high score on variable 1 and a moderate score on variable 2. The scores vary on variable 3. An examination of the figure shows that variables 1 and 2 are physically closer than either variables 1 and 3 or variables 2 and 3. Therefore, the first two would load the same factor in a d^2 analysis.

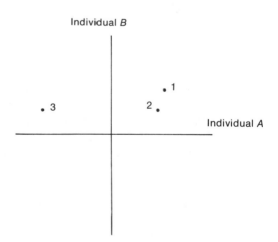

FIG. 14.1. Three variables in a space defined by two individuals.

The distance between the end points of any two vectors is given by the use of the generalized Pythagorean rule. The formula for an individual d^2 is:

$$d_{12}^2 = (y_{n1} - y_{n2})^2 \tag{14.3.4}$$

where d^2 is the square of the distance between variables 1 and 2, y_{n1} are the individuals' scores on variable 1, and y_{n2} are the individuals' scores on variable 2. Distances can be factored (Osgood, Suci & Tannenbaum, 1957, pp. 332–335).

Another matrix that is based on the same information as d^2 is the cross-product matrix. The cross-product matrix is defined as follows:

$$A_{vv} = Y_{vn}' Y_{nv} \tag{14.3.5}$$

where A_{vv} is the cross-product matrix from the raw data matrix, Y_{nv}. Nunnally (1962) has pointed out that d^2 and A_{vv} analyses generally lead to the same interpretations, although the analytic procedures differ.

In actual practice, it is convenient to rescale the data matrix by dividing each element in it by n:

$$A_{vv} = Y_{vn}' Y_{nv} n^{-1} \tag{14.3.6}$$

A_{vv} is then the average cross-product matrix. The average cross-product matrix has two advantages over the plain cross-product matrix: it has smaller numbers and is independent of the number of individuals. Because the number of subjects is common to all variables and cannot differentially influence their interrelationships, it is irrelevant. The same factors will result from the raw cross-product matrix and from the average cross-product matrix. Only the average cross-product matrix will be discussed here.

A common approach to factoring the average cross-product matrix is to treat it as one would a correlation matrix. The initial factors are extracted so that the following holds true:

$$A_{vv} = B_{vf} B_{fv}' \tag{14.3.7}$$

where B is considered to be the factor matrix. (In most notations, B is represented by F, but this notation has been avoided because confusion with factor scores could result in the present context.) **B is a factor pattern matrix within the multivariate linear model only if the factors are assumed to have average cross products of 1.0 with themselves and zero cross products with all other factors.** This can be seen by the following derivations.

Substituting in the factorial definition of Y into Eq. (14.3.6) gives:

$$A_{vv} = B_{vf} F_{fn}' F_{fn} n^{-1} B_{fv}' \tag{14.3.8}$$

When A_{ff} is the average cross product between the factor scores:

$$A_{vv} = B_{vf} A_{ff} B_{fv}' \tag{14.3.9}$$

In the $A = BB'$ type of equation it is assumed that A_{ff} is an identity matrix. The calculation of other matrices, such as the correlations of the factors with the variables, can also be derived.

When analyzing cross products, most of the standard factor-analytic programs and procedures can be used. However, any computer program would need to be checked to assure that it could print appropriate results and that it did not assume the diagonal elements of the matrix being factored were 1 or were to be set equal to 1. The loadings in cross-products analysis will usually be greater than 1. In addition, the usual calculation of R_{ff} and S will make inappropriate assumptions when applied to A. Ross (1963) gives the formulas for calculating both the factor pattern and factor scores. Horn (1969a) discusses the method from a more general perspective. Nunnally (1978) presents an example of a cross-products analysis.

*14.3.4 Other Indices of Association

Numerous other indices of association could be utilized in a factor analysis. In most cases, a matrix of such indices could be factored by the $A = BB'$ approach. However, the relationships of such B's to factor patterns and factor structures would need to be theoretically examined to determine the exact impact of such procedures. The difficulties in relating the results to the multivariate linear model generally make them less preferable than the standard correlation coefficient.

One possible index that may occasionally be useful is a rank-order correlation coefficient. Whereas the correlation coefficient itself eliminates the impact of means and variances on the index of association, the rank correlation goes further by reducing the impact of skewness and kurtosis. The rank coefficient is calculated by first transforming all of the raw data to rank orders and then correlating these rank orders by the product-moment formula. The reproduced data matrix contains, of course, the rank orders and not the original raw data. The impact of skewness and kurtosis can also be reduced by normalizing the variables. The choice between normalizing and rank ordering lies in whether or not there are meaningful differences between scores in the middle of the range as compared to the extremes of the range. In rank-order correlations, it is assumed that the differences in the middle are as important as those in the tails of the original distribution. However, when rank orders or normalizing are needed the most, they are often not applicable. For example, when a large number of individuals receive the same score, neither rank ordering nor normalizing will spread them out.

*15 Two- and Three-Mode Factor Analysis

Factor analysis has been presented as a procedure for analyzing a two-dimensional data matrix. The first dimension has been the individuals who formed the rows of the data matrix. The second dimension is associated with the columns of the data matrix and has consisted of the variables. The term **dimension** is, however, a poor term because it is often a synonym for the term **factor.** In its place, the term **mode** is commonly used.

Traditional factor analysis has a two-mode data matrix with the first mode being individuals and the second mode being variables. However, other modes could be considered as a replacement for either the individuals or the variables. In Section 15.1, Two-Mode Factor Analysis, variations on traditional factor analysis that occur when another mode replaces one of the regular modes are considered.

In some situations, the investigator is explicitly concerned with more than two modes. Three modes are often of concern in psychological research that includes variations not only in variables and individuals but that also in the conditions under which the observations are made. For example, the same data may be collected from the same individuals on different days or by different measuring devices, or the investigator may feel that the responses change when the individuals perceive themselves as being in different situations. When scores for the same variables are collected under several sets of circumstances, a three-mode factor analysis may be appropriate. Three-mode factor-analytic procedures are discussed in Section *15.2.

Two- and three-mode factor analyses are special cases of multimode factor analysis that may have four, five, or more modes. However, the procedures for multimode factor analysis are insufficiently developed for consideration here.

---

*Optional.

15.1 TWO-MODE FACTOR ANALYSIS

A factor analysis is based on the model $Z = FP'$. There is nothing in the model that limits what can be considered as the rows and columns of Z. The rows could be individuals, variables, occasions, methods of measurement, or any other mode that made sense for the problem at hand. In the same manner, the columns could be variables, individuals, or any other mode that it seemed advisable to factor. The restrictions on Z are that the same mode cannot occur as both rows and columns and that the mode that is to be factored forms the columns of Z. The mode that forms the basis for computing the index of association forms the rows of Z. In Section 15.1.1 factor analyses of some of the more popular modes are discussed.

Although the data matrix is usually evaluated for the factors that underlie the relationships among the columns, it can be transposed so that columns become rows (and vice versa) and then refactored. If the first analysis identified factors of the variables, the second analysis would identify factors of the individuals. The factor analysis of a transposed data matrix is discussed in Section 15.1.2.

15.1.1 Alternatives for Two-Mode Analysis

A factor analysis can be of individuals, variables or conditions (where conditions would be further specified as, for example, occasions across time or methods of measurement). The simplest situation is where most modes not being factored are held constant. The usual factor analysis is of this type. The variables are factored over individuals with the variables being collected under only one of the possible conditions. Thus, modes of little interest are held constant, either implicitly or explicitly. The assumption made is that any generalization from the factor analysis will be only to the conditions under which the variables were collected for the initial factor analysis or to a condition sufficiently similar so that little loss of accuracy would occur.

Because any mode may be factored, a number of factor-analytic techniques exists. For example, taking all possible permutations of individuals, variables, and occasions when the data were collected gives a set of research designs. Cattell (1966b) has summarized the set for the standard data matrix, Z_{nv}, as a series of "techniques." These are given in Table 15.1.1. From the table, it can be seen that factoring a set of variables collected at the same time from a number of individuals is referred to as R technique. As Cattell points out, Table 15.1.1 only contains samples of the various possible modes for a two-mode factor analysis. Cattell (1966b, Chapter 3) and Sells (1963) present lists of variables and conditions that could form modes for a social scientist. Because a mode such as measurement technique may be substituted for some other mode, such as occasions or variables, the possibilities are infinite.

In psychology, the typical focus of a factor analysis varies and so does the appropriate technique. A factor analysis of variables is concerned with states or

TABLE 15.1.1
Techniques for Two-Mode Factor Analysis

Technique	Mode Being Factored (v)	Mode Across Which Indices of Association are Computed (n)	Mode Held Constant
O	occasions	variables	All data are from one individual.
P	variables	occasions	All data are from one individual.
Q	individuals	variables	All data are from one occasion.
R	variables	individuals	All data are from one occasion.
S	individuals	occasions	All data are from one variable.
T	occasions	individuals	All data are from one variable.

traits. The focus is on states if the analysis is across time, as in *P* technique, and on traits if the factors are assumed to generalize across time. If individuals are being factored, then the focus is a typological one. When the factors are of situations or conditions, the focus is ecological. Thus techniques *P* and *R* seek the identification of states and traits, *Q* and *S* seek to identify types of individuals, and *O* and *T* look for similar situations or environments. Each of these pairs is a transposed factor analysis of the other, and the conclusions regarding comparisons of *R*- and *Q*-technique analyses in Section 15.1.2 also hold for comparisons between *O* and *P* techniques or between *S* and *T* techniques.

P technique is the forerunner of and multivariate approach to what is currently called *single subject design* or *N of 1 analysis*. *P* technique differs in that it is multivariate. This means that the behaviors or other variables of interest are defined by using several measurement operations instead of one, and the factor analysis integrates these several multiple measures as is appropriate. Because there are no significance tests in exploratory factor analysis, the fact that correlated error may exist across time is irrelevant because such correlated errors only affect the significance test and not the estimates of parameters such as *P* and *S*. Confirmatory factor analysis allows correlated error of certain types to be included in models. Mintz and Luborsky (1970) show how exploratory *P* technique can be used to analyze patient–therapist interaction. An overview of exploratory *P* technique is given in Luborsky and Mintz (1972) and in Cattell (1978), with practical suggestions by Cattell and Birkett (1980).

The limit to generalizability is determined by the mode held constant. For example, *P*-technique analysis is adequate as long as the only interest is in generalizing to the population of conditions for this one individual or in species characteristics that can be assumed to exist in identical form for all individuals. *O* looks promising for analysis of situational data like that summarized by Sells (1963). *S* and *T* techniques are virtually never used because the generalization would be limited to one variable. One suspects that the lack of *S* and *T* applications is a function of the fact that factor analysis comes, historically, from the individual difference approach to psychology and therefore experimentalists interested in only one characteristic have not been aware of its possibilities.

R and *Q* techniques are more often used than the others. The mode that is not varied is that of conditions, and the assumption of most of these analyses is that the conditions are much the same for all individuals or are implicitly sampled by the sampling of individuals. When psychologists factor ability data collected from a set of school children, it can generally be assumed that the children themselves are under a variety of conditions regarding fatigue, motivation, and other relevant variables. In such a study, conditions are sampled with subjects and the results can be generally applied to other samples of children in the same type of school system on other days. Similar assumptions can often be made for the other techniques previously listed.

Example

P technique has been used to analyze changes in a given nation over time. A study by Cattell and Adelson (1951) examined the century of 1845–1945 for the United States. They collected the available data for variables such as cancer death rate, density of population, and number of immigrants for each year of the century. The data matrix consisted of 100 individual years as rows and 44 variables as columns. The analysis was by an exploratory multiple-group factor analysis (common factor procedures were not readily available at that time). The correlations were examined for clusters and factors extracted for what seemed to be major clusters; six factors were extracted. The factors were rotated visually to simple structure.

A similar analysis of data from Great Britain, 1837 to 1937, was also carried out (Cattell, 1953). It had 44 variables and 100 individual years, and nine multiple-group factors resulted.

Each of these analyses is important in its own right. One would not expect the same factors to necessarily appear because each country followed a unique course across the century. Nevertheless, several factors did appear in both *P*-technique studies. One such factor was "Cultural Pressure" and was loaded by variables such as high cancer and suicide death rates, along with a large population. Another factor in each analysis was marked by the number of men in the armed forces and expenditures for their support; it was particularly clear in the British data. The factors are plotted in Fig. 15.1 and show the expected trends but, of course, identify them more exactly than the usual historical approach.

15.1.2 *Q* Technique as a Transposed Factor Analysis

Q technique arose from problems where the central issue was the grouping of individuals. The individuals to be grouped could be clinical cases, organizations, people in general, or any other individual unit that would usually define the rows of the data matrix. The intent is to identify classes of individuals. Any new individual can then be placed in that group which she or he most resembles as defined by the factor-analytic research.

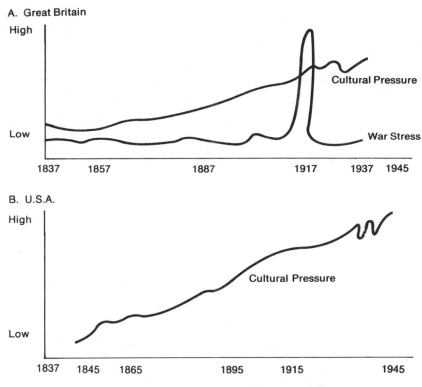

FIG. 15.1.   Fluctuations of P-technique factors for two countries.

In Q technique, individuals are factored to determine how they should be grouped. The definition equation is:

$$Z'_{vn} = F_{vf}P'_{fn} \qquad (15.1.1)$$

Where Z is a data matrix standardized by rows (n), F the factor scores of the v variables on the f factors, and P contains the weights by which each of the n individuals' variable scores can be reproduced from the factor.[1]

The factor loadings of P indicate to what extent each individual resembles a hypothetical prototype. If the prototype individual actually existed, then he or she would clearly load this and only this factor. The result differs considerably from traditional typology because the factor matrix gives the relationship of each individual to each of the hypothetical types and, unless an exceptionally good simple structure is found, many individuals are related to more than one of the typological factors.

---

[1]For a conceptually simpler approach to classifying individuals, see Section *12.3.

All of the factor-analytic theory developed in earlier chapters can be applied to transposed factor analysis. The equivalency follows from the fact that the matrix being factored is simply the transpose of the data matrix factored in the usual analysis. Because factor-analytic theory is not concerned with how the rows and columns are defined, all factor theory applies to it and all the procedures apply to it. The analysis can use averaged cross products, covariances or correlations. **However, to gain stable measures of relationship, the data matrix should have a large number of columns (v) relative to the number of rows (n) before it is transposed.**

Some of the interpretations do shift when Q technique is used rather than R technique. For example, significance testing would assume a random sampling of variables from a population of variables, an assumption that would be difficult to defend. Significance tests do not, therefore, generally apply to transposed factor analysis.

Example

Cattell and Coulter (1966) were interested in exploring Q technique for taxonomic purposes. The plasmode they chose consisted of British naval vessels. *Jane's Fighting Ships* was the source of the data for their analyses.

Each ship was correlated with every other ship across normative variables. The variables included such characteristics as the number of light guns, submersibility, and the number of personnel. Their analyses and some reanalyses by Guertin (1971) resulted in one factor for aircraft carriers and another for destroyers. Frigates were a class unto themselves. Depending on the type of analysis, the submarines form their own factor or load negatively on the destroyer factor. Somehow, submarines and destroyers being at the opposite ends of the same dimension has intuitive appeal. They form a type of ecological balance, just as cats and mice, men and women, and top and bottom also "balance" each other.

Effects of Transformations. To compare individuals on a set of variables by a single index, such as the correlation coefficient, it is necessary that the variables have comparable score units. In some cases, the score units are not directly comparable because one variable is measured in meters, another in liters, and so forth. The same numerical value may have a different meaning for different variables. These cases can be resolved by normalizing the variables of the matrix so that their means and standard deviations are the same.

If the mean differences were not eliminated and correlations between individuals were used for the analysis, the differences in means from the several variables would lead to high correlations between all individuals and one general factor representing the high average correlation. Cattell has referred to the general factor that results from differences in the means of the variables as a species factor (Cattell, 1952, p. 99). The loadings on it will indicate which individuals are most like, and which individuals are most discrepant from, the average or typical individual in that sample. Gollob (1968a, 1968b, 1968c) suggests that removal of the species factor by equating all means may produce a clearer analysis. Normalizing has the advantage of reducing the species factor sufficiently so that individual difference factors may appear.

In most transposed factor analyses, the data are ipsatized after they are normalized. Usually, the ipsatization is implicit because correlations are computed across a data matrix that has been normalized. The effect of the ipsatization is to remove any mean differences among the individuals from the analyses. Because a general factor is a function of the same differences occurring across all variables, a general factor is associated with a difference in the individuals' mean scores on the variables. By ipsatizing, the general factor is minimized because the mean differences are eliminated. A normalized-ipsatized data matrix has almost all of any general factor eliminated from it.

A problem unique to transposed factor analysis is that arising from the possible reversal of variables. When the definition of variables is arbitrary in terms of the direction of scoring, the direction selected can affect the correlation coefficient that results. For example, Cohen (1968a, 1969) gives an example where one of five variables is reversed in scoring and the correlation coefficient between individuals shifts from .67 to $-.37$. The effect is not found in R-technique analysis because individuals cannot be "reversed." To overcome the problem, Cohen suggests a new correlation coefficient, r_c, which is invariant across shifts in the direction of the variables.

The easiest procedure for calculating r_c is to extend the data matrix. For each variable in the original data matrix, Z_{nv}, a new column is added with that variable's scores reflected (Cohen, 1968a, 1969). The correlation coefficients among rows are then calculated across all of these columns, both the original ones and the reflected ones. The r_c is therefore an average across the reflected and unreflected variables.

Although the coefficient r_c would appear to be useful in some special cases, the problem of the arbitrary direction of variables will not arise in all transposed factor analyses. In some cases, the direction is not arbitrary but can be readily defined. In other cases where the direction is not quite so apparent, some definition can be worked out. For example, all variables could be reflected so as to produce the maximum number of positive correlations.

Similarity of Results Between Regular and Transposed Analyses. Burt (1937) was able to show that the factors from an R analysis and from a Q analysis of a double-centered matrix could be directly translated one for the other. Except for a variance adjustment, the factor scores from one analysis were the same as the factor loadings from the other analysis.

Burt's conclusion has been generally upheld and further formulas developed to relate the factors from R and Q techniques (Holley, 1970a, 1970b; Holley & Harris, 1970; Jones, 1967; Ross, 1963; Ryder, 1964; Sandler, 1949) with Gollob's (1968a, 1968b) discussion reconfirming Burt's conclusions from a different perspective. The analyses apply, however, to the unrotated factors. Because the configuration of individuals will usually be different from the configuration of variables, the rotated factors need not be the same. Each will be rotated to its own simple structure and factor scores will no longer equal the factor loadings of the other analysis.

The preceding discussion applied to component analysis of double-centered matrices where all the means and variances of the variables are brought to the same values and all of the means and variances of the individuals are brought to the same values. If the R technique is analyzed in the usual manner (i.e., by correlating columns of the data matrix) and the Q technique is performed in the usual manner (i.e., by correlating rows of a normatized data matrix) then the results will not be the same. **The R-technique analysis will include information on mean differences between individuals that is excluded from the Q-technique analysis.** Therefore, the R technique has the possibility of finding a general factor. The general factor may be large or small depending upon whether or not the mean differences across the individuals are large or small, but there will be differences in the results.

If the data underlying the measures of the relationship include the same information, then the results will be mathematically similar. The usual R-technique correlational analysis has its counterpart in a cross-products Q-technique analysis of a normalized data matrix. As Broverman (1961, 1963), Gollob (1968a, 1968b), and McAndrew and Forgy (1963) have indicated, the major differences resulting from R- and Q-component analyses lie in the way the data matrix has been altered and in the measures of association that have been calculated. However, as Ross (1963) has also pointed out, the differences in rotated matrices may be much greater because of the different configurations formed by individuals and by variables.

Example

The ability data can be factored to illustrate an inverse or Q-technique factor analysis. Because the number of individuals included must be smaller than the number of variables, 16 individuals were selected from the 145 students on whom ability data were available. Correlations among the students across the 26 variables—a dangerously small number of variables on which to base a Q-technique analysis—were factored by the principal axis procedure. Four factors were extracted for comparability with the R-technique analysis of the ability data. Squared multiple correlations were used as initial communality estimates and the solution was iterated twice.

Promax rotations were carried out with $k = 4$ and $k = 2$, but neither increased the hyperplane count of the simple structure more than 1% over varimax. Therefore, the varimax factors were accepted and are presented in Table 15.1.2. No general factor occurred because mean differences among the individuals were excluded. Note that the factors cannot be interpreted without knowing the characteristics of the individuals in-

TABLE 15.1.2
Varimax Factor Pattern for 16 Individuals

| Individuals | Factors | | | |
	A	B	C	D
6	.02	−.06	.74	−.27
35	.63	−.10	−.01	−.13
55	.06	.72	.16	.11
57	−.22	.72	−.05	−.14
69	−.13	.38	−.18	.10
75	−.54	−.64	−.09	.46
76	.18	−.71	.01	.05
79	−.12	−.02	.88	.00
85	−.68	−.12	−.22	−.56
99	−.57	.22	.15	−.01
102	−.05	−.13	−.18	.55
104	.09	−.02	−.29	.26
109	.42	−.23	−.01	−.57
113	.55	−.38	−.33	−.24
114	.42	.38	−.42	−.33
167	−.06	.00	−.09	.71

volved. Generally, most Q solutions are interpreted by the scores the individuals receive on the variables.

Although the preceding analysis used normative scores, a second analysis used the raw scores. Otherwise, it was factored in an identical fashion as the normalized data. The first principal factor was strong; each individual had a loading of at least .95. The major source of correlation was from the differences in the means of the variables, and the first factor was a species factor that reflected the fact that everyone scores higher on some of the tests than on other tests. Mean differences among individuals did not affect the solution because the correlations were not affected by such differences; therefore, a general ability factor did not occur at either the primary or secondary level for either of these analyses.

Whether Q or R technique should be used depends upon where the theoretical interest lies. If the concern is with the similarity of variables, then R technique is appropriate. If the concern is with developing a typology, then Q technique and the procedures of Section *12.3 will need to be explored. Both techniques have been used (Skinner, 1978).

The literature comparing Q and R techniques is generalizable to comparing any pair of analyses where one analysis involves the transposed data matrix of the other. The results from the two analyses cannot be expected to be the same unless a double-centered matrix is factored for the same number of factors. In most research situations, the question prompting the study will determine which mode should be factored.

15.2   THREE-MODE FACTOR ANALYSIS

Investigators' interests may not be restricted to just two modes. Instead, they may be interested in several modes. The present section contains a discussion of factoring data with three modes. To simplify the discussion, one mode will be assumed to be individuals, another to be variables, and the third to be the conditions under which the observations are made. (There is no logical requirement that three-mode analyses always include any one mode, such as individuals.) It will be assumed that all possible combinations of the modes occur. For example, all individuals will be considered to have a score for every variable under all conditions where data are collected.

A three-mode analysis could be concerned with several different questions. First, the concern may be with the factors which are found under both of two conditions where a variable is measured (Section 15.2.1). Or, the investigator may wish to evaluate the factors in each of several modes, and then relate the factors to each other. The former is considered in Section 15.2.2 and the latter in Section 15.2.3.

Multimode factor analysis has received less attention than standard factor-analytic techniques and little research experience has been gained with it. Three-mode factor analysis is still experimental. The goal of the present section is to present the basic principles of analysis when three-mode data are available. Acquaintance with the basic principles allows an investigator to determine if further study is warranted and to understand research involving three-mode analyses.

15.2.1 Factors Extending Across Two Modes

Interbattery Factor Analysis.   Interbattery factor analysis (Tucker, 1958) is a procedure by which factors appearing across two sets of variables can be found when they have been collected from the same individuals by different measuring devices, on different occasions, etc. The interest lies in those factors that appear from the correlations between the two sets of variables and not in factors that appear from the correlations among the variables of only one set. Each set of variables may be collected underneath a different condition, the case that is of primary interest for two-mode factor analysis. Or, each set of variables may simply represent a different domain of variables, the traditional case where interbattery analysis has been used. Nicewander, Urry, and Starry (1969) suggest a procedure for factoring large numbers of items that is a variant upon interbattery factor analysis.

In interbattery factor analysis, only the correlations between the two sets of variables are factored. If there are v_1 variables in the first set and v_2 in the second set, then a v_1 by v_2 correlation matrix is formed from the data matrix, $Z_{n(v_1 + v_2)}$.

It is conceptually part of a larger matrix that has an order of $v_1 + v_2$. The total matrix, $R_{(v_1 + v_2)(v_1 + v_2)}$—of which the matrix of interest, $R_{v_1 v_2}$, is a part—is shown in Fig. 15.2.

$R_{v_1 v_2}$ is asymmetrical and has no diagonal element problem. If the variables are the same for both the v_1 and v_2 conditions and if they are ordered the same, the diagonals of the resulting square matrix will be the "across-condition reliability coefficients," although the off-diagonals will still be asymmetrical. Because of the asymmetry, it is obvious that any factor analysis program used for such data must operate upon the entire matrix (the usual computer procedures analyze only half of the correlation matrix because it is generally assumed that a symmetrical matrix is being factored).

The general factor-analytic model is used with each set of variables:

$$Z_{nv_1} = F_{nf}P'_{fv_1}$$
$$Z_{nv_2} = F_{nf}P'_{fv_2}$$

(15.2.1)

The present concern is to find only those columns of P that appear in both P_{v_1f} and P_{v_2f}. Because $R_{v_1 v_2}$ is composed of the correlations between the two sets of variables, the reproduced correlation matrix will be a function of the factors that they have in common. The two factor patterns reproduce the correlations between the two sets of variables:

$$R_{v_1 v_2} = P_{v_1f}R_{ff}P'_{fv_2}$$

(15.2.2)

In Eq. (15.2.2), both factor patterns have the same factors and thus the basic concern is made explicit.

Interbattery factor analysis solves for the two patterns in Eq. (15.2.2) to find

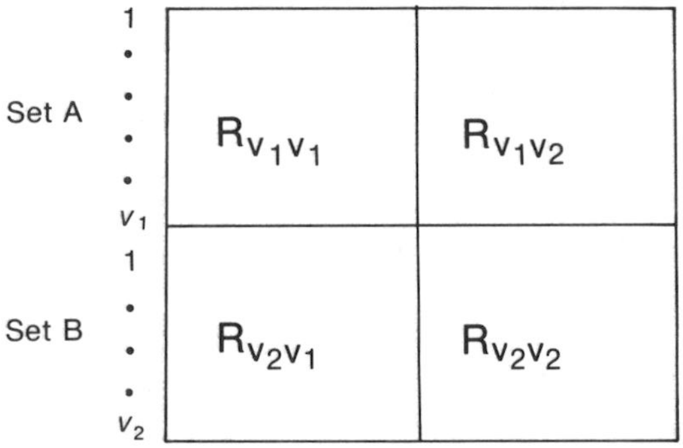

FIG. 15.2.   The correlation matrix for interbattery factor analysis.

that common set of factors, f, which extends across both variable sets. It may be that a factor will appear in $R_{v_1 v_1}$ or $R_{v_2 v_2}$ that is not necessary to reproduce $R_{v_1 v_2}$; these factors can be solved for independently by factoring the residuals within any particular variable set after the variance attributable to the joint factors defined from Eq. (15.2.2) has been removed. The variance from the interbattery factors is removed by computing $\hat{R}_{v_1 v_1}$ from $P_{v_1 f}$ and R_{ff}. $\hat{R}_{v_1 v_1}$ is subtracted from $R_{v_1 v_1}$ and the resulting residuals factored by the usual procedures.

$R_{v_1 v_2}$ can be factored by various techniques. For example, theoretical considerations could suggest diagonal or multiple group factoring. In the diagonal approach, a pair of variables from the two sets would be selected as the first definers of a factor. The square root of their joint element in $R_{v_1 v_2}$ would be the loadings of both variables on that factor. The loadings would be placed in both $P_{v_1 f}$ and $P_{v_2 f}$ and the other elements of the P's evaluated by the diagonal formula.

Both Tucker (1958) and Horst (1965) present procedures to solve for the principal factors of $R_{v_1 v_2}$. The number of factors can be decided by the scree test; criteria such as Guttman's roots are not used. The number of factors cannot exceed v_1 or v_2, whichever is smaller. Both of the P's may be rotated separately or by augmenting the two P's into a $P_{(v_1 + v_2) f}$ matrix. Seeking simple structure in the combined matrix would be consistent with the total approach. Factor scores can also be calculated. However, problems can also occur in a principal factor solution, particularly if the two sets of variables have few factors in common (Gibson, 1960); in that case, other procedures may be more appropriate (Gibson, 1963b; Taylor, 1967).

Maximum Likelihood Analysis Across Several Modes.   Jöreskog (1969c) has been generalizing both exploratory and confirmatory maximum likelihood procedures to the multimode case. His analysis begins with the entire $R_{(v_1 + v_2), (v_1 + v_2)}$. Jöreskog then sets up various hypotheses about factors that may be appearing in particular modes and about factors that may cut across modes. The hypotheses are then tested by the confirmatory maximum likelihood procedure. If the initial hypotheses do not reproduce the correlation matrix adequately, then additional hypotheses are generated and an exploratory search conducted. Any factors found by the exploratory procedure would need to be confirmed in another sample of the individuals.

In Jöreskog's approach, it is not necessary that the same variables appear under the different conditions, nor is it necessary that their number be the same. Inasmuch as the variables are all unique, the procedure collapses back into ordinary two-mode factor analysis but with a greatly enlarged domain of variables being sampled. Jöreskog's procedure includes interbattery factor analysis as a special case. Further discussion and examples are given in Boruch, Larkin, Wolins, and MacKinney (1970) and Boruch and Wolins (1970) (also see Chapter 7).

15.2.2 Factoring Each of Three Modes

Separate Analyses.   When it is desirable to find factors that appear in both of two modes, the variables collected under each mode can be factored separately. For example, Nottingham, Gorsuch, and Wrightsman (1970) were interested in identifying those factors that appeared in the items of the Philosophies of Human Nature Scale across the mode of sex (i.e., for both males and females). Separate factor analyses were conducted for each sex and those factors that appeared regardless of the mode were noted.

The procedures of Chapter 13 are used to compare the factors of each mode with those derived from the other modes. If the same factor (or factors) appears across the modes, then evidence for that factor's generalizability across the modes being considered has been found.

Instead of rotating the factors from each of several modes independently, they can be jointly rotated to the same position so that the several factor patterns are proportional or congruent (cf. Section *10.4.2; Cattell & Cattell, 1955; Evans, 1971; Meredith, 1964a). The similarity between the several solutions is thereby maximized even though some capitalization on chance may occur in the maximization process.

If it is suspected that the factor structure is different under the various conditions, then separate two-mode factor analyses should be performed for each condition. A significance test for determining whether or not covariance matrices differ is available (Maxwell, 1959; Boruch & Dutton, 1970). Only if significant differences are found can one conclude that the underlying factors represent nonchance variations. Conditions for the proper application of this technique are in Holthouse (1970).

Collapsing Across Modes.   In three-mode factor analysis, variables are measured on each individual underneath the conditions that are thought to represent those to which the conclusions are to be generalized. The result is a cube of data that can be collapsed into a set of two-mode data matrices. For example, X_{nvc_1}, X_{nvc_2}, X_{nvc_3} are three slices where c_1 refers to the slice giving the first condition, c_2 refers to the second condition, and so forth. They can be combined into a two-mode matrix, $X_{nv.}$, where the dot indicates that the c mode has been collapsed.

There are several approaches to summarizing by collapsing across the conditions so that an ordinary two-mode factor analysis can be computed. The one to choose depends upon the conditions involved. The first approach is to sum up or average the various matrices. In that case:

$$X_{nv.} = X_{nvc_1} + X_{nvc_2} + X_{nvc_3} + \ldots X_{nvc_c} \qquad (15.2.3)$$

where X_{nvc_c} refers to the last matrix in the series.

Summing elements may not be appropriate. For example, individuals may differ from condition to condition because an individual in the first condition is "contaminated" so that he cannot appear in the second condition. There is no way to average across the various condition matrices if the individuals differ.

If the individuals differ, the data matrices are extended instead of summed or averaged. In extending the matrices, each data matrix collected under a new condition is placed at the bottom of the other matrices and the columns are correlated for the factor analysis. The matrix submitted for correlation appears in Fig. 15.3. Note that if the number of rows in each of the condition matrices is not the same, the resulting correlation coefficients will be more influenced by the matrix with the greater number of rows. If the number of individuals is considerably different but equal weights are desired, procedures such as averaging the covariance matrices may need to be considered.

Because the focus is on the relationships among the variables across the modes making up the individuals and the conditions, differences in means and standard deviations introduced by the different conditions may not be of interest. However, differences in means or standard deviations introduced by the conditions can affect the correlations in the extended data matrix approach. Indeed, variables that correlate not at all under each separate condition can have high correlations if they both have the same large mean differences across the conditions. On the other hand, two variables that are highly correlated but have means that are affected differentially by the conditions may have that correlation wiped out. In such a situation, each variable can be standardized so that it has the same mean and standard deviation in every condition, thus reducing the effects of mean differences.

So far the discussion has implied that the data are factored only once. However, with three modes the data may be factored several times. The data can be factored once from the perspective of each mode of theoretical interest. For example, variables could be factored by collapsing across individuals and the individuals factored by collapsing across variables or occasions. Cattell (1978) gives a detailed presentation of this approach, which he calls N-way analysis.

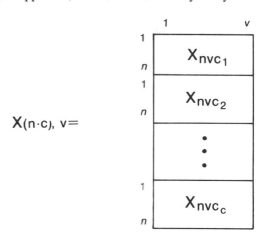

$$X_{(n \cdot c), \, v} =$$

FIG. 15.3.   Extended data matrices.

Example

Osgood, Ware, and Morris (1961) were confronted with a three-mode problem. One mode was Morris's Ways of Life Scale. Each of the 13 "Ways" stressed the value of a different mode of living. The ways range from "humble obedience to cosmic purposes" to "abandonment to sensuous enjoyment." The second mode consisted of semantic differential adjectives; each Way was rated on a continuum from interesting to uninteresting, from kind to cruel and so forth, for 26 adjective pairs. The third mode was individuals; its levels were 55 male college students.

To factor the Ways they first excluded subject variance by averaging the responses across all individuals. The resulting data matrix had the 13 Ways as variables and the 26 scales as "individuals" across which the variables were correlated. The analysis was of the generalized perception of the Ways by the average college student. For a second analysis each individual's scores on each scale were added to the data matrix so that there was one row for each individual's use of each adjective scale. Although the variables were still the 13 Ways, the correlations were calculated across the 338 responses by each of the 55 individuals on the 26 scales. Analyzing the extended matrix allowed mean differences among individuals to influence the results whereas analyzing the averaged matrix did not.

In both cases centroid factors were extracted (this procedure is no longer recommended because principal factor solutions are readily available) with unities for the estimated communalities (highly questionable with only 13 variables when the variables had been selected because the author thought each Way was independent of the others). It appears that only four factors were extracted because the authors felt that number accounted for most of the variance. The factors were rotated to the quartimax solution (thus assuming the factors would be unrelated even though the Ways are defined as in the same basic area, but also allowing for a possible general factor).

The factors from each approach are given in Table 15.2.1. It can be seen that each analysis led to similar factors, a finding that means there were no major mean differences among the individuals.

The only major difference was in the variance accounted for in the analyses. In the averaged data, the four factors accounted for 95% of the total variance; in the extended data matrix the four factors accounted for only 61% of the total variance. The difference in variance accounted for suggests that (a) group data are more stable than individual data; and that (b) the mean differences may have produced some minor factors that were not extracted.

Osgood, Ware, and Morris also wanted to examine the semantic differential space of the scales used to rate the Ways. Being unsure as to the theoretical importance of individual means, they again analyzed the data by both extended and averaged data matrix procedures. The semantic differential scales were the variables for this analysis. Again their factors were quite similar.

If they had wanted to factor individuals by averaging across one mode, they would have needed to decide whether the indices of association would be calculated across the Ways or across the semantic differential scales. The factors from analyzing averaged semantic differential ratings for the Ways need not be the same as those found when analyzing average responses to semantic scales. The first would tend to place together individuals who saw the same Ways in the same light. The latter would place together

TABLE 15.2.1
Salient Loading Patterns for Ways of Life

Ways	Factor A Dynamism		Factor B Social-ization		Factor C Control		Factor D Venturesome	
	I	II	I	II	I	II	I	II
1. Preserve the best in society	—	—	X	X	X	X	—	—
2. Self-sufficiency, reflection and meditation	—X	—X	—	—	X	X	—	—
3. Altruistic affection and concern for others	—	—	X	X	—	—	—	—
4. Abandonment to sensuous enjoyment	X	—	—	—	—	—	X	X
5. Group action toward common goals	X	—	—	—	—	—	—	X
6. Progress through realistic solution of problems	X	X	—	—	—	—	—	X
7. Integration of diversity	X	—	X	—	—	—	—	X
8. Wholesome enjoyment of simple comforts	—X	—	X	X	—	—	—	—
9. Quiet receptivity to experience	—X	—X	—	—	—	—	—	—
10. Dignified self-control	—	—	—	—	X	X	—	—
11. Contemplation of the rich inner life	—X	—X	—	—	—	—	—	—
12. Dynamic physical interaction with the environment	X	X	—	—	—	—	—	X
13. Humble obedience to cosmic purposes	—X	—X	—	—	—	—	—	—

Note: An X indicates a definite relationship was observed. (I) was the first analysis from the averaged data; (II) was the second analysis which included individual differences. (Adapted from Tables 1 and 3 of Osgood, Ware, & Morris, 1961).

those individuals who had used the same scales in the same way. Because of the difficulties in knowing how to collapse across what mode, theoretical guidance is needed at this point.

15.2.3 Relating Factors Across Modes

If each of the modes has been factored, it may be of interest to relate the factors across modes. An examination of the interrelationships might show the same factor to be appearing in different modes, that scores for a factor shift as a function of the conditions, or that a type of person is characterized by having high or low scores on factors of another mode.

In many situations, the factors of two modes can be related by computing factor scores for individuals. One factor analysis would be for variables with conditions collapsed and the other for conditions with variables collapsed. Individuals would receive factor scores for both the factors of the variables and the factors of the conditions. The two sets of factors could then be correlated together to evaluate when, for example, a type of response tended to occur (Cattell, 1970a).

Computing factor scores for individuals also allows other types of analyses. Analysis of means would be particularly appropriate if the factors had been of variables with conditions collapsed. The question would be whether the individuals had different mean factor scores under the different conditions. Scores for the factors from the variables would be computed separately for each condition and the means analyzed by the usual statistical procedures.

Another variant would be to select out the individuals with the purest factor loadings in the typological factoring. One group would be selected for each typological factor, and they could then be compared for mean differences on factor scores for the variables. The possible ways of comparing the factors are many.

The above procedures are for situations where the factor scores are actually computed. Usually, appropriate equations can be derived so that the correlations between sets of factor scores or means for groups of individuals can be evaluated for several conditions without computing the factor scores. Tucker (1963, 1964, 1966, 1967) has provided basic equations for calculating the relationships among the factors from each of three modes (for computer programs see Kroonenberg, Pieterm, & deLeeuw, 1980; McCloskey & Jackson, 1979; Walsh & Walsh, 1976; Zenisek, 1978).

His procedure gives a "core" matrix that defines the intermode relationships. Tucker (1964) has also provided illustrations of three-mode factor analyses, with core matrices, for multitrait–multimethod and learning research. Further developments of this approach are given by Bentler and Lee (1978, 1979) and Snyder and Law (1979). Lastovicka (1981) extends the model to four-mode matrices.

Example

Tucker (1964) reports several three-mode analyses. In one case Levin (1965) analyzed data collected by Endler, Hunt, and Rosenstein (1962). One mode consisted of the situations in which a person might find himself. The situations varied from taking a competitive exam to being with a new date. Each situation was rated on a number of scales for possible reactions, such as perspiring or wanting to avoid the situation. The scales formed the second mode. The students doing the ratings formed the third mode.

The results are summarized in Table 15.2.2, which gives only illustrative results rather than the full matrices. In the first section of the table the three factors are presented that resulted from analyzing the responses. The second section contains the factors from the situations. The person factors are not given, but three were extracted.

TABLE 15.2.2
A Three-Mode Analysis

A. *Mode 1: Responses*

Variables	*A. Distress*	*B. Exhilaration*	*C. Autonomic*
		Factors	
Get "uneasy feeling"	X	—	—
Heart beats faster	X	—	—
Enjoy the challenge	—	X	—
Seek experiences like this	—	X	—
Have loose bowels	—	—	X
Need to urinate frequently	—	—	X

B. *Mode 2: Situations*

Variables	*A. Interpersonal*	*B. Inanimate*	*C. Unknown Situation*
		Factors	
Speech before large group	X	—	—
Job interview	X	—	—
Ledge high on mountain side	—	X	—
Alone in woods at night	—	X	—
Psychological experiment	—	—	X
Auto trip	—	—	X

C. *Core Box*

Variable Factors	*Interpersonal*	*Situation Factors* *Inanimate*	*Unknown*
1. For type A person.			
Distress Response	X	X	—
Exhilaration Response	—	—	—
Autonomic Response	X	X	—
2. For type B person.			
Distress Response	—	X	—
Exhilaration Response	X	X	X
Autonomic Response	—	—	X
3. For type C person.			
Distress Response	—	X	—
Exhilaration Response	X	—	—
Autonomic Response	—	X	—

Note: An X indicates a definite relationship was observed. Adapted from Tucker's (1964) presentation of analyses by Levin (1965) on data from Endler, Hunt, and Rosenstein (1962).

The final section contains the core, which shows major relationships of each of the factors with the other factors. It can be seen that the interpersonal situations are associated with distress for one type of person and exhilaration for the other types.

16
The Replication and Invariance of Factors

A crucial question for the design of an investigation is how to maximize the generalizability of the results. The question is more important for factor analysis than for the usual statistical procedure because significance tests are rare and because many possibilities exist for capitalizing on chance. This chapter is concerned with noting the conditions under which the results from a factor analysis can be generalized across samples of individuals or variables so that recommendations for the design of factor-analytic studies can be made.

In the first part of the chapter, Section 16.1, we discuss when factors can be expected to generalize across *random* sets of individuals drawn from the same population, and our concern is with **replication.** In Section 16.2 the discussion is extended to the case of *systematic* selection of either variables or individuals, a problem called that of the **invariance,** hardiness, or robustness of factors.

In the present context, factorial invariance refers to replicating factors across systematic variations in the selection of variables or subjects. The fact that the samples are assumed to be from differing populations distinguishes factorial invariance from factorial replication; replication, as discussed in Section 16.1, refers to the finding of the same factors across random samples. It should be noted that Thurstone (1947), Henrysson (1960), and others used the term invariance for the concept of replication as well.

16.1 THE REPLICATION OF FACTORS ACROSS RANDOM SAMPLES OF INDIVIDUALS

If factors are extracted from the same variables measured on several random samples of individuals drawn from the same underlying population, when will the factors from two samples match? The more often factors match, the more

328

worthwhile the factor-analytic procedure is for achieving its task. The less a factor analysis leads to replicable factors, the less desirable it is. This section considers when the factors resulting from one research study are more likely to replicate in another study; it is assumed that each study is based on a random sample of individuals drawn from the same population. In Section 16.1.1, the impact of the method of factoring on the likelihood of replicating the results is considered. In Section 16.1.2, the impact of the design characteristics of the study on replication is assessed. Some brief comments on the extent to which replication appears to be possible are given in Section 16.1.3. The sections all deal only with the effects of random sampling of individuals when the variables are assumed to be identical; the effects of nonrandom selection are considered in Section 16.2 under the topic of invariance.

16.1.1 Impact of the Method of Factoring

With the wide variety of factor-analytic procedures available, several questions can be raised: Do some procedures lead to more replicable factors than others? Do minor changes in procedures lead to major differences in the generalizability of the factors across random samples of individuals? Evidence on these questions has been referred to at numerous points in the preceding chapters and is only briefly summarized here.

From theoretical considerations and the empirical studies that have been done (Bechtoldt, 1961; Browne, 1968a; Gorsuch, 1970; Hakstian, 1971; Harris, 1967; Horn, 1963, Rosenblatt, 1969), it appears that the following conclusions can be drawn:

1. When some variables do not correlate well with any other variables and the number of variables is low (e.g., 10 or 20), use of the component model leads to a different solution than the common factor model. Except for unusual cases, the various procedures for estimating communalities lead to essentially the same results. There is suggestive evidence that the common factor model may lead to more replicable factors than the component model when the communalities are actually low (i.e., when the communalities from a truncated component analysis are considerably less than unity).

2. Principal factor and maximum likelihood analyses lead to essentially the same factors, provided that the diagonals of R_{vv} are similar. Therefore, it is expected that the replicability of these factors will also be quite similar.

3. The number of factors extracted interacts with the rotation. If only a very few factors have been extracted the larger rotated factors shift considerably when an additional factor is added to the rotation. But when a moderate number of factors have been extracted, adding one or two more factors does not alter the larger rotated factors. Extracting a large number of factors again shifts the results. It appears that extracting too few factors decreases the replicability of

those factors, whereas extracting a moderate number with one or two extra factors—and only one or two—does not.

4. The differences between the analytic procedures for rotating to simple structure are primarily found in the differences between orthogonal and oblique rotations. Most of the oblique procedures lead to the same factors, but biquartimin and maxplane may produce less replicable factors. Some evidence does suggest that the rotated factors are more stable than the unrotated factors. Evidence on the replicability of orthogonal versus oblique factors is not sufficient to draw any conclusions; the problem is complicated by the fact that both procedures give the same results when the underlying factors are "actually" orthogonal.

5. In factor analysis, one has numerous possibilities for capitalizing on chance. Most extraction procedures, including principal factor solutions, reach their criterion by such capitalization. The same is true of rotational procedures, including those that rotate for simple structure. Therefore, the solutions are biased in the direction of the criterion used. It is, for example, easy to show that even random data produce a reasonably simple structure (Cattell & Gorsuch, 1963) that can be interpreted (Armstrong & Soelberg, 1968; Horn, 1967; Humphreys et al., 1969). The impact of chance is particularly important in Procrustean rotation where Horn and Knapp (1973) note that support can be found for randomly determined theories even when variables are reliable, the sample contains several hundred individuals, and only loadings greater than .3 are interpreted.

The effects of capitalization upon chance in the interpretation can be reduced if a suggestion by Harris and Harris (1971) is followed: Factor the data by several different analytical procedures and hold sacred only those factors that appear across all the procedures used.

16.1.2 The Importance of the Communalities, Number of Variables per Factor, and Number of Individuals

Given the same variables and true random sampling from the population, the possibility of replicating the factors will be influenced by the same phenomena that influence the replicability of any research. The primary parameters influencing the replicability of statistical conclusions are: the accuracy of measurement, the strength of the phenomena, the number of variables, and the number of individuals on which the statistic is based. The first two, accuracy of measurement and the strength of the phenomena, are manifested jointly in the communalities of the variables in the factor-analytic study.

Communalities.   Several factor-analytic principles previously discussed suggest that the communalities may be important for replicability:

(1) Under the truncated component model, the communalities are an indication of how well the data fit the model. If the communalities are high, then the model is more appropriate. If the communalities are not high, the model is less appropriate for the data and probably would not replicate as well.

(2) Under the common factor model, the communalities are also important. When they are high, the unique factor weights are low. In Section 3.5.1, it was noted that the theoretical common and unique factors have zero correlations in the population but chance correlations in the sample. The chance correlations are multiplied by the unique weights and will be low when the unique weights are low (i.e., when the communalities are high). The reduction of chance correlations among the variables can only enhance the replicability.

Humphreys et al. (1969) have shown that as the number of random variables increases, the loadings are generally higher because of capitalization upon chance and thus more impressive. They do not, however, replicate any better than low loadings unless the replication capitalizes on chance. It appears that adding variables that correlate poorly with the other variables (i.e., variables with low communalities) does not increase the replicability of the factor but may, through increasing the possibilities of capitalization upon chance, actually *decrease* the possibility of replicating the results.

Other empirical work also confirms the theoretical expectation: the factor loadings become more stable and replicable as the communalities increase (Cliff & Pennell, 1967; Pennell, 1968). High communalities occur only when both the reliabilities are high and the variables correlate with some of the other variables in the analysis. **Therefore, variables without a prior history of good reliability estimates and good correlations with other variables in the analysis are not desired in a factor analysis.** If it is necessary to develop new variables for the analysis, they should be tested in a pilot study and revised if necessary.

Ratio of Variables to Factors.   In addition to the communalities, the strength of a factor is also manifested by the number of salient variables per factor. Several factor-analytic principles suggest that there should be more than the minimum number of variables necessary to assure the factor's appearance:

(1) As the number of variables increases, the number of diagonal elements becomes a smaller percentage of the total matrix and the solution is less influenced by the decision of what should be in the diagonals. The resulting factors are more model free and will probably replicate better.

(2) As the number of salient variables per factor increases, the rotational position will be more uniquely determined and will involve less capitalization on chance. The less capitalization on chance occurs, the more replicable the results should be.

(3) Under the common factor model, the factor scores are progressively better determined as the number of variables per factor increases. Better determined factor scores can be expected to be more replicable than indeterminate factor scores.

The empirical evidence supports the conclusion that factors should have sufficient salient variables to be clearly determined (Browne, 1968a; Cliff & Pennell, 1967; Gorsuch, 1970; Humphreys et al., 1969; Nesselroade & Baltes, 1970; Nesselroade, Baltes, & LaBouvie, 1971). It appears that it is generally difficult to replicate factors with fewer than five or six salient variables per factor. Replication should generally be attempted with at least four, and preferably six, variables per factor. The only exception to the four to six variables per factor rule would be some confirmatory factor analyses where the factor had been exceptionally well defined in previous research. For example, the concern in diagonal factor analysis may not be in replicating the factor but in extracting a well-established factor from the data on the basis of one widely recognized measure of that factor.

Number of Individuals. The number of individuals has the expected relationship to the replicability of factors: the more the better (Browne, 1968a; Cliff & Pennell, 1967; Humphreys et al., 1969; Nesselroade & Baltes, 1970; Nesselroade et al., 1971; Pennell, 1968). For example, Cliff (1970) factored 12 and 20 variables in a Monte Carlo study and found all of the four factors to be recoverable with an n of 600, but only two to three of the factors were identifiable with an n of 200.

Unfortunately, no one has yet worked out what a safe ratio of the number of subjects to variables is, probably because it varies depending upon the strength of the phenomena. A present suggested absolute minimum ratio is five individuals to every variable, but not less than 100 individuals for any analysis. The Barrett and Kline (1981) results suggest that when the number of subjects is indeed large, the ratio of number of individuals to number of variables is less crucial; the absolute minimum of 100 even if only a few variables are being factored is also consistent with their conclusions. The suggested minimum applies only when the expected communalities are high and there are many variables per expected factor. But if the variables have low reliabilities or the phenomena are weak, then many more individuals will be needed. It appears that the only safe conclusion is that any factors of interest should be based upon n's greater than the aforementioned rate and should be highly significant by the tests given in Chapter 8, poor as the tests may be.

Higher-Order Factors.   Higher-order factors may be more difficult to replicate than lower order factors because the correlations among factors appear to be
more unstable than correlations among variables. Also, each is generally defined
by only a few variables and therefore the rotational position is not as well
defined. However, no analysis of the replicability of higher-order factors has
been conducted.

16.1.3 The Expected Level of Replication of Factors

When factors are matched in a substantive area, some replicate and others do not.
This is true of all statistics but factor analysis lacks the usual significance tests to
predict the results more likely to replicate. How easy is it to replicate factors?

Replicable factors have been found in many areas. Some samples from psychology are:

(1) Norman (Norman, 1963; Passini & Norman, 1966) has been able to
consistently replicate five factors from ratings of personality variables.

(2) Cattell (Cattell, 1957; Hundleby, Pawlik, & Cattell, 1965) indicates that
most of his numerous personality factors replicate when careful analyses are
carried out; however, others (Peterson, 1965; Sells, Demaree, & Will, 1970) feel
that only the major factors replicate in Cattell's data.

(3) Bechtoldt (1961) found reasonable replication when factoring ability
scales; Ryckman and Wiegerink (1969) also found replicable factors, although
the degree of replication was less because few of the studies reviewed contained
a sufficient number of individuals.

(4) Gorsuch (1967) indicated that about half the factors from an adjective
checklist replicated.

(5) Struening and Cohen (1963) present data on items concerned with mental
illness; they suggest that all five of their factors replicated, but it could be argued
that only three of the five were replicated sufficiently to warrant use of the term.

None of the studies referenced used a significance test to evaluate replication
or specified in advance a level of replication that was systematically applied to
the data, although Hundleby, Pawlik, and Cattell (1965) came close to doing so.
Therefore, replicated versus nonreplicated decisions are difficult to make, and
the degree of replication to expect is difficult to judge on the basis of past
performance in psychology.

The studies cited are only samples of the factor-analytic studies that have
attempted replication; most investigators appear to assume all their results will
replicate. Although no comprehensive review of factor-analytic studies has been
attempted, it does appear that about two-thirds of the factors in a study meeting
the requirements previously noted can be expected to replicate.

Because of the possibility of interpreting factors that will not replicate, **it is worthwhile to build a replication into the initial factor-analytic study.** The replication would proceed by randomly splitting the sample in half, factoring both halves and identifying the factors that match across the two samples. Only the matching factors would be reported. Each half of the sample would need to be sufficiently large so that all factors of interest would be statistically significant in each analysis. **If a statistic were needed for another study, such as the weight matrix for computing factor scores, the statistic would then be computed from the full sample for only the replicated factors.** It can be expected that factors that appear in both samples will have a very high probability of replicating again. The double-factoring procedure should be a standard practice until better significance tests are more widely available.

16.2   THE INVARIANCE OF FACTORS

The invariance of a factor solution across changes in the selection of variables or individuals is defined in terms of the loadings for a variable included in all of the analyses. A solution is invariant when a variable has the same factor pattern in the new study as it does in other solutions containing the same factors. When the solution is invariant, the factor patterns of the two studies would produce highly correlated reproduced variables when used with the factor scores of an appropriate sample of individuals.

Example

The ability data might be expected to show a fair degree of invariance when only a few variables are changed. The Grant-White data allow some changes in variables. The usual factoring procedure has been to include variables 25 and 26 while excluding variables 3 and 4. In Table 13.5.1 are the results when the data were factored with variables 3 and 4 instead of 25 and 26. The individuals were the same and only 2 of 24 variables had been changed; those that were replaced had their own parallel forms for substitutes. Factorial invariance is certainly expected with only minor changes in the variables, and the problem can be used to illustrate invariance.

The factor pattern for variable 1 is taken from Table 9.3.2:

$$v_1 = -.08A + .03B + .77C - .04D \text{ (analysis with variables 25 and 26).}$$

The second factor pattern for variable 1 is from the analysis that gave Table 13.5.1:

$$v_1 = -.05A' - .02B' + .76C' - .02D' \text{ (analysis with variables 3 and 4).}$$

Are the loadings factorially invariant? They are in the sense that the same factor would be used in both cases to predict the variable. Chance fluctuations did occur and should discourage interpretation of the second digit in any factor pattern. The chance fluctuations would, of course, have been much greater if the second analysis was on a different sample of individuals.

Factor invariance can be more precisely defined. Note that invariance occurs when the same factor relates to the same variables in two studies. Because the variables are defined operationally and are hence identical for the two studies, the same factors can only reproduce these variables if they correlate the same with the variables in both studies. This occurs only if factor score estimates from the two studies are highly correlated when scored for the same sample. Hence **invariance occurs across two studies when factor scores based on those studies correlate highly in a new sample.**

Factorial invariance across systematic variations of the samples is distinct from replication across random samples. When the results differ slightly across random samples, it can be assumed that the differences are chance fluctuations around the population values. When the results differ across samples that vary nonrandomly, the differences could be either from chance fluctuations or from actual differences. Major differences between studies in a replication design lead to a questioning of the adequacy of both studies or of the analytic procedures being used. But major differences between studies utilizing samples drawn from distinct populations could also mean that the populations are different and, indeed, help to identify the manner in which they are different. A psychological test that measures the ability to add numbers in children will often measure only a clerical speed factor in adults. When this same test loads on two different factors in children and adults, the results are a meaningful description of the differences between the samples.

However, to the extent that invariance can be found across systematic changes in either the variables or the individuals, then the factors have a wider range of applicability as generalized constructs. The subpopulations over which the factor occurs could—and probably would—differ in their mean scores or variances across the groups, but the pattern of relationships among the variables would be the same. The factors would be applicable to the several populations and could be expected to generalize to other similar populations as well.

Historically, the stress on solutions leading to invariant factors developed when factor analysis was used to define the concepts for a domain. Thurstone in particular felt the purpose of factor analysis was to establish concepts within an area to help conceptualize future research. He proposed simple structure as an aid in the search for invariant factors across samples of variables. Although the question of the ''real'' dimensions underlying a domain is relatively fruitless, it is still true that more invariant factors will be more useful than less invariant factors.

Invariance is a function of sampling across all modes, including individuals, variables, and conditions, but this section will consider invariance of only two modes: the variables and the individuals. Sections 16.2.1 and 16.2.2 are concerned with the effects of the selection of variables (i.e., that which the indices of association interrelate). The effects of selection of individuals are discussed in Section 16.2.3.

In the discussion of the sampling of variables, it is assumed that the sampling of individuals presents no problem, whereas it is assumed that the sampling of variables presents no problem in the discussion of the sampling of individuals. Generally, "no problem" means that either the sampling is not a problem because the same variables or individuals are used in both analyses or that the sampling of individuals is random from the same population.

The concept of invariance is generally operationalized by stating that two factor patterns are the same, but more exact measures can be used. An appropriate statistical measure of invariance is noted in Section 16.2.4 along with the situations where that index, and therefore factorial invariance, is likely to be high.

16.2.1 The Effects of Variable Selection on the Occurrence of a Factor

As a set of variables is expanded, reduced, or has some variables replaced, the factors underlying the resulting data matrix may be the same. It is apparent that if the factors remain unchanged, the factor pattern for any given variable occurring in all the solutions should be the same. Because all factors appear in each solution, the factor scores for two individuals included in all the analyses will place them in the same rank order except for chance fluctuations. (It is assumed that the factors' rotated positions are the same in each analysis, an assumption that is made throughout this section).

If the identical factors are not found in each and every analysis, however, a variable's factor pattern could change. Naturally, the elimination of a column will eliminate that loading, but the disappearance of a factor correlated with the factors loading the variable could have an effect even though it loaded the variable zero. As Gordon (1968) has pointed out, the correlation between two factors need not be very large to occasionally produce a noticeable effect on some weights in the factor pattern.

Whether or not a given factor appears in a particular study is a direct function of the selection of variables. Any factor appearing in any analysis can have a sufficient number of its identifying variables deleted so that it does not occur in the next analysis, and not all of its salient variables need be deleted for it to be too insignificant or trivial to be extracted in an exploratory study.

Increasing the number of variables for a given factor may also influence the results. With a heavy sampling of variables from a narrow area, a factor that previously appeared as a single factor may be split into several factors with the desired factor appearing only in higher-order analyses. The factor pattern for a variable would then appear to be considerably different from that of a prior study.

For example, assume that two sets of variables are being factored and that these two sets of measurements were taken on several sections of an earth-like planet's surface. (The measurements form the variables for the factor analysis

and the sections form the individuals). The first set of variables contains numerous measurements reflecting variations that are characteristic of land bodies.
These measurements may be as diverse as humidity at half a meter above the
surface, distance of the surface from the center of the planet, forms of life found
in between the surface and one meter below the surface, or the presence of
various chemicals. The first variable set contains only three variables that reflect
characteristics primarily variable across bodies of water, such as current. Factors
appearing from an analysis of this first variable set would primarily differentiate
among sections of land and types of soil, although one factor could appear
distinguishing, for example, still bodies of water from moving bodies of water.

A second variable set may reverse the ratio of land-oriented variables to
water-oriented variables. If only three variables that reflected differences characteristic of land bodies were included, only one land-oriented factor might occur.
However, because numerous variables reflecting differences in bodies of water
were included, several water-oriented factors might appear. In the second set of
variables, the distinction between still and moving bodies of water might be
found in a second- or third-order factor.

The effects of the selection of variables upon the occurrence of factors may be
further illustrated by considering Figs. 16.1 to 16.5. A common factor model is
assumed for these figures. The factorial composition of all seventeen variables is
given in Fig. 16.1. The term **stratum** will be used to refer to each level as
abstracted in the theory presented in Fig. 16.1 and **order** reserved for the levels
observed in a particular analysis. The straight lines indicate the loadings of the
various factors. The variables labeled 1 through 17 are loaded by a set of 5 first-
stratum factors, labeled A through E. A through E are correlated and produce
second-stratum factors, I and II. The second-stratum factors are moderately
correlated and lead to a third-stratum single factor, again labeled 1. The structure
given in Fig. 16.1 is the "actual" structure in the sense that a complete common
factor analysis of the 17 variables would produce it. (Other theories could insist
that the 17 variables are not the appropriate sample and therefore its strata are
inappropriate; the differences between the two theories would need to be resolved on the basis of their usefulness in relating to new data.)

Figure 16.2 is the probable result of factoring one variable subset selected
from the 17 original variables. At the first order, factors A and B appear as they
do in the theoretical stratum because all of their variables were included. Howev-

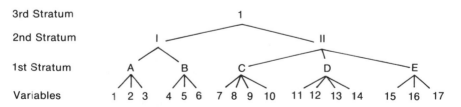

FIG. 16.1.   Structure from factoring 17 variables.

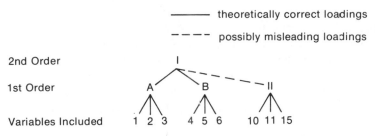

FIG. 16.2. Structure from factor variable set 1.

er, only one variable was included from each of the primary stratum factors C, D, and E and one variable is insufficient to produce a primary factor. The variables are still moderately correlated because the primary stratum factors to which they are related correlate. The moderate correlation will produce a factor which is, in essence, Fig. 16.1's II but occurs at the primary level. In a second-order analysis of these three factors, II would appear to be loaded by I even though the full model indicates that both factors are at the same stratum.

Figure 16.3 is a summary of the results from another selection of variables. Here only variables from factors C, D, and E were included and factors D and E occur at the first-order level. The first-order factors combine to give the second-stratum factor, II. Variable 10 is a problem because it is the only variable from its primary factor, C. It does have some affinity for factors D and E because these factors are correlated with C, and so it will have minor correlations with both factors D and E.

Figure 16.4 portrays still a third set of variables. Each variable is from a separate primary factor. None of the primary factors appears in the analysis because an insufficient number of variables is included to identify any of them. Instead, the third-stratum factor occurs in the first-order analysis.

In Fig. 16.5 still a fourth set of variables is presented. Here it is assumed that the experimenter unwittingly included three variants of variable 10. Because these will have all their variance in common except that produced by random error, the three variable 10's produce a factor of their own. The factor, labeled simply 10, will correlate with factor C to the extent to which variable 10 correlated with first-stratum factor C. If the correlation is sufficiently high, it will help produce a new factor, C', at the second-order level in this analysis. C' will be

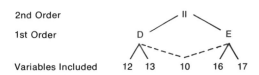

FIG. 16.3. Structure from variable set 2.

FIG. 16.4. Structure from variable set 3.

composed of proportional parts of C and 10. C' would then probably load the third-order factor as indicated.

From an examination of only Figs. 16.2 through 16.5, what would be the conclusion as to the nature of variable 10? Even a thoughtful examination of the solutions may not be sufficient for the experimenter to unravel this puzzle.

In research situations, there is seldom a paradigm that would define the "real structure." Because of the problems in defining and selecting variables, several investigators may produce what are apparently different primary factors related to the same variable, as was the case for variable 10 in the examples previously given. What appears as a primary factor in one analysis may be a second-order factor in another, provided the rotation is oblique in each case.

A variation in levels for the same factor also results from the fact that factors can usually be subdivided into finer factors by including more variables loading it in the analysis. The only case where this would not be so is when the reliability of each major loading of a given factor equals the square root of the variable's reference vector correlation with that particular factor. It is doubtful that such a factor could be subdivided by increasing the density of sampling.

If only uncorrelated factors are extracted, no higher-order factors will appear. Otherwise, the same effects as shown in the figures would occur: light sampling would collapse factors and heavy sampling would split the factor. However, the results of the four studies (Figs. 16.2–16.5) would be more difficult to untangle because the assumption of orthogonality would prevent a split factor from reappearing in a second-order analysis. Without the higher-order factors, the effects of the sampling of variables would be less apparent when reviewing the literature.

Because of the effects of the selection of variables upon the factors, the order of a factor has been distinguished from its stratum. The orders are simply a

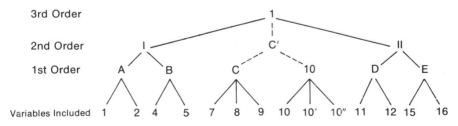

FIG. 16.5. Structure from variable set 4.

presentation of empirical results but the strata are the theoretical integration of the present results with any previous results—including information from non-factor-analytic studies—into the conceptual levels of generalizability. **Once strata have been suggested and a paradigm established, the strata are a guide to selecting variables so as to produce the factors of major importance for the study at the primary level.** Depending upon the problem at hand, such an analysis might resemble *any* of the figures for the five sample sets previously given.

The discussion of the impact of the selection of variables upon the appearance of a factor has been partially oversimplified. Besides assuming that any factor that does appear will have the same rotated position, it implies that strata are noncontinuous. For example, Fig. 16.1 has each factor either in a particular stratum or not in it. However, a more complete conceptualization would have factors at various strata blending into each other. The sampling of variables could produce factors at stratum 1.3, 1.5, or 1.95 as well as at stratum 1, 2, or 3. However, it is likely that the simpler, noncontinuous strata model will be the more efficient for present theory building.

16.2.2 The Effects of Variable Selection on Rotation

The foregoing section assumed that the selection of variables did not appreciably affect the rotated position of the factors. When a factor appeared, it appeared in the same position and was therefore easily identifiable as the same factor. The next question asked is how the selection of variables might affect the positions of the factors.

The procedures that base the factor's position upon all the variables in the solution will shift slightly to accommodate a new variable or adjust to a dropped variable. The degree of change in the solution will be a function of: (1) the relationship of the variable that is dropped or added to the other variables in the total set; and (2) the impact of that variable in the total set as measured by the percentage of variance it contributes to the solution. For example, if variables 1 and 2 were dropped from Fig. 16.6, the principal factor would shift some 35 degrees. Most of the ways of extracting the initial factors, such as the principal factor and maximum likelihood solutions, base the solution on all the variables and so would be affected in the manner described here. Procedures which base the factor on a limited number of variables (e.g., a diagonal or a multiple-group analysis) would be affected only if one of the defining variables was involved.

The advantage of simple structure is that each factor is influenced by a relatively small subset of variables. The position of any one factor is less likely to change with adding, deleting, or replacing one or two variables, unless, of course, these variables are crucial to its position. In that case, it could undergo a major shift in position. Generally, a simple structure factor would be somewhat more invariant. The possibility of increased invariance was the reason Thurstone

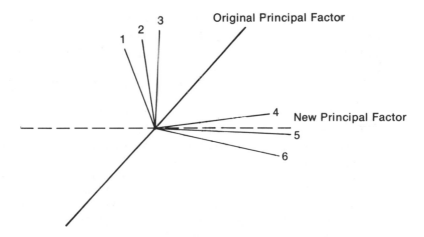

FIG. 16.6.   Shift in a principal factor when variables 1 and 2 are dropped.

originally suggested simple structure. In Fig. 16.6, the two simple structure factors would be placed near variables 2 and 5. Dropping 1 and 2 would only shift the first factor closer to variable 1.

In a simple structure solution, the correlations among factors can be expected to be particularly susceptible to shifts in variables. For example, if variable 7 were added one-third of the way from variable 4 to variable 3 in Fig. 16.6, then the factor passing through the cluster of variables defined by 4, 5, and 6 would shift somewhat toward the other cluster. The shift would increase the correlation between the factors. If R_{ff} is ignored, an oblique rotation for this figure is more factorially invariant than an orthogonal one because the factor from variables 1, 2, and 3 would not have its position affected at all by the addition of variable 7. In an orthogonal rotation, both factors would be slightly affected because shifting either factor would cause a shift on the other to maintain the 90 degree angle between them. Examples can be easily drawn where the correlated factors are considerably more invariant in the sense that they would still produce the same factor scores, whereas the uncorrelated factor scores would shift more. However, in oblique rotation there is more opportunity for capitalizing on chance. Whether or not oblique or orthogonal factors are more generally invariant across sampling of variables remains a question for empirical determination.

Occasionally, it is suggested that any set of factors desired could be produced simply by selecting variables appropriately. Although it is true that factors can be drastically changed through the systematic creation of new variables in appropriate positions, theoretically the general statement is not completely true. Uncorrelated variables always remain uncorrelated and highly correlated ones remain highly correlated. Because it can be assumed that two factors would never be placed through two variables that correlated .9 with each other, a factor defined by such variables could not be split. However, because the factors could be shifted 45 degrees or so by including different variables, considerable thought must be given to the variables selected and their probable influence on the rotation. Pilot factoring may be valuable, and using extension analysis, so that all the variables need not be included in the definition of the factors, may also be helpful.

Example

To illustrate the effects of altering the sample of variables, the ability data from Grant-White School were factored for only 15 of 26 possible variables. The variables selected were primarily from factor C(1, 2, 3, 4, 20, 21, 22, 23, 25, and 26), while two were from A (5 and 8), one from B (13) and two from D (16 and 18). Four factors were extracted to compare with the other solution. The principal axis method with two iterations for communalities after beginning with squared multiple correlations for the initial estimates was used. The factors were rotated to promax ($k = 4$), and the factor pattern and correlations among factors are given in Table 16.2.1; they can be compared with Table 9.3.2.

Factor C is much the same. Factor A is also identifiable. Factor B' has shifted somewhat to "borrow" variance from the original C. Factor D' is different.

To what extent do the loadings survive such a drastic redefining of the variable pool? Here are some factor patterns with the results of the complete variable analysis given first for comparison.

$$v_1 = - .08A + .03B + .77C - .04D \quad \text{(all variables)}$$
$$v_1 = - .07A' + .20B' + .52C' + .19D' \quad \text{(reduced variable set)}$$
$$v_{13} = - .01A + .54B + .41C - .16D \quad \text{(all variables)}$$
$$v_{13} = + .09A' + .46B' + .27C' - .01D' \quad \text{(reduced variable set)}.$$

Some noticeable shifts do occur even when the correct number of factors was known in advance.

16.2.3 The Effects of Selection of Individuals

Whenever individuals are selected from a different population, by definition the samples differ. The differences may be in means, variances, rank orders, the shape of the distributions, or in the relationships among variables. If the populations are completely different, little can be said. However, if one sample was drawn from a restricted part of the population from which the original sample was drawn, some conclusions can be reached.

Univariate selection occurs when the samples differ because one sample has been selected on the basis of its scores on only one variable. Univariate selection may occur directly upon an already defined variable or upon a new variable that is a linear composite of several previously defined variables. For example, college students may be selected from the total pool of applicants on the basis of an entrance exam or on the basis of a score formed by adding standard scores from the exam and from high school grades. **Multivariate selection** occurs when the effect cannot be identified with a simple linear combination of the variables.

TABLE 16.2.1
Promax ($k = 4$) Solution for Altered Set of Ability
Variables

A. *Factor Pattern*

	A'	B'	C'	D'
1. Visual Perception	−.07	.20	.52	.19
2. Cubes	−.07	−.03	.44	.18
3. Paper Form Board	.01	.48	.07	.23
4. Lozenges	.07	.21	.44	.09
5. General Information	.66	.18	−.01	−.01
8. Word Classification	.65	.28	−.09	.09
13. Straight and Curved Capitals	.09	.46	.27	−.01
16. Figure Recognition	−.10	.04	.58	.07
18. Number-Figure	−.04	.15	.55	−.11
20. Deduction	.35	−.19	.47	.05
21. Numerical Puzzles	.11	.23	.62	−.28
22. Problem Reasoning	.36	−.14	.49	−.06
23. Series Completion	.38	−.04	.37	.14
25. Paper Form Board	.08	.13	−.01	.59
26. Flags	.02	.18	.42	.10

B. *Correlations Among 4 Factors*

	A'	B'	C'	D'
A'	1.00			
B'	.29	1.00		
C'	.59	.43	1.00	
D'	.39	.36	.57	1.00

The effect of the selection will be partially a function of the index of association used. If the selection of individuals alters the variability or distribution of a particular variable, then both covariances and correlations will be affected. Although correlations correct for arbitrary differences in standard deviations, selection procedures directly affecting the variance or distribution do reduce correlation coefficients. For example, if the selection is such that a large number of individuals receive the same score, then the correlation coefficient with another variable that remains continuous will usually be reduced.

The effect of restricting the range of scores on factor analysis is shown in Fig. 16.7. The figure shows a set of variables in two-dimensional space both before and after selection has occurred. For the purpose of illustration, a component solution is shown where each variable has a length, before selection, of 1.0. The letters A through I represent variable vectors. If F is the variable of selection and the selection procedure reduces the variance in half, the resulting end points of the vectors are given by variables A, B', C', etc. through H' and I. Variables A and I are uncorrelated with F and are therefore not affected. The effect is strongest on those variables, such as E, that are close to F. Note that in Fig. 16.7

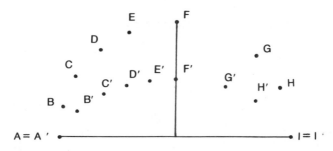

FIG. 16.7.   Effects of restriction of range on variable F.

configural invariance occurs; that is, the variables are still projected in the same direction and therefore the position of the factors would not, it appears, be adversely affected.

The effect in Fig. 16.7 is one of partial selection because the restriction of range was not such as to completely eliminate variable F. If complete selection occurred on variable F so that all subjects received the same score, then all of the points would fall on the line A–I and the number of factors would be reduced by 1. Disappearance of a factor occurs when complete selection occurs.

Figure 16.7 is an incomplete representation of the component solution for the correlations after selection. In the case of a component analysis, each variable vector would be extended out toward unity as far as possible. F' would be extended to unit length, as would the other variables. However, because the correlations have been and are still reduced, the position of the vectors in space would also be altered (cf. Chapter 4).

Figure 16.8 represents both the original variables and the new variables based on the attenuated correlations but extended out to communalities of 1.0. Fewer variables are represented in the second figure in order to simplify the drawing. The variables shift their positions because the cosines are reduced by the restriction of range effect. In the component case, it is obvious that the configural

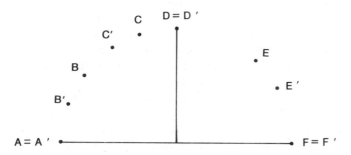

FIG. 16.8.   Effects of restriction of range on variable D when vectors are then extended to unity.

invariance is much less. Because of the shifting of vectors away from the vector on which selection occurred, **any factor whose natural position is close to the variable of selection would be more difficult to locate.** A factor is usually placed through a cluster of points; as the points scatter out, the position is less uniquely defined. A common factor model would not attempt to extend the vectors as far and hence their positions would shift less than is shown by Fig. 16.8. The common factor model, which makes some allowance for error, can be expected to be somewhat more invariant in this sense.

When the selection occurs on an individual variable, the variable is seldom orthogonal to all factors but one. In that case, the shifts in the vectors that are correlated with the selection variable will alter both factors somewhat.

In the previous discussion it was assumed that the selection of individuals leaves the shape of the score distributions essentially unaltered. Many selection procedures introduce some skew into a distribution. If skew is introduced, the correlations are lowered even more and the position of a variable is even more indefinite than is suggested by the preceding discussion (Brewer & Hills, 1969).

In Figs. 16.7 and 16.8, the variable upon which selection occurs could be considered to be a factor. The same conclusions would be drawn but, in addition, it can be noted that the zero elements in the factor matrix would remain the same for that factor. Nonzero elements could be reduced to zero elements if the selection were severe enough. In the case of extreme selection, the amount of variance attributed to the data matrix by the factor on which selection occurred may be negligible and it may not be extracted.

Thompson (1939; Thompson & Ledermann, 1939), Thurstone (1947), Ahmavaara (1954), and Meredith (1964a) have derived equations concerned with the various instances of selection. Bloxom (1968) has extended these analyses to three-mode factor-analytic situations. The following conclusions appear warranted:

1. Multivariate selection can be considered to be successive univariate selections on each of several variables. Therefore, the illustrations given previously can be used to draw some conclusions regarding multivariate selection as well.

2. The number of common factors remains the same upon partial selection, providing that the variables on which a selection occurs are not included in the analysis. If they are included, then spurious factors can result in the case of multivariate selections. Complete selection may reduce the number of factors.

3. The same simple structure can be found in any selected subpopulation as in the parent population when selection does not directly occur on the variables in the analysis and does not reduce the number of factors extracted. Note that this says that the same simple structure *can* be found but does not say that the same simple structure *will* occur. Several suggestions have

been made for rotational procedures to give invariant structures (Cattell, 1944; Cattell & Cattell, 1955; Evans, 1971; Meredith, 1964a, 1964b), but these do not appear sufficiently advanced for regular use.

Insufficient data exist to know the robustness of the preceding conclusions. It may be that present analytic rotation procedures are sufficiently invariant to provide approximate solutions or it may be that even minor selection produces enough distortion in the configuration to seriously affect invariance.

Because selection usually reduces correlations, it appears that selection is more likely to eliminate factors than to produce them. In addition, the reduction in the correlations reduces the length of the variable vectors and thus makes them somewhat more subject to error fluctuations. For reasons such as these, **the usual recommendation is to randomly sample as broadly as possible so that individuals are included from all of the population to which the results might be generalized.** It is generally assumed that variables on which any selection might have directly occurred have not been included in the analysis.

Example

Half the subjects were removed from the Grant-White sample for the ability data. The half eliminated consisted of the upper and lower quarters of variable 9, the major marker for the factor with the highest salients, A. The usual principal axis–promax analysis was carried out for four factors. The resulting correlations among factors and factor pattern are given in Table 16.2.2.

The correlations among the factors are relatively unaffected by the restrictions on the solution. The factor patterns did shift. For example, variables 1 and 13 have the following patterns:

$$v_1 = -.08A + .03B + .77C - .04D \quad \text{(all individuals)}$$
$$v_1 = .00A' - .10B' + .75C' + .10D' \quad \text{(restricted sample)}$$
$$v_{13} = -.01A + .54B + .41C - .16D \quad \text{(all individuals)}$$
$$v_{13} = -.26A' + .39B' + .51C' + .19D' \quad \text{(restricted sample)}$$

Factor C's contributions remain relatively unchanged but the other factors have shifted their contributions. For the selected sample, the fourth root is small. It is questionable whether or not the last factor would have been rotated. Extreme selection can eliminate a factor.

16.2.4 Indices and Conditions of Invariance

Comparison of the factor patterns gives a feel for the invariance of the solutions, but what if an index is desired? In that case, invariance can be defined as follows: **The factors are invariant to the degree that they produce the same factor scores when scored for the same individuals.**

Under this definition, the derivations of Chapter 13 can be brought to bear. It is then apparent that Eq. (13.2.3) applies here if the weight matrices are the result of the two different analyses and the correlation matrix is from the sample in

TABLE 16.2.2
Promax (k = 4) Ability Factors When Individuals
Have Been Systematically Selected

A. Factor Pattern

	A'	B'	C'	D'
1. Visual Perception	.00	−.10	.75	.10
2. Cubes	−.14	−.14	.63	.33
5. General Information	.29	.17	.05	.31
6. Paragraph Comprehension	.68	.06	−.02	.08
7. Sentence Completion	.68	−.05	.07	.21
8. Word Classification	.16	.15	.28	.32
9. Word Meaning	.45	−.17	.02	.40
10. Add	−.09	.96	−.21	.07
11. Code	.06	.54	−.05	.19
12. Counting Groups of Dots	−.10	.48	.16	.27
13. Straight and Curved Capitals	−.26	.39	.51	.19
14. Word Recognition	.23	.04	−.11	.82
15. Number Recognition	.06	.17	.07	.65
16. Figure Recognition	.09	.02	.20	.70
17. Object-Number	.25	.66	−.21	−.19
18. Number-Figure	.10	.51	.31	−.26
19. Figure-Word	.00	.41	.09	.16
20. Deduction	.27	−.14	.68	−.26
21. Numerical Puzzles	−.14	.46	.50	−.10
22. Problem Reasoning	.16	.09	.52	−.12
23. Series Completion	.07	−.02	.72	−.20
24. Woody-McCall Mixed Fundamentals, Form I	.08	.56	−.01	.23
25. Paper Form Board	.06	−.19	.65	.21
26. Flags	−.03	−.16	.71	.13

B. Correlations Among Factors

	A'	B'	C'	D'
A'	1.00			
B'	.56	1.00		
C'	.51	.60	1.00	
D'	.50	.55	.59	1.00

which the check for invariance is to be made. Equation (13.2.5) would apply only if one set of factors was assumed to be perfectly scored and the match made in that sample.

Example

The factors from the example computed from a reduced set of ability variables can be related to the original factors by Eq. (13.2.3). A weight matrix for the solution from the reduced set of variables was developed by the idealized variable method. The weight matrix was used with the 26-variable correlation matrix for the full sample to obtain the standard deviations. Weights of zero were given to those variables not in the factor analysis.

TABLE 16.2.3
Correlations Between Factor Scores for Full and
Reduced Variable Sets

		Factors From Reduced Variable Set			
		A'	B'	C'	D'
Factors	A	.88	.25	.40	.22
From Full	B	.38	.54	.41	−.14
Variable	C	.50	.38	.87	.62
Set	D	.39	.13	.67	.14

The weight matrix for the original factors was given in Table 12.1.2. It was used with R to determine the standard deviations.

All of the data were then used in Eq. (13.2.5). The result is given in Table 16.2.3. Factors A and C matched across the samples. Factors B and D did not match. The fourth factor from the reduced variable set appears to be more of a variant of the original factor C than of the original factor D. The effects of variable selection are not easily predicted.

From the discussion in Sections 16.2.1 and 16.2.2, the following conclusions may be drawn for the designing of a study to reproduce a previously found factor even though some selections of variables or individuals will occur:

1. The conditions set forth in Section 16.1 for the replication of the factor must be met. Too few variables, variables with low communalities, or too few individuals will guarantee that the results will look different. A study seeking invariance even though some selection will occur should be careful that the conditions for replicability are more than met. Otherwise, the differences could be from either a shift in the factors under the new conditions or from random fluctuations.

2. The selection of the variables must cover the same area as in the previous study so that the same factors have an opportunity to appear. Sampling the same factors will also prevent mislabeling when a previously found factor reappears in a new set of variables. To cover the same factor domain, four to six clear marker variables need to be included for each previous factor so that the factor can appear. If many new variables are also expected to load a factor then the new variables would probably be included in an extension analysis (cf. Section 10.5) to avoid splitting the factor in an exploratory analysis. If the selection of individuals is likely to reduce the correlations among the marker variables for a factor, then the variables should be carefully chosen so that they will cluster together even under the limits imposed by the sample of individuals. Pilot data may be needed to assure that an appropriate selection of variables has been made.

3. The selection of individuals cannot occur on any variable included in the analysis or unduly reduce the variance of the marker variables. If pilot data

suggest that the variance for a marker variable will be half that of the prior study, then serious problems may occur in the new study.

4. Selection of variables and individuals should not occur in the same study. It is difficult to predict the effects of either, and their combined effects are unknown. The problem can be reduced by limiting the factor analysis to the marker variables and holding all new variables for an extension analysis.

An implication of the conditions for factor pattern invariance is that **the selection of variables is a crucial and time-consuming step in a factor analysis.** The variables must be carefully selected and pilot work conducted to assure their adequacy. The interpretation of factors may even shift upon minor changes in the variables, as when a continuous variable is dichotomized at different points. It is no wonder that factor analysts such as Thurstone devoted as much time to variable selection and development as to the rest of the factor analysis (and this was before computers when all of the statistics were laboriously computed by clerks).

Example

The most elementary of facts about variables cannot be assumed. For example, many would assume that several measures of how well rats learn mazes would be highly correlated. Vaughn (1937) found otherwise. Table 16.2.4 gives the correlations among three measures of the performance of rats running mazes. Vaughn's (1937) conclusions on the correlations among 34 variables of rat performance were:

"In general (the correlations) are low. About 30% have an absolute value equal to or greater than .20. Only 22 of the 561 correlations are greater than .40. These small values are in accord with those ordinarily found in animal studies."

The problems are fewer in a confirmatory factor analysis. When the factors are predefined, the factor will be extracted and its position will not be as influenced by the changes in selecting variables and individuals. For example, the factor will occur at the desired order in a confirmatory analysis. Therefore, confirmatory multiple-group and maximum likelihood procedures are recommended when the design of a new study necessitates some selection. After the hypothesized factors have been extracted, the residuals can be explored for new factors.

TABLE 16.2.4
Correlations Among Measures of Rat Performance
in Mazes

	6.	7.	8.
6. Time	1.00		
7. Trials to Criterion	.22	1.00	
8. Errors	.17	.29	1.00

(Adapted from Vaughn, 1937.)

17 Factor Analysis as a Research Technique

Research proceeds by utilizing operational referents for the constructs of a theory to test if the constructs interrelate as the theory states. As previously discussed (e.g., Section 5.3), factor analysis can be used to select a representative subset of the variables, directly test interrelationships of constructs, and so forth. The present chapter includes several research applications of factor analysis that have not been sufficiently discussed in prior chapters.

A prime use of factor analysis has been in the development of both the theoretical constructs for an area and the operational representatives for the theoretical constructs, applications that are discussed in Section 17.1. But factor analysis also has other uses. On the one hand, an investigator may desire to orthogonalize his set of independent or dependent variables before computing appropriate significance tests; orthogonalization may involve factor-analytic procedures (Section 17.2). On the other hand, the data may need to be explored for potential relationships from which a theory could be built, and part of the exploration may be by factor-analytic procedures (Section 17.3). Other applications for factor analysis also exist (Section 17.4), and a concluding note is given (Section 17.5).

17.1 OPERATIONALIZATION OF CONSTRUCTS

The first task of any research program is to establish empirical referents for the abstract concepts embodied in a particular theory. Until operational representatives are developed for the constructs, it is impossible to test a theory. Or, it may be that the theory is not explicit about the constructs that are actually needed but simply refers to an area of interest. In that case the area itself will need to be analyzed for appropriate constructs before research can proceed.

Once the basic constructs in an area have been developed, then new variables can be built that will, it is hoped, measure the construct with great accuracy. It is also hoped that the measuring instruments will not be unduly correlated with other variables as identified by the theory, that is, that they will not be biased. It has been suggested that factor analysis can be helpful both in the development of the basic concepts in an area (Section 17.1.1) and in the development of appropriate composite variables, or scales, to represent the constructs (Section 17.1.2).

17.1.1 Development of Basic Concepts in an Area

If a theory has clearly defined constructs, then scales can be directly built to embody those constructs. However, it is often the case that the theories in a particular area are sufficiently undeveloped so that the constructs are not clearly identified. Whereas confirmatory factor-analytic procedures would be used if the constructs had already been defined and were being tested, exploratory factor analysis is generally used when the constructs are less well defined. Factor analysis has often been used to aid in developing appropriate constructs for an area.

It has been suggested that factor analysis is *the* way to develop constructs because it bases them on empirical data. "No more need man be a slave to the arbitrary dictates of his own theoretical biases—let the data give the constructs—factor analyze." Such advice is only partially warranted. The problem is that the selection of variables is a crucial one (cf. Section 16.2), and such an approach seldom takes this into account. When the selection of variables is poor, the results will be difficult to interpret and more of a hindrance than a help. Nowhere is the computer adage of "GIGO" (i.e., "Garbage In-Garbage Out") more warranted than in random factoring of random data.

Variable Selection for Concept Development by Factor Analysis. The factorial development of the basic concepts in a given domain needs to be based upon the proper selection of variables. To select variables, it is necessary to identify a set of potential operational representatives for whatever constructs emerge. Therefore, some theoretical perspective is necessary to select the initial set of variables just as it is necessary for gathering data to be analyzed by other techniques. The role of factor analysis is to provide an empirical analysis for the clarification of the constructs for the area.

Fortunately, almost every area of interest has had some prior research. An examination of related studies will suggest potential constructs of interest either because past findings suggest they are useful or because others who do research in the area naturally think with these constructs. **Proper variable selection**

always begins by identifying marker variables from related analyses in the literature. Ignoring the marker variable step prevents science from building upon itself.

Further selection of variables is then defined by the explication of the implicit theories in the area. Usually, the investigator proceeds by constructing the logical categories cutting across the domain. The logical categories are often multidimensional in the sense that they cut across the domain in several different and independent ways. The intersection of the categories of these dimensions forms cells or facets, each one of which is a logical area to be sampled. The hope is that sampling each cell will lead to an adequate sampling of the entire area.

Example

Guilford's (1965b) work on the nature of intelligence illustrates the facet approach. His three dimensions of logical categories are given in Fig. 17.1 and lead to a systematic sampling across the domain of intelligence. He reports reasonable success in finding a factor for many cells, although that is not a necessary result of facet sampling.

Another approach to selecting variables is to base the variable selection upon how people who have intimate contact with the domain approach it. It is assumed

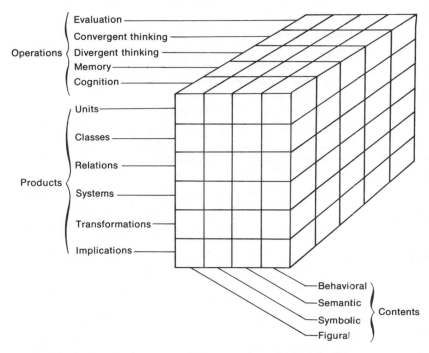

FIG. 17.1.   Theoretical model for the complete structure of intellect. (Adapted from Guilford, 1965b.)

that their experiences would have led to a consideration of the important variables within an area. The informants may be formally interviewed for their views as to the important variables or the literature might be searched for variables preexisting within the area. The question would then be that of determining exactly what constructs could be used to summarize the numerous constructs—and their variants—developed by the individual experts. The answer would be found by factoring the reported constructs. In areas such as psychology and sociology that have a proliferation of scales that knows no bounds, such analyses may be quite helpful in establishing the operational equivalency of the variables derived from many perspectives.

Example

A systematic sampling procedure was followed by Cattell (1946) in his initial research on personality. He defined his area of interest as the description of human personality and his variable domain as the descriptive terms that the English language has for personality. Factor analyzing samples from the domain of terms resulted in a limited number of dimensions that reflected the variations in laymen's descriptions of personality. Cattell also sampled the experts' constructs by factoring a representative sample of the personality questionnaires developed by psychologists. The resulting factors then summarized the culture's view of personality in as few dimensions as possible, but from both lay and psychological perspectives.

Factor-Analytic and Other Approaches to Concept Development. It can be argued that factor analysis is not the proper way to develop constructs within an area. Instead, the development of theoretical constructs could proceed first from the intuitively obvious ones. The intuitive categories would be used to explain as much of the empirical phenomena in an area as possible. And when these intuitively obvious constructs broke down, then a new construct would be suggested and analyzed.

Although such a critical position has some validity, factor analysts answer that what is "intuitively obvious" to one is not to another, and that intuitively obvious distinctions may not be empirically verifiable. Psychology, with its history of "faculties," then "instincts," and finally "personality traits," could be cited as an example of an area that needs help in the development of constructs. Unfortunately, the factor-analytic solutions offered for the personality area have not been widely accepted even though several factors have been widely confirmed (Sells, Demaree, & Will, 1970). Therefore, the power of factor analysis to aid in the development of constructs cannot be proved in this area. Whether this is the fault of the factor analyses or of most psychologists' continued faith in their own intuition is debatable, but the latter is certainly a factor.

It is true that within some areas of psychology factor analysis has had reasonable success in developing constructs. Thurstone's (1938) primary mental abilities, which consist of such dimensions as verbal comprehension, word fluency, numerical ability, visual relations, reasoning, and so forth, are widely accepted as is his second-order factor that matches Spearman's general intelligence. Further work in intelligence (Cattell, 1963; Horn, 1972; Horn & Cattell, 1967) has improved on Thurstone's constructs by adding those of fluid and crystallized intelligence. Osgood's (Osgood, Suci, & Tannenbaum, 1957) analysis of meaning, which gave rise to factors such as evaluation, activity, and potency, has been helpful and widely accepted in the areas of human judgment and social psychology. Although those technically competent in these areas will continue to develop and improve the concepts, the factors have established themselves as part of psychology's general paradigms. Factor analysis can be expected to be useful in establishing other conceptual paradigms as well.

Factor-Analytic Theories.   When factor analysis is extensively used in a given substantive area, the results are often subsumed under the general heading of a "factor-analytic theory." In the area of intellectual development, factor theories have been associated with names such as Spearman, Burt, Thompson, Thurstone, Cattell, and Guilford. Cattell and Eysenck are said to have factor-analytic theories of personality. The name arises from the prominent use of factor analysis in establishing the taxonomy of a given domain and indicates the similarity of technique across the several investigators.

However, the term factor-analytic theory is a misnomer. Factor-analytic theory by definition refers to the statistical procedure of analyzing data by factor analysis and not to theories of any substantive area. The results of factor analyses give rise to a set of variables that will, hopefully, be interrelated in causative and explanatory ways by a theoretical–empirical analysis. The result, a theory whose constructs are represented by a set of measurement operations, is a theory just as any other theory that was not developed with the aid of factor analysis. Indeed, after the theory is completely developed, **the student being given an elementary introduction to the substantive area need never know that factor analysis was prominent in the development of the constructs used.** Naturally, the advanced student will need to evaluate the appropriateness of the procedures used to establish the constructs, just as she or he would need to evaluate how any other set of constructs arose.

To have found the factors in a given area does not explain that area. As Thurstone (1947) and Cattell (1946, 1957) have pointed out, research on constructs is only the preliminary step in a thorough investigation and understanding of the phenomena. Although the descriptive results are an important addition to man's knowledge, a full scientific program follows description with explanation to build the actual theory.

Example

Wimberley (1978) was interested in construct development in two areas: religion and politics. Because he felt that both areas would function the same as they both were manifestations of values, he established equivalent variables in each of the areas. Because two domains of possible constructs were involved, he factored each separately although the data were collected from everyone. First-order factor analyses suggested that there were six domains within each of the two areas: belief, knowledge, experience, private behavior, behavior, and social interaction. Although the exact items differed from religion to politics, the items in each area could be grouped under these headings. For example, the factor of religious private behavior included Bible reading and private prayer, whereas this factor in the area of politics was composed of items concerned with voting, a behavior that is private in the sense that no one else knows how we vote unless we tell them. Wimberley's conclusion is, therefore, that the same basic factors could be found in both the religious and political areas although, of course, the manifestation of each was unique to its own domain.

The factors in each domain were intercorrelated, and second-order factors extracted. The second-order factors were distinct and different for each of the two domains. In the domain of religion, the first second-order factor grouped conservative belief with experience and behavior. The second factor was principally a knowledge factor. In the domain of politics, the first factor combined knowledge and active behavior with social interactions, whereas the second factor was principally liberal versus conservative.

Analyzing two domains led Wimberley to conclude that the constructs were the same for both domains at the first-order level but diverged at the second-order level. He was further curious about the relationship between the two domains, so Wimberley computed factor scores within each domain and found the correlations between religious and political factor scores. Because the correlations between the two domains were not influenced by the factor analyses, these were ordinary correlation coefficients and were tested for significance. The highest correlation was found between political liberalism and religious liberalism.

This study illustrates several worthwhile points. First, the study was heavily based on the past literature regarding the conceptualization of the religious domain. The items were selected to represent possible dimensions as suggested by other investigators . The factors that resulted were then directly related to the conceptualizations of the past investigators, with the results being of considerable interest for the construct development of the areas. Second, the two domains were factored separately so that the intercorrelations among them would not influence the factors, and hence the resulting factors were appropriate to each domain. Third, higher-order factor analyses were also carried out. Fourth, the relationships between the two domains were found by correlating factor scores. Thus the study provides an example not only of using factor analyses of items based upon past investigations to test for proposed factors in a domain but also provides very distinctive information regarding the interrelationships between two domains.

17.1.2 Factor Analysis in the Development of New Variables

Using factor analysis to aid in developing operational representatives for the constructs differs from the use of factor analysis to develop the basic constructs only in emphasis. The two are inseparable because any factor analysis will provide some test of the constructs in the area whereas that same factor analysis can be used to evaluate methods of measuring the factor. Using factor analysis for measurement development assumes that some constructs are already outlined in the area; it is an attempt to sharpen those constructs sufficiently so that they can be adequately measured.

In a series of factor analyses, the emphasis often shifts more and more to the finding and identifying of a composite variable for each factor that would measure the factor so well that only the composite would be needed in future research. Although each future study could define the factor by computing a factor analysis, the development of a composite variable for each concept allows a wider range of statistical analyses to be conveniently conducted. The composite variable is often in the form of a scale (cf. Nunnally, 1978, for the characteristics of a scale).

Factor-Analytic Scale Development.   No special factoring procedures are necessary for scale development. The techniques discussed earlier would be used as appropriate. Usually the series of studies would begin with exploratory factor analyses. As knowledge of the possible factors and scales accumulated, particular factors would come to be expected. The later stages of such a series of factor analyses would use confirmatory factor-analytic procedures to test the quality of potential scales.

If factor analysis is used to develop scales from a set of individual items in, for example, a survey questionnaire, the lower reliabilities of individual items as compared to the usual factor-analytic variable must be recognized. The low reliabilities place an upper bound on the communalities, and the common factor model would be more appropriate than the component model. As previously noted, factors from variables with lower communalities will be more difficult to replicate due to the error components. Therefore, factors are extracted more cautiously from items and more research is needed that focuses upon the replicating of the factors. For this reason, it is not good to identify the constructs in an area by the factoring of items and then build scales from the same factor analysis. One study should factor the items simply to define the constructs in the area, and another study, with new items written to test the interpretations of these constructs, should be used to develop the scales. Because of possible difficulty factors, oblique rotation with higher-order factor analysis is essential.

A common error is to fail to consider the interaction of the selection of initial variables and the definition of the factor(s). For example, if all the variables in the analysis are attempts to measure just one concept, then the first unrotated principal factor will define the concept as a function of all the variables in the analysis. The principal factor can be used as a criterion by which a composite variable would be formed to represent the construct. However, it could be that a subset of the variables is known to be closely related to the construct and that the construct would be better expressed as a function of the subset than as a function of all the variables in the total matrix. The other variables are included in the hope of finding some of them that may be more related to the construct defined by the subset than is any variable from within the subset itself. The appropriate procedure would be to place a multiple-group factor through that subset. Simple structure rotation would *only* be appropriate for scale construction if the variables were assumed to represent a set of qualitatively distinct constructs at the first-order level with any broader construct appearing in a higher-order analysis.

Potential Advantages of Factor-Analytically Developed Measures.   The expected advantages of using factor analysis in the development of measuring instruments are several. For example, each variable is correlated with the factor it is expected to measure and with all the other factors at the same time in S_{vf}. This allows a ready analysis of the extent to which a given variable may measure more factors than is desirable. Few item analysis programs compute a matrix of this nature; instead they compute only the correlations of the items with a single factor as represented by the total score or an outside criterion.

The most important characteristic expected of factor-analytically developed variables is that they would include a maximum amount of the area's information in a minimum number of constructs. This is definitely advantageous for future research because the number of variables that need to be included in any study is thereby kept at a minimum.

Factor-analytic variables are also expected to have lower correlations among variables than would variables developed by other procedures. Low correlations among scales are expected even when the factors are rotated obliquely because the correlations among factors are never allowed to be very high.

The low correlations among composite variables based on factors make the usual statistical procedures, such as regression analysis, analysis of variance, and profile analysis, easier to apply. If the correlations among scales are low, then a variable's correlation and beta weight with the criterion will be more alike and the interpretation easier. If two variables correlate highly and an analysis of variance is to be computed, many individuals must be dropped from the analysis to gain the necessary equal or proportional cell frequencies. Variables with lower intercorrelations will fit into such research designs more efficiently.

The expected advantages of factor-analytically developed scales do not necessarily include, it should be noted, greater ease of interpretation. Unless a program of factor-analytic studies is pursued, the usual analysis would leave several factors with, at best, tentative interpretations. Although such difficulties of interpretation temporarily increase the theoretical problems, they may be offset by the more limited number of variables that result from a factor-analytic study. With fewer variables, each variable may be researched more carefully.

Factor-Analytic and Other Approaches to Variable Development.   There have been several studies comparing scales developed from a factor-analytic approach with those developed from some other approach. The results are generally as expected. For example, Hase and Goldberg (1967) found the factor scales to have the highest internal consistency reliability. Butt and Fiske (1968) also found factorial scales to have adequate internal consistencies; the correlations among scales were somewhat lower than scales developed by an intuitive, rational procedure. They pointed out that when the sampling of variables was guided by a systematic facet model, rather than simply including a group of items thought to possibly measure the concept, the internal consistencies were somewhat higher. In both studies the scales from factor-analytic procedures had correlations with other variables outside of the domain that were as high as or higher than scales from other procedures. Horst (1968b) also examined personality data for both rational and factor scales and argues for the latter.

Goldberg (1972) does note that the preceding conclusions hold only if capitalization on chance is kept to a minimum in the factor-analytic studies. Factor-analytic scales can be expected to be advantageous only if the factors are clearly defined, the sample of individuals is large, and the scoring procedures are kept simple because these conditions reduce possibilities for capitalizing on chance (Wackwitz & Horn, 1971).

A decision to use or not use factor-analytic procedures in the development of new variables to represent constructs appears to center around two questions: How easily interpretable should the scales be in the immediate future for the uninitiated? To what extent should the area be covered with a relatively few scales? To the extent that the second question is more critical than the first, the usual factor-analytic procedures would need to be followed. To the extent that the first is more important than the second, then rationally based scales may be more appropriate. The use of factor analysis after a systematic rational analysis to guide item selection is essentially a facet approach; it tends to give some of the advantages of pure factor scales and pure rational scales.

In the present discussion, "factor analysis" has been used to refer to procedures such as principal axis factoring and rotation. From the broader concept of the multivariate linear model presented in Chapter 2, it is apparent that most traditional procedures recommended for scale development, as in Nunnally (1978), are basically factorial in nature. When, for example, a set of correlations is calculated between individual items and a total score from those items, it is the same as correlating the items with an equivalently defined factor. Indeed, if the variables are all converted to standard scores before they are summed to give the total score, the results of a centroid factor analysis and the usual item analysis procedure would be identical.

Another example of an implicit factor analysis would be the case where the variables are correlated with an outside criterion, and those variables correlating highest are selected to form a new variable. The procedure is identical to placing a diagonal factor through the criterion in a correlation matrix that includes all the variables and the criterion as well. Personality tests such as the MMPI and the California Personality Inventory are of this type.

Indeed, it seems that the choice is not between factor-analytically developed scales and scales developed by "ordinary" statistical procedures but rather in the kind of factor-analytic scales that are developed. **The usual scale development procedures are implicit factor analyses.**

17.2 FACTOR ANALYSIS OF INDEPENDENT AND DEPENDENT VARIABLES

A factor analysis of the variables may be useful before other statistical procedures are applied to the data. The factor scores would then be submitted for an analysis of variance, multiple discriminate analysis, multiple regression analysis, chi-square, or some other statistical procedure. The aim is to produce a more powerful or more interpretable basic analysis. Factor analysis can be used with either the independent or dependent variables (Sections 17.2.1 and 17.2.2, respectively) or both (Section 17.2.3).

17.2.1 Factor Analysis of Independent Variables

To Increase the Degrees of Freedom.   In a multiple regression analysis, the combination of the independent variables or predictors that will best predict the dependent variable or criterion is computed. Because the procedure uses any and all variables that might help, there is the possibility of capitalizing upon chance: A variable with a chance correlation with the criterion will be given an unwarranted weight. The more variables available as predictors, the more likely it is that one with a high but chance correlation with the dependent variable will occur. For this reason, the degrees of freedom of a multiple correlation are corrected for the number of predictors.

Inasmuch as the same information can be conveyed in a smaller number of variables, the possibilities of capitalizing upon chance will be decreased and the degrees of freedom will be increased. Goldberg (1972) points out that the degrees of freedom problem is more serious than even statisticians generally assume it to be.

Horst (1965) has suggested that factor analysis be used to increase the degrees of freedom by reducing the number of independent variables or predictors. The total set of predictors would be factored into a smaller number of factors and the resulting factor scores used to predict the criterion. The factor scores are often computed by one of the more accurate procedures in which a score is based on all the variables.

Following Horst's suggestion assumes that all of the predictive variance is also variance that overlaps among the predictors. Such would be the case only if predictors had been deliberately selected so that they were multiple attempts to measure the predictor variance and not selected so that they were mutually exclusive attempts to measure that variance. If the former is the case, common factor analysis is used, and there will probably be little loss in predictability. In the latter case a factor analysis is inappropriate to increase the degrees of freedom.

Another approach to increasing the degrees of freedom would be to use factor analysis to identify a representative subsample of the total set of variables. Each selected variable would be as pure a measure of the factor as could be found among that factor's salients or by the procedure of Chapter 5. The result would be a representative set of predictors with very little overlap that would use as few degrees of freedom as possible. Note, however, that one may also want to carry along any variable with high reliability but low communality because the specific factor in such a variable could be quite important in predicting the criterion.

In the case where the predictors do share variance and most of the predictable variance of the criterion comes from overlap among the predictors, Horst argues that factor analysis would usually reduce error variance more than predictive variance. He does not discuss any possible loss of degrees of freedom because of capitalizing upon chance in the factor analysis. If the factor analysis is performed upon the same data on which the multiple regression is finally run, some capitalization upon chance would occur that would not be taken into account in the formula for degrees of freedom. It would appear to be better to factor the variables in a separate sample and then score for the factors in a new sample to evaluate the prediction. Morris and Guertin (1977) evaluated this technique and found only negligible loss of prediction by using factors instead of variables, and also found better generalization to a new sample for the factor weights than for the variable weights, particularly when the implicit multiple-group factor scoring procedure was used (Morris, 1979, 1980). This has been confirmed by Cotter and Raju (1982).

To Combine and Divide Overlapping Variances. When a study involves several independent variables, they are often intercorrelated. The correlations indicate variance that two or more of the variables have in common. Factor analyzing the variables before the prediction study encourages combining measures that have overlapping variance. As Gordon (1968) and Gorsuch (1973b) have pointed out, multiple regression analysis leads to a selection of only one variable from several essentially parallel forms and does not indicate that increased accuracy and interpretability may occur if the parallel forms are combined. A factor analysis would indicate how to combine the overlapping variables to gain that increased accuracy and interpretability.

It may also be useful to divide the overlapping variances among the independent variables. When several overlapping predictors all correlate with a criterion, it is difficult to know if each adds significant variance to the prediction or if each is significant solely because the variance they share is related to the criterion. Factor-analytic techniques can divide the overlapping variances so that this ambiguity is reduced. As Gorsuch (1973b) shows, the distributing of the overlapping variances to the variables often allows for more interpretable significance tests.

If diagonal analysis is used to extract the factors, they are extracted according to a predetermined order to distribute the overlapping variance. Two different principles could guide the ordering by which the factors are extracted. First, the variables could be subdivided according to the theoretical level of causation. If, logically, variable X can overlap with Y because X can produce Y but never vica versa, then the overlapping variance in prediction would need to be attributed to X. Such might be the case in the study of genetic and environmental influences on behavior. The environment cannot affect the genetic structure except under unusual circumstances, and any individuals subjected to such situations would be systematically eliminated from the data matrix. The overlap between genetic and environmental variables could then be generally attributed to the genetic component, and so any genetically oriented variables would be extracted before the environmentally oriented ones.

Second, the ease of manipulation and control of the variables may determine the distribution of overlapping variance. Here the direction of causation is assumed to be reversible. For example, the attempt may be to predict and control erosion along a river. If the study included an easily changed variable, such as the rate of water flow through a valley, and a difficult-to-change variable, such as the amount of rain falling in a valley, all of the overlap between these two predictor variables would probably be attributed to the variable that is easier to change. In this case the rate of water flow through the valley would be the first factor because it is easier to build dams than it is to stop the rain. The residual variance attributable to the rainfall factor would also be correlated with the criterion as a second variable uncorrelated with the first. The weight given the easier-to-control variable would indicate the maximum impact one could exert through it; the weight given to the other variable would indicate the extent of increased control gained from manipulating the more-difficult-to-control variable after the easier-to-control variable had already been used.

A variation on the second principle is to divide the variance according to the ease of data collection. Using ease of data collection as a criterion is particularly helpful in a situation requiring a selection of individuals, such as employment or college admissions. Usually the question is to find the additional variance that can be predicted from adding a battery of new variables to that data which is always collected and available. The collected and available data would include such variables as sex, age, and, in a job selection situation, the applicant's previous employment history. By knowing the additional prediction that occurs from a new procedure, its usefulness in applied situations can be evaluated. The result would be an analysis where the first diagonal factor would be placed through the easiest-to-collect and most readily available data of theoretical importance, the second factor would be defined by the next-easiest-to-collect variable, and so on. The results would indicate the increased prediction gained by moving to the more expensive data collection procedures.

Note that although the present discussion includes only diagonal factors, successive multiple-group factors would be extracted by the same principles guiding diagonal factor analysis. The ordering could, for example, specify extracting one diagonal factor, then three group factors to be extracted as a set, and so forth. Gorsuch (1973b) indicates how other factor-analytic procedures—such as higher-order image analysis—can be useful aids to dividing variance that several predictors have in common.

As can be seen from the several ways that have been suggested as illustrations of how factor analysis may be used with independent variables, the exact procedure would differ depending upon the situation. Although this might initially appear to be a disadvantage, it is better conceptualized as an advantage or a fact of life. One's theory always influences the research, and the point would be to test the efficacy of different theoretical decompositions of the overlapping variance to compare their usefulness. It is also an advantage in the same sense that several theories may need to utilize the same data from different perspectives, and a flexible factoring approach allows differential utilization.

Examples

Fleishman and Hempel (1954) were interested in the relationships of factorially derived dimensions of abilities as independent variables in analyzing a complex tracking task. Their analysis included factoring abilities, and the factors appeared to confirm those previously found in the analysis of Air Force men's abilities.

They then related the abilities to performance on the task at different stages. Some of their results are summarized by Fig. 17.2 where each line represents the percentage of variance in the task accounted for by that factor at each of eight stages of practice. Examination of the figure shows, for example, that the several factors of visual ability are predictive at early stages but not at later stages. Perhaps the most important change in contribution by a factor is that of an ability specific to this complex coordination task; this experience-oriented ability increases sharply in the first five trial blocks and then levels off. Fleishman and Hempel's type of analysis can be used to answer questions such as the importance of generalized traits and job specific abilities in predicing performance at different points in time.

Another example where factor analysis has clarified the independent variables is the area of physique where psychologists have been concerned with the relationship of physique to personality. Some have seen both physique and personality as having common biological roots, but such approaches are not currently popular. Instead, contemporary views of the relationship between physique and personality stress, for example, the role that a person's physique has in determining how others relate to him—that is, the social stimulus value of one's physique to others—and how the treatment that results shapes one's own personality.

To analyze the relationship of physique to personality requires that physique be measured. Because physique can be measured in numerous ways, factor analyses have been conducted to determine the dimensions that need to be considered. One of the examples previously used in this book factored the dimensions of physique. The results of our factor analyses are similar to others in the field that show that it can be represented with two dimensions: height and circumference (Eysenck, 1969). The two dimensions correlate and form a second-order factor of size. These dimensions are the basis for many scores computed in contemporary psychological theory concerned with physique. The factor analyses of physique, therefore, have provided a basis for a set of simple, independent variables that are being used in further research.

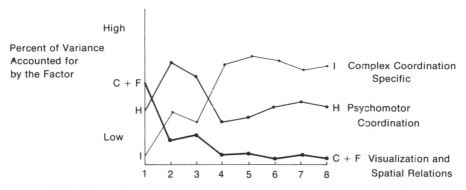

FIG. 17.2.   Predictive power of factors at different stages of learning. (Adapted from Fleishman & Hempel, 1954.)

17.2.2 Factor Analysis of Dependent Variables

In many studies, there are multiple dependent variables. The impact of the independent variables on the dependent variables is sought through the use of significance tests. A problem arises when the various dependent variables are intercorrelated, as often occurs. In that case, a series of tests of significance to each of the dependent measures will not produce independent significance tests. Because the dependent variables overlap, each significance test is examining the effect of the independent variables on both that portion of the variable that overlaps with the other dependent variables and the independent portion. The overlap is tested numerous times when statistical analyses are run on each of the correlated dependent variables.

When dependent variables overlap, the significance levels cannot be interpreted in the usual fashion. If 20 dependent variables were involved, then finding the hypothesized relationship between the independent variable and 10 of the dependent variables to be significant could mean more or less than it seems. For illustration, consider the case where the 10 variables that produce significant results all correlate 1.0. Then the same significance test is repeated 10 times and the significance of the total result would be the p value of the statistic for any individual test. However, if these 10 variables were all uncorrelated, the analyses would provide 10 independent confirmations of the hypothesis. If each significance level were exactly .05, the probability of all these occurring by chance would be lower than the probability of any one occurring. In this case, the actual significance is estimated to be less than .001 (Winer, 1962, pp. 43–45).

Orthogonalization of the dependent variables will provide for independent tests significance. Although the number of possible orthogonalizations through factor-analytic procedures is limited primarily by man's imagination, several specific procedures appear to be natural candidates for use in this situation.

First, the dependent variables could be orthogonalized with each variable as a factor. The easiest procedure is to simply extract all principal components from the correlations, rotate the components to varimax simple structure, and compute factor scores. The full component model is used because all the variance of each variable is to be included. In every case that has extracted as many factors as variables and rotated to varimax, the rotated factors were each loaded by one obviously salient variable. Thus, each factor represented an orthogonalized version of one of the original dependent variables. Component scores would be orthogonal and would represent the best simple structure orthogonal approximation to the original set of variables.

Another procedure would be to extract principal components and leave the components unrotated. A test of the first principal component would then test whether or not the maximum variance in common among the variables was significantly predicted by the experimental conditions or other independent variables. Additional tests could be run on each of the successive principal components. The procedure would be similar to a multivariate analysis of variance, but it is difficult to see the results as interpretable unless a general factor could be assumed to exist.

The standard factor-analytic procedures with rotation to orthogonal simple structure and the calculation of factor scores could be used (Gorsuch, 1973b). Inasmuch as simple structure factors are considered to be more interpretable, the significance test results should also be more interpretable. If the common factors are scored, Anderson and Rubin's procedure for generating truly uncorrelated factor scores would be used (cf. Section 12.1.2). Only well-replicated factors should be used so that the findings are interpretable.

Examples

A detailed analysis of the dependent variables for a complex tracking task has been reported by Tucker (1967). He used data from Parker and Fleishman (1960) in a three-mode factor analysis.

Each individual subject was required to keep a marker on a moving target by adjusting a rudder stick and foot pedals, much as in flying a small airplane. Several measures of accuracy were taken across 10 sets of trials for use as the dependent variables.

Factor analyses indicated that there were two kinds of accuracy: accuracy of direction and accuracy introduced by proper hand–foot coordination. Analyses of accuracy factors in relationship to the trials showed an interesting phenomenon: in the early practice stages the two accuracy factors were negatively correlated because, it appears, attending to one type of accuracy prevents attending to the other. In the later practice stages the factors were positively correlated as attending to them became more automatic. The types of accuracy and their changing relationship to the trials may not have been noted if the accuracy measures had not been factored before being related to the trials.

Eysenck (1969) has produced factor analyses of personality. These analyses have produced factors such as anxiety and extraversion that parallel second-order factors in Cattell's personality questionnaires and that have been used as dependent measures for research. For example, one of Eysenck's interests has been in the relationship of physique to personality. Rather than taking a large number of arbitrary measures of the independent and dependent variables, he has chosen to use the factor-analytically based measures of both physique and personality. By so doing, he has been able to concentrate the research on the major dimensions of both areas.

The research on the relationship of physique to personality has usually contrasted the slim person (i.e., one who has a high score on the height factor relative to his score on the circumference factor) with the stout person (who has a high score on the circumference factor relative to the height factor). Although the relationships are generally too small to have significance in everyday affairs, the trend is clear: slim people tend to be more introverted and anxious than others, whereas the stout person tends to be more extroverted. In addition, slim people tend to be slightly brighter (Eysenck, 1969). These findings are consistent with and probably caused by society's stereotypes.

17.2.3 Factor Analysis of Both Independent and Dependent Variables

A major problem with multivariate techniques such as MANOVA and canonical correlations is the difficulty of interpretation. Canonical variables, for example, show the same interpretation problems as do unrotated principal factors. Separate factor analysis of independent and dependent variables followed by canonical analysis of factor scores results in greater interpretability because each variable set is orthogonalized and fewer variables are in the canonical analysis. Morris and Guertin (1975) provide an example of such an analysis. Skinner (1977) discusses other techniques to apply in this situation, including interbattery factor analysis.

Confirmatory factor analysis is the most powerful technique available for analyzing the relationship between sets of independent and dependent variables [Bentler (1980) and Kenny (1979) present these causal model analyses in detail]. This technique has the advantage of reducing the impact of random error of measurement and, for many cases, of reducing bias in measurement as well. The result is a more elegant test of hypotheses than is available with almost any other technique.

17.3 USING FACTOR ANALYSIS TO SUGGEST NEW LEADS FOR FUTURE RESEARCH

Exploratory factor analyses are usually undertaken to examine the area so that the next research study might be more powerful. A thorough analysis of the pilot data often suggests many new leads that can be followed up in the next study. An examination of the predictors and criterion variables by factor analysis will often help in an exploratory study.

When the predictors or independent variables are not perfectly related to the criteria or dependent variables, the lack of prediction can come from several sources. Among the causes may be the fact that the independent variables contain unwanted variance that is confusing the prediction. Or it may be that the criteria have variance among themselves that is unrelated to the predictor variables. A factor analysis of the criteria and predictors together will aid in teasing out these two sources of possible error.

The procedure for factoring could be the usual simple structure approach applied to a matrix containing both the predictors and the criteria. Table 17.3.1 presents a hypothetical factor matrix from such an analysis. The first set of variables load factors *A*, *B*, and *C*. The second set, the criteria or dependent variables, load factors *A*, *B*, and *D*. Factor *C* is unwanted but reliable variance in the predictors and suggests that a new variable is needed that is either pure *A* or *C*. If the new variable loaded only *A*, it should predict better than the present variables because it is uncontaminated by factor *C*. If the new variable were predominantly *C*, then it would be used to correct the present variables for the unwanted variance. Factor *D* is predictable variance presently missed for which a new predictor is needed.

Other factoring procedures could also be used. For example, the prime interest may lie in one of the criteria rather than in the overlapping variance among criteria, as was assumed in the preceding paragraph. In that case, a diagonal factor would be extracted for the criterion and the predictor variables examined in relationship to it. Successive diagonal factors could be extracted for each of the criteria so that the relationship of the predictors to each of these successive criterion factors could be examined. Factors among the criteria not currently predicted would be obvious. Unwanted variance among the predictors would be in the residual matrix of predictors after all the diagonal factors for the criteria

TABLE 17.3.1

Variables		*Factors*			
		A	*B*	*C*	*D*
Independent	1.	X		X	
	2.	X		X	
	3.	−X	X		
	4.		X		
	5.	X		X	
Dependent	1.	X			X
	2.	X	X		
	3.	X			X
	4.	X			X

had been extracted. The residual matrix could be factored and rotated to simply structure to better understand the unwanted variance so that tests can be designed without it or to correct for it.

17.4   OTHER USES OF FACTOR ANALYSIS

Numerous other applications of factor analysis have occasionally appeared. Boruch, Larkin, Wolins and MacKinney (1970), and Boruch and Wolins (1970), as well as others, utilize factor analysis to separate the variance in variables that comes from the method used to measure the construct as opposed to the variance from the construct itself. Cattell (1970b), Hegmann and DeFries (1970), and Royce (1957) divide the variance of behavior into genetic and environmental components by factor analysis. Woodbury, Clelland, and Hickey (1963), and Horst (1968a) solve for missing elements of a data matrix by factor analysis. Haertzen (1966) examined the effects of LSD-25 on factor structures. The imaginative mind finds many applications for factor analysis.

Example

Barnard has been using factor analysis in a manner somewhat different than that previously described. He and his associates use it to score the individuals in his research. For example, Gardner and Barnard (1969) were interested in the impact of intelligence on the perception of others. The independent variable was intellectual ability; mentally retarded, normal, and intellectually gifted children formed the levels of this variable.

The dependent measures were factorially derived scores but in an unusual sense. Each individual rated a series of 34 pictures on 15 semantic differential scales. Each individual's data were separately factored and rotated. One score computed was the degree to which a standard number of factors accounted for the variance on each individual subject's use of the adjective scales.

An analysis of variance showed that the retardates had a weaker structure than did nonretardates. Even though the retardates used the semantic scales just as reliably or consistently as did the nonretardates, their perceptions were less organized because the same number of factors accounted for less variance than was the case with the brighter groups.

However, just because a formal factor analysis can be applied does not mean it should be applied. Because capitalization on chance can occur and estimates of how the solution would vary across samples are lacking, other statistic procedures will often be given preference over factor analysis. A simple sum of standard scores across a set of variables is, for example, usually as useful a measure of a general factor as is the first principal component, but the scoring procedure is more generalizable and the analyses are easier to follow. Such simple factor analyses are to be preferred if a choice is available and the interpretations can be expected to be the same.

17.5   CONCLUDING NOTE

The discussions in this chapter have been principally illustrated with exploratory factor analyses for historical reasons. Exploratory factor analysis has developed first and therefore more examples are available with it. However, none of the uses outlined previously are intrinsically related to exploratory factor analysis rather than confirmatory factor analysis. Confirmatory factor analysis is necessary for each of the purposes outlined.

When operationalizing constructs, a theoretical model of the construct is often available and can be readily developed. Whenever that is the case, then confirmatory factor analysis is the appropriate technique to choose over exploratory factor analysis. This includes cases of establishing constructs and of scale development. Such confirmatory factor analyses will often allow for many of the advantages of rational scale construction as well as the empirical data-based analyses, for there are always multiple rotation positions in exploratory analyses that fit the data and it is best to take the position that fits our constructs; confirmatory factor analysis allows one to do this explicitly.

Confirmatory factor analysis is also appropriate when analyzing independent and dependent variable sets. Here again, a particular factor structure can often be hypothesized and then tested with the confirmatory model. Confirmatory factor analysis is particularly important for analyzing the relationships between a set of factors that function as independent variables and a set of factors representing dependent variables through causal modeling (Bentler, 1980).

18 Epilogue

The usefulness of factor analysis for research has been and is debated. Indeed, there are those who would question whether it can be used in research at all. It seems appropriate at this point to examine present practices and their criticisms in the light of the recommendations made in the preceding chapters. Some of the criticisms are examined in a discussion of the present usage of factor analysis (Section 18.1). It will be found that a number of the criticisms that have been applied are quite appropriate, given the way factor analysis is often utilized. We shall then move boldly in Section 18.2 and outline the steps to be involved in a standard factor analysis, steps that will hopefully avoid some of the pitfalls seen in past research. Some brief comments on the future of factor analysis are given in Section 18.3.

18.1   CRITICISMS OF PRESENT FACTOR-ANALYTIC PRACTICES

Because of the versatility of factor analysis, the complexities in selecting the proper procedures, and the readily available "little jiffy" computer programs,[1] there is a wide range in the quality of factor-analytic studies currently reported. Although numerous studies are well thought out and make solid contributions, it is still true that studies are reported in the literature where factor analysis has probably been misused (Comrey, 1978; Skinner, 1980).

---

[1]A "little jiffy" computer program extracts the principal components with roots ≥ 1 and rotates them to the varimax criterion (Kaiser, 1970). It is often the only factor-analytic program available at a computer center.

seen factor-analytic studies that reported a higher-order analysis from arimax factors. The investigators seem to have done the impossible by from an identity matrix. It appears that the varimax factors were scored by an est... procedure. Because the estimation procedure did not compute the factor scores exactly, the resulting estimated factor scores were somewhat correlated and these correlations were factored. Theoretically, either the error in the estimation procedure was factored or the correlations among implicit multiple-group factors were analyzed. There was nothing in the articles that suggested that the investigators knew that the varimax factor loadings were inconsistent with their higher-order analysis or that told the reader why higher order factors were appropriate.

McNemar (1951) has reported his view of what could be called "errors by factor analysts." Although he based his critique on the research of that period, most of the criticisms still hold true for contemporary research. They are points that any investigator expecting to use factor analysis should ponder. McNemar's criticisms are as follows:

1. The results vary considerably across studies because of unstable correlations from small sample sizes.
2. The lower bounds for interpreting the results are not based on any sampling considerations.
3. Although a general factor solution is warranted by the data, a rotation procedure such as varimax was used that carefully avoids it. The opposite error is to use the first factor as a general factor even though nonchance evidence for the existence of a general factor does not exist in the data.
4. Numerous variables of low reliability are included in the analysis. The variables are usually factored by a component analysis.
5. The postulates of the particular factor-analytic procedure used, particularly that of the experimental independence of the variables, are ignored.
6. The results must be predestined because every time two or three variables marking a factor go into the data matrix, that factor always occurs in the interpretation.
7. At one extreme, the variables being factored come from an area so small that nothing is learned. The other extreme consists of studies that include variables from such a wide range of areas that nothing is intercorrelated.
8. Some variables are carefully chosen to aid in interpreting the factors, whereas others are just as carefully ignored. The variable selection involves "super insight" or ESP into the operations of chance so that a .10 loading is interpreted but a .20 loading on the same factor is ignored as random.

McNemar also notes the general struggle in which all factor analysts are involved. The struggle is that of interpreting the factors. The struggle of interpretation forms McNemar's most telling criticism and one that is still applicable to many studies.

The struggle to interpret factors reflects what is probably the prime contribution of factor analysis that has been overlooked. The concepts identified by factor analysis that are the same as previous concepts do not add greatly to an area, but the serendipitous results could, with further research, aid in the development of the substantive area. However, many factor analyses are not part of an ongoing research program. So even though a new factor is identified, it is not the target of research studies designed to clarify its nature and meaning, and the serendipitous results are lost.

Studies to tease out the meaning of a new factor may be factor analytic or could consist of analyses of variance between appropriate groups or other standard research procedures. Once the factor is clarified and appropriate measurement techniques are available, then the causes producing the factor and the factor's impact in the area can be further investigated.

Other criticisms can also be made of the way factor analysis is practiced. These include:

1. **It is assumed that the factors from one particular research study are** *the* **factors.** As Overall (1964) and Armstrong (1967) have empirically demonstrated, one need not find the dimensions that best summarize the data from a known theoretical perspective. Indeed, interpretable factors can be easily found in random data (Horn, 1967; Armstrong & Soelberg, 1968) if appropriate precautions are not taken. Factors become recognized factors only upon replication and integration into a theoretical network.

2. **Insufficient attention is given to the selection of variables.** The factors are interpreted by examining the variables, and so the variables aid the interpretations only if they are interpretable. Proper selection of variables also determines what factors can appear and at what level. Considerable thought needs to be given to the inclusion of each variable and its probable impact on the solution.

3. **Research studies often fail to report what was actually done in sufficient detail so that the analysis can be approximated in another study.** In 40 factor-analytic studies published during 1966 in A.P.A. journals, less than half indicated how the number of factors were decided or what was used in the main diagonal of the correlation matrix. Approximately three-fourths of the studies indicated the method by which the factors were initially extracted and the type of rotation, but a full fourth did not. Even the number of individuals was not reported in several studies. Although some of the studies were brief reports where detailed discussions would not be expected, it does appear that other investigators would have a difficult time replicating many factor-analytic studies published in the major psychological journals. We simply would not know how they were done. This appears to be, in part, a fault of journal editors because they have failed to request that the appropriate information be included.

4. **There appears to be a heavy reliance on programmed factor-analytic procedures used because of their availability rather than because the study was designed for that type analysis.** To use a programmed factor-analytic

procedure is more desirable than writing a new one because the costs are greatly reduced, but the investigator should understand the programs available and design his research accordingly. Usually designing for a type of analysis is easy in the early stages of the development of the study. Perhaps it should be mandatory that a computer quiz a researcher on the appropriateness of his data for the program's procedures before the computer allows those data to be run.

5. **Factors already well replicated in a standard area are often rediscovered and given a new name.** This seems to happen regularly in an area generating many factor analyses and may be a function of the tendency to publish rather than to read. Personality research, for example, often produces factors that appear to be what others have called intelligence, emotionality (anxiety), extraversion, or conscientiousness. There is a simple solution to this problem. An investigator in a particular area should always include marker variables for those factors that have already been well substantiated. Research in the area of intelligence has utilized such marker variables to great advantage. The problem is not, of course, unique to factor analysis because throughout the psychological literature—if not in other areas—investigators invent new measures of the same concepts or of a concept only slightly different from that already well investigated. The failure to overlap one's own research with that previously completed certainly retards the theoretical development of any field.

Underlying all these criticisms is the major culprit: the lack of a theoretical approach that integrates the data collection, factor analysis, and interpretation, and which leads to future use of the results. Sometimes the integration fails to occur because the investigators seem to be without intelligent theories for the area. On other occasions, it may be because they fail to sufficiently understand the variants of factor analysis and do not find a consultant who can integrate the theory and the analysis. The lack of integration is undoubtedly the reason why so few hypothesis-testing factor analyses are done relative to the number of exploratory—or even "shotgun"—analyses. The lack of integration forms the basis for contemporary critiques of the use of factor analysis (Lykken, 1971). The problem does not lie in the procedures but in the level of sophistication of some users.

18.2 RECOMMENDED PROCEDURES FOR SELECTED RESEARCH DESIGNS

Although factor analysis is a versatile technique and can be used in numerous situations, four situations occur often. With such situations it is possible to recommend reasonably standard factor analytic designs that can be used for analysis. The first factor analytic design is to orthogonalize a set of variables for further statistical analysis of that same data set (Section 18.2.1).

In some situations the purpose of a factor analysis may be to reduce the number of variables so that the domain might be covered in another research study more efficiently or so that a comprehensive but efficient test battery might result. This situation is met by Design II: reducing the variable set (Section 18.2.2).

Another common situation has been the factor analysis of individual items to check the dimensionality of a potential scale, to evaluate bias in an item set, or to develop a multidimensional set of scales for a particular domain. Design III, scale analysis by factoring items, is discussed in Section 18.2.3.

Perhaps the most common use of factor analysis is met by Design IV: dimensional analysis (Section 18.2.4), which is appropriate when the concern is in examining a set of variables to establish their dimensionality for theoretical purposes. The distinction between Design IV and Design III is sometimes a fine one because either analysis can be used for dimensional purposes; the emphasis in Design III is on constructing scales and uses items as the "variables" in the factor analysis, which means that there is considerably more error in the analysis and that must be taken into account in the procedures. In Design IV, the variables are assumed to be well defined and validated so that error is less of a problem.

Our discussion of each case assumes that proper preliminary design principles have been followed. This includes building of this study upon the conclusions from past literature, selecting participants who range broadly enough so that any factor of interest would occur with sufficient strength to be identifiable, selecting variables (or items) carefully and including marker variables from past studies, directly relating the results of this study to past literature so that factors being confirmed across several studies can be identified, and assuring that the project has direct import for theory or practice. The discussion does not contain details of the rationale for particular recommendations because those rationales are covered extensively in preceding chapters.

Perhaps the most important assumption of this particular section is that literature and theory in the area are somewhat sparse, thus necessitating an exploratory factor analysis. If there is reasonably substantial research or a reasonably strong theory, then confirmatory factor analysis should be the first choice (Chapters 5 and 7). Exploratory factor-analytic procedures are replaced by the more powerful confirmatory procedures whenever possible.

18.2.1 Design I: Orthogonalization

It is occasionally desirable to orthogonalize variables in a study, thus eliminating correlations among them. The independent variables of the study could be orthogonalized, or the orthogonalization could be of dependent variables, or both could be orthogonalized. Section 17.2 contains further discussion for determining if this is a suitable procedure. The intent is to keep the orthogonalized variables as close to the original variables as possible, and there is no interest in using factors to reduce the number of variables or summarize them more succinctly. (If there is need both for orthogonalization and for having fewer factors than variables, see Design III or IV.)

Table 18.2.1 contains a summary of procedures for Design I and the other designs. It can be seen that no significance test is recommended for Design I because the interest is in generating orthogonal versions of the original variables, not in analyzing their common overlap. The number of factors is predetermined as the number of variables.

Any component extraction procedure could be used because all procedures will result in extracting 100% of the variance when there are as many variables as factors. Principal component analysis is widely available and so would be generally used. Do note that only component procedures are appropriate, for the interest is in extracting all the variance for every variable and thus communalities of the solutions must be 1.0.

Any component solution will do because results are then rotated by varimax. Except with unusually complex data, varimax places one factor close to each of

TABLE 18.2.1
Recommended Procedures for Exploratory
Factor Analysis

Design	Significance test of R_{vv}, f (C. 8)	No. of Factors (C. 8)	Factor Extraction (C. 5–7)	Rotation (C. 9–10)	Higher Order? (C. 11)
I. Orthogonization	None	v	Any component technique	Varimax	No
II. Reducing variable set	None	Scree	Maximal decomposition multiple group	No	No
III. Scale analysis by factoring items or miniscales	Bartlett's; Humphreys'	Scree or Wrigley's	Any principal factor if $v >$ 40; otherwise any common principal factor technique	Varimax– Promax (or other oblique); test if orthogonal	Yes to check for general factor, reduce difficulty factors
IV. Dimensional analysis	Bartlett's; Humphreys'	Scree & root $\geq$ 1	Any principal factor if $v >$ 30; otherwise any common principal factor technique	Varimax– Promax (or other oblique); test if orthogonal	Yes if oblique

Note: Confirmatory factor analysis is a more powerful techique if it can possibly be used in the above situations. The ''C'' 's refer to the appropriate chapter in this book.

the variables in this type solution, and the result is orthogonalized versions of the original variables. Any overlap between two variables is split between those two variables; split variance is described by the minor loadings on each factor.

18.2.2 Design II: Reducing Variable Sets

The prime purpose of the factor analysis may be to reduce the number of variables in an economical manner. Reduction of the number of variables may be to increase the degrees of freedom of a particular analysis or simply to adequately represent the domain represented by the original variable set in another study but at less cost. It is assumed that the variables would be administered in the next study just as they were in the original study.

The need is to carry the minimum number of original variables necessary to represent the area into the next set of studies. The procedure that is most suitable for this analysis is maximal decomposition multiple-group factor analysis (Chapter 5). The first factor is defined as that variable which best reproduces all the information in the original data matrix. The second factor is defined as that variable which accounts for the maximum amount of variance in the original data matrix in addition to the first factor/variable. Additional factors continually add new variables that account for new sources of information so that the maximum amount of variance is reproduced by the minimum number of factors/variables at each step.

Maximum decompositional multiple-group factor analysis is a more efficient procedure than principal factors under the restriction that factors are to be measured by as few of the original variables as possible. (Any principal factor is extracted without regard to this restriction and generally can be measured only by using a weighted composite of several of the original variables.)

Significance tests for the number of factors are not available for this situation because it is a stepwise procedure that may involve some capitalization upon chance. To establish the number of factors the scree test is used as an aid in identifying the amount of additional variance that can be accounted for by adding one more factor/variable to the solution. Factor extraction may be stopped based upon the normal scree criteria but it is often profitable in this situation to consider the cost of administering the extra variable that represents the additional factor before deciding whether to keep it or not. If the next variable, which represents the next factor, is readily collected, then that factor might well be kept whereas another variable representing a factor accounting for the same amount of variance that was quite difficult to collect might be dropped. Rotation is not relevant because the factors are already in the desired form.

18.2.3 Design III: Scale Analysis by Factoring Items

A common use of factor analysis is to factor analyze a set of items to evaluate the number of subscales for a particular test and which items define each. However, individual items are generally unreliable—which is why we usually combine several into a scale—and difficulty factors are common due to differential skews. Because of the special problems, scale analysis by factoring items has a different set of recommended procedures than Design IV, dimensional analysis.

Because of the unreliability of items, it is essential that significance tests be included. Bartlett's and Humphreys' significance tests are recommended (Chapter 8). Any factor identified as insignificant by either of these two techniques should be neither extracted nor rotated.

For Design III, numerous items are sampled from the same general domain. To be considered important within that domain, a given factor should therefore have several items loading it. Any factor that does not reach this criterion is considered trivial and is excluded in the analysis. Wrigley's criterion is a direct index of the number of factors with several loadings and the scree test can also be used in this situation. (The root-greater-than-one criterion is inappropriate because it functions as if there were an average of three to five items per factor; in most item analyses there is more likely to be an average of ten to twenty items per factor. Experience with the root-greater-than-one criterion has found it seriously overestimates the number of factors for Design III (Gorsuch, 1974; Lee & Comrey, 1979).

The type of factor extraction procedure to use will be a function of the number of items in the factor analysis. As noted in Chapter 6, any of the principal factor exploratory analyses result in much the same factors if communalities are high and the number of variables are reasonably large. However, with items the reliabilities are not high and so the communalities will be at most moderate; hence the number of items included in analysis should, as a rule of thumb, be greater than 40 before one simply uses the most convenient program. If the number of items are less than 40, then a common factor technique should be used. If there are less than approximately 20 items, serious consideration should be given also to the means by which communalities are estimated.

The purpose of Design III is to generate scales that can be useful in further research studies, where those scales have known properties. One of the major properties that needs to be known before going into another study is whether the scales are correlated or not. For this reason, compute both varimax and promax (or other equivalent oblique procedure) to evaluate the degree to which the scales are likely to be correlated. If the oblique rotation does definitely increase hyperplane count over the orthogonal rotation, there is evidence that any scale constructed from these items is likely to be correlated in future samples.

It would be nice to use an orthogonal rotation and then assume that any future scales would be orthogonal, but the latter occurs only if the orthogonal rotation is approximately as good as the oblique rotation. Whenever the oblique rotation improves the hyperplane count, there is a strong possibility that the orthogonal rotation is keeping the factors orthogonal by capitalizing upon chance in this sample. Due to such capitalization upon chance, the orthogonality will seldom generalize to a new sample, and the scales are correlated anyway. It is better to know in advance that the scales will be correlated so that fact can be included in the research design, and hence an oblique rotation needs to be examined. Of course, if the oblique rotation does not add over the orthogonal rotation, then the orthogonal rotation is accepted and the scales will probably be orthogonal within chance variations in the new sample.

If the oblique solution is accepted, then it is essential to extract higher-order factors. Examining higher-order factors overcomes limits of simple structure rotation used by the analytic procedures for rotating exploratory factors. Use of simple structure procedures *assumes* there is no broad, general factor and avoids rotating to such a position whenever possible. However, it might be that a broad, general factor does exist in the data. That broad, general factor will occur in the higher-order analysis. This is the only appropriate procedure if the original author of the test scored all items as a single scale (all other procedures *assume* the author was incorrect).

Rotating obliquely and computing higher-order analyses reduces the major problem of item factor analyses: difficulty factors. Difficulty factors occur because the distributions on different items reflect the mean level response on those items—that is, their difficulty—and only those items with the same type distributions can be correlated highly with each other. Hence items with high means tend to correlate more highly with each other than do items with low means even though they have the same factor composition (see Chapter 16). Rotating obliquely allows the difficulty factors to appear at the first-order level; the higher-order factor analyses then reflect the more general factors that are usually the ones of primary interest.

18.2.4 Design IV: Dimensional Analysis

Classical development of factor analysis has focused on Design IV. Whereas Designs I, II, and III are pragmatic ones to aid in a particular research process, Design IV is used for more theoretical questions regarding the appropriate number and type of distinctions to be made within the area. The primary concern in Design IV is representing as much of the domain as possible in as few factors as possible.

A primary assumption of Design IV is that the variables have indeed been *sampled* to represent the domain of interest. This is more difficult than it initially seems, for defining a domain has some difficulties of its own and knowing how to sample from that domain of variables is also problematic, and an individual investigator simply selecting a set of variables on an intuitive basis lacks the rigor necessary to truly do a dimensional analysis. Instead, there needs to be systematic boundaries for the domain and some procedure identified for sampling within the domain. For examples of such domain sampling, consult the work of Cattell wherein he defines the personality domain as the terms of the English language that refer to personality and sampled therefrom, or consider Guilford who developed a facet model of intelligence by which to sample the domain. It is assumed that the variables are well constructed, having good-to-excellent reliabilities and validities (although it is occasionally worthwhile to include variables for which reliability and validity are essentially unknown, such variables should be a very small percentage of the total variables in the analysis or else the resulting factors will probably be uninterpretable).

The first step in Design IV analysis is to evaluate the correlation matrix for significance by Bartlett's significance test. That test and Humphreys' test are also used for all of the extracted factors. A factor deemed insignificant by either test is not rotated. (If an insignificant factor were of sufficient size to be judged nontrivial by a scree or root-greater-than-one test, that would indicate the sample size was too small to be profitable. Withhold further analysis until the sample size can be enlarged.) When the upper bound for the number of factors is established by the significance tests, the root-greater-than-one and scree tests are examined to determine the number of nontrivial factors to include. If these tests both agree, that is the number of factors. If these tests do not both agree, then several different numbers of factors are rotated to see which factors are robust across the number-of-factors decision.

Because the variables have been carefully selected, the communalities would generally be from moderate to high. In that situation, all principal factor-based exploratory analyses result in highly similar factors if there are at least 30 variables, and so any of these techniques might be used. With less than 30 variables, common factor techniques would be preferred to avoid the inflated loadings given by component analyses because the assumption made by component analysis that the communalities are all 1.0 is not actually true.

For rotation, start with varimax and then add a major oblique procedure such as promax. If promax adds to the hyperplane count over varimax, then an oblique solution is worth examining. If varimax is equal to promax, then accept the orthogonal solution as the most appropriate solution. However, if the oblique solution is better than the orthogonal—for example, produces higher hyperplane count—then the assumption that orthogonal factors are best is rejected and the oblique solution accepted. An oblique solution is likely to be a better representation of the data because it suggests that none of the factors could be measured in a new sample without correlations among factor scores; if this is the case, then it should be included theoretically in the original Design IV analysis.

If oblique rotation does give a better solution, then proceed with a higher-order analysis. The higher-order factor analysis allows for more detailed examination of the relationships among the factors within the domain. Higher-order analysis also helps to overcome a major handicap of simple structure: the assumption that several domains are actually represented. If several domains are indeed represented—such as intelligence and extroversion—then the factors will be orthogonal across domains because they are distinct. If it happens that the domains are not as distinct as originally hypothesized when selecting variables, then they may all be interrelated, just as measures of abilities generally correlate somewhat with each other even though they form separate factors. This information will be identified and analyzed in the higher-order factor analysis for a more complete understanding of the area. As noted in Chapter 16, higher-order analysis increases the possibility of matching factors with other studies that used a different variable sampling plan.

18.3   THE FUTURE OF FACTOR ANALYSIS

The future of factor analysis is partially dependent on the ways in which it is used. If it is often used for problems where it is not appropriate or only because it can "massage" the data, its future is dim. If it is predominately used in more creative ways—as, indeed, it occasionally has been—then it will spread as a valuable methodological tool.

The possibility of improvement in the factor-analytic studies reported in the literature can be viewed as an educational problem. The prime limitation on present usage is, one suspects, that relatively few of the users have received an appropriate background. Such a background has been difficult to obtain because factor analysis is an advanced statistical topic, and thus the recent textbooks are generally oriented toward the mathematically sophisticated reader interested in factor analysis as a statistical technique rather than toward the behavioral scientist with research objectives.

The possibilities for gaining a background sufficient to do factor-analytic research have been complicated by the fact that some graduate schools do not regularly offer a full semester course in the area. Covering factor analysis in, for example, two weeks as part of another course is insufficient because it only encourages superficial analysis by canned programs.

Even if the student never did a factor analysis himself, systematic study of the area would produce side benefits in terms of greater sophistication for research in general. Although factor-analytic research design does not touch upon such vital research issues as random assignment to treatment and control groups or quasi-experimental designs, it does confront the student with many problems faced implicitly by every investigator in every area. These include:

1. What is the area from which the data are to be collected? Should the area be defined broadly or narrowly? How are the variables to be selected to represent the area and how are the theoretical distinctions to be operationalized?
2. Should variables, individuals, or conditions be analyzed? What is to be done with the modes not directly included?
3. Is the ordinary linear approach adequate or should interactive and cur-

vilinear relationships be considered? How much information should the indices of association take into account?

4. How many constructs are warranted for the area? Can the constructs be organized as, for example, in a higher-order analysis? If so, what is the most profitable resolution of the generality versus accuracy tension?

5. What is the best way to summarize the relationships among the variables? How can a choice be made between the multiplicity of alternative solutions? What external evidence can aid in deciding between, for example, the rotational positions or alternative theories?

One value of the study of factor analysis is that such questions are explicitly recognized. It should be emphasized, however, that *every* study faces the same questions, regardless of whether or not the data are factored. Factor analysis only makes the problems more explicit than multiple regression analysis, analysis of variance, and other such procedures.

Another educational mechanism is provided by journal editing. As previously noted and found independently (Armstrong & Soelberg, 1968; Skinner, 1980), journals have been unusually lax in requiring sufficient detail so that the reader can know how the analysis was performed. No article should be published that does not provide sufficient information to replicate the study. The following data should be included: size and characteristics of the sample; reference for each variable used, or the item or scale itself if it is not accessible through a public source; the index of association used; the kind of communality estimation; the method by which the number of factors was determined; how the factors were extracted; the method of rotation with at least the factor structure and correlations among factors, and similar data on any higher-order analyses. Making the means, standard deviations and indices of association publicly available would also be a helpful practice. Many articles already include most of this information; adding the other information can often be accomplished by using appropriate adjectives at appropriate places in the article. A statement such as "the principal components with roots greater than 1.0 were extracted from the product-moment correlation matrix, and the promax factor structure and factor correlations are given Table 3" contains most of the basic information in surprisingly little space. A discussion of the rationale for the analysis employed should be encouraged and even required in some cases. It is vital that the reader know how factor analysis fits into the theoretical structure of the research program.

More information is particularly needed in regard to questions of replication, invariance, and robustness. One could even dream of an informal moratorium on new rotation procedures and other such developments until it is determined how the present ones contribute to replication and invariance. Fortunately, these are areas where Monte Carlo simulation studies and plasmodes are being profitably employed. Although such analyses will ultimately be replaced, one hopes, by mathematical proofs, empirical studies can provide working guidelines for contemporary research and evaluate the importance of subtle mathematical distinctions.

Despite the widespread misuse of factor analysis, it has still contributed to psychology. Indeed, among the top 18 contributors to psychology across the period of 1950 to 1975, three used factor analysis extensively or exclusively (Daniel, 1979). Factor-analytic techniques can be recommended that will lead to replicable factors. As knowledge of principles for designing good factor-analytic studies spreads, factor-analytic research can be expected to contribute substantially to psychology and other similar fields.

Appendix A

DATA FOR EXAMPLES

The tables in this appendix present the means and standard deviations for each of the major examples used throughout the book. These tables are included so that the examples can be used to evaluate local computer programs or as exercises.

APPENDIX A.1
Box Plasmode: Means and Standard Deviations

Variables	Mean	Standard Deviation
1. Length squared	8675	7990
2. Height squared	3655	6581
3. Width squared	4449	6566
4. Length plus width	139.0	73.0
5. Length plus height	129.7	76.9
6. Width plus height	100.8	76.5
7. Longest inner diagonal	97.3	54.0
8. Shortest inner diagonal	73.0	45.9
9. Space inner diagonal	109.5	58.7
10. Thickness of edge	15.4	29.0

Note: Measurements are to the nearest centimeter as computed from measurements to the nearest inch. Thickness of edge is computed to the nearest millimeter. The correlations are given in Table 1.3.1.

APPENDIX A.2

Twelve Physique Variables: Means and
Standard Deviations

Variables	Mean	Standard Deviation
1. Stature	161.29	6.262
2. Symphysis height	80.95	4.641
3. Breadth of skull	13.34	0.568
4. Length of skull	17.31	0.844
5. Biacromial diameter	33.53	1.997
6. Transverse chest diameter	23.52	1.556
7. Sagittal chest diameter	17.24	1.206
8. Bicristal diameter	24.13	1.654
9. Length of sternum	16.30	1.118
10. Chest circumference (at expiration)	89.16	6.190
11. Hip circumference	82.86	6.533
12. Weight	55.74	7.710

Note: The correlations are presented in Table 5.1.1. (Adapted from Rees, 1950.)

APPENDIX A.3

Twenty-Four Ability Variables: Means, Standard
Deviations and Reliabilities

	Grant-White (N = 145)			Pasteur (N = 156)		
Variables	Mean	Standard Deviation	Reliability Coefficient	Mean	Standard Deviation	Reliability Coefficient
1. Visual Perception	29.60	6.89	.7563	29.65	7.09	.7661
2. Cubes	24.80	4.43	.5677	23.94	4.91	.6105
3. Paper Form Board	14.30	2.81	.4396	14.16	2.84	.3628
4. Lozenges	15.97	8.29	.9365	19.90	9.28	.9542
5. General Information	44.85	11.62	.8077	36.60	11.70	.7969
6. Paragraph Comprehension	9.95	3.36	.6507	8.47	3.45	.7499
7. Sentence Completion	18.85	4.63	.7536	15.98	5.23	.8297
8. Word Classification	28.20	5.34	.6802	24.20	5.27	.6793
9. Word Meaning	17.28	7.92	.8701	13.45	6.91	.8472
10. Add	90.18	23.70	.9518	101.94	25.88	.9586
11. Code	68.59	16.61	.7116	69.69	14.67	.6228
12. Counting Groups of Dots	109.75	20.92	.9374	111.26	19.51	.9164
13. Straight and Curved Capitals	191.78	36.91	.8889	193.82	38.18	.8765
14. Word Recognition	176.28	10.79	.6483	174.73	12.86	.7619
15. Number Recognition	89.37	7.52	.5070	90.60	7.85	.5169
16. Figure Recognition	103.40	6.78	.5997	101.71	8.24	.6633
17. Object-Number	7.21	4.55	.7248	9.19	5.03	.3952

(continued)

APPENDIX A.3—(*Continued*)

Variables	Grant-White (N = 145)			Pasteur (N = 156)		
	Mean	*Standard Deviation*	*Reliability Coefficient*	*Mean*	*Standard Deviation*	*Reliability Coefficient*
18. Number-Figure	9.44	4.49	.6101	9.38	4.30	.6036
19. Figure-Word	15.24	3.58	.5686	12.85	4.28	.7185
20. Deduction	30.34	19.71	.6492	23.67	18.34	.6946
21. Numerical Puzzles	14.46	4.82	.7843	14.06	4.29	.8018
22. Problem Reasoning	27.73	9.79	.7866	24.85	8.34	.7348
23. Series Completion	18.75	9.33	.9310	17.56	8.89	.9246
24. Woody-McCall Mixed Fundamentals, Form I	25.83	4.70	.8362	22.81	4.27	.8134
25. Paper Form Board	15.65	3.08	.5437			
26. Flags	36.30	8.31	.9215			

Note: The number of cases varies for the r_{xx}'s from 143 to 152 for Grant-White and from 158 to 165 for Pasteur. The reliabilities are as published but the other statistics have been recomputed and occasionally vary from that reported by Holzinger and Swineford (1939: 17). The raw data are given in the original report; the correlations are presented in Table 6.2.1.

maximum
likelihood

Computers and Factor Analysis

B.1 COMPUTER PROGRAMS FOR FACTOR ANALYSIS

B.1.1 "Mainframe" Computers

Factor analyses are, as noted in the text, calculated through computer programs rather than with a hand calculator. The major computer packages—including SPSS, BMD, and SAS—all have special sections of programs for factor analysis on university computers.

Using a program someone else has developed and tested for your computer is highly desirable. Program development is time consuming and has many "tricks of the trade" that make for an accurate, easy to use program.

There are several aspects of available computer programs that, despite the programming expertise, need to be watched closely. They arise because programmers sometimes have their own views about factor analysis, views that may not be informed by even one course in the area. In addition, such programs are complex and it is difficult to even know if all the possible options are completely error free.

Few factor analytic packages seem to be inaccurate. While some, such as maximum likelihood as noted in the text, have special problems, most do what they say they will do and do it accurately within the bounds described in Appendix B.2.

The major problem to watch for with factor analytic computer programs is hidden assumptions. For example, the BMD program has an option for extracting those factors with roots greater than 1. For principal components this option works fine. For principal axes the number of factors is the number of roots greater than 1 when the roots are from the correlation matrix with communalities in the diagonals rather than unities. As noted in Chapter 8 there is a definite

387

rationale for using the roots greater than 1 criterion when the roots are of the correlation matrix but there is *no* rationale for using the roots of the matrix with communalities, as found in BMD. To properly use the root criterion with BMD, two passes are necessary. First a principal component analysis is necessary to obtain the roots of the correlation matrix to determine the number of factors. Then on the next pass the principal axes are extracted for the number of factors determined in the first pass. Hopefully, by the time you read this the package will be corrected.

Another common but erroneous assumption can be found in the SPSS factor analysis programs. For principal axis analysis, the defaults are for iteration of the communalities to occur until the estimates converge or until a large number of iterations have been computed. But there is no evidence that what the estimates converge to is any more accurate than a "good guess," as noted in Chapter 6. The proper default, as shown in the literature, is two iterations from initial estimates of squared multiple correlations. Hopefully, the SPSS default will be changed to such a value.

Most packages allow a parameter to be stated which controls the degree of correlation among the factors in an oblique rotation. Read this section carefully, for the parameter varies depending upon which method is used in the rotations and how the formula is applied. Sometimes a positive value increases correlations among factors and sometimes it decreases the correlations. Check the manual carefully.

Because of the complexity of many of the programs, it is always useful to run some test problems. The examples given in this book and detailed in Appendix A are included to allow test runs for data that have been extensively analyzed with known results. The output should agree within rounding error (that, with some iteration procedures can, unfortunately, sometimes be seen in the second decimal place).

Most packages lack two useful factor analytic procedures. The first one lacking is confirmatory factor analysis. Surprisingly few packages contain the easily programmed confirmatory multiple group procedure. This analysis can be approximated by computing linear composites for the factors and then using the linear composites with an ordinary correlation program.

It is less surprising that only a few centers have a confirmatory maximum likelihood program since the program is expensive, difficult to install, and difficult to use. Special programs to aid in the use of the program itself are being developed, and hopefully these will lead to wider availability and greater usability of the procedure.

The second useful procedure lacking is the Schmid-Leiman type solution for higher order analysis. The higher order analyses generally must be computed by submitting the correlations among factors just as any other correlation matrix. The Schmid-Leiman transformation can then be computed by hand. Vanderbilt University and several other universities compute higher order factors with Schmid-Leiman transformations whenever factors are rotated obliquely.

B.1.2 Microcomputers

The earlier discussion was of "mainframe" computers as currently found at universities. They utilize second generation programs (the first generation was submitting the program with the data, and the second was having all the programs stored in the computer and requesting the desired program under the direction of a master program).

Microcomputers allow for a third generation of factor analytic programs. Such programs will dialogue with the user to determine the appropriate procedure. For example, in deciding between orthogonal and oblique rotation, the program may ask "Is there prior evidence that it is appropriate to assume the factors will be uncorrelated (or do you wish to evaluate whether they are uncorrelated)?" The answer would then determine the rotation procedure. Since the microcomputer program will be "people literate," there will be no need for a manual or for the user to be "computer literate."

A further advantage to microcomputing is the immediate access that the investigator has. The same computer used for word processing can be used in one's office or home to conduct a factor analysis. While the microcomputer operates at a slower speed than a mainframe, the time from the investigator's beginning of the analysis to when results are in usable form will be faster. The increased "throughput" speed comes from several aspects: no time taken to travel across campus to use a terminal, no terminal lag due to multiple users, immediate correction of a mistake (the micro program can detect a mistake and wait for the user to return and correct it without having to start over), and no time needed to study a manual to determine how to obtain the desired output.

Because microcomputers are smaller than mainframes, some feel that they can only process smaller data sets. This depends on programming. Most microcomputers should easily process 50 or so variables, and more with special programming procedures (but that increase time considerably). Hence, they are capable of analyzing all but the largest of problems.

Note that the above comments apply only to a properly developed program. Some of the programs now available are attempts to transfer traditional packages to microcomputers. These will continue to be more limited versions of what is now available on mainframes. Only programs that are completely designed for microcomputing can capitalize on the possibilities.

B.2 ACCURACY OF COMPUTER PROCESSING

When a program does run and gives some output, there is a tendency to automatically assume the answers are correct. Unfortunately, this is often not the case. While most gross errors are a function of the user's incorrect submission of data to the program, there are four conditions that place inherent limitations on the accuracy of computer processing. These are: unnoticed errors in the programs, the accuracy of the input data (Section B.2.1), inaccuracies from subtraction, divisions, etc., in the calculation algorithm (Section B.2.2), and limitations in the accuracy with which computers store and operate upon numbers (Section B.2.3).

Most programs will have been checked before they are used by the consumer, but checking all the possible combinations of options in a program is so complex that it is never completed. Many computer centers and programmers rely upon problems discovered by the user to uncover subtle errors. This means that the output of any program must be carefully examined for all possible errors; processing sample data where the solution is already known is a necessity.

B.2.1 Accuracy of the Input Data

It is assumed that the data are collected as accurately as possible. But the accuracy with which data are collected is often not great and may be considerably less than it appears to be from the number of digits in a column of X_{nv}. For example, the psychologist's IQ test reports a score which is three digits in length (e.g., 120), but may be based on a test with less than 100 items. Obviously, the IQs three digits may not all be accurate. However, even if each IQ point stands for one item answered correctly, its three digits are three digits of accuracy only in terms of an observed score. They could be considered accurate to the third digit only for a component model. In a common-factor model, the reliability of the test would also be of interest and this reliability, expressed as a standard error, indicates that a person taking a parallel form of an IQ test could easily receive a score five to ten points different from the original one. Therefore, an IQ score's conceptual accuracy is greater than one digit but certainly less than three digits.

Simple data errors can also affect the results. For example, if two cards are out of order in a 100-individual analysis involving 2 cards per subject, correlations can change .05 to even .10. Double checks are needed at each step of the analysis, even with computers.

B.2.2 Inaccuracies from the Calculation Algorithm

Errors introduced by the calculation procedures can often be found only by an examination of the procedure. Some familiarity with the algorithm being used and the running of one's own checks on the output are definitely desirable for data analysis. This, of course, is true whether or not the analysis is carried out on a computer.

The following sources of calculation errors are particularly important:

1. Rounding errors from reducing the number of digits (for truncation error cf. Section B.2.3). Rounding errors can be avoided by carrying out the calculations to at least three more places than one has significant digits.

This will allow the rounding error to accumulate in the last digit or two and not seriously affect the one which will determine the final rounding. But note that even more digits may need to be carried if the calculations are extensive as in iterative procedures. Rounding errors can, and often will, accumulate.

2. Calculation errors introduced by such procedures as subtracting or dividing nearly equal sums of cross-products or squares can be reduced by utilizing procedures which keep these to a minimum (cf. Section B.2.3 where this error can be particularly problematic).

3. Iteration criteria should be set sufficiently low so as to assure an adequate degree of accuracy. The best way to determine this is to run a procedure with the same set of data but with varying degrees of accuracy. When the last stage of data calculation gives the same results for the interpretable digits even though the accuracy criterion is increased, then the proper criterion has been found. But note that the trial data should be relatively problematic. It should require a high number of iterations for this to be a meaningful basis for generalization.

B.2.3 Computer Accuracy

Since computer programs use standard data and calculation procedures, they are limited by all the ways in which such procedures are limited. But, in addition, they have another major limitation. Computers carry numbers by recording the digits and the number of decimal places separately. For example, 73.0469 would be 730469+02 where the 2 represents the decimal's position. The range of the decimal place that can be recorded is sufficiently great on most computers so that this presents no problem. However, the number of digits retained is sufficiently small so that this can affect the results. Computers vary in the number of digits used. Most computers generally have 6- to 7-digit accuracy.

The digits that are not kept are simply dropped; no rounding occurs. Therefore, the error introduced is greater than would be normally expected. Also note that this truncation means that anytime a number appears with more digits than can be stored by the computer, the right-most digits are dropped.

Whenever a cross-product or sum of squares adds up to more than the permissible number of digits, it is no longer adequately represented. The last digits are lost. So when one such number is subtracted from another of almost identical size the result may be inaccurate. For example, suppose the two sums of squares are 5807963 and 5807001; subtracting the latter from the former in a computer may give zero, not 962. Further calculations will retain, or even magnify, the degree of inaccuracy.

Computer accuracy is particularly a problem where the initial input has the major variation in the right-most digits. For example, this would be true of scores ranging from 9001 to 9099. The cross-products become quite large, but the variation is in the right-most digits that tend to be lost. Answers can be wildly inaccurate under such conditions. Howard and Lissitz (1966) found correlations of 1.0 becoming .99, .62, 50, 0.0, and even 1.42 as the errors increased.

The problem can be reduced if the computer programs avoid the normal raw data calculation formulas and, instead, use formulas keeping the sums of squares and cross-products to a minimum. Such formulas create a little error through more division, but the introduction of that error is of lesser magnitude than the error which can be encountered from truncation effects. A common procedure for achieving this goal is to use the following three formulas for the mean, variance, and covariances:

$$\text{Mean of } X = \frac{\Sigma \, (X_i - X_1)}{N} + X_1 \tag{B.2.1}$$

$$\text{Variance of } X = \frac{\Sigma \, (X_i - X_1)^2}{N} - \left(\frac{\Sigma \, (X_i - X_1)}{N} \right)^2 \tag{B.2.2}$$

Covariance of X and $Y =$

$$\frac{\Sigma \, (X_i - X_1) \, (Y_i - Y_1) - N \left(\dfrac{\Sigma \, X_i - X_1}{N} \right) \left(\dfrac{\Sigma \, Y_i - Y_1}{N} \right)}{N} \tag{B.2.3}$$

where X_1 and Y_1 are the first individual's scores on variables X and Y succeeding, and each individual's score is calculated as a deviation from the first person's score; the statistics are then corrected in the final operation. Similar formulas should be used in calculating correlation coefficients and other such statistics.

Example

To test for truncation effects in the computations of correlation coefficients, a standard set of data can be run. One hundred "individuals" are generated with each individual being assigned one of the scores from 1 to 99. The first variable is simply the assigned score; the second variable is the assigned score plus 900; the third is the original score plus 9000 and so on. Ten decks of these 100 subjects are reproduced so that varying numbers of subjects can be run.

The effects of large numbers on means and variances calculated by the standard procedures can be seen by examining Table B.2.1. This table gives the means and variances as computed for two different numbers of individuals. Note that even a four-digit input may produce inaccurate variances. Use of the formulas in the text gave the correct results even when the data were five digits in length. Entering more digits than the computer can record will always lead to erroneous results in the last digits.

Many computers and programs print by truncating the digits. All digits to the right of those printed out are simply dropped. No rounding occurs. Therefore, the user must round off his numbers to fewer digits than are printed out in such cases. Programmers and computer center personnel often do not know whether their compilers automatically provide for rounding or whether rounding is writ-

TABLE B.2.1
Truncation Error Effects

Range of Raw Data	N = 100		N = 1000	
	Mean	Variance	Mean	Variance
01–99	50.5	833.25	50.5	833.25
9,001–9,099	9,050.5	796.00	9,050.5	452.00
90,001–90,099	90,050.5	−2,400.00	90,050.5	−37,500.00
900,001–900,099	900,050.5	−350,000.	900,046.5	2,880,000.
9,000,001–9,000,099	9,000,046.	30,000,000.	9,000,005.5	396,000,000.

Note: The correct means equal 50.5 plus the appropriate constant. The correct variance for each set of data equals 833.25.

ten into any given program; the easiest and only accurate way to find out is to run your own check.

The effects of errors can be devastating. In trial runs of one regression problem, some computer programs were accurate only as to sign of the regression weights although others were accurate to 6 or 7 digits (Longley, 1967). At this stage of development of computer statistical libraries, the user must bear the responsibility for checking the programs and the output to assure that programming or computer error has not affected his results.

References

Adams, R. C. On the use of a marker variable in lieu of its factor-analytic construct. *Perceptual and Motor Skills,* 1975, *41,* 665–666.

Ahmavaara, Y. Transformation analysis of factorial data. *Annales Academiae Scientiarum Fennical,* Series B, (Helsinki) 1954, *88*(2), 54–59.

Anderson, R. D., Acito, F., & Lee, H. A simulation study of three methods for determining the number of image components. *Multivariate Behavioral Research,* 1982, *17,* 493–502.

Anderson, T. W., & Rubin, H. Statistical inference in factor analysis. *Proceedings of the Third Berkeley Symposium on Mathematical Statistics and Probability* 1956, *5,* 111–150.

Archer, C. O. A look by simulation, at the validity of some asymptotic distribution results for rotated loadings. *Psychometrika,* 1976, *41*(4), 537–541.

Archer, C. O., & Jennrich, R. I. Standard errors for rotated factor loadings. *Psychometrika,* 1973, *38,* 581–592.

Armstrong, J. S. Derivation of theory by means of factor analysis or Tom Swift and his electric factor analysis machine. *American Statistician* 1967, *21*(5), 17–21.

Armstrong, J. S., & Soelberg, P. On the interpretation of factor analysis. *Psychological Bulletin,* 1968, *70*(5), 361–364.

Arthur, A. Z. Kelley's non-parametric factor analysis. *Psychological Reports,* 1965, *16*(3), 922.

Baehr, M. E. A comparison of graphic and analytic solutions for both oblique and orthogonal simple structures for factors of employee morale. *Psychometrika,* 1963, *28*(2), 199–209.

Bailey, J. P., & Guertin, W. H. Test item dependence of several oblique factor solutions. *Educational and Psychological Measurement,* 1970, *30*(3), 611–619.

Bargmann, R. *Signifikantz-untersuchungen der einfachen Struktur in der Factoren analyse. Mitteilungs blatt fur Mathematische Statistik.* Wurzburg: Physica Verlag, 1954.

Barrett, P. T., & Kline, P. The observation to variable ratio in factor analysis. *Personality Study and Group Behavior,* 1981, *1,* 23.

Bartlett, M. S. The statistical conception of mental factors. *British Journal of Psychology,* 1937, *28,* 97–104.

Bartlett, M. S. Tests of significance in factor analysis. *British Journal of Psychology,* 1950, *3*(2), 77–85.

Bartlett, M. S. A further note on tests of significance in factor analysis. *British Journal of Psychology*, 1951, *4*(1), 1–2.

Bechtoldt, H. P. An empirical study of the factor analysis stability hypothesis. *Psychometrika*, 1961, *26*, 405–432.

Bentler, P. M. Alpha-maximized factor analysis (alphamax): Its relation to alpha and canonical factor analysis. *Psychometrika*, 1968, *3*(3), 335–345.

Bentler, P. M. A comparison of monotonicity analysis with factor analysis. *Educational and Psychological Measurement*, 1970, *30*(2), 241–250.

Bentler, P. M. Multistructure statistical model applied to factor analysis. *Multivariate Behavioral Research*, 1976, *11*, 3–25.

Bentler, P. M. Multivariate analysis with latent variables: Causal modeling. *Annual Review of Psychology*, 1980, *31*, 419–456.

Bentler, P. M., & Lee, S. Y. Statistical aspects of a three-mode factor analysis model. *Psychometrika*, 1978, *43*, 343–352.

Bentler, P. M., & Lee, S. Y. A statistical development of three-mode factor analysis. *British Journal of Mathematical and Statistical Psychology*, 1979, *32*, 87–104.

Bentler, P. M., & Weeks, D. G. Linear structural equations with latent variables. *Psychometrika*, 1980, *45*(3), 289–308.

Bentler, P. M., & Wingard, J. Function-invariant and parameter scale-free transformation methods. *Psychometrika*, 1977, *42*, 221–240.

Bentler, P. M., & Woodward, J. A. A Head Start re-evaluation: Positive effects are not yet demonstrable. *Evaluation Quarterly*, 1978, *2*, 493–510.

Bentler, P. M., & Woodward, J. A. Regression on linear composites: Statistical theory and applications. *MBR*, Monograph 1979, 79.1.

ten Berge, J. M. F. Orthogonal procrustes rotation for two or more matrices. *Psychometrika*, 1977, *42*(2), 267–276.

ten Berge, J. M. F. On the equivalence of two oblique congruence rotation methods, and orthogonal approximations. *Psychometrika*, 1979, *44*(3), 359–364.

Bisher, J. W., & Drewes, D. W. *Mathematics in the Behavioral and Social Sciences*. New York: Harcourt, Brace & World, Inc., 1970.

Bloxom, B. A note on invariance in three-mode factor analysis. *Psychometrika*, 1968, *33*(3), 347–350.

Borg, I. Procrustean analysis of matrices with different row order. *Psychometrika*, 1978, *43*, 277–278.

Borgatta, E. F. Difficulty factors and the use of r_{phi}. *Journal of General Psychology*, 1965, *73*(2), 321–337.

Boruch, R. F., & Dutton, J. E. A program for testing hypotheses about correlation arrays. *Educational and Psychological Measurement*, 1970, *30*, 719–721.

Boruch, R. F., Larkin, J. D., Wolins, L., & MacKinney, A. C. Alternative methods of analysis: Multitrait-multimethod data. *Educational and Psychological Measurement*, 1970, *30*, 833–853.

Boruch, R. F., & Wolins, L. A procedure for estimation of trait, method, and error variance attributable to a measure. *Educational and Psychological Measurement*, 1970, *30*(3), 547–574.

Bottenberg, R. A., & Ward, H. J., Jr. *Applied multiple linear regression*. Technical Documentary Report No. PRL-TD-63-6. Washington, Clearinghouse for Federal Scientific and Technical Information, 1963.

Brewer, J. K., & Hills, J. R. Univariate selection: The effects of size of correlation, degree of skew, and degree of restriction. *Psychometrika*, 1969, *34*(3), 347–361.

Brewer, M. B., Campbell, D. T., & Crano, W. D. Testing a single factor model as an alternative to the misuse of partial correlations in hypothesis-testing research. *Sociometry*, 1970, *33*(1), 1–11.

Brogden, H. E. Pattern, structure, and the interpretation of factors. *Psychological Bulletin*, 1969, *72*(5), 375–378.

Bromley, D. B. Rank order cluster analysis. *British Journal of Mathematical and Statistical Psychology*, 1966, *19*(1), 105–123.

Broverman, D. M. Effects of score transformation in *Q* and *R* factor analysis techniques. *Psychological Review*, 1961, *68*, 68–80.

Broverman, D. M. Comments on the note by McAndrew and Forgy. *Psychological Review*, 1963, *70*, 119–120.

Browne, M. W. On oblique procrustes rotation. *Psychometrika* 1967,*32*(2), 125–132.

Browne, M. W. A comparison of factor analytic techniques. *Psychometrika*, 1968, *33*(3), 267–334. (a)

Browne, M. W. A note on lower bounds for the number of common factors. *Psychometrika*, 1968, *33*(2), 233–236. (b)

Browne, M.W., & Kristof, W. On the oblique rotation of a factor matrix to a specified pattern. *Psychometrika*, 1969, *34*, 237–248.

Burt, C. L. Methods of factor analysis with and without successive approximation. *British Journal of Educational Psychology*, 1937, *7*, 172–195.

Burt, C. L. The factorial study of physical types. *Man*, 1944, *44*, 82–86.

Burt, C. L. Factor analysis and physical types. *Psychometrika*, 1947, *12*, 171–188.

Burt, C. L. The factorial study of temperamental traits. *British Journal of Psychology*, (Statistical Section) 1948, *1*,178–203.

Butler, J. M. Simple structure reconsidered: Distinguishability and invariance in factor analysis. *Multivariate Behavioral Research*, 1969, *4*(1), 5–28.

Butt, D. S., & Fiske, D. Comparison of strategies in developing scales for dominance. *Psychological Bulletin*, 1968, *70*(6), 505–519.

Campbell, D. T., & Fiske, D. W. Convergent and discriminant validation by the multitrait-multi-method matrix. *Psychological Bulletin*, 1959, *56*, 81–105.

Carroll, J. B. An analytic solution for approximating simple structure in factor analysis. *Psychometrika*, 1953, *18*, 23–38.

Carroll, J. B. Biquartimin criterion for rotation to oblique simple structure in factor analysis. *Science* 1957, *126*, 1114–1115.

Carroll, J. B. IBM 704 program for generalized analytic rotation solution in factor analysis. Harvard University, unpublished, 1960.

Cattell, R. B. Parallel proportional profiles and other principles for determining the choice of factors by rotation. *Psychometrika*, 1944, *9*, 267–283.

Cattell, R. B. The description of personality: Principles and findings in a factor analysis. *American Journal of Psychology*, 1945, *58*, 69–90.

Cattell, R. B. *The description and measurement of personality*. New York: World Book Co., 1946.

Cattell, R. B. A note on factor invariance and the identification of factors. *British Journal of Psychology*, (Statistical Section) 1949, *2*(3), 134–138.

Cattell, R. B. *Factor analysis*. New York: Harper & Brothers, 1952.

Cattell, R. B. A quantitative analysis of the changes in culture patterns of Great Britain, 1837–1937, by P-technique. *Acta Psychologica*, 1953, *9*, 99–121.

Cattell, R. B. Validation and intensification of the sixteen personality factor questionnaire. *Journal of Clinical Psychology*, 1956, *12*, 205–214.

Cattell, R. B. *Personality and motivation structure and measurement*. New York: World Book Co., 1957.

Cattell, R. B. The basis of recognition and interpretation of factors. *Educational and Psychological Measurement*, 1962, *22*, 667–697.

Cattell, R. B. Theory of fluid and crystallized intelligence: A critical experiment. *Journal of Educational Psychology*, 1963, *54*, 1–22.

Cattell, R. B. Higher order factor structures and reticular vs. hierarchical formulae for their interpretation. In C. Banks & P. L. Broadhurst (Eds.), *Studies in psychology*. London: University of London Press, Ltd., 1966. (a)

Cattell, R. B. The data box: Its ordering of total resources in terms of possible relational systems. In R. B. Cattell (Ed.), *Handbook of multivariate experimental psychology*. Chicago: Rand-McNally, 1966. (b)

Cattell, R. B. The meaning and strategic use of factor analysis. In R. B. Cattell (Ed.), *Handbook of multivariate experimental psychology*. Chicago: Rand-McNally, 1966. (c)

Cattell, R. B. The scree test for the number of factors. *Multivariate Behavioral Research*, 1966, *1*(2), 245–276. (d)

Cattell, R. B. The isopodic and equipotent principles for comparing factor scores across different populations. *British Journal of Mathematical and Statistical Psychology*, 1970, *23*(1), 23–41. (a)

Cattell, R. B. Separating endogenous, exogenous, ecogenic, and epogenic component curves in developmental data. *Developmental Psychology*, 1970, *3*, 151–162. (b)

Cattell, R. B. Real base true zero factor analysis. *Multivariate Behavioral Research Monographs*, 1972, No. 72–1.

Cattell, R. B. *The scientific use of factor analysis in behavioral and life sciences*. New York: Plenum Press, 1978.

Cattell, R. B., & Adelson, M. The dimensions of social change in the U.S.A. as determined by P-technique. *Social Forces*, 1951, *30*, 190–201.

Cattell, R. B., Balcar, K. R., Horn, J. L., & Nesselroade, J. R. Factor matching procedures: An improvement of the *s* index; with tables. *Educational and Psychological Measurement* 1969, *29*, 781–792.

Cattell, R. B., & Baggaley, A. R. The salient variable similarity index for factor matching. *British Journal of Statistical Psychology*, 1960, *13*, 33–46.

Cattell, R. B., & Birkett, H. Can P-technique diagnosis be practicably shortened? Some proposals and a test of a 50-day abridgement. *Multivariate Experimental Clinical Research*, 1980, *5*(1), 1–16.

Cattell, R. B., & Brennan, J. The practicality of an orthogonal confactor rotation for the approximate resolution of oblique factors. *Multivariate Experimental Clinical Research*, 1977, *3*(2), 95–104.

Cattell, R. B., & Burdsal, C. A. The radial parcel double factoring design: A solution to the item-vs-parcel controversy. *Multivariate Behavioral Research*, 1975, *10*, 165–179.

Cattell, R. B., & Cattell, A. K. S. Factor rotation for proportional profiles: Analytic solution and an example. *British Journal of Statistical Psychology*, 1955, *8*(2), 83–86.

Cattell, R. B., & Coulter, M. A. Principles of behavioral taxonomy and the mathematical basis of the taxonome computer program. *British Journal of Mathematical and Statistical Psychology*, 1966, *19*, 237–269.

Cattell, R. B., & Foster, M. J. The rotoplot program for multiple, single-plane, visually-guided rotation. *Behavioral Science*, 1963, *8*, 156–165.

Cattell, R. B., & Gorsuch, R. L. The uniqueness and significance of simple structure demonstrated by contrasting organic "natural structure" and "random structure" data. *Psychometrika*, 1963, *28*, 55–67.

Cattell, R. B., & Gorsuch, R. L. The definition and measurement of national morale and morality. *Journal of Social Psychology*, 1965, *67*, 77–96.

Cattell, R. B., & Jaspers, J. A general plasmode (No. 30-10-5-2) for factor analytic exercises and research. *Multivariate Behavioral Research Monographs*, 1967, No. 67–3.

Cattell, R. B., & Muerle, J. The "Maxplane" program for factor rotation to oblique simple structure. *Educational and Psychological Measurement*, 1960, *20*(3), 569–590.

Cattell, R. B., & Vogelmann, S. A comprehensive trial of the scree and KG criteria for determining the number of factors. *Multivariate Behavioral Research*, 1977, *12*, 289–325.

Christoffersson, A. Factor analysis of dichotomized variables. *Psychometrika*, 1975, *40*, 5–32.

Cliff, N. The relation between sample and population characteristic vectors. *Psychometrika*, 1970, *35*(2), 163–178.

Cliff, N., & Hamburger, C. D. The study of sampling errors in factor analysis by means of artificial experiments. *Psychological Bulletin*, 1967, *68*(6), 430–445.

Cliff, N., & Pennell, R. The influence of communality, factor strength, and loading size on the sampling characteristics of factor loadings. *Psychometrika*, 1967, *32*(3), 309–326.

Cohen, J. r_c: A profile similarity coefficient invariant over variable reflection. *Proceedings of the 76th annual convention of the American Psychological Association*, 1968, *3*(1), 211–212. (a)

Cohen, J. Multiple regression as a general data-analytic system. *Psychological Bulletin*, 1968, *70*, 426–443. (b)

Cohen, J. A profile similarity coefficient invariant over variable reflection. *Psychological Bulletin*, 1969, *71*(4), 281–284.

Cohen, J., & Cohen, P. *Applied multiple regression/correlation analysis for the behavioral sciences*. Hillsdale, N.J.: Lawrence Erlbaum Associates, Inc., 1975.

Coles, G. J., & Stone, L. A. An exploratory direct-estimation approach to location of observers in percept space. *Perceptual and Motor Skills*, 1974, *39*(1, Part 2), 539–549.

Comrey, A. L. The minimum residual method of factor analysis. *Psychological Reports*, 1962, *11*, 15–18.

Comrey, A. L. Tandem criteria for analytic rotation in factor analysis. *Psychometrika*, 1967, *32*, 143–154.

Comrey, A. L. Common methodological problems in factor analytic studies. *Journal of Consulting and Clinical Psychology*, 1978, *46*(4), 648–659.

Comrey, A. L., & Ahumada, A. Note and Fortran IV program for minimum residual factor analysis. *Psychological Reports*, 1965, *17*(2), 446.

Cotter, K. L., & Raju, N. S. An evaluation of formula-based population squared cross-validity estimates and factor score estimates in prediction. *Educational and Psychological Measurement*, 1982, *42*, 493–519.

Crawford, C. B. Determining the number of interpretable factors. *Psychological Bulletin*, 1975, *82*, 226–237.

Crawford, C. B., & Ferguson, G. A. A general rotation criterion and its use in orthogonal rotation. *Psychometrika*, 1970, *35*(3), 321–332.

Crawford, C. B., & Koopman, P. Note: Inter-rater reliability of scree test and mean square ratio test of number of factors. *Perceptual & Motor Skills*, 1979, *49*, 223–226.

Cronbach, L. J. Coefficient alpha and the internal structure of tests. *Psychometrika*, 1951, *16*, 297–334.

Cureton, E. E. Communality estimation in factor analysis of small matrices. *Educational and Psychological Measurement*, 1971, *31*(2), 371–380.

Cureton, E. E. Studies of the promax and optres rotations. *Multivariate Behavioral Research*, 1976, *4*, 449–460.

Cureton, E. E., Cureton, L. W., & Durfee, R. C. A method of cluster analysis. *Multivariate Behavioral Research*, 1970, *5*(1), 101–116.

Cureton, E. E., & Mulaik, S. A. The weighted varimax rotation and the promax rotation. *Psychometrika*, 1975, *40*(2), 183–195.

Daniel, R. S. Biblometrics and scholarly impact. *Acta Psychologica*, 1979, *34*, 725–726.

Darlington, R. B. Multiple regression in psychological research and practice. *Psychological Bulletin*, 1968, *69*, 161–182.

Dielman, T. E., Cattell, R. B., & Wagner, A. Evidence on the simple structure and factor invariance achieved by five rotational methods on four types of data. *Multivariate Behavioral Research*, 1972, *7*, 223–242.

Digman, J. M. The procrustes class of factor-analytic transformation. *Multivariate Behavioral Research*, 1967, *2*(1), 89–94.

Dingman, H. F., Miller, C. R., & Eyman, R. K. A comparison between two analytic rotational solutions where the number of factors is indeterminate. *Behavioral Science*, 1964, *9*, 76–80.

DuBois, P. H. An analysis of Guttman's simplex. *Psychometrika*, 1960, *25*, 173–182.

DuBois, P. H., & Sullivan, R. F. Some experiences with analytic factor analysis. Paper presented at the Psychometric Society annual meeting, 1972.

Dwyer, P. S. The determination of the factor loadings of a given test from the known factor loadings of other tests. *Psychometrika*, 1937, *2*, 173–178.

Dziuban, C. D., & Harris, C. W. On the extraction of components and the applicability of the factor model. *American Educational Research Journal*, 1973, *10*, 93–99.

Eber, H. W. Toward oblique simple structure: Maxplane. *Multivariate Behavioral Research*, 1966, *1*(1), 112–125.

Elashoff, J. D. Analysis of covariance: A delicate instrument. *American Educational Research Journal*, 1969, *6*(3), 383–401.

Endler, N. S., Hunt, J., & Rosenstein, A. J. An S-R inventory of anxiousness. *Psychological Monographs*, 1962, *76*(536).

Evans, G. T. Transformation of factor matrices to achieve congruence. *British Journal of Mathematical and Statistical Psychology*, 1971, *24*, 22–48.

Eyman, R. K., Dingman, H. F., & Meyers, C. E. Comparison of some computer techniques for factor analytic rotation. *Educational and Psychological Measurement*, 1962, *22*, 201–214.

Eysenck, H. J. *Dimensions of personality*. London: Kegan Paul, 1947.

Eysenck, H. J. *The structure of human personality*. (3rd Ed.) London: Methuen, 1969.

Ferguson, G. A. The concept of parsimony in factor analysis. *Psychometrika*, 1954, *19*(4), 281–290.

Filsinger, E. E. Differences in religious structures between empirically derived types. *Review of Religious Research*, 1981, *22*(3), 255–267.

Fleishman, E. A., & Hempel, W. E., Jr. Changes in factor structure of a complex psychomotor test as a function of practice. *Psychometrika*, 1954, *19*, 239–252.

Fuller, E. L., Jr., & Hemmerle, W. J. Robustness of the maximum-likelihood estimation procedure in factor analysis. *Psychometrika*, 1966, *31*(2), 255–266.

Gardner, T., & Barnard, J. Intelligence and the factorial structure of person perception. *American Journal of Mental Deficiency*, 1969, *74*(2), 212–217.

Gebhardt, F. Maximum likelihood solution to factor analysis when some factors are completely specified. *Psychometrika*, 1971, *36*, 155–163.

Gerbing, D. W., & Hunter, J. E. The return to multiple groups: Analysis and critique of confirmatory factor analysis with LISREL. Unpublished manuscript, 1980.

Geweke, J. F., & Singleton, K. J. Interpreting the likelihood ratio statistic in factor models when sample size is small. *Journal of the American Stat. Association*, 1980, *75*, 133–137.

Gibson, W. A. Remarks on Tucker's interbattery method of factor analysis. *Psychometrika*, 1960, *25*, 19–25.

Gibson, W. A. Factoring the circumplex. *Psychometrika*, 1963, *28*, 87–92. (a)

Gibson, W. A. On the symmetric treatment of an asymmetric approach to factor analysis. *Psychometrika*, 1963, *28*(4), 423–426. (b)

Gibson, W. A. A latent structure for the simplex. *Psychometrika*, 1967, *32*(1), 35–46.

Glass, G. V. Alpha factor analysis of infallible variables. *Psychometrika*, 1966, *31*(4), 545–561.

Glass, G. V., & Maguire, T. Abuses of factor scores. *American Educational Research Journal*, 1966, *3*(3), 297–304.

Goldberg, L. R. Parameters of personality inventory construction and utilization: A comparison of prediction strategies and tactics. *Multivariate Behavioral Research Monograph* 1972, No. 72-2.

Gollob, H. F. A statistical model which combines features of factor analytic and analysis of variance techniques. *Psychometrika*, 1968, *33*(1), 73–115. (a)

Gollob, H. F. Confounding of sources of variation in factor-analytic techniques. *Psychological Bulletin*, 1968, *70*(5), 330–344. (b)

Gollob, H. F. Rejoinder to Tucker's "Comments on 'Confounding of sources of variation in factor-analytic techniques.'" *Psychological Bulletin,* 1968, *70*(5), 355–360. (c)

Gordon, R. A. Issues in the ecological study of delinquency. *American Sociological Review,* 1967, *32*(6), 927–944.

Gordon, R. A. Issues in multiple regression. *American Journal of Sociology,* 1968, *73,* 592–616.

Gorsuch, R. L. The clarification of some superego factors. Unpublished doctoral dissertation, University of Illinois, 1965.

Gorsuch, R. L. The general factor in the Text Anxiety Questionnaire. *Psychological Reports,* 1966, *19,* 308.

Gorsuch, R. L. Dimensions of the conceptualization of God. *In* J. Matthes (Ed.), *International yearbook for the sociology of religion,* Vol. III 1967.

Gorsuch, R. L. A comparison of Biquartimin, Maxplane, Promax, and Varimax. *Educational and Psychological Measurement,* 1970, *30,* 861–872.

Gorsuch, R. L. Using Bartlett's significance test to determine the number of factors to extract. *Educational and Psychological Measurement,* 1973, *33,* 361–364. (a)

Gorsuch, R. L. Data analysis of correlated independent variables. *Multivariate Behavioral Research,* 1973, *8*(1), 89–107. (b)

Gorsuch, R. L. *Factor analysis.* Philadelphia: W. B. Saunders Company, 1974.

Gorsuch, R. L. Factor score reliabilities and domain validities. *Educational & Psychological Measurement,* 1980, *40*(4), 895–898.

Gorsuch, R. L. & Nelson, J. *CNG scree test: An objective procedure for determining the number of factors.* Presented at the annual meeting of the Society for Multivariate Experimental Psychology, 1981.

Gorsuch, R. L., & Yagel, C. Item factor analysis. Presented at the annual meeting of the American Educational Research Association, 1981.

Gottwald, N. F. *A light to the nations.* New York: Harper & Row, 1959.

Gower, J. C. Generalized Procrustes analysis. *Psychometrika,* 1975, *40,* 33–51.

Green, B. F. The orthogonal approximation of an oblique structure in factor analysis. *Psychometrika,* 1952, *17,* 429–440.

Gruvaeus, G. T. A general approach to procrustes pattern rotation. *Psychometrika,* 1970, *35*(4), 493–505.

Guertin, W. H. Typing ships with transpose factor analysis. *Educational and Psychological Measurement,* 1971, *31,* 397–405.

Guertin, W. H., & Bailey, J. P. *Introduction to modern factor analysis.* Ann Arbor: Edwards Brothers, Inc., 1970.

Guilford, J. P. *Fundamental statistics in psychology and education.* (4th Ed.) New York: McGraw-Hill, 1965. (a)

Guilford, J. P. Intelligence: 1965 model. *American Psychology* 1965, *21,* 20–26. (b)

Guilford, J. P. *The nature of human intelligence.* New York: McGraw-Hill, 1967.

Guilford, J. P. Factors and factors of personality. *Psychological Bulletin,* 1975, *82,* 802–814.

Guilford, J. P. The invariance problem in factor analysis. *Educational and Psychological Measurement.* 1977, *37,* 11–19.

Guilford, J. P. Higher-order structure-of-intellect abilities. *Multivariate Behavioral Research,* 1981, *16,* 411–435.

Guilford, J. P., & Hoepfner, R. Comparisons of varimax rotations with rotations to theoretical targets. *Educational and Psychological Measurement,* 1969, *29*(1), 3–23.

Guilford, J. P., & Hoepfner, R. *The analysis of intelligence.* New York: McGraw-Hill, 1971.

Guilford, J. P., & Zimmerman, W. S. Some variable-sampling problems in the rotations of axes in factor analysis. *Psychological Bulletin,* 1963, *60,* 269–301.

Guttman, L. Multiple group methods for common-factor analysis: Their basis, computation, and interpretation. *Psychometrika,* 1952, *17,* 209–222.

Guttman, L. Some necessary conditions for common factor analysis. *Psychometrika*, 1954, *19*(2), 149–161.

Guttman, L. A general nonmetric technique for finding the smallest coordinate space for a configuration of points. *Psychometrika*, 1968, *33*, 469–506.

Haertzen, C. A. Changes in correlation between responses to items of the Addiction Research Center Inventory produced by LSD-25. *Journal of Psychology and Pharmacology*, 1966, *1*, 27–36.

Hakstian, A. R. A computer program for oblique factor transformation using the generalized Harris-Kaiser procedure. *Educational and Psychological Measurement*, 1970, *30*(3), 703–705. (a)

Hakstian, A. R. A computer program for generalized oblique procrustes factor transformation. *Educational and Psychological Measurement*, 1970, *30*(3), 707–710. (b)

Hakstian, A. R. A comparative evaluation of several prominent methods of oblique factor transformation. *Psychometrika*, 1971, *36*(2), 175–193.

Hakstian, A. R. Optimizing the resolution between salient and non-salient factor pattern coefficients. *British Journal of Mathematical and Statistical Psychology*, 1972, *25*, 229–245.

Hakstian, A. R., & Boyd, W. M. An empirical investigation of some special cases of the general "orthomax" criterion for orthogonal factor transformation. *Educational and Psychological Measurement*, 1972, *32*, 3–22.

Hakstian, A. R., Rogers, W. T., & Cattell, R. B. The behavior of number-of-factors rules with simulated data. *Multivariate Behavioral Research*, 1982, *17*, 193–219.

Halperin, S. The incorrect measurement of components. *Educational and Psychological Measurement*, 1976, *36*, 347–353.

Hamburger, C. D. Factorial stability as a function of analytical rotation method, type of simple structure, and size of sample. Unpublished doctoral dissertation, University of Southern California, 1965.

Hamilton, M. Notes and correspondence. *British Journal of Mathematical and Statistical Psychology*. 1967, *20*(1), 107–110.

Harman, H. H. On the rectilinear prediction of oblique factors. *Psychometrika*, 1941, *6*, 29–35.

Harman, H. H. *Modern factor analysis*. Chicago: The University of Chicago Press, 1960.

Harman, H. H. *Modern factor analysis*. Chicago: The University of Chicago Press, 1967.

Harman, H. H. *Modern factor analysis* (3rd ed. rev.). Chicago: The University of Chicago Press, 1976.

Harman, H. H., & Jones, W. H. Factor analysis by minimizing residuals (minres). *Psychometrika*, 1966, *31*(3), 351–368.

Harman, H. H., and Fukuda, Y. Resolution of the Heywood case in the minres solution. *Psychometrika*, 1966, *31*,(4), 563–571.

Harris, C. W. Some recent developments in factor analysis. *Educational and Psychological Measurement*, 1964, *24*(2), 193–206.

Harris, C. W. On factors and factor scores. *Psychometrika*, 1967, *32*(4), 363–379.

Harris, C. W., & Kaiser, H. F. Oblique factor analytic solutions by orthogonal transformations. *Psychometrika*, 1964, *29*(4), 347–362.

Harris, M. L. & Harris, C. W. A factor analytic interpretation strategy. *Educational and Psychological Measurement*, 1971, *31*(3), 589–606.

Hase, H. D., & Goldberg, L. R. Comparative validity of different strategies of constructing personality inventory scales. *Psychological Bulletin*, 1967, *67*(4), 231–248.

Heeler, R. M., & Whipple, T. W. A Monte Carlo aid to the evaluation of maximum likelihood factor analysis solutions. *British Journal of Mathematical and Statistical Psychology*, 1976, *29*, 253–256.

Heermann, E. F. Univocal or orthogonal estimators of orthogonal factors. *Psychometrika*, 1963, *28*(2), 161–172.

Hegmann, J. P., & DeFries, J. C. Maximum variance linear combinations from phenotypic, genetic, and environmental covariance matrices. *Multivariate Behavioral Research*, 1970, *5*(1), 9–18.

Hendrickson, A. E., & White, P. O. Promax: A quick method for rotation to oblique simple structure. *British Journal of Statistical Psychology,* 1964, *17*(1), 65–70.

Henrysson, S. *Applicability of factor analysis in the behavioral sciences.* Stockholm: Almquist & Wiksell, 1960.

Henrysson, S. Methods of adjustment of item-total correlation for overlapping due to unique item variance. Research Bulletin, Institute of Educational Research, University of Stockholm, 1962, No. 8.

Hicks, M. M. Applications of nonlinear principal components analysis to behavioral data. *Multivariate Behavioral Research,* 1981, *16,* 309–322.

Hofmann, R. J. The oblimax transformation. Unpublished doctoral dissertation, State University of New York at Albany, 1970.

Hofmann, R. J. Complexity and simplicity as objective indices descriptive of factor solutions. *Multivariate Behavioral Research,* 1978, *13,* 247–250.

Hofmann, R. J. Multiple hierarchical analysis. *Applied Psychological Measurement,* 1980, *4*(1), 91–103.

Holley, J. W. On the generalization of the Burt reciprocity principle. *Multivariate Behavioral Research,* 1970, *5*(2), 241–250. (a)

Holley, J. W. On the Burt reciprocity principle: A final generation. *Psychological Research Bulletin,* 1970, *9*(7), 9. (b)

Holley, J. W., & Harris, C. W. The application of the Harris bridge in the generalization of the Burt reciprocity principle: A demonstration study. *Scandinavian Journal of Psychology,* 1970, *11,* 255–260.

Hollingshead, A. B., & Redlich, F. C. *Social class and mental illness: A community study.* New York: Wiley, 1958.

Holthouse, N. D. *An empirical analysis of selected procedures for testing the equality of variance-covariance matrices.* Unpublished doctoral dissertation, Ohio University, 1970.

Holzinger, K. J., & Swineford, F. *A study in factor analysis: The stability of a bi-factor solution.* University of Chicago: Supplementary Educational Monographs. No. 48, 1939.

Horn, J. L. Second-order factors in questionnaire data. *Educational and Psychological Measurement,* 1963, *23,* 117–134.

Horn, J. L. An empirical comparison of methods for estimating factor scores. *Educational and Psychological Measurement,* 1965, *25*(2), 313–322. (a)

Horn, J. L. A rationale and test for the number of factors in factor analysis. *Psychometrika,* 1965, *30*(2), 179–185. (b)

Horn, J. L. On subjectivity in factor analysis. *Educational and Psychological Measurement,* 1967, *27,*(4), 811–820.

Horn, J. L. Factor analyses with variables of different metric. *Educational and Psychological Measurement,* 1969, *29*(4), 753–762. (a)

Horn, J. L. On the internal consistency reliability of factors. *Multivariate Behavioral Research* 1969 *4*(1), 115–125. (b)

Horn, J. L. The structure of intellect. Primary abilities. In R. M. Dreger (Ed.), *Multivariate personality research.* Baton Rouge: Claitor's, 1972.

Horn, J. L. *Concepts and methods of correlational analyses.* New York: Holt, Rinehart & Winston, 1973.

Horn, J. L., & Cattell, R. B. Age differences in fluid and crystallized intelligence. *Acta Psychologia,* 1967, *26,* 107–129.

Horn, J. L., & Engstrom, R. Cattell's scree test in relation to Bartlett's chi-square test and other observations on the number of factors problem. *Multivariate Behavioral Research,* 1979, *14,* 283–300.

Horn, J. L., & Knapp, J. R. On the subjective character of the empirical base of the structure-of-intellect model. *Psychological Bulletin,* 1973, *80,* 33–43.

Horn, J. L., & Miller, W. C. Evidence on problems in estimating common factor scores. *Educational and Psychological Measurement*, 1966, *26*(3), 617–622.

Horst, P. *Matrix algebra for social scientists*. New York: Holt, Rinehart & Winston, 1963.

Horst, P. *Factor analysis of data matrices*. New York: Holt, Rinehart & Winston, 1965.

Horst, P. The missing data matrix. *Journal of Clinical Psychology*, 1968, *24*(3), 286–306. (a)

Horst, P. *Personality: Measurement of dimensions*. San Francisco: Jossey-Bass, 1968. (b)

Howard, K. I., & Cartwright, D. S. An empirical note on the communality problem in factor analysis. *Psychological Reports*, 1962, *10*, 797–798.

Howard, K. I., & Gordon, R. A. Empirical note on the "number of factors" problem in factor analysis. *Psychological Report*, 1963, *12*(1), 247–250.

Howard, K. I., & Lissitz, R. W. To err is human: Effects of a computer characteristic. *Educational and Psychological Measurement*. 1966, *26*, 199–203.

Humphreys, L. G. Number of cases and number of factors: An example where *N* is very large. *Educational and Psychological Measurement*, 1964, *24*, 457–466.

Humphreys, L. G., & Ilgen, D. Note on a criterion for the number of common factors. *Educational and Psychological Measurement*, 1969, *29*, 571–578.

Humphreys, L. G., Ilgen, D., McGrath, D., & Montanelli, R. Capitalization on chance in rotation of factors. *Educational and Psychological Measurement*, 1969, *29*(2), 259–271.

Humphreys, L. G., Tucker, L. R., & Dachler, P. Evaluating the importance of factors in any given order of factoring. *Multivariate Behavioral Research*, 1970, *5*(2), 209–215.

Hundleby, J. D., Pawlik, K., & Cattell, R. B. *Personality factors in objective test devices: A critical integration of a quarter of a century's research*. San Diego: Robert T. Knapp, 1965.

Hunter, J. E. Maximal decomposition: An alternative to factor analysis. *Multivariate Behavioral Research*, 1972, *7*, 243–268.

Hurley, J., & Cattell, R. B. The procrustes program: Producing direct rotation to test a hypothesized factor structure. *Behavioral Science*, 1962, *7*(2), 258–262.

Irwin, L. A method for clustering eigenvalues. *Psychometrika*, 1966, *31*(1), 11–16.

Jackson, D. N. & Skinner, H. A. Univocal varimax: An orthogonal factor rotation program for optimal simple structure. *Educational and Psychological Measurement*, 1975, *35*, 663–665.

Jenkins, T. N. Limitations of iterative procedures for estimating communalities. *Journal of Psychological Studies*, 1962, *13*, 69–73.

Jennrich, R. I. Orthogonal rotation algorithms. *Psychometrika*, 1970, *35*(2), 229–235.

Jennrich, R. I., & Robinson, S. M. A Newton-Raphson algorithm for maximum likelihood factor analysis. *Psychometrika* 1969, *34*(1), 111–123.

Jennrich, R. I., & Sampson, P. F. Rotation for simple loadings. *Psychometrika*, 1966, *31*(3), 313–323.

Johnson, S. C. Hierarchical clustering schemes. *Psychometrika*, 1967, *32*(3), 241–254.

Jones, K. J. Relation of R-analysis factor scores and Q-analysis factor loadings. *Psychological Reports*, 1967, *20*(1), 247–249.

Jöreskog, K. G. On the statistical treatment of residuals in factor analysis. *Psychometrika*, 1962, *27*(4), 335–354.

Jöreskog, K. G. Testing a simple structure hypothesis in factor analysis. *Psychometrika*, 1966, *31*(2), 165–178.

Jöreskog, K. G. A computer program for unrestricted maximum likelihood factor analysis. *Research Bulletin*, Princeton, Educational Testing Service, 1967.

Jöreskog, K. G. A general approach to confirmatory maximum likelihood factor analysis. *Psychometrika*, 1969, *34*(2), 183–202. (a)

Jöreskog, K. G. Efficient estimation in image factor analysis. *Psychometrika*, 1969, *34*(1), 51–75. (b)

Jöreskog, K. G. Factoring the multitest-multioccasion correlation matrix. *Research Bulletin*, Princeton, Educational Testing Service, 1969. (c)

Jöreskog, K. G. Statistical analysis of sets of congeneric tests. *Psychometrika*, 1971, *36*(2), 109–133.

Jöreskog, K. G. Structural analysis of covariance and correlation matrices. *Psychometrika*, 1978, *43*, 443–477.

Jöreskog, K. G., & Gruvaeus, G. A computer program for restricted maximum likelihood factor analysis. *Research Bulletin*, Princeton, Educational Testing Service, 1967.

Jöreskog, K. G., Gruvaeus, G., & Thillo, V. ACOUS: A general computer program for analysis of covariance structures. *Research Bulletin*, Princeton, Educational Testing Service, 1970.

Jöreskog, K. G., & Lawley, D. N. New methods in maximum likelihood factor analysis. *British Journal of Mathematical and Statistical Psychology*, 1968, *21*(1), 85–96.

Jöreskog, K. G., & Sörbom, D. *LISREL V users guide*. Chicago: National Educational Research, 1982.

Kaiser, H. F. The varimax criterion for analytic rotation in factor analysis. *Psychometrika*, 1958, *23*(3), 187–200.

Kaiser, H. F. Formulas for component scores. *Psychometrika*, 1962, *27*(1), 83–87.

Kaiser, H. F. A second generation Little Jiffy. *Psychometrika*, 1970, *35*(4), 401–415.

Kaiser, H. F. Image and anti-image covariance matrices from a correlation matrix that may be singular. *Psychometrika*, 1976, *41*, 295–300. (a)

Kaiser, H. F. Review of Lawley, D. N., & Maxwell, A. E. Factor analysis as a statistical method. *EPM*, 1976, *36*, 586–589. (b)

Kaiser, H. F., & Caffrey, J. Alpha factor analysis. *Psychometrika*, 1965, *30*(1), 1–14.

Kaiser, H. F., & Cerny, B. A. Casey's method for fitting hyperplanes from an intermediate orthomax solution. *Multivariate Behavioral Research*, 1978, *13*, 395–401.

Kaiser, H. F., & Dickman, K. W. Analytic determination of common factors. Unpublished manuscript, University of Illinois, 1959.

Kaiser, H. F., Hunka, S., & Bianchini, J. Relating factors between studies based upon different individuals. *Multivariate Behavioral Research*, 1971, *6*, 409–422.

Kalimo, E. Notes on approximate procrustes rotation to primary pattern. *Educational and Psychological Measurement*, 1971, *31*(2), 363–369.

Kallina, H., & Hartman, A. Principal component analysis versus classical factor analysis. *Psychologische Beitrage*, 1976, *18*, 84–98.

Kazelskis, R. A correction for loading bias in a principal components analysis. *Educational and Psychological Measurement*, 1978, *38*, 253–257.

Keil, D., & Wrigley, C. Effects upon the factorial solution of rotating varying number of factors. *American Psychologist*, 1960, *15*, 383–394.

Kelly, F. J., Beggs, D. L., & McNeil, K. A. *Multiple regression approach*. Carbondale: Southern Illinois University Press, 1969.

Kenny, D. A. An empirical application of confirmatory factor analysis to the multitrait multimethod matrix. *Journal of Experimental and Social Psychology*, 1976, *12*, 247–52.

Kenny, D. A. *Correlation and causality*. New York: Wiley, 1979.

Kenney, B. P., Vaughan, C. E., & Cromwell, R. E. Religiosity among ethnic minorities. *JSSR*, 1977, *16*(3), 237–244.

Knapp, T. R., & Swoyer, V. H. Some empirical results concerning the power of Bartlett's test of the significance of a correlation matrix. *American Educational Research Journal*, 1967, *4*(1), 13–17.

Korth, B., & Tucker, L. R. Procrustes matching by congruence coefficients. *Psychometrika*, 1976, *41*, 531–535.

Kristof, W., & Wingersky, B. A generalization of the orthogonal procrustes rotation procedure to more than two matrices. *Proceedings of the 79th Annual Convention of the American Psychological Association*, 1971, *6*(1), 89–90.

Kroonenberg, P., & de Leuw, J. Principal component analysis of three-mode data by means of alternating least square algorithms. *Psychometrika*, 1980, *45*, 69–97.

Kruskal, J. B., & Carroll, J. D. Geometrical models and badness-of-fit functions. *Multivariate Analysis*, 1969, *2*, 639–671.

Lastovicka, J. L. The extension of component analysis to four-mode matrices. *Psychometrika*, 1981, *46*, 47–57.

Laux, D. F., & Tucker, R. K. The effects of differentially computed factor scores on statistical decisions. *The Psychological Record*, 1979, *29*, 501–516.

Lawley, D. N. The estimation of factor loadings by the method of maximum likelihood. *Proceedings of the Royal Society of Edinburgh*, 1940, *60*, 64–82.

Lawley, D. N. Further investigations in factor estimation. *Proceedings of the Royal Society of Edinburgh*, 1941. *61*, 176–185.

Lawley, D. N. A statistical examination of the centroid method. *Proceedings of the Royal Society of Edinburgh*, 1955, *64*, 175–189.

Lawley, D. N., & Maxwell, A. E. *Factor analysis as a statistical method*, London: Butterworth, 1963.

Ledermann, W. The orthogonal transformation of a factorial matrix into itself. *Psychometrika*, 1938, *3*, 181–187.

Ledermann, W. On a shortened method of estimation of mental factors by regression. *Psychometrika*, 1939, *4*, 109–116.

Lee, H. B., & Comrey, A. L. An empirical comparison of two minimum residual factor extraction methods. *Multivariate Behavioral Research*, 1978, *13*, 497–508.

Lee, H. B., & Comrey, A. L. Distortions in a commonly used factor analytic procedure. *Multivariate Behavioral Research*, 1979, *14*, 301–321.

Levin, J. Three-mode factor analysis. *Psychological Bulletin*, 1965, *64*(6), 442–452.

Levonian, E., and Comrey, A. L. Factorial stability as a function of the number of orthogonally-rotated factors. *Behavioral Science*, 1966, *11*(5), 400–404.

Lindell, M. K., & St. Clair, J. B. Tukknife: A jacknife supplement to canned statistical packages. *Educational and Psychological Measurement*, 1980, *40*, 751–754.

Lingoes, J. C., & Guttman, L. Nonmetric factor analysis: A rank reducing alternative to linear factor analysis. *Multivariate Behavioral Research*, 1967, *2*(4), 485–505.

Lingoes, J. C., Roskam, E. E., & Borg, I. *Geometric representations of relational data*. Ann Arbor, MI: Mathesis, 1979.

Linn, R. L. A Monte Carlo approach to the number of factors problem. *Psychometrika*, 1968, *33*(1), 37–72.

Lissitz, R. W., Schönemann, P. H., & Lingoes, J. C. A solution to the weighted procrustes problem in which the transformation is in agreement with the loss function. *Psychometrika*, 1976, *41*, 547–550.

Longley, J. W. An appraisal of least squares programs for the electronic computer from the point of view of the user. *Journal of the American Statistical Association*. 1967, *62*, 819–841.

Loo, R. The orthogonal rotation of factors in clinical research: A critical note. *Journal of Clinical Psychology*, 1979, *35*(4), 762–765.

Lord, F. M. Large sample covariance analysis when the control variable is fallible. *Journal of American Statistical Association*, 1960, *55*, 309–321.

Luborsky, L., & Mintz, J. The contribution of P-technique to personality, psychotherapy, and psychosomatic research. In R. M. Dreger (Ed.), *Multivariate personality research: Contributions to the understanding of personality*. Baton Rouge, LA: Claitor's Publishing Division, 1972.

Lykken, D. T. Multiple factor analysis and personality research. *Journal of Experimental Research in Personality*, 1971, *5*, 161–170.

MacDonell, W. R. On criminal anthropology and the identification of criminals. *Biometrika*, 1902, *1*, 178–227.

Maxwell, A. E. Statistical methods in factor analysis. *Psychological Bulletin*, 1959, *56*(3), 228–235.

McAndrew, C., & Forgy, E. A note on the effects of score transformations in Q and R factor analysis techniques. *Psychological Review*, 1963, *70*, 116–118.

McCloskey, J., & Jackson, P. R. Three-mode: A fortran IV program for three-mode factor analysis. *Behavior Research Methods & Instrumentation*, 1979, *11*(1), 75–76.

McDonald, R. P. A general approach to non-linear factor analysis. *Psychometrika*, 1962, *27*(4), 397–415.

McDonald, R. P. The common factor analysis of multicategory data. *British Journal of Mathematical and Statistical Psychology*, 1969, *22*(2), 165–175. (a)

McDonald, R. P. A generalized common factor analysis based on residual covariance matrices of prescribed structure. *British Journal of Mathematical and Statistical Psychology*, 1969, *22*(2), 49–163. (b)

McDonald, R. P. The theoretical foundations of principal factor analysis, canonical factor analysis, and alpha factor analysis. *British Journal of Mathematical and Statistical Psychology*, 1970, *23*, 1–21.

McDonald, R. P. Some checking procedures for extension analysis. *Multivariate Behavioral Research*, 1978, *13*, 319–325.

McDonald, R. P., & Burr, E. J. A comparison of four methods of constructing factor scores. *Psychometrika*, 1967, *32*(4), 381–401.

McDonald, R. P., & Mulaik, S. A. Determinacy of common factors: A nontechnical review. *Psychological Bulletin*, 1979, *86*(2), 297–306.

McNemar, Q. The factors in factoring behavior. *Psychometrika*, 1951, *16*, 353–359.

McNemar, Q. Lost: Our intelligence? *American Psychologist*, 1964, *19*, 871–882.

McQuitty, L. L. Rank order typal analysis. *Educational and Psychological Measurement*, 1963, *23*(1), 55–61.

Meredith, W. Notes on factorial invariance. *Psychometrika*, 1964, *29*(2), 177–185. (a)

Meredith, W. Rotation to achieve factorial invariance. *Psychometrika*, 1964, *29*(2), 187–206. (b)

Mintz, J., & Luborsky, L. P-technique factor analysis in psychotherapy research: An illustration of a method. *Psychotherapy*, 1970, *7*, 13–18.

Montanelli, R. G., Jr., & Humphreys, L. G. Latent roots of random data correlation matrices with squared multiple correlations on the diagonal: A Monte Carlo study. *Psychometrika*, 1976, *41*(3), 341–347.

Morris, J. D. A comparison of regression prediction accuracy on several types of factor scores. *American Educational Research Journal*, 1979, *16*(1), 17–24.

Morris, J. D. The predictive accuracy of full-rank variables vs. various types of factor scores: Implications for test validation. *Educational and Psychological Measurement*, 1980, *40*, 389–396.

Morris, J. D., & Guertin, W. H. Relating multidimensional sets of variables: Canonical correlations or factor analysis? *Psychological Reports*, 1975, *36*, 859–862.

Morris, J. D., & Guertin, W. H. A computer program to relate factors across separately factor analyzed variable domains. *Educational and Psychological Measurement*, 1976, *36*, 171–174.

Morris, J. D., & Guertin, W. H. The superiority of factor scores as predictors. *Journal of Experimental Education*, 1977, *45*, 41–44.

Moseley, E. C., & Klett, C. J. An empirical comparison of factor scoring methods. *Psychological Reports*, 1964, *14*(1), 179–184.

Mosier, C. I. A note on Dwyer: The determination of the factor loadings of a given test. *Psychometrika*, 1938, *3*(4), 297–299.

Mosier, C. I. Determining a simple structure when loadings for certain tests are known. *Psychometrika*, 1939, *4*, 149–162. (a)

Mosier, C. I. Influence of chance error on simple structure. *Psychometrika*, 1939, *4*, 33–44. (b)

Mote, T. A. An artifact of the rotation of too few factors: Study orientation vs. trait anxiety. *Revista Interamericana de Psicologia*, 1970, *4*(3–4), 171–173.

Mulaik, S. A. Inferring the communality of a variable in a universe of variables. *Psychological Bulletin*, 1966, *66*(2), 119–124.

Neill, J. J., & Dunn, O. J. Equality of dependent correlation coefficients. *Biometrics*, 1975, *31*, 531–543.

Nesselroade, J. R., & Baltes, P. B. On a dilemma of comparative factor analysis: A study of factor matching based on random data. *Educational and Psychological Measurement*, 1970, *30*(4), 935–948.

Nesselroade, J. R., Baltes, P. B., & LaBouvie, E. W. Evaluating factor invariance in oblique space: Baseline data generated from random numbers. *Multivariate Behavioral Research*, 1971, *6*, 233–241.

Neuhaus, J. O., & Wrigley, C. The quartimax method: An analytical approach to orthogonal simple structure. *British Journal of Statistical Psychology*, 1954, *7*, 81–91.

Nicewander, W. A., Urry, V. W., & Starry, A. R. Composite components analysis: A method for factoring large numbers of items. *Proceedings of the 77th Annual Convention of the American Psychological Association*, 1969, *4*(1), 111–112.

Norman, W. T. Toward a taxonomy of personality attributes: Replicated factor structure in peer nomination personality ratings. *Journal of Abnormal and Social Psychology*, 1963, *66*, 547–583.

Nosal, M. A note on the minres method. *Psychometrika*, 1977, *42*(1), 149–151.

Nottingham, J., Gorsuch, R. L., & Wrightsman, L.: Factorial replication of the theoretically derived subscales on the Philosophies of Human Nature Scale. *Journal of Social Psychology*, 1970, *81*, 129–130.

Nunnally, J. C. The analysis of profile data. *Psychological Bulletin*, 1962, *59*, 311–319.

Nunnally, J. C. *Psychometric theory*. New York: McGraw-Hill, 1967.

Nunnally, J. C. *Psychometric theory* (2nd ed.). New York: McGraw-Hill, 1978.

Olsson, U. Maximum likelihood estimation of the polychoric correlation coefficient. *Psychometrika*, 1979, *44*, 443–460.

Osgood, C. E., Suci, G. H., & Tannenbaum, P. H. *The measurement of meaning*. Urbana: The University of Illinois Press, 1957.

Osgood, C. E., Ware, E. E., & Morris, C. Analysis of the connotative meanings of a variety of human values as expressed by American college students. *Journal of Abnormal and Social Psychology*, 1961, *62*, 62–73.

Overall, J. E. Note on the scientific status of factors. *Psychological Bulletin*, 1964, *61*(4), 270–276.

Owen, G. *Mathematics for the social and management sciences: Finite mathematics*. Philadelphia: W. B. Saunders Co., 1970.

Parker, J., Jr., & Fleishman, E. A. Ability factors and component performance measures as predictors of complex tracking behavior. *Psychological Monographs, General and Applied*, 1960, *74*(16–503).

Passini, F. T., & Norman, W. T. A universal conception of personality structure. *Journal of Personality and Social Psychology*, 1966, *4*(1), 44–49.

Pennell, R. The influence of communality and *N* on the sampling distributions of factor loadings. *Psychometrika*, 1968, *33*(4), 423–439.

Peterson, D. R. Scope and generality of verbally defined personality factors. *Psychological Review*, 1965, *72*, 48–59.

Pinneau, S. R., & Newhouse, A. Measures of invariance and comparability in factor analysis for fixed variables. *Psychometrika*, 1964, *29*(3), 271–281.

Pinzka, C., & Saunders, D. R. Analytic rotation to simple structure, II: Extension to an oblique solution. *Research Bulletin*. Princeton: Educational Testing Service, 1954.

Quereshi, M. Y. Patterns of psycholinguistic development during early and middle childhood. *Educational and Psychological Measurement*, 1967, *27*, 353–365.

Rao, C. R. Estimation and tests of significance in factor analysis. *Psychometrika*, 1955, *20*(2), 92–111.

Rees, L. A factorial study of physical constitution in women. *Journal of Mental Science*, 1950, *96*(1), 619–631.

Rees, L. Constitutional factors in mental abnormality. In H. J. Eysenck (Ed.), *Handbook of abnormal psychology*. London: Pitman, 1960.

Revelle, W., & Rocklin, T. Very simple structure: An alternative procedure for estimating the optimal number of interpretable factors. *Multivariate Behavioral Research*, 1979, *14*, 403–414.

Rippe, D. D. Application of a large sampling criterion to some sampling problems in factor analysis. *Psychometrika*, 1953, *18*(3), 191–205.

Rock, D. A., Werts, C. E., Linn, R. L., & Jöreskog, K. G. A maximum likelihood solution to the errors in variables and errors in equations model. *Multivariate Behavioral Research*, 1977, *12*, 187–198.

Roff, M. Some properties of the communality in multiple factor theory. *Psychometrika*, 1935, *1*, 1–6.

Rosenblatt, S. M. Empirical study of the sampling error of principal components and varimax rotation factor loadings. *Proceedings of the 77th Annual Convention of the American Psychological Association*, 1969, *4*(1), 115–116.

Ross, J. The relation between test and person factors. *Psychological Review*, 1963, *70*(5), 432–443.

Royce, J. R. Factor theory and genetics. *Educational and Psychological Measurement*, 1957, *17*, 361–376.

Royce, J. R. The development of factor analysis. *Journal of General Psychology*, 1958, *58*, 139–164.

Ryckman, D. B., & Wiegerink, R. The factors of the Illinois Test of Psycholinguistic Abilities: A comparison of 18 factor analyses. *Exceptional Children*, 1969, *36*(2), 107–113.

Ryder, R. G. Profile factor analysis and variable factor analysis. *Psychological Reports*, 1964, *15*(1), 119–127.

Sandler, J. The reciprocity principle as an aid to factor analysis. *British Journal of Psychology* (Stat Section), 1949, *2*, 180–187.

Saunders, D. R. An analytic method for rotation to orthogonal simple structure. *Research Bulletin*. Princeton, Educational Testing Service, 1953.

Saunders, D. R. Transvarimax: Some properties of the ratiomax and equamax criteria for blind orthogonal rotation. Paper delivered at the American Psychological Association meeting, 1962.

Schmid, J., & Leiman, J. The development of hierarchical factor solutions. *Psychometrika*, 1957, *22*(1), 53–61.

Schmidt, F. L. The relative efficiency of regression and simple unit predictor weights in applied differential psychology. *Educational and Psychological Measurements*, 1971, *31*, 699–714.

Schönemann, P. H. A generalized solution of the orthogonal procrustes problem. *Psychometrika*, 1966, *31*(1), 1–10.

Schönemann, P. H. The minimum average correlation between equivalent sets of uncorrelated factors. *Psychometrika*, 1971, *36*, 21–30.

Schönemann, P. H. Factorial definitions of intelligence: Dubious legacy of dogma in data analysis. In I. Borg (Ed.) *Multidimensional data representations: When and why*. Ann Arbor, MI: Mathesis Press, 1981.

Schönemann, P. H., & Steiger, J. H. Regression component analysis. *British Journal of Mathematical and Statistical Psychology*, 1976, *29*, 175–189.

Schönemann, P. H., & Steiger, J. H. On the validity of indeterminate factor scores. *Bulletin of the Psychonomic Society*, 1978, *12*(4), 287–290.

Schönemann, P. H., & Wang, M. M. Some new results on factor indeterminacy. *Psychometrika*, 1972, *37*, 61–91.

Scott, W. A. *Values and organizations: A study of fraternities and sororities*. Chicago: Rand McNally, 1965.

Sells, S. B. *Stimulus determinants of behavior*. New York: Ronald Press, 1963.

Sells, S. B., Demaree, R. G., & Will, D. P., Jr. Dimensions of personality. I. Conjoint factor structure of Guilford and Cattell trait markers. *Multivariate Behavioral Research*, 1970, *3*, 391–422.

Shaycoft, M. F. The eigenvalue myth and the dimension reduction fallacy. Presented at the American Educational Research Association Annual Meeting, Minneapolis, 1970.

Shepard, R. N., & Carroll, J. D. Parametric representation of nonlinear data structures. In P. R. Krishnaiah (Ed.), *Multivariate analysis*. New York: Academic Press, 1966.

Shepard, R. N., & Kruskal, J. B. Nonmetric methods for scaling and for factor analysis (abstract). *American Psychologist*, 1964, *19*, 557–558.

Sherin, R. J. A matrix formulation of Kaiser's varimax criterion. *Psychometrika*, 1966, *31*, 535–538.

Skinner, H. A. Exploring relationships among multiple data sets. *Multivariate Behavioral Research*, 1977, *12*, 199–220.

Skinner, H. A. The art of exploring predictor-criterion relationships. *Psychological Bulletin*, 1978, *85*(2), 327–337.

Skinner, H. A. Factor analysis and studies on alcohol. *Journal of Studies on Alcohol*. 1980, *41*(11), 1091–1101.

Smith, P. A. A comparison of three sets of rotated factor analytic solutions of self-concept data. *Journal of Abnormal and Social Psychology*, 1962, *64*, 326–333.

Sokal, R. R. A comparison of five tests for completeness of factor extraction. *Transactions of the Kansas Academy of Science*, 1959, *62*, 141–152.

Steiger, J. H. Multicorr: A computer program for fast, accurate, small-sample testing of correlational pattern hypotheses. *Educational and Psychological Measurement*, 1979, *39*, 677–680.

Struening, E., & Cohen, J. Factorial invariance and other psychometric characteristics of five opinions about mental illness factors. *Educational and Psychological Measurement*, 1963, *23*(2), 289–298.

Synder, C. W., Jr., & Low, H. G. Three-mode common factor analysis: Procedure and computer programs. *Multivariate Behavioral Research*, 1979, *14*, 435–441.

Taylor, P. A. The use of factor models in curriculum evaluation: A mathematical model relating two factor structures. *Educational and Psychological Measurement*, 1967, *27*, 305–321.

Tenopyr, M. L., & Michael, W. B. A comparison of two computer-based procedures of orthogonal analytic rotation with a graphical method when a general factor is present. *Educational and Psychological Measurement*, 1963, *23*(3), 587–597.

Tenopyr, M. L., & Michael, W. B. The development of a modification in the normal varimax method for use with correlation matrices containing a general factor. *Educational and Psychological Measurement*, 1964, *24*(3), 677–699.

Thompson, G. H. *The factorial analysis of human ability*. (5th Ed.) London: University of London Press, 1939.

Thompson, G. H., & Ledermann, W. The influence of multivariate selection on the factorial analysis of ability. *British Journal of Psychology*, 1939, *29*, 288–305.

Thurstone, L. L. *The vectors of the mind*. Chicago: University of Chicago Press, 1935.

Thurstone, L. L. Primary mental abilities. *Psychometric Monographs*, 1938, No. 1.

Thurstone, L. L. *Multiple factor analysis*. Chicago: University of Chicago Press, 1947.

Timm, N. H. The estimation of variance-covariance and correlation matrices from incomplete data. *Psychometrika*, 1970, *35*(4), 417–437.

Tobias, S., & Carlson, J. E. Brief report: Bartlett's test of sphericity and chance findings in factor analysis. *Multivariate Behavioral Research*, 1969, *4*(3), 375–377.

Trites, D. K., & Sells, S. B. A note on alternative methods for estimating factor scores. *Journal of Applied Psychology*, 1955, *39*, 455–456.

Tryon, R. C., & Bailey, D. E. *Cluster analysis*. New York: McGraw-Hill, 1970.

Tucker, L. R. *A method for synthesis of factor analysis studies*. Personnel Research Section Report No. 984. Washington, D.C., Department of the Army, 1951.

Tucker, L. R. An inter-battery method of factor analysis. *Psychometrika*, 1958, *23*(2), 111–136.

Tucker, L. R. Implications of factor analysis of three-way matrices for measurement of change. In C. W. Harris (Ed.), *Problems in measuring change*. Madison: University of Wisconsin Press, 1963.

Tucker, L. R. The extension of factor analysis to three-dimensional matrices. In N. Frederiksen & H. Gulliksen, (Eds.), *Contributions to mathematical psychology*. New York: Holt, Rinehart & Winston, 1964.

Tucker, L. R. Some mathematical notes on three-mode factor analysis. *Psychometrika*, 1966, *31*(3), 279–311.

Tucker, L. R. Three-mode factor analysis of Parker-Fleishman complex tracking behavior data. *Multivariate Behavioral Research*, 1967, *2*(2), 139–151.

Tucker, L. R. Comments on "Confounding of sources of variation in factor-analytic techniques." *Psychological Bulletin*, 1968, *70*(5), 345–354.

Tucker, L. R. Relations of factor score estimates to their use. *Psychometrika*, 1971, *36*(4), 427–436.

Tucker, L. R., Koopman, R. F., & Linn, R. L. Evaluation of factor analytic research procedures by means of simulated correlation matrices. *Psychometrika*, 1969, *34*, 421–460.

Van Driel, O. P. On various causes of improper solutions in maximum likelihood factor analysis. *Psychometrika*, 1978, *43*(2), 225–243.

Van Hemert, M., Van Hemert, N. A., & Elshout, J. J. Some simulations of orthogonal rotation of factors: 2. Real factors and random hypotheses. Some simulations of targeted orthogonal rotations of factors: 1. Real factors and random hypotheses. In G. Bruchman, F. Ferschel, & L. Schmetter (Eds.), *COMSTAT 1974. Proceedings in computational statistics*. Wien: Physics Verlag, 1974.

Vaughn, C. L. Factors in rat learning: An analysis of the intercorrelations between 34 variables. *Comparative Psychology Monographs*, 1937, *14*, 41 pp.

Veldman, D. J. *Fortran programming for the behavioral sciences*. New York: Holt, Rinehart & Winston, 1967.

Velicer, W. F. An empirical comparison of the stability of factor analysis, principal component analysis, and image analysis. *Educational and Psychological Measurement*, 1974, *34*, 563–572.

Velicer, W. F. The relation between factor score estimates, image scores, and principal component scores. *Educational and Psychological Measurement*, 1976, *36*, 149–159.

Velicer, W. F. An empirical comparison of the similarity of principal component, image, and factor patterns. *Multivariate Behavioral Research*, 1977, *12*, 3–22.

Velicer, W. F., Peacock, A. C., & Jackson, D. N. A comparison of component and factor patterns: A Monte Carlo approach. *Multivariate Behavioral Research*, 1982, *17*, 371–388.

Wackwitz, J. H., & Horn, J. L. On obtaining the best estimates of factor scores within an ideal simple structure. *Multivariate Behavioral Research*, 1971, *6*(4), 389–408.

Walsh, J. A., & Walsh, R. A revised FORTRAN IV program for three-mode factor analysis. *Educational and Psychological Measurement*, 1976, *36*, 169–170.

Ward, J. H. Hierarchical grouping to optomize an objective function. *Journal of the American Statistical Association*, 1963, *58*, 236–244.

Weeks, D. G., & Bentler, P. M. A comparison of linear and monotone multidimensional scaling models. *Psychological Bulletin*, 1979, *86*(2), 349–354.

Wellhausen, J. *Prolegomena to the history of ancient israel* (Black, J. S., & Menzies, A., trans.) Edinburgh: A. and C. Black, 1885. Reprinted, Cleveland: World Press, 1957.

Wherry, R. Hierarchical factor solutions without rotation. *Psychometrika*, 1959, *24*(1), 45–51.

White, O. Some properties of three factor contribution matrices. *Multivariate Behavioral Research*, 1966, *1*(3), 373–378.

Wimberley, R. C. Dimensions of commitment: Generalizing from religion to politics. *Journal for the Scientific Study of Religion*, 1978, *17*, 225–240.

Winer, B. J. *Statistical principles in experimental design*. New York: McGraw-Hill, 1962.

Woodbury, M. A., Clelland, R. C., & Hickey, R. J. Applications of a factor-analytic model in the prediction of biological data. *Behavioral Science*, 1963, *8*(4), 347–354.

Wrigley, C. Objectivity in factor analysis. *Educational and Psychological Measurement*, 1958, *18*, 463–476.

Wrigley, C. *A procedure for objective factor analysis*. Paper presented at the first annual meeting of the Society of Multivariate Experimental Psychology, 1960.

Wrigley, C. S., & Neuhaus, J. O. The matching of two sets of factors. *American Psychologist*, 1955, *10*, 418–419.

Young, F. W., Takane, Y., & de Leeuw, J. The principal components of mixed measurement level multivariate data: An alternating least squares method with optimal scaling features. *Psychometrika*, 1978, *43*, 279–281.

Zak, I. Constancy and variability of the HSPQ across two Israeli cultures. *Multivariate Experimental Clinical Research*, 1979, *4*(3), 81–92.

Zenisek, T. J. Three-mode factor analysis via a modification of Tucker's computational method-III, *Educational and Psychological Measurement*, 1978, *38*, 787–792.

Zwick, W. R., & Velicer, W. F. Factors influencing four rules for determining the number of components to retain. Unpublished, University of Rhode Island, 1980.

Author Index

Numbers in *italics* denote pages with complete bibliographic information.

A

Acito, F. 164, 170, 171, *395*
Adams, R. C. 267, *395*
Adelson, M. 313, *398*
Ahmavaara, Y. 283, 345, *395*
Ahumada, A. 116, *399*
Anderson, R. D. 164, 170, 171, *395*
Anderson, T. W. 265, *395*
Archer, C. O. 210, *395*
Armstrong, J. S. 149, 330, 371, 380, *395*
Arthur, A. Z. 120, *395*

B

Baehr, M. E. 202, *395*
Baggaley, A. R. 285, 288, *398*
Bailey, D. E. 9, 211, 270, *410*
Bailey, J. P. 205, 211, *395, 401*
Balcar, K. R. 285, *398*
Baltes, P. B. 290, 332, *407*
Bargmann, R. 181, *395*
Barnard, J. 367, *400*
Barrett, P. T. 332, *395*
Bartlett, M. S. 149, 150, 152, 264, *395, 396*
Bechtoldt, H. P. 329, 333, *396*
Beggs, D. L. 17, *405*

Bentler, P. M. 117, 120, 139, 140, 203, 255, 266, 276, 295, 306, 326, 365, 368, *396, 411*
ten Berge, J. M. F. 233, 234, *396*
Bianchini, J. 284, *405*
Birkett, H. 312, *398*
Bisher, J. W. 37, 46, *396*
Bloxom, B. 345, *396*
Borg, I. 119, 233, *396, 406*
Borgatta, E. F. 293, *396*
Boruch, R. F. 16, 129, 321, 322, 367, *396*
Bottenberg, R. A. 17, *396*
Boyd, W. M. 202, *402*
Brennan, J. 234, *398*
Brewer, J. K. 302, 345, *396*
Brewer, M. B. 89, *396*
Brogden, H. E. 208, *396*
Bromley, D. B. 9, 211, *397*
Broverman, D. M. 317, *397*
Browne, M. W. 107, 123, 153, 154, 163, 233, 329, 332, *397*
Burdsal, C. A. 295, *398*
Burr, E. J. 260, *407*
Burt, C. L. 13, 285, 316, *397*
Butler, J. M. 185, *397*
Butt, D. S. 357, *397*

413

Subject Index